EUROPEAN MANAGEMENT GUIDES

Contracts and terms
and conditions
of employme

GW00363577

European Management Guides

The European Management Guides, written and researched by the International Department of Incomes Data Services, provide a reliable and up-to-date overview of employment law and practice in Europe. They now include Austria, Sweden and Switzerland as well as the eleven major member states of the European Union. There will be three volumes:

**Contracts and Terms and Conditions of Employment
Employee Relations and Collective Bargaining
Recruitment, Training and Development.**

EUROPEAN MANAGEMENT GUIDES
General editor: Pete Burgess

Contracts and terms and conditions of employment

Incomes Data Services

Institute of Personnel and Development

© Institute of Personnel and Development 1995

Published 1995

Phototypeset by The Comp-Room, Aylesbury
and printed in Great Britain by
Short Run Press, Exeter

British Library Cataloguing in Publication Data
A catalogue record for this book is available
from the British Library

ISBN 0 85292 559 X

INSTITUTE OF PERSONNEL
AND DEVELOPMENT

IPD House, Camp Road, London SW19 4UX
Tel: 0181 946 9100   Fax: 0181 947 2570
Registered office as above. Registered Charity No. 1038333
A company limited by guarantee. Registered in England No. 2931892

Contents

General Introduction

European Management Guides

The internationalisation of businesses within the European Union (EU), the creation of new corporate entities as a result of mergers and acquisitions across national boundaries, and the complexities of meshing cultures and practices – often accompanied by painful rationalisation – are set to continue unabated in the 1990s. The management of the human resource dimension to these processes will continue to pose fresh challenges to personnel practitioners, especially those confronted with international personnel issues for the first time.

The programme to realise a Single European Market by 1993 triggered a new raft of European-level legislative proposals intended to complement the commercial and economic aspects of European integration with a 'social dimension'. Although influential, and occasionally decisive, in a number of areas of employment regulation, EU legislation has left the diverse institutional structures of the member states largely untouched. Substantial differences in cultures, institutions, law and practice will persist for the foreseeable future, tempered more by broader economic exigencies than by legislative intervention from the European Commission. Indeed, the philosophy behind the 1993 Treaty on European Union (the Maastricht Treaty) and the European Commission's more recent approach to employment policy is that greater scope should be left to negotiation and local implementation rather than monolithic prescription from Brussels.

Understanding and working with national diversity will therefore continue to be vital for personnel or line managers entrusted with European responsibilities. Although professional advice is indispensable when approaching a European venture or major personnel decision, access to basic and structured information can help in shaping the agenda for decisions – as well as saving precious time and money. The European Management Guides series aims to meet this need for accessible and comprehensive information on employment in the major economies of Western Europe. The second edition of the series, researched and written by Incomes Data Services Ltd (IDS) and published by the Institute of Personnel and Development (IPD), consists of three volumes covering:

- Contracts and terms and conditions of employment.
- Employee relations and collective bargaining.
- Recruitment, training and development.

European Management Guides are based on research carried out by the International Department of IDS using original national sources: this embraces the business press, specialist publications (including those from employer associations, trade unions, and personnel management organisations), legislation, collective agreements, and material on policy and practice supplied by companies and consultants, including extensive and regular face-to-face interviews with specialists and practitioners. The main sources, including published secondary material, are listed at the end of each country chapter.

Each volume presents information on a country-by-country basis, structured to allow easy comparative reference. Appendices detail local organisations which can provide further help and information. However, European Management Guides are not intended as a substitute for expert advice tailored to an individual situation and provided in the context of a professional relationship. Every effort has been made to ensure that the information contained in them is accurate and relevant. The publishers and authors offer them to readers on the understanding that neither organisation seeks to take the place of a lawyer or a consultant.

Incomes Data Services

Incomes Data Services has monitored employment developments in Europe since 1974. IDS's International Service publishes:

- *IDS European Report*, a monthly subscription journal on pay and employment law and practice in existing and prospective members of the European Union. Each issue includes news on pay, collective bargaining and legal developments in EU member states, a Country Profile drawing together trends and developments in the economy, pay, employment law, labour costs and executive remuneration for an individual country, together with regular supplements on European Union-level legislation and issues, with features, and regular statistics on pay trends and prices.
- *IDS International Documents* comprise two series of in-depth reference sources on an individual country basis covering i) Pay and Conditions, ii) Recruitment and Dismissal. Updated regularly, each series provides both context and detail in these crucial areas of personnel management.

For more details contact: IDS Subscriptions, 193 St John Street, London EC1V 4LS (tel. 071-250 3434, fax 071-608 0949).

Acknowledgements

European Management Guides are researched and written by the staff and contributors of the International Department of Incomes Data Services Ltd, London. Individual country chapters were prepared by Andrea Broughton, Angela Bowring, Pete Burgess, Sally Marullo, Tony Morgan, Steve Steadman, George Tsogas and Caroline Welch. The series editor is Pete Burgess. The authors would like to thank the many individuals and companies who helped in the research for their time and co-operation; the staff of the publishing department of the Institute of Personnel and Development for their patient and scrupulous editorial input; and the national committees of the IPD for their support and advice.

The authors are grateful to Monks Partnership Limited for permission to use data drawn from their surveys *Management Remuneration in Europe*, *Incentives and Benefits in Europe*, and *European Company Car Survey*.

Introduction

Contracts and terms and conditions
of employment

Contracts and Terms and Conditions of Employment is the first volume of the new, three-volume edition of the IDS/IPD European Management Guides. It sets out to provide detailed information and context for fourteen EU member countries on the following subjects:

- Contracts of employment.
- Working time and time off.
- Pay and benefits.
- Equal opportunities.
- Retirement.
- Individual and collective dismissals, and transfer of undertakings.

The second volume of the series will cover *Employee Relations and Collective Bargaining* and the third *Recruitment, Training and Development*.

The mid- to late-1980s saw a growing period of internationalism in Europe's businesses, spurred on by the moves towards the Single European Market, but also beyond Europe by the pressures of global competition and the need for presence in growing markets. Cross-border mergers and acquisitions reached an all-time high in Europe, spawning a new generation of international undertakings and joint ventures. Many medium-sized companies also embarked on an intense phase of international development, exposing personnel practitioners schooled in their own national contexts to a first taste of cross-cultural, and cross-jurisdictional, management.

The surge of investment-led growth in Europe, given a further fillip by German unification, initially confronted personnel managers with the problems of expansion and strains on capacity – including human resources. For example, heightened international recruitment efforts were not only directed towards creating a cadre of multicultural managers but also reflected worries about the abrupt drying-up – at least in some European countries – of the supply of fresh graduates.

The recession that swept through Europe in 1992/93 penalised overhasty expansion or ill-considered acquisitions and also put the international personnel manager at the sharp end of managing the often painful processes of rationalisation, redundancies and reducing labour costs. Three particular areas for action emerged: dismissals, restraining pay and benefits, and reorganising working time. Each is regulated in highly diverse ways in different European countries. Although all three are dealt with in this volume they are also profoundly affected by collective bargaining and statutory forms of employee representation in many EU member states – issues taken up in Vol. 2 of this series, on employee relations and collective bargaining.

Dismissals

Handling dismissals in a way that is socially responsible towards those affected, cost-effective for the employer and in line with local laws, agreements, norms and cultural sensitivities undoubtedly presents international personnel managers with one of their greatest challenges. Procedures for handling dismissal, be it individual or collective, are complex in every EU member state, but there are a number of national peculiarities which, if not properly taken into account, could prove costly and introduce additional delays to the process.

- *Workforce consultation.* Workforce consultation is mandatory in several countries, and failure to inform elected employee representatives may render dismissals not merely unfair but null and void. Under EU directives on collective dismissals and transfer of undertakings, employee representatives – and failing that, individual employees – must be informed before decisions are taken.
- *Official authorisation.* The past few years have seen a gradual withdrawal of official bodies from mechanisms for recruitment and dismissal. However, official authorisation, as well as notification, remains mandatory in some countries and elected employee representatives can delay or entirely halt decisions pending an official review of rationalisation plans.
- *Selection for redundancy.* The employer's freedom to determine the selection of employees for redundancy, and to swap employees around to fill posts vacated by redundant employees, varies from country to country. In Germany and Austria, for example, selection for redundancy must ensure that those least able to manage socially are most protected from dismissal – meaning that the employer may not be able to dismiss poor performers or less able workers during a redundancy exercise. Failure to abide by prescribed selection criteria can lead to a legal challenge on grounds of unfair or unwarranted dismissal, and in several countries employee representatives have a statutory right to negotiate over such selection criteria.
- *Notice and severance pay.* The length of required notice varies substantially between countries, as does the form of regulation: virtually every country provides for a statutory minimum notice period, but collective agreements, with widespread application, may offer substantially more generous arrangements for employees. In some countries, long periods for non-managerial as well as (more typically) for managerial employees effectively function as a means of providing severance pay, especially in the absence of statutory arrangements. However, how such payments mesh with the tax system varies considerably, and is largely outside the scope of this book.

Restraining pay and benefits

The response of pay-setting arrangements to the recession has exposed both the rigidities and flexibilities of different national systems. In the UK, for example, the process of steady movement towards widespread decentralisation of bargaining begun in the mid-1980s has continued. The major response of UK employers to the recession was to embark on dramatic cost- and sometimes drastic capacity-cutting, often involving several waves of redundancies. On pay, settlements were squeezed, and many employers negotiated or imposed pay pauses or freezes of varying length and severity. The relatively centralised bargaining systems of mainland Europe, often combining industry-level bargaining with company top-ups, were obliged to take another course – but one that would appear, provisionally at least, to have delivered an effective short-term response to the demands of recession. In Belgium and the Netherlands state-ordained or agreed incomes policies came into force in 1993/94. In Germany cuts in real pay were negotiated at industry level in 1993 and 1994, in some instances accompanied by pay pauses for up to five months. At company level, employers took the axe to many long-established benefits, and sought to tie elements of the pay package and bonuses to performance objectives. In Italy pay indexation was abolished in 1992 and an effective pay freeze at company level has been imposed through a restructuring of the bargaining system.

Reorganisation of working time

The reorganisation of working time as a response to recession has been put on the political and bargaining agenda in several EU member states. In Italy and France changes to the law on working hours and contracts gave fresh scope for job creation and preservation through the expansion of part-time work and cuts in hours. In France employers can claim reductions in social insurance contributions in return for negotiating new working-time arrangements, and the trade-off between pay and jobs through company-level agreements has been a major feature of recent bargaining rounds. In Germany alarm about spiralling unemployment in 1993 led the trade unions to attempt to bargain over measures to save jobs – typically by working-time cuts – in return for concessions on pay. And in 1994 the German government launched a publicity initiative to encourage more part-time working.

Relationship between law, collective agreement and individual contracts

Every system of employment law and regulation contains a hierarchy of laws, most of which exhibit similar contours. However, systems in mainland Europe do have features that can appear perplexing to a practitioner schooled in UK traditions. *First*, collective agreements are legally binding and enforceable in virtually every EU member state: that is, in order to be effective they do not have to be written into ('incorporated') into individual contracts of employment, although this frequently takes place in part simply as a means of clarification. The EU Directive on Proof of an Employment Relationship, currently being transposed into national law in member states, also requires an individual statement of terms and conditions to be given to the employee. *Second*, as an autonomous source of law in most countries, collective agreements may provide for certain terms and conditions that are poorer for the employee than those offered by statute law – but which may be offset in the contract as a whole by other terms and conditions which, on balance, are accepted as satisfactory by the negotiating parties. The underlying philosophy is that employees represented by trade unions are sufficiently protected to allow them to negotiate a greater degree of flexibility than that contained in the statutory minimum. In Germany such derogation is permitted regarding notice periods. In a number of countries, including Germany and Belgium, it is also allowed regarding working time. *Third*, there are some statutory frameworks, most notably in Switzerland, that contain three types of provision: mandatory laws, which may not be deviated from under any circumstances; statutory provisions, which may be deviated from provided this benefits the employee (the principle of *faber laboratoris* – customary in most jurisdictions); and provisions which only apply if no other (usually written) determination has been made, irrespective of whether it is a collective or individual one, and irrespective of whether the new provision is better or worse from the standpoint of the employee.

Currency conversions

Currency conversions are provided at average rates applicable in mid-summer 1994, in some cases further rounded up or down where rates have oscillated considerably.

The European Union Context

The background

Prior to the 1985 Single European Act, which marked the beginning of a new phase of European integration through the decision to advance towards a Single European Market (SEM), the influence of legislation passed by the European Community (since 1993, the European Union) and its associated case law was already pervasive, if not always immediately apparent, on the individual employment relationship. The directives introduced during the 1970s and 1980s on equal pay and aspects of equal treatment, on collective dismissals, acquired rights on the transfer of an undertaking or employer insolvency and freedom of movement have been – and continue to be – fundamental in shaping the terms of individual employment contracts, and have provided the material for a number of major employment law controversies, especially in the United Kingdom. And by adding a 'social dimension' to the Single Market, the 1989 Community Charter of the fundamental social rights of workers (the 'Social Charter') substantially augmented the actual, and potential of, European-level provisions input to the area of contractual terms through a new raft of legislation proposals under the Charter's associated Action Programme. The Single European Act also opened the door to new procedures for the passage ('adoption') of European Union legislation by removing the veto rights of individual member states over proposals intended to bring about the Single Market or regulate the health and safety of employees. Reservations about the operation of the procedure – both by member states enthusiastic for greater European-level activity as well as those with fundamental doubts, such as the UK – led to a further reshaping of these procedures under the 1993 Treaty on European Union (the Maastricht Treaty), as well as some rethinking about the required overall philosophy. (An Appendix to this Chapter outlines European Union legal instruments and procedures: see pages 17–19).

National systems under pressure

Notwithstanding the requirement upon member states to transpose the growing body of European Union law into domestic legislation, movement towards convergence of employment standards has been tentative. Clear national differences remain in the form and degree of regulation in the social and employment field area, and personnel practitioners in different member states are confronted with varying degrees of scope for exercising policy prerogatives – still a potent source

1

of difficulty for internationally-operating firms attempting to establish consistent practices. The principle of 'subsidiarity', now formally enshrined in the Treaty on European Union, is intended to ensure that harmonisation between countries is pursued only where a need for it can be established.

Irrespective of moves towards formal harmonisation recent economic pressures have had the effect both of moving national systems closer together and of necessitating convergent outcomes – such as downward pressure on labour costs – through differing institutional arrangements. The combined forces of recession, rising unemployment, new technology and stiffer global competition have brought about important changes in virtually every national industrial relations system, with important repercussions on how employment terms and conditions are determined. Government responses to pressure have been diverse, ranging from attempts at wholesale social deregulation – most notably in the United Kingdom – to shifting more responsibility for setting terms and conditions from national and sectoral level to that of the enterprise, and creating more scope for flexible working arrangements. The cycle of recession, boom and a return to recession over the past ten to fifteen years has put enormous strains on traditional bargaining systems and tested the capacity of trade unions to respond effectively in a period of unprecedently fast industrial restructuring and change. Both boom and recession have seen a shift to more individualised employment relationships than in the past. Despite this, however, collective bargaining, reinforced by mechanisms to extend agreements to non-signatory employers in many EU member states, remains the foundation for terms and conditions of employment for the bulk of the labour force throughout Europe.

At the European level, the Agreement on Social Policy, part of the Treaty on European Union (see page 4), can be regarded as one expression of this more flexible approach to employment regulation through its express acknowledgement and advocacy of collective agreements as a way to implement or as an alternative to Euro-legislation. The Working Time directive, for example, is one European regulation which offers plentiful scope for adapting its core provisions to the circumstances of the individual workplace.

The 1989 Social Charter

The broad objective of the Social Charter was to complement the moves to economic and commercial freedom in the Single Market with a range of binding minimum standards in defined areas of employment. Under the Social Charter Action Programme, which implemented the Charter's principles over 1990–94, a number of key directives were adopted. According to the provisions of the Single European Act, which allowed for qualified majority voting on health and safety proposals, these included a number of non-technical health and safety measures covering, for example, working time, young people and maternity rights. (These and other directives are outlined on pages 8–10.)

A number of non-legislative proposals was also approved, such as a five-year programme for equal opportunities and recommendations on childcare, equity sharing and financial participation, all of which have exerted an indirect influence on the shaping of employment terms. The impact of such non-statutory measures should not be overlooked. According to the European Court of Justice (ECJ), national courts should take account of recommendations in resolving legal disputes where these give guidance to employers about the interpretation of European law.

At the close of the five-year Social Charter Action Programme a number of measures concerning individual conditions was still outstanding, notably those on equal treatment of 'atypical' workers, on the temporary posting of workers to another EU country and parental leave. These are likely to be resubmitted and adopted – in some form – under the new five-year European social policy programme set to begin in 1995.

A new European social programme

The effects of the 1990s recession in Europe, which pushed up unemployment to levels unprecedented in the post-war period, stimulated a rethink within the European Commission about approaches to the management of economic and social change. In particular, the Commission sought to respond to the charge that the social model that characterised most member states was inimical to job creation, when set against the apparent employment successes of the USA. The Commission's White Paper on *Growth, Competitiveness, Employment*, published at the end of 1993, set out a number of policies intended to foster sustained economic growth and tackle the seemingly inexorable rise in European unemployment levels.

Focusing further on reducing unemployment, the Commission's White Paper on *European Social Policy – A Way Forward for the Union*, published in July 1994, develops the policy debate and in particular highlights the change in emphasis of the Commission. The social policy White Paper argues that employment creation is the policy priority, but one that must be achieved within the context of the distinct features of the 'European social model', rooted in high social standards and social cohesion. However, the Commission emphasises that diversity within the European Union must be respected and that 'total harmonisation of social policies is not an objective of the Union'. The Commission argues instead for continued progress towards common objectives, based on minimum standards. New legislative proposals will be brought forward in accordance with the principles of 'subsidiarity and proportionality' – that is, only when national measures are inadequate or inappropriate, and when the means are proportional to the desired ends. Moreover, based on the new possibilities offered by the Treaty on European Union for social dialogue, the Commission hopes to strike 'a new balance . . . between the legislator at Community level and collective agreements between the social partners'.

Although the next five-year social programme is widely expected to be less prescriptive than its predecessor, certain projects are bound to carry implications for individual employment terms. The European Commission is already committed to consolidating progress in areas where some action has already been taken, and to achieve more rapid and effective transposition of existing directives into national law. (At the end of 1993 the United Kingdom and Portugal were found to have the best record in implementing European measures.) Areas in which further legislative activity can be expected are:

- Occupational pension and social security schemes.
- Transfer of undertakings.
- Sex equality, for example through the issuing of a Code of Practice on equal pay; tackling occupational segregation by gender through targeted education and training measures; making it easier to bring sex discrimination cases.
- Data protection. Although the 1990 draft directive on the protection of individuals with regard to personal data processing has yet to be adopted, the Commission is currently conducting research on other aspects of workers' privacy not covered by existing European regulations.
- Discrimination. When the new Treaty on European Union (see below) is reviewed in 1996 it may be amended to allow legislation prohibiting race, religious, age and disability discrimination to be introduced, to complement existing provisions on sex discrimination..

The Treaty on European Union

The Maastricht Treaty, which came into effect as the Treaty on European Union (TEU) on 1 November 1993, is set to have a major impact on the social area through new powers conferred on the various Community institutions and through one of the annexes to the main treaty: the Social Protocol (commonly known as the Social Chapter). Under new procedures for the passage of European legislation, the European Parliament will have the right to require the Commission to present proposals on matters which it considers worthy of EU action – possibly giving rise to an increased volume of legislative proposals – as well as a restricted right of veto over Community legislation. The 1996 review of the Treaty will give scope for further changes to be introduced, and perhaps clarify the legal uncertainty that still surrounds the precise legal status of the Social Protocol, and any measures binding only the eleven member states.

The Social Protocol

The Treaty's Social Protocol provides a new basis for regulating employment issues beyond the possibilities offered by articles 117–22 of Title II of the Treaty (essentially the employment articles of the Treaty of Rome, as amended by the Single European Act). The Protocol constitutes an agreement between the EU member states which empowers all members, save the United Kingdom, to act on certain matters in accordance with the Agreement on Social Policy (usually dubbed the Social Chapter), which is part of the Protocol. (The remaining part sets out the United Kingdom's 'opt-out' from the Social Chapter.) Under the terms of the United Kingdom's opt-out, any measure passed under the new procedure will apply only to the territory of the eleven member states who have accepted the Social Chapter, together with any of the new member states (Austria, Finland, and Sweden) due to join in 1995. The Agreement also allows legislation blocked through insufficient agreement under existing Treaty articles, and in particular by the United Kingdom's veto, to be advanced.

The agreement on Social Policy offers two options for the passage of legislation: unanimity or a qualified majority (of the eleven currently subject to its provisions), depending on subject matter. Prior to the Agreement, qualified majority voting (of the twelve) was permissible only for employment measures linked to health and safety or completion of the single market. However, under the Agreement qualified majority voting can also apply to working conditions, employee information and consultation, equal opportunities and measures to integrate those currently excluded from the labour market measures, in theory making it easier to adopt such legislation. Unanimity is still required in the areas of social security and social protection of workers, protection against dismissal, representation and co-determination between employers and employees. The Agreement expressly excludes pay, rights of association, the right to strike and the right to impose a lock-out from the scope of European legislation.

Following past criticism of the lack of flexibility and consultation in the formulation and implementation of European legislation, the Agreement on Social Policy also promotes social dialogue between employers and employee representatives. There will be greater scope for consultation before European-level action is taken, together with the option of regulating an issue by means of collective agreement at European Union level instead of legislation.

By the middle of 1994 the proposal on information and consultation in multinational companies (European works councils) was the only measure to be advanced through the Agreement, following the previous UK veto of the project. However, it is possible that other measures still outstanding from the Social Charter Action Programme, such as that on 'atypical workers', could take this route in 1995.

Fears have been expressed about the dangers of a twin-track social Europe, with the United Kingdom an outsider. The Commission certainly prefers that all member states should continue to act together, and has indicated that it would prefer to bring forward proposals under the provisions of the Treaty of Rome (as amended by the Single European Act) rather than reinforce UK isolation by using the Social Protocol. The need for international companies to develop consistent policies, possibly urged on by employees and their representatives looking for comparable treatment, is also likely to prove a major factor in weakening the impact of the United Kingdom's formal exclusion. The UK employers' organisation, the Confederation of British Industry (CBI), has suggested for example that these considerations might lead it to change its view of the United Kingdom's opt-out on some social policy issues.

The European Court of Justice

Given the now considerable body of European law (termed the *acquis commau-nitaire*), which takes precedence over national law, the European Court of Justice constitutes a powerful force for change in shaping personnel practices. The Court's powers of law enforcement – that is, bringing to book member states that fail to implement directives, or implement them incorrectly – have been strengthened under the Treaty on European Union by allowing it to impose fines on member states that fail to comply with its judgments.

Moreover, in some important areas, the provisions of Community law may have a direct effect in law and can be relied on by plaintiffs irrespective of whether a member state has transposed them into national law. For example, article 119 of the Treaty of Rome, which provides for equal pay, and parts of the Equal Treatment directive have been held by the European Court of Justice to be directly applicable. As yet there have been no decisions that establish the direct applicability of the Equal Pay directive.

The most influential role of the Court is interpreting EU law on the basis of preliminary references from national courts. For their part, national courts are obliged to ensure that domestic law is interpreted in line with the obligatory provisions of EU law, even if this involves conflicts with domestic legislation or constitutional principles that existed prior to the relevant European provisions being brought into force.

The main areas in which European law shapes the individual employment relationship are set out below. In each case the European directive must be transposed into national legislation in a way that gives effect to the meaning of the directive, either through new domestic legislation or the amendment of existing statutes. How (and whether) this is accomplished in the following areas is indicated in the appropriate individual country chapters.

Contracts of employment

Proof of an employment relationship

Council directive 91/533/EEC (14 October 1991) obliges an employer to give to an employee working at least eight hours a week on a contract lasting a month or more written notification of the 'essential aspects of the contract or employment relationship'.

This information must be supplied to a new recruit within two months of starting work and should include details of the contracting parties, the place of work, job category and description of duties, the date the employment commenced, the expected duration of the contract (if for a fixed term), the probationary period, pay rate and frequency of payment, working hours, paid leave, and reference to any appropriate collective agreements. Where employees are required to work abroad, they are entitled – before departure from the home base – to be informed of the length of the assignment, the currency to be used for salary payment, any benefits due, and conditions concerning the return to the home base.

Temporary posting of workers

The outstanding draft directive on the temporary posting of workers aims to clarify which national employment rules should apply where employees are temporarily posted from their home base to another EU member state. Pressure for the directive has come in particular from the trade unions and some employers' organisations in northern Europe who fear that high national employment standards might be undermined by subcontracted workers from countries with poorer wages and conditions. The draft directive establishes a 'hard core' of mandatory rules which companies using posted workers in a host country for more than three months must observe, provided such rules are in the form of legislation or generally binding agreements in the country concerned. The areas covered by such rules are working time, leave, minimum pay rates, health and safety, equal treatment and hiring of temporaries. Progress towards adopting this proposal has been tardy, but the threads are likely to be picked up in the new social programme if it fails to make headway in its present form.

Non-standard forms of employment

As part of the Social Charter Action Programme, three draft directives were issued in 1990 on various aspects of 'atypical' employment broadly covering part-time, temporary and agency employment. One of the proposals, guaranteeing health and safety protection for such employees, was adopted by the Commission in 1991. Agreement on the other two has proved highly contentious.

One of the outstanding proposals concerns equal access of 'atypical' workers to training, company and non-contributory benefits and priority consideration for full-time vacancies. Such employees would be included in thresholds used for establishing workplace employee representative bodies, which would also be informed by the employer where they were planning to use 'atypical' workers. The original proposal requires unanimous approval. The second deals with establishing minimum conditions for 'atypicals' to prevent distortions of competition arising through disparities in rules governing this type of employment. It requires qualified majority for adoption.

Deadlock on these proposals, essentially due to the UK government's view that regulation of this sort discourages job creation, has led to two further attempts – one by the Belgian EU Presidency in July 1993, the other by the

German Presidency a year later – to amalgamate the proposals into a single text. In both cases the aim was to establish equal treatment in employment terms between full-time permanent staff and 'atypical' workers, and ensure that such employees are taken into account in the constitution of workers' representative bodies. Notwithstanding the revised texts, the proposal remains subject to unanimous approval under main Treaty articles. Should the United Kingdom maintain its opposition the matter could be switched to the Agreement on Social Policy in 1995: this would allow other EU member states to adopt a proposal applying only in their national territories.

Data protection and workers' privacy

A proposal for a directive on protection of individuals with regard to the processing of personal data and on freedom of movement of such data was first presented in 1990. By the summer of 1994 the Council of Ministers had still to reach a 'common position' on the proposal. The proposal would establish a high level of protection throughout the European Union, and ensure free movement and prevent distortion of competition arising from existing differences in provision. The proposal covers computerised and manual personnel files and would limit transfer to third countries with less rigid standards of protection. It emphasises the rights and privacy of the individual by requiring, for example, individual consent to be given before health records can be accessed.

The European Commission is concurrently examining other aspects of workers' privacy with a view to action at EU level. However, unlike the United Kingdom, many other member states already have statutes protecting the individual's right to privacy in various contexts.

Terms and conditions of employment

Working time

In November 1993 an EU directive on the organisation of working time was adopted, giving member states until November 1996 to implement most of its provisions.

The directive specifies a minimum rest break after six hours' continuous work, minimum daily and weekly rest periods, and annual paid leave. Maximum weekly working hours, normally to be averaged over four months, are limited to forty-eight including overtime, with longer reference periods applying in the case of derogations foreseen in the directive (six months) or where a collective agreement is signed (up to twelve months). Night work may not exceed eight hours in normal circumstances and must never exceed this limit where hazardous work is performed. Health and safety protection for night and shift workers is tightened up. Derogations from stated limits (except the forty-eight-hour week) are allowed for particular activities, provided workers affected are given an equivalent alternative rest period.

In order to meet objections from the UK government, the directive offers member states the option (until 2003 at least) of not applying the maximum forty-eight-hour limit, provided an employee has freely consented to work longer hours. Nevertheless, in 1994 the UK government instituted proceedings in the European Court of Justice challenging the lawfulness of using the health and safety article of the Treaty of Rome (article 118a) as the legal base for the directive. Until the matter is resolved the UK government will take no steps to implement the directive. Other member states are however in the process of transposing provisions into national law, often incorporating the scope for flexibility offered by the directive.

The transport and sea-fishing industries, trainee doctors and other work at sea, are excluded from the directive's scope. Consultations in some of these sectors have been launched with a view to framing regulations that complement the main directive, either by means of a generally applicable agreement between the social partners, or via European legislation.

Directive on young people

A directive on protection of young people at work is to be implemented by June 1996. It prohibits child labour, sets a minimum working age of 15 (save in exceptional circumstances), and requires that working conditions for adolescents (i.e. those aged between 15 or minimum school leaving age and 18) be adapted to protect their physical, mental, moral and social development. Adolescents are barred from certain types of work and risk assessments must be conducted before employment commences. Daily and weekly working-time limits are laid down for working children (i.e. performing 'light work' or under training) and adolescents. Adolescents over school age must work no longer than eight hours daily and forty weekly. Night work is forbidden to children and greatly restricted for adolescents. Rest periods of fourteen hours in twenty-four are set for children, twelve in twenty-four for adolescents, with an entitlement to two consecutive days' rest a week which may not be reduced below thirty-six in any circumstances. A thirty-minute rest break must be given after four and a half hours' work. The UK government secured a longer transposition period for complying with maximum weekly working times; however, when this concession is reviewed by the Council after four years it is unlikely to be continued.

Maternity rights, parental and other forms of leave

One major proposal to be approved under the 1989 Social Charter Action Programme, with implementation due by October 1994, was the directive aimed at enhancing health and safety protection for pregnant workers and workers who have recently given birth and/or who are breastfeeding. This introduces a requirement for employers to conduct risk assessments of the work environment and to transfer women onto other work where necessary and compulsorily in the case of night work. It also gives pregnant employees the right to fourteen weeks' maternity leave during which they are entitled to 'maintenance of a payment' and/or 'entitlement to an adequate allowance'. In addition the contract of employment will be maintained during the maternity leave period, with protection against dismissal on the grounds of pregnancy guaranteed from the beginning of a pregnancy to the completion of maternity leave. Individuals had previously to pursue cases involving dismissal on the grounds of pregnancy under the provisions of the 1976 Equal Treatment directive.

Proposals on parental leave have been on the European agenda since 1983 but have not advanced. A revised text was presented by the Belgian Presidency to the Council of Ministers in 1993. This called for three months' parental leave in the year following a child's birth, ten days' leave a year for urgent family reasons and protection from dismissal for reasons connected with taking such leave. This new initiative has fared no better than previous proposals, and the new EU social programme for 1995–99 may feature a framework directive covering issues for reconciling professional and family life, including career breaks and parental leave.

Individual pay and benefits

Financial participation   In 1992 the Council approved a non-binding recommendation (92/443/EEC) aimed at promoting equity sharing and financial participation schemes. Member states were specifically called upon to ensure that legal structures permit the development of such schemes, to consider the granting of incentives to boost the introduction of certain schemes and to ensure that the choice of schemes be made 'as close as possible to the employed person and the enterprise'.

Right to a fair, or equitable, wage   Contrary to popular belief, under the Treaty on European Union – including the Agreement on Social Policy – there is no legal basis for the European Commission to introduce legislation on a statutory minimum wage, and the Commission has not sought to pursue such a goal. The nearest the Commission has come to acting in this area was its adoption, in September 1993, of a non-binding opinion on an equitable, or fair wage, in the context of one of the principles of the 1989 Social Charter: 'All employment shall be fairly remunerated . . . workers shall be assured of an equitable wage i.e. a wage sufficient to enable them to have a decent standard of living.'

One of the opinion's recommendations is that the right to an equitable wage must be protected in member states. Consequently it urges them to re-assess the adequacy of existing mechanisms for establishing minima and to strengthen bargaining arrangements as appropriate. However, due to the cool winds of recession over recent years the reality has been adjustments to national minimum wage systems – both agreed industry minima and statutory minima – which in many cases weaken the basis for an equitable wage.

In the United Kingdom, for example, wages councils which set industry minima for 2.6 million employees were abolished in 1993, with the exception of the body setting rates in agriculture. Mechanisms for uprating pay in line with inflation applying to all employees have also been altered. In Italy, meanwhile, the *scala mobile* partial wage-indexation system was abolished altogether in 1992, and Belgium's automatic indexation mechanism effectively marked time for a period in 1994. The system for linking increases in Dutch statutory pay minima with increases in average earnings has been severed, although subsequently the minimum wage system was extended to all part-time workers. In other countries with a statutory minimum wage the operation of uprating mechanisms has also allowed the value of minima to decline relative to average earnings. And in Germany fears have been expressed that the collective bargaining system which delivered almost universal application of agreed industry minima to the former West German Länder has become somewhat eroded, especially since unification.

The problem of low pay has become acute under adverse economic conditions and represents a major source of poverty. Increasing earnings disparities have been well documented, with women employees bearing the brunt. As a result further action to strengthen the application and enforcement of EU equal pay and treatment law is likely in the future.

Equal pay and equal treatment directives

Equal pay is the only aspect of remuneration regulated by EU legislation. Equal pay between men and women performing the same or similar work is embodied as a fundamental principle of Community law under article 119 of title 11 of the Treaty on European Union (incorporating the Treaty of Rome). This obliges member states to guarantee equal pay for equal work, with 'pay' covering payments in cash or kind received directly or indirectly in respect of employment. 'Equal pay' requires that pay for the same work at piece rates must be calculated on the same unit of measurement, and pay for work at time rates must be for the same job. Article 119 is directly applicable and can be relied on by plaintiffs in national courts of law if national law does not provide a remedy.

In order to tackle the undervaluing of women's work which arose out of the segregation of the jobs market, the 1975 directive (75/117/EEC) applies the equal pay principle to 'equal pay for work of equal value'. It also requires the elimination of sex discrimination from all aspects and conditions relating to remuneration, including provisions in collective agreements, wage scales, wage agreements or individual employment contracts. Any provisions contrary to the equal pay principle may be declared null and void or amended.

The Equal Treatment directive (adopted in 1976) extends the principle of equal treatment to matters relating to access to employment, vocational training and promotion, and working conditions. Some key cases brought before the

European Court of Justice under the directive include rulings on pregnancy dismissals and women's night work (see page 14). Council directives 79/7 and 86/378 require the application of equality in matters of social security and occupational social security schemes respectively (see pages 16–17).

The concept of pay   Through rulings of the European Court of Justice the concept of 'pay' has been extended to include post-retirement benefits (*Garland v. British Rail*, 1982), employer contributions to and benefits arising from supplementary occupational pension schemes (*Bilka Kaufhaus v. Weber von Hartz*, 1986 and *Barber v. Guardian Royal Exchange*, 1990), sick pay due under a statutory scheme (*Rinner-Kuhn v. FWW Spezial-Gebäudereinigung*, 1989) and pay for attending training courses (*Bötel v. Arbeiterwohlfahrt der Stadt Berlin*, 1992).

The Barber judgment confirmed that the equal pay principle must be applied to all elements of pay. However, to date far less attention has been drawn to aspects of payment systems such as job supplements, and performance and merit pay, even though research has established their potential for discrimination.

Court rulings on EU equal pay legislation have also affected the conditions of distinct categories of employee such as part-timers through the principle of indirect sex discrimination. The test for indirect sex discrimination is clearly set out in the important Bilka-Kaufhaus case: namely, does the use of a criterion which is ostensibly sex neutral affect in practice a considerably greater number of one sex than the other? If it does, two further questions arise: can the use of the criterion be objectively justified, i.e. is it based on factors unrelated to discrimination on the grounds of sex? And has the principle of proportionality been respected? In other words, is the aim pursued by use of the criterion a legitimate one, and is the means used necessary to achieve that aim proportional to it?

The Court ruled in the Bilka-Kaufhaus case that the exclusion of part-time workers, mostly women, from a company's occupational pension scheme would be unlawful under article 119 unless the difference in treatment could be objectively justified. A similar approach was adopted in the Rinner-Kuhn judgment where national legislation allowed the exclusion of workers employed for fewer than a number of hours per week, again predominantly women, from a sick leave scheme. The Court did not accept that the existence of such legal provisions in itself justified the employer's practice. The Federal German government subsequently legislated to rectify the problem, following a ruling by the German Constitutional Court and a gap of some five years. Two further cases (*Kowalska v. Freie und Hansestadt Hamburg*, 1990, and *Nimz v. Hansestadt Hamburg*, 1991) concerned indirect discrimination arising from clauses in collective agreements – in one instance denying a part-timer temporary severance benefit, in the other requiring a part-timer to accumulate longer length of service in order to qualify for promotion to a higher pay grade.

Job evaluation and job classification   The 1975 directive states that where a system of job classification is used for determining pay, it must apply the same criteria to men and women. Two key European Court judgments have interpreted how the law should be applied. In the case of *Rummler v. Dato-Druck GmbH*, 1986 the Court ruled that the directive required that the criteria used in weighting various factors in job evaluation systems should not, when the system was taken as a whole, be discriminatory, for example by giving muscular strength greater value than dexterity. The second ruling, the Danfoss case, (*Handels- of Kontorfunktionærernes Forbund i Danmark (HKF) v. DA* [on behalf of Danfoss] 1989) concerned an agreed pay system where all employees on the same grade received the same basic pay rate. However, merit increases were awarded on the basis of 'flexibility', seniority and training criteria, resulting in different earnings for staff on the same grade. The staff were unable to identify how criteria had been used to arrive at different pay amounts. The Court ruled that if an employee can establish on a statistical basis that the average pay of women workers is lower than that of men on the same grade, and where the pay structure in operation is not 'transparent', it is up to the employer to prove the pay practice was not discriminatory – i.e. that the distribution of payments was objective.

The preliminary ruling requested by the UK Court of Appeal in the case of *Enderby v. Frenchay Health Authority* 1992 is also important. It concerns (predominantly female) speech therapists who were paid less than principal pharmacists (predominantly male), even though the jobs were deemed of equal value. Again, the Court decided that it was for the employer to show the pay differential was objectively justified. It accepted that market forces could constitute an objective justification for paying differentially but only in relation to the proportion attributable to market forces.

Until the implications of these and other judgments are fully understood both industry- and company-based job evaluation and payment systems could well be operating in breach of European law, not only contributing to the perpetuation of unequal pay but also exposing the employer to the possibility of legal challenge by those affected. A number of major reviews of job grading and evaluation systems has taken place, certainly in Northern Europe, as a consequence of these rulings.

The volume of equal pay cases referred to the ECJ is small, a fact attributed to the complexities and inadequacies of national and European law. Consequently, in June 1994, the European Commission adopted a Memorandum on Equal Pay for Work of Equal Value. This defines the scope and concept of equal pay for work of equal value, and provides guidance on the criteria to be taken into account on job evaluation and job classification. The Memorandum identifies four areas for action: the need for more up-to-date pay data to allow adequate wage comparisons between men and women to be made, better dissemination of information about key cases based on Community law, improved training on aspects of European law and the publication of a Code of Practice for implementing equal pay for work of equal value. This task will be part of the forthcoming European social programme.

European Court of Justice rulings based on the equal treatment directive have been important for the development of equality law in a number of areas. For example:

- *Night work.* In the case of *Ministère public v. Alfred Stoeckel* 1991 the Court found that French law infringed the equal treatment directive in that it prohibited women's night work, albeit with numerous exceptions, whereas night work for men was not banned. As a result of this judgment the European Commission launched infringement proceedings in 1994 against five member states which had failed to bring their national provisions into line with the directive as required. In addition, the French state launched an appeal which concerned its international obligations as a result of its adherence to conventions of the International Labour Organisation. In Germany legislation was passed in 1994 that abolished the ban on industrial night work for women but, in parallel, introduced a number of important health and safety provisions to protect all night- and shiftworkers.
- *Discrimination on appointment and award limits.* In the case of *von Colson and Kamann v. North-Rhine Westphalia* 1984 the European Court of Justice ruled that any compensatory award made in the event of discrimination on appointment, where the actual incurred damages might be small, needed to go beyond a symbolic amount and had to constitute a sufficient and effective deterrent to an employer. In Germany, where the case originated, the ruling was initially interpreted as sanctioning awards for discrimination of up to six months' pay, although this has subsequently been reduced by a 1994 statute to three months. In *Marshall v. Southampton and South West Hampshire Area Health Authority* (No. 2), 1993, the Court ruled that the United Kingdom's statutory limit on compensation was in breach of the directive as awards had to be adequate – i.e. enable the loss and damage actually sustained as a result of discrimination to be made good.
- *Dismissal on grounds of pregnancy.* European Court rulings have consistently held that dismissals, and refusals to hire, on the grounds of pregnancy constitute direct discrimination on the grounds of sex under article 2(1) and 3(1) respectively of the 1976 equal treatment directive, even though no comparison with a man is possible. This effectively means that national courts cannot take into account the grounds, which may be available under national law, that justify the discrimination, nor the (national) requirement of fault.

    One leading case here is *Dekker v. Stichting Vormingscentrum voor Jong Volwassenen Plus* (No. C-177/88), which involved an organisation's decision not to appoint a women on the grounds of her pregnancy. Despite the fact that pregnancy dismissals are prima facie directly discriminatory, a Court judgment in the case of (*Handels- of Kontorfunktionærernes Forbund i Danmark v. DA [Aldi]*, 1992) confirmed, however, that the directive does not preclude dismissals after the maternity protection period, as defined in national law, which are the result of absence due to an illness attributable to pregnancy and confinement. The circumstances involved an employee who was absent on grounds of sickness connected with her pregnancy in the year following her return to work after maternity leave.

In the case of *Habermann-Beltermann v. Arbeiterwohlfahrt, Bezirksverband* 1994 the Court ruled that an employment contract signed without either party being aware that the employee was pregnant could not subseqently be declared null and void, nor could it be terminated on the grounds of pregnancy without infringing the provisions of the 1976 equality directive. This judgment overrode two specific aspects of German law. The employee concerned was hired specifically to perform night work, which under German law is forbidden to pregnant women. Moreover, German law also allows either party to challenge a contract if 'fundamental facts' about one of the parties subsequently come to light which, had they been known at the time of signing the contract, would have led the other party not to conclude a contract.

A similar line of argument was pursued by the European Court in the case of *Webb v. EMO Air Cargo (UK) Ltd* Case 1994 where it took the view that the equal treatment directive precluded the dismissal of a permanent employee who becomes pregnant on the grounds that she is temporarily prevented from performing her work. The background here was that the plaintiff had been recruited on an open-ended contract, although initially with a view to replacing an employee taking maternity leave. She was then dismissed when the employer discovered her pregnancy. As far as UK case law is concerned, the European Court held that pregnancy cannot be classed with other reasons such as illness in deciding whether an employee is unable to perform their job, as had been argued by the UK courts.

The 1992 directive on the protection of pregnant workers may serve to put an end to some uncertainties surrounding the lawfulness of pregnancy dismissals. Article 10 states that special protection against dismissal is granted to women from the beginning of their pregnancy to the end of their maternity leave, save in exceptional cases not connected with their condition. However, the directive provides no remedy for non-appointment to jobs on pregnancy grounds.

Sexual harassment

In 1991 the European Commission adopted a recommendation on the protection of the dignity of men and women at work, and a Code of Practice on measures to be taken to combat sexual harassment (92/131/EEC). The recommendation calls upon member states to promote awareness that sexual harassment is unacceptable and may infringe the equal treatment principle. It also urges employers and unions to devise measures to implement the Code of Practice. In September 1993 the Commission published a guide to implementing the Code of Practice.

The overall approach is to prevent harassment as far as possible by changing attitudes and behaviour, and to deal with complaints through established policies and procedures. To this end the Code urges that all employers should produce a policy statement, including a complaints procedure, to be communicated to employees. Although efforts should be made to stop harassment at an early stage, where such behaviour is established the company's disciplinary procedure should be invoked and where necessary sanctions applied.

Various approaches have been adopted in the different EU member states to deal with this problem. In France and Belgium specific legislation has been adopted. In Belgium works rules must specify how such behaviour is to be dealt with, state a designated person to support a complainant, lay down a complaints procedure and disciplinary action which can be applied. In other states, such as the United Kingdom, non-discrimination provisions may be invoked. In yet other cases general provisions on the civil and contractual liability of employers must be used. In Denmark, for instance, employers have an obligation to guarantee safe and healthy working conditions. German law provides for both criminal and civil law sanctions against sexual harassment. The 1994 Employee Protection Act draws together the various elements of employment law on sexual harassment in a new statutory framework in which the problem is explicitly addressed, in part by attempting a statutory definition of sexual harassment. It requires the employer to protect employees from sexual harassment, including taking preventive action. Should the employer fail to do so, the employee has a right to complain and ultimately to refuse to work, with no loss of pay, until the problem is resolved.

Older workers

There is no EU legislation outlawing age discrimination as such. Most expert organisations and surveys indicate that the problem is widespread and has worsened with the deterioration of the European economy in the early 1990s. This has given rise to early retirement and other labour-market exit policies that often oblige older workers to withdraw from economic activity long before official retirement age. Such policies largely continue in force even though early exit is creating difficulties in social security schemes designed to suit circumstances that prevailed several decades ago.

At present the only scope for redress is through article 119 of the Treaty of Rome and the 1976 Equal Treatment directive where age discrimination results in unequal pay or unfair treatment on the grounds of sex. Despite pressure from the European Parliament the Commission has been reluctant to act in this matter.

Retirement pensions and policies

As far as private pension schemes are concerned, one of the most crucial judgments is that of *Barber v. Guardian Royal Exchange* 1990 which ruled that retirement benefits paid under a private contracted-out occupational pension scheme fall under the scope of article 119, and that unequal pension ages for men and women are therefore unlawful. The ramification of this judgement continues to be felt, and a number of other controversial cases are still before the European Court of Justice.

A Protocol attached to the Treaty on European Union limited the retrospective impact of the Barber judgment by providing that pension benefits attributable to employment before 17 May 1990 are not to be considered as remuneration, unless legal proceedings were pending before that date. Various European Court judgments issued since Barber have clarified other aspects of occupational pension schemes, such as the use of differential actuarial calculations in working out benefits. The Court ruled on a further six cases referred from UK and Dutch courts in September 1994. It confirmed that the exclusion of part-timers from schemes may be unlawful, and that married men and women must be treated equally. Furthermore it held that claims for scheme membership (and the payment of back contributions) could in principle be backdated to 1976. Schemes may raise women's pension age to achieve equality even where this worsens women's pension benefits. Where pension rights are transferred from one scheme to another when an employee changes job, it is up to the second scheme to ensure the employee is paid their full benefits under the first scheme to eliminate any discrimination. Although the rulings will initially promote equal pension ages and wider part-timers access to schemes, uncertainty remains over issues such as backdating claims for scheme membership, the lawfulness of a minimum hours qualifying limit and the calculation of transfer values.

Apart from this, a measure which could potentially influence personnel practice in the longer-term is a non-binding recommendation adopted by the Council of Ministers in 1982 that calls for flexible retirement to become a principle of member states' social policy. In addition it urges a gradual reduction in working hours prior to retirement, the establishment of pre-retirement programmes, measures permitting pensioners to undertake paid employment and the abolition of temporary incentives promoting early retirement due to economic conditions as part of a flexible retirement scheme. The European Commission is also planning to issue a new draft law on occupational pensions mobility.

Appendix

European Union legislation

The European Union has three instruments through which to create binding legislation:

- Regulations: these are directly binding on member states.
- Directives: these provide a framework and are binding on member states 'as to the results to be achieved', with the precise form of implementation ('transposition') at national level left to each member state.
- Decisions: these are binding on selected member states.

The European Commission may also issue recommendations and opinions, neither of which are binding. However, according to the European Court of Justice (which rules on the application of European legislation) these non-binding instruments should be borne in mind, and may be considered by the court, in the event of a dispute over the implementation or interpretation of a Directive.

The procedure that the institutions of the European Union have to follow in passing an item of legislation differs depending on the issue and the legal base under which it is advanced. In developing legislation, the right to take an initiative rests with the European Commission; legislative proposals are considered, and ultimately adopted, by the Council of Ministers which directly represents member states through their governments, and effectively acts as the European legislature; the European Parliament has consultative rights, rights of initiative, rights to propose amendments and determine voting procedures in the Council of Ministers, and in some cases a right of veto depending on the legal basis on which the proposal is being advanced. The three paths are as follows:

- The Treaty of Rome, as amended by the Single European Act (now incorporated in Articles 189a and 189c of the Treaty on European Union). This provides for measures applicable to all EU member states to be passed either by unanimous vote in the Council of Ministers or, in certain cases, by qualified majority voting. Where unanimity is required, the European Parliament's role is confined to giving an opinion at the first (and only) reading of the proposal.

  Qualified majority voting is possible on some social and employment matters under changes made under the Single European Act. These embrace proposals designed to complete the Single European Market (some of which, such as proposals on 'atypical' workers, have employment implications) and proposals connected with the working environment, and health and safety at work (chosen as the legal basis for the directive on working time). Where a measure is proposed under this provision, it must obtain the support of fifty-four out of a possible seventy-six votes in the Council of Ministers of the twelve member states (as of 1994): countries are allocated votes broadly in proportion to their size (based on Germany's pre-unification population).

  The European Parliament has a greater role in proposals selected for adoption by qualified majority voting under the 'co-operation' procedure. If the European Parliament rejects by an absolute majority a proposal agreed in the Council of Ministers (a 'common position'), the Council can only subsequently pass the proposal by unanimity. The Parliament may also propose amendments to the original proposal. If the Commission accepts them, they are incorporated into the proposal and may be voted on by qualified majority vote on the Council. If the Commission rejects the Parliament's amendments, the Council can only accept them by unanimous vote.

- The Treaty on European Union. Under a new provision set out in Article 189b of the Treaty and termed the 'co-decision' procedure the European Parliament has an effective veto over some types of proposed legislation. Under this procedure (set out in Article 189b of the Treaty) if proposals to be decided on by qualified majority voting are rejected by the Parliament a Conciliation Committee is called to resolve differences between the Council and Parliament. If the Parliament insists on rejecting the proposal by an absolute majority after the intervention of the Committee, and following a protracted period of consultation, then the proposal will be deemed not to have been adopted.

- The Agreement on Social Policy (the 'Social Chapter'). This part of the Treaty on European Union makes a number of innovations. First, it allows for the possibility of qualified majority voting solely amongst the eleven member states (i.e. excluding the United Kingdom) who accepted the Social Chapter on health and safety matters, working conditions, information and consultation of workers, sex equality, and the integration of people excluded from the labour market. These eleven member states may also adopt measures unanimously on social security, protection against dismissal, and employee representation and co-determination. Second, the Agreement sets out to promote social dialogue at European level between management and labour, and creates enhanced scope for consultation with them by the Commission before any legislative proposal is envisaged. In addition, management and labour may opt to pursue a Commission objective through the form of a collective agreement rather than legislation, with any such agreement implemented either through national arrangements or via a decision of the Council of Ministers.

1

Austria

Basic rights and labour jurisdiction

The Austrian constitution assigns responsibility for employment law to the federal authorities. Basic employee rights, such as the freedom of association and the right to equal treatment, are guaranteed through individual pieces of legislation and via Austria's ratification of the European Convention on the Protection of Human Rights and Fundamental Freedoms. Some of the main labour laws, statutes such as the Law on Association, date from the nineteenth century. Some elements of employment law were codified in 1973 as the Works Constitution Act (*Arbeitsverfassungsrecht*), which is mainly concerned with collective employment relations. In most cases, however, legal provisions are still effected through a multiplicity of laws and ordinances, combining public and private law.

Hierarchy of legal provisions

Below the level of general constitutional law (*Verfassungsgesetz*), the highest tier of provision on employment is that of statute law. In most cases this is automatically binding but departure from it is permissible so long as it is the employee and not the employer who benefits. In a small number of instances statutes may contain categorical provisions, which must be complied with absolutely. Austrian law also contains some provisions which may be departed from even where this is prejudicial to the employee, provided the contractual parties have agreed. In such cases the law offers a provision which can be fallen back on in the absence of any other agreement. Statute law can be implemented via regulations (*Verordnungen*) or other official Acts – for example, to set minimum pay rates in industries where there are no representative employers' associations or to establish rates for trainees.

Collective agreements (*Kollektivverträge*) are negotiated between employers' organisations and industrial unions at industry level. They set out minimum pay and other terms and conditions for their particular industry. The sole trade union confederation in Austria, the Österreichischer Gewerkschaftsbund (ÖGB), consists of fourteen affiliates, organised along industrial lines for blue-collar workers and with a white-collar union which crosses sectoral lines of demarcation. Not only is the ÖGB itself competent to conclude collective agreements, but its affiliated unions are not wholly independent organisations. In effect they operate as sections of the ÖGB, and sign collective agreements in its name. Collective agreements are binding upon all signatory parties. In addition, a collective agreement may be extended (*Satzung*) by the labour authorities to cover all other companies in the sector, whether they are members of a signatory organisation or not. In practice, however, the vast majority of companies find themselves covered by collective agreements because such agreements are negotiated on their behalf by the relevant industry section of the statutory organisation, representing employers, the Federal Economic Chamber (*Bundeswirtschaftskammer*), to which all companies must belong. (These issues and the structure of collective bargaining and employee representation are dealt with in another volume in the series, *Employee Relations and Collective Bargaining*.)

Company agreements (*Betriebsvereinbarungen*) are negotiated within individual firms by the employer and workplace employee representatives, works councils, and may improve upon terms and conditions set out in the industry collective agreement. However, they may regulate only those areas of employment which the industry collective agreement has expressly delegated to the company agreement.

In itself the individual contract of employment may only govern areas not covered by law, or by industry or company agreement, although it may improve upon existing provisions at any of these levels. Contracts deemed contrary to good morals are null and void. Should a contract contain a provision which is contrary to a statutory or agreed provision, this does not mean that the whole contract is null and void. The relevant provision is simply replaced by the statutory or agreed provision. As a rule, contracts of employment refer to the relevant sections of collective agreements where the agreed provision applies (see below).

Labour jurisdiction

There is a separate system of labour jurisdiction governed by the Labour and Social Courts Act (*Arbeits- und Sozialgerichtsgesetz*), which came into force in 1987. It deals with disputes arising out of the employment relationship, including the application of laws on employee representation, and social security matters. The system operates at three levels. Disputes which cannot be resolved between the parties at company level can be heard before a local court (*Kreisgericht*), sitting as a first instance labour and social court (*Arbeits- und Sozialgericht*). Vienna has its own separate labour court. When handling employment matters the court will consist of an independent stipendiary justice and two lay magistrates, one each from the employer and the employee side. The parties may either represent themselves or elect to be represented. Contested decisions of the labour and social courts may be taken on appeal to the regional court (*Oberlandesgericht*), sitting on employment and social matters. The parties must be represented by a lawyer, a trade union representative or a member of one of the statutory representative organisations. Appeals must be lodged within four weeks. This court consists of three stipendiary magistrates and one lay magistrate each from the employer and employee side. Rulings may be appealed to the national High Court (*Oberster Gerichtshof in Arbeits- und Sozialrechtssachen*), sitting on employment and social matters, made up of seven stipendiary magistrates and two lay magistrates each from the employer and employee side. Representation must be by a lawyer.

Contracts of employment

Types of employee

Non-managerial   Dependent employees are generally categorised as blue-collar (*Arbeiter*) or white-collar (*Angestellte*). The 1859 Industrial Code (*Gewerbeordnung*) and the 1921 Salaried Employees Act (*Angestelltengesetz*) include definitions of blue- and white-collar employees. These categories in turn are further broken down into specific occupational groups. Subsequent legislation has harmonised many provisions covering the terms and conditions of blue- and white-collar workers – for example, on holiday entitlement and sick pay. However, pay bargaining is still conducted separately for each group, and, as noted above, the make-up of the Austrian trades union confederation, the ÖGB, continues to reflect status differences.

Managing directors and executives   Board members (*Vorstandsmitglieder*) of stock corporations (*Aktiengesellschaften*) are not, in general, deemed to be employees because, in Austrian company law, they enjoy an employer's power to supervise and direct and cannot, therefore, be deemed subordinate: as a rule they will carry out their duties under a freely negotiated contract of service (*freier Dienstvertrag*). The exclusion of this type of contract from the scope of employment law means that many aspects of the employment relation which in the case of employees are governed by legislation, such as holiday rights and severance entitlement, must be written into the individual contract. The employment status of managing directors (*Geschäftsführer*) of private limited liability companies (*GmbH*) depends primarily on the extent of their share ownership, and in particular on whether they can block resolutions of the general shareholders' meeting. Where an MD works subject to instructions issued by the shareholders, case law has generally ruled that he or she is an employee.

Executives are counted as employees but may be excluded from the scope of some employment legislation. There is no single statutory definition of an executive (*leitende Angestellte*). Rather, individual pieces of legislation offer slightly varying definitions, mainly concerning the exclusion of executives from various aspects of employment law. According to the legislation on employee representation (*Arbeitsverfassungsgesetz*), executives – who are not represented on works councils – are those employees who exercise 'decisive influence on the management of the establishment'. This provision also excludes executives from the right to contest dismissal. Moreover, company-level agreements between management and a works council do not apply to executives who fall within this definition, although substantive terms and conditions may become part of the contract implicitly or through the conduct of the parties. However, unless they are specifically excluded, executives may fall within the scope of industry-level collective agreements.

With slightly varying definitions, executives are also excluded from statutory regulations on working hours.

Form of the contract

There is no statutory requirement for formal contracts of employment to be in writing: a contract may be oral or implied from the conduct of the parties. In practice, however, virtually all contracts for managers, for salaried employees and, in many cases, for manual employees are in that form. Employees must be given a written statement of particulars (*Dienstzettel*) of their employment which must specify, among other things, the relevant collective agreement covering the workplace, job classification and duties, and pay provisions. Many employers prefer to confine themselves to written particulars rather than draw up a formal contract of employment, as written contracts are subject to stamp duty of ASch 60 (£3.40) for annual pay of ASch 42,000–ASch 140,000 (£2,400–£8,000) and ASch 400 (£22.85) for annual pay of ASch 140,000 and above. As part of its commitment to implement European Union social legislation on joining the European Economic Area, Austria implemented the EC Directive on Proof of an Employment Contract with effect from July 1993, requiring all employers to give new employees written particulars of their employment relationship and to supply particulars to existing employees on request. Under the Works Constitution Act (*Arbeitsverfassungsgesetz*) employers must inform works councils of all new hirings.

Typical content of a contract

A contract will typically contain the following:

- Personal details of the employee.
- Details of the place of work.
- Details of the type of work to be carried out and whether the employee may be transferred to different work within the company.
- Job title and grading.
- Type of contract, probationary period and duration of the contract, if it is fixed-term.
- Pay levels and payment arrangements.
- Hours of work and overtime arrangements.
- Holiday provision.
- The employee's duties of fidelity and confidentiality.
- Any non-competition arrangements.
- Periods of notice and severance pay arrangements.

Express and implied terms

In addition to the express terms laid down by the contract, employers and employees are automatically subject to a number of terms implicit in the employment relationship. These include, on the employee side:

• The duty to perform the agreed tasks.
• A duty of fidelity to the employer.
• The duty to inform the employer of any irregularities at the workplace or in the production process.
• Liability to make good any wilful damage to the employer's property.

On the employer's side they include:

• The duty to pay the employee the agreed wages, but not necessarily to provide actual employment at all times, so long as the agreed wages are paid.
• The duty to allow agreed holidays and rest periods.
• The duty to ensure the safety of the employee at the workplace.
• The duty to treat employees fairly and equally.

Types of contract

Fixed-term contracts   Fixed-term contracts may be agreed under a number of statutory provisions, some of which are general in character whilst others relate to particular occupations. In principle, a fixed-term contract may be limited either by setting a specific date or the attainment of a stated objective. However, some collective agreements, which may apply throughout an industry, only allow fixed-term contracts to be concluded when a starting and a finishing date are stipulated. In general, if employment continues beyond the agreed period, the contract will be deemed to have become permanent. The law does not require any particular reason to be adduced for using a fixed-term contract. However, case law does demand justification on economic or social grounds for employing anyone on a succession of fixed-term contracts, and the reasons must be demonstrated on each individual occasion. An automatic succession of fixed-term contracts – *Kettenarbeitsverträge*, as the device is called – will be null and void as far as the fixed-duration element is concerned and the contract will be deemed to be permanent. (For termination provisions, see below.)

Agency employment   Temporary work agencies are permitted and agency employment is regulated by the 1988 Temporary Employment Act (*Arbeitnehmerüberlassungsgesetz*). The Act also applies to situations where a company makes its employees temporarily available to a third party in exceptional circumstances. Temporary workers are permanent employees of the agency, not of the client company, and are protected by a number of statutory provisions intended to shield the employee from the business risks entered into by the employer. These include a ban on their income being linked to the length of an assignment with a client company, a ban on fixed-term contracts – unless there is a material reason – and a ban on any clause which prevents the employee taking up a full-time job with a client.

Agency employees are subject to most of the collective or customary provisions applying in the client company (for example, as regards hours of work) but not necessarily to those affecting pay. There is also a collective agreement for the sector, laying down minimum terms and conditions. Temporary staff often prove cheaper to use than permanent employees, as the rates paid by the agencies tend to be the minimum specified in the collective agreement, and this is likely to be below contractual pay in a client company, which will include company-level supplements.

Part-time contracts   Part-time work is work for hours shorter than those set by law or collective agreement for full-time workers. Individual statutes may include specific provisions on minimum hours of work and/or minimum eligibility for coverage by legislation. Employers may not treat part-time workers differently from full-time workers without a material reason.

Women have a right to return to work on a part-time basis after maternity leave. The right is usually taken up. The employer may contest the right on economic grounds. In cases which have come before the courts, the ruling has been that companies with ten or more employees would normally be expected to offer a part-time position to a returning employee.

Census figures for 1991 revealed that 20 per cent of the female work force and 1.2 per cent of the male work force worked part-time.

Probationary periods

Probationary periods at the beginning of a contract of employment are common. They are limited by law to one month, during which either party can terminate the contract without notice, justification or severance payment. Longer probationary periods can be agreed for some employee groups, such as domestic servants. Collective agreements may also stipulate the length of probationary periods, and these may also be complemented by company-level agreements. Probationary periods are not customary at management level.

Non-competition clauses

Austrian law differentiates between competition with the employer during and competition after the termination of a contract. While the employment relationship lasts the employee is subject to a duty of fidelity and under para. 7 of the Salaried Employees Act must not enter into a competitive relationship (*Konkurrenzverbot*) with the employer, either in connection with their employment or quite independently of it, except by prior agreement. In case law, doing so has been deemed valid grounds for summary dismissal. However, the encroachment on the business interests of the employer must be shown to have been substantial. Similar statutory provisions apply to board members of public corporations and managing directors of private limited liability companies.

Restrictions on competition following the termination of the employment relationship are regulated by non-competition agreements (*Konkurrenzklauseln*). These agreements are usually written into the employment contract, and specify restrictions regarding time, geographical area, field of competence or may take the form of the former employee agreeing not to approach the former employer's clients within a certain period. Reasonable limits in these areas have been set by case law. In addition, the Salaried Employees Act states that non-competition clauses must not run for a period of more than one year, must not unreasonably hinder the professional advancement of the ex-employee, and must not be unduly onerous (*gegen die guten Sitten*), for example by imposing draconian penalties.

A non-competition agreement will not be valid if the employer terminates the employment without the employee having given cause through 'culpable behaviour'. However, the agreement can be upheld if the employer undertakes at the time of giving notice to go on paying the employee throughout the term of the covenant. A covenant will remain in force should the employee resign, except where resignation can be interpreted as constructive dismissal, or in the event of termination by mutual agreement. Should a covenant involve a financial consideration, there is no obligation on the employee to offset any earnings from a new employer. A covenant may include an agreed penalty in the event of breach by the employee: any such penalty must be reasonable and subject to review by the courts. Where an employee breaches the agreement, the employer may only demand the agreed penalty, and does not have the right to seek damages or insist on the employee refraining from the activity in question. The former employer may decide to waive the non-competition clause, and the employee may not insist upon it being adhered to by the company.

In practice, such clauses are common only in the case of managers and specialists and normally last for twelve months following employment. It is customary, but not obligatory, for the employer to compensate the employee for agreeing to the clause, usually to the tune of one year's salary, payable on the termination of the contract. If the employee breaks the agreement the sum becomes repayable. In certain circumstances a new employer may settle any dispute by repaying it himself.

Employee inventions

The 1970 Patent Act (*Patentgesetz*) states that an invention is generally the property of the inventor, but allows that ownership of employee inventions may be regulated by agreement, which must be in writing. Employee inventions are defined in the Patent Act as those which occur during normal employment, those arising out of ideas developed during working hours, or those which are made possible by the use of company tools or processes. Any inventions outside these criteria are designated free inventions of the employee (*freie Erfindungen des Arbeitnehmers*) and belong to the employee. Inventions offered to the employer but not accepted remain the exclusive property of the employee.

Workplace discipline

Disciplinary procedures may be agreed at industry level in an industry-wide collective agreement, or at enterprise level, where the agreement of the works council must be obtained. Enterprise-level agreements may improve upon but not detract from the provisions of industry-wide agreements. Typical sanctions are verbal or written warnings, loss of promotion, transfer and dismissal. Employees may be fined, but the money is usually paid into a fund, not to the employer.

Individual workplace rights

The Works Constitution Act provides for a number of rights which are exercised collectively through works councils but which protect the individual employee in several important areas. For example, questionnaires which collect information about individual employees are subject to co-determination by works councils and management. Irrespective of works councils' consent, no questions which intrude into the personal sphere or touch on individuals' political or religious beliefs are permissible. Works council consent is also required for the introduction of systems intended to monitor and control the performance and behaviour of employees.

Grievances

Under the Works Constitution Act each individual employee has the right to put grievances to the works council or direct to the employer. The employer has the right to set up an enterprise grievance procedure (*betriebliches Beschwerdewesen*), with or without the involvement of the works council. If the works council is involved, this procedure is formally incorporated into the company agreement.

Data protection   Under the Data Protection Act (*Datenschutzgesetz*), employees' personal data must be kept secret, regardless of how they are stored. Systems intended to collect and process data on employees through EDP equipment require the consent of works councils.

Smoking   There are no statutory regulations governing smoking in the workplace and formal company policies on smoking are not particularly widespread. However, many companies have informal approaches which consist of asking, at interview stage, whether a potential employee smokes, and trying to accommodate the needs of smokers and non-smokers in the workplace.

Terms and conditions of employment

Hours of work

Hours of work are regulated by the 1969 Working Time Act (*Arbeitszeitgesetz*). This provides for a normal working day of eight hours and a normal working week of forty hours. However, the Act does provide for certain more flexible arrangements, such as reorganising hours of work in order to achieve the forty-hour average over a specified reference period to permit longer weekends, subject to a maximum nine-hour day. It is also possible to set up 'bridging' holidays (making Friday a holiday following a public holiday on a Thursday) by employees working longer at other times, provided the average is achieved over a seven-week period and the working day does not exceed ten hours. A derogation permits a working day of up to nine hours and a working week of up to forty-four hours in commerce, provided the statutory forty-hour week is achieved on average over a four-week reference period.

Collective agreements   In practice hours of work are governed by industry-wide collective agreement. There has been a general movement towards a shorter working week over the past few years, and many industry-level collective agreements, such as those covering commerce, banking and metalworking, now provide for a 38.5 hour working week.

The working week may also be extended by industry collective agreement by up to twenty hours for those employees who are not working at full capacity for the entirety of their working hours, such as taxi drivers and night porters, subject to a maximum working day of twelve hours for men and ten hours for women. If there is no collective agreement, an extension may be authorised by the labour inspectorate (*Arbeitsinspektorat*).

Companies are free to set their own working hours within the framework of the law and/or the relevant collective agreement. Whilst most companies adhere to collectively agreed provisions with regard to the length of the working week, it is common practice to agree, formally or informally, a system of flexitime. Such systems can range from complete flexitime from 07.00 to 19.00, with no core time, to systems of flexible starting and finishing times within a two- or three-hour range. Most systems stipulate that hours worked over one month may not differ by more than ten either side of normal monthly working hours.

Rest periods   Daily rest is fixed by the 1983 Rest Periods Act (*Arbeitsruhegesetz*) and consists of an entitlement to thirty minutes' break after six hours' work. There is no obligation for this to be a paid break, nor is it included in the calculation of working hours. The law stipulates a minimum eleven-hour break between working days, although this may be shortened to ten hours for male workers by collective agreement. Weekly rest periods are set by law at thirty-six consecutive hours, including a Sunday, in any calendar week, and should begin at 13.00 on a

Saturday or at 15.00 for workers such as cleaners and maintenance staff. Derogations are provided for by law or collective agreement. For example, workers on continuous shifts may have weekly rest shortened to twenty-four hours, provided an average of thirty-six hours per week is achieved over a four-week period.

Annual leave and public holidays

All employees are entitled by law to thirty working days' paid holiday a year (including Saturdays, i.e. five weeks'), rising to thirty-six days after twenty-five years of working life. Holiday pay should be paid to the employee in advance of the holiday to be taken. Industry collective agreements or company agreements usually adhere quite closely to these provisions, although some may award the enhanced provisions after twenty years instead of the twenty-five stipulated by law. There are thirteen public holidays in Austria: 1 January (New Year), 6 January (Epiphany), Easter Monday, 1 May, Ascension Day, Whit Monday, Corpus Christi, Assumption, 26 October (National Day), 1 November (All Saints' Day), 8 December, Christmas Day and Boxing Day.

Maternity and parental leave

Pregnant women have a right to be put on to lighter physical duties and cannot work overtime or work at night, at weekends or on public holidays. Daily and weekly working time limits are nine hours and forty hours respectively for pregnant women. There is also protection against dismissal, except for economic reasons or gross misconduct during pregnancy and for four months following the birth, or, if parental leave is taken, until four weeks after the end of the maternity leave, whichever is the greater. In the event of dismissal on economic grounds, or where the woman voluntarily accepts notice of dismissal, court permission must be obtained.

Maternity leave is sixteen weeks in all, eight weeks before the expected date of birth and eight weeks afterwards. The latter can be extended to twelve weeks in the event of premature or multiple births, or delivery by Caesarian section. Women have the right to go back to work part-time eight weeks after the birth or after one year's maternity leave. This right extends until the child's fourth birthday, or up to the child's second or third birthday if both parents take advantage of the part-time working provisions. In principle the employer cannot reasonably refuse to take an employee back on a part-time basis, although the courts have allowed concessions to companies with fewer than ten employees.

Parental leave (*Elternkarenzurlaub*) is available to both father and mother and may follow either birth or adoption. It may be taken by one parent only or shared between the two. In practice the vast majority of leave is taken exclusively by women. Parents have the right to take up to two years' leave from the birth or adoption of a child. This leave is paid by the state, at the 1994 rate of ASch 5,424

(£309.95) monthly or ASch 8,049 (£459.95) monthly for lone parents. It is not usual for companies or collective agreements to top up these payments. Employees returning from parental leave have a right to re-engagement, but not to reinstatement.

Other time off

Care leave   Since 1 January 1993 all employees have had a statutory right to one week's paid care leave per year to look after close members of the family. There is no length-of-service requirement to qualify for this leave, which is paid for by the employer. The law states that employees should inform the employer as soon as possible that they wish to take the leave. There is no statutory requirement for proof of illness to be provided, and employers who wish to see such proof must bear the financial cost of obtaining a doctor's report. The leave may be extended to two weeks a year in certain cases.

Staff representative duties and training   The Works Constitution Act (*Arbeitsverfassungsgesetz*) sets out staff representatives' right to paid time off in order to carry out duties and functions related to the position. In firms with 150 or more employees the law provides for one employee to be a full-time staff representative, the figure rising to two full-time representatives in firms of 700 employees or more, three in firms of 3,000 or more and one further full-time representative for each additional 3,000 employees. Furthermore, staff representatives have a right to paid time off for training in connection with their duties, up to three weeks annually, unless the firm has under twenty employees, in which case time off for staff representative training is unpaid. Training leave may be extended to five weeks annually in some cases.

Promotion and transfer

Many companies have an explicit policy of internal promotion and career development, often outlined in collective agreements, to fill most positions up to middle management level. Job classification systems and incremental scales provided for in collective agreements are widely followed by companies, providing an automatic salary progression system. Senior managers tend to be appointed from outside.

Under para. 101 of the Works Constitution Act, works councils must be informed of any transfer of employees either to different positions or different places of work. Where any worsening of terms is involved, the consent of the works council must be obtained. Transfers are either deemed to be provided for within the contract of employment, as an implicit component of the employer's right to supervise and direct, or constitute a variation in the contract. In the latter case the employee is justified in refusing the transfer and such refusal does not constitute just grounds for dismissal. However, the employer is entitled to issue a notice of termination in order to modify the contract, which is subject to normal dismissal procedures and can be challenged by the employee.

Individual pay and benefits

Statutory pay determination

There is no statutory national minimum wage. Industry collective agreements, concluded between the relevant industry sections of the Federal Economic Chamber (*Bundeswirtschaftskammer*), the statutory body representing employers, membership of which is compulsory, and the union confederation, the ÖGB, set out minimum rates of pay for jobs in their particular industry. Employers may not pay below these rates. In occupations where there is no representative employer organisation, such as domestic service, caretaker or private tutor, employee or union representatives may apply to the Federal Conciliation Office (*Bundeseinigungsamt*) for a decree setting minimum wage rates for the employees (*Mindestlohntarif*). Over the past few years the ÖGB has been pushing for a ASch 10,000 (£571) monthly minimum wage to be adopted by industry collective agreements. The campaign has been widely successful, with the majority of industries complying. The number of workers earning less than ASch 10,000 monthly fell from 430,000 in 1989 to 150,000 in 1992. The ÖGB is now campaigning for the minimum to be raised to ASch 12,000 (£686) monthly.

The law on pay

The 1859 Industrial Code (*Gewerbeordnung*) requires wages to be paid in cash as opposed to goods or payment in kind. The Works Constitution Act states that works councils have an enforceable right to conclude company agreements, subject to any provisions already agreed at industry level, on frequency of payment, date of payment, advance payments and the form of payment, which may be cash, cheque or transfer into the employee's bank or building society account.

White-collar workers, supervisors and managers are usually paid by way of an annual salary, paid monthly into a bank account. Blue-collar workers are paid either weekly, in cash or otherwise, or monthly.

Levels of pay determination

As noted above, there is no statutory national form of pay determination. Binding collective agreements at industry level set out minimum rates of pay for job categories in the industry, which are increased once a year through collective bargaining. Well over 90 per cent of employees are covered by industry collective agreement, as by law employers must belong to the Federal Economic Chamber, which negotiates for the employers' side. Employees not covered by industry collective agreement are either very small groups with no industry agreement, such as dental assistants, or small groups in an industry, such as blue-collar workers in banking and finance, where there is a white-collar agreement only.

Industry collective agreements set an enforceable minimum for pay rates. Company pay rates usually exceed the collectively agreed minima by a substantial margin, typically 20–5 per cent. This divergence is also taken account of in collective bargaining at industry level, which specifies an increase not only in the industry minima (the *KV-Lohn*) but also in company rates (*Ist-Lohn*). The increase in the minimum is usually higher than the increase in company pay. This conclusion of binding agreements on increases in company-level pay limits employers' freedom to negotiate the local element of pay, for example by eating into accumulated wage drift at times when business is difficult. There is no significant difference between the rates of pay offered by Austrian companies and those offered by Austrian branches of multinationals.

Make-up of the pay package

The pay package consists of a basic sum, consisting of the company rate for the job, usually above the minimum rate set out by collective agreement, plus any regular supplements, such as productivity or performance payments, or additions for particular skills. Pay in the Vienna area tends to be higher than elsewhere in Austria.

Many companies have incremental scales with automatic progression based on seniority, although companies are increasingly looking to replace seniority-based payments with supplements more closely tied to employee performance. The vast majority of collective agreements stipulate that monthly salaries must be paid fourteen times a year. Some collective agreements provide for fifteenth and sixteenth payments. Extra monthly payments are usually made at Christmas time and in the summer, and are subject to favourable tax treatment.

Pay increases

As mentioned above, a two-tier system of minimum rates is collectively agreed at industry level. The bargaining round begins in the autumn each year, with most pay agreements lasting for one year. Many industries agree separate scales for blue-collar workers (*Arbeiter*) and white-collar workers (*Angestellte*). The lead settlement is in the engineering industry, which usually sets rates as from 1 November each year. Around two-thirds of settlements are reached in the autumn, and one-third in the spring, beginning with the chemical industry agreement, which is usually renewed from 1 May each year. Companies may then agree their own increase with the staff representatives, if any, in addition to the collectively agreed increase, and are free to set their own rates, as long as they are above the collectively agreed minimum. Annual bargaining typically sets increases in minimum rates both for the industry and in company-level pay. One innovation in the 1993/94 bargaining round was a clause in the engineering industry agreement allowing companies not to implement actual rate (*Ist-Lohn*) increases, after due consultation with staff representatives, in cases of financial difficulty and/or where other social measures (including job guarantees) can be offered in place of the increase. This option of an 'enabling clause' (*Öff-nungsklausel*) was not widely taken up by companies, however, despite a more difficult economic situation.

Overtime and weekend working

Overtime is generally held to be any hours worked in excess of forty hours weekly and must by law be remunerated at 150 per cent of normal rates. There are statutory limits on overtime: in the first instance, five hours a week, with the possibility of a further sixty hours a year, subject to a limit of ten hours in any one week and a maximum ten-hour day. However, provided it is allowed for in a collective agreement a further five hours of overtime can be worked in any one week (i.e. a maximum of fifteen) which may be extended to twenty hours a week in all for some groups of employees, provided the working day does not exceed thirteen hours for men and ten hours for women, and the working week does not exceed sixty hours. All these limits may be suspended in a serious emergency. Many collective agreements provide for a working week of 38.5 hours and time worked beyond that, up to forty hours, is classified as additional time (*Mehrarbeit*) rather than as overtime, and is often not remunerated as overtime.

It is normal practice for collective agreements and companies to remunerate normal overtime hours at 150 per cent, and weekend working (Saturday after-noon to Sunday evening) and work on public holidays at 200 per cent of normal rates. Many companies have a system under which a fixed monthly amount is paid to compensate overtime (*Überstundenpauschale*) for some employees, es-pecially managerial staff, irrespective of how much is worked. The average allowance is twenty hours a month. Some companies will adjust the amount if overtime worked is regularly above or below the fixed amount.

Night work

Night work is defined as at least six hours' work carried out between 22.00 and 06.00. Women are banned from working nights, but Austria is committed to reviewing the ban by 2001. There are many derogations from the ban, however, e.g. for nurses and other health professionals, in hotels and catering, in entertain-ment and for managers. Remuneration for night work is covered by law for some employees, such as agricultural workers and those in the baking industry, stipu-lating that night work must be remunerated at 200 per cent of normal rates. Most collective agreements and company agreements provide for remuneration at 200 per cent.

Shift work

Rest periods during shift work are governed by law: employees involved in continuous shift processes may take their statutory thirty-minute break (see above) in smaller, more frequent pauses. Employees doing arduous work on night shift (working at least six hours between 22.00 and 06.00) on a regular basis are governed by the 1981 Arduous Night Work Act (*Nachtschwerarbeitsgesetz*), as amended in 1993, which provides for certain enhanced provisions for night workers, such as two extra days' holiday a year for those who have worked fifty or more such night shifts a year, rising to four extra days if the employee has worked the night shifts for five years, and six extra days after fifteen years. These workers also have a right to early retirement and enhanced protection against dismissal. Payment for shift work is regulated by collective agreement or company agreement. Rates of 150–200 per cent are common, with 200 per cent usually paid for night shifts. Some companies pay a fixed enhanced rate for availability to work shifts, plus a supplement for shift work actually done.

Bonuses

Employees almost universally receive holiday and Christmas payments, which commonly take the form of thirteenth and fourteenth monthly salary payments, under the terms of collective agreements. Some agreements also provide for fifteenth and sixteenth monthly payments. Collective agreements or company agreements may also provide for employees to receive a presentation to mark length of service anniversaries, typically jewellery or shares in the company.

Pay for performance

There has been a growing trend over the past few years for a larger element of pay to be tied to individual performance, principally in the case of managerial staff. Around 80 per cent of senior managers have a variable element in their pay, with the amount at risk typically accounting for some 25 per cent of total remuneration.

There is some movement towards the introduction of performance-related elements in white-collar pay. One initiative in the banking sector, for example, provides for a performance-related supplement of up to two months' salary for top performers. However, such approaches remain, as yet, largely undeveloped.

Managers' pay

As noted above, there has been a growing tendency for managers' pay to include a performance or incentive element. However, the amount of variable pay for all but top management remains fairly small. Whereas top managers might have a bonus element approaching 25 per cent, incentives for senior managers tend to be in the 10–15 per cent range, or lower in some cases.

In general, company size and performance are more important than industry in determining managerial salaries. Function pay differences, as revealed by the Monks Partnership survey *Management Remuneration in Europe* and based on total earnings, suggest a substantial differential between senior and top management, but with a fairly close bunching of senior managers without major function differentials. Whereas managing directors were earning nearly double senior managers' pay, with sales the next highest paid, the range between function heads was almost insignificant.

Car provision is above 90 per cent for top and senior management, but tails off rapidly below that level.

Profit-sharing and financial participation

Profit-share schemes may be set up for all or part of the work force, and linked to all or a particular part of company profits. By law, employees have the right to check the company results taken by the employer as the basis of the profit-share pay-out. There is no legally prescribed formula which profit-share schemes must follow, although employees in profit-share schemes must be informed of calculation methods. Such schemes are most common for managerial staff and board members.

Sick pay

There is a dual system of sick pay entitlement for employees who cannot work owing to illness. Initially, employees are entitled to a period of full pay for a service-related period, followed by four weeks at half pay, paid by the employer. Employees then move on to statutory sickness benefit, paid by the state sickness insurance fund.

Service-related sick pay   White-collar employees (*Angestellte*) are entitled to fixed rates of sick pay, paid by the employer. The period of entitlement varies according to length of service, from six weeks at full pay (the average of pay received over the previous twelve months) for up to five years' service, rising to eight weeks after five years' service, ten weeks after fifteen years' service and twelve weeks for over twenty-five years' service. All the above are also entitled to an extra four weeks at half pay. There is also a basic right to eight weeks' full sick pay for work-related illnesses and accidents. If the employee falls ill once more within six months of returning to work, entitlement to sick pay is halved.

Blue-collar employees (*Arbeiter*) have a right, under the law governing sick pay (*Entgeltfortzahlungsgesetz*) to four weeks' sick pay after fourteen days' service, rising to six weeks' after five years' service, eight weeks' after fifteen years' service and ten weeks' after twenty-five years' service. Employees who fall ill once more within one year of returning to work are entitled to whatever remains to them from the previous period of sick pay. The employer may claim back amounts of sick pay paid out to blue-collar workers from the sick pay fund which is financed by employer and employee contributions of 3.95 per cent each of gross salary. Employers also receive a lump sum from the fund to cover all social security contributions for the employee in question. It is not usual company practice to grant longer entitlement, although some of the older, traditional firms may have schemes.

Sickness benefit   When entitlement to employer sick pay has run out, employees may claim state sickness benefit (*Krankengeld*) after a waiting period of four days. State sickness benefit is paid for a maximum of twenty-six weeks, which can be extended to seventy-eight weeks in some cases. The benefit is equivalent to 50 per cent of daily pay (taking account of non-working days), increasing to 60 per cent after forty-three days' illness.

Maternity and parental leave benefit

Maternity benefit, available under the statutory sickness insurance scheme, is payable during the period of maternity leave (eight weeks before and usually eight weeks after the birth). The benefit is equal to normal weekly earnings over the thirteen weeks before leave is taken.

Parental leave benefit (*Karenzurlaubsgeld*) is paid for up to two years after the birth of the child, at a rate of ASch 180.80 (£10.33) daily or ASch 5,424 (£309.95) monthly, and at an enhanced rate of ASch 268.30 (£15.33) daily or ASch 8,049 (£460) monthly for lone parents or those on low incomes. The rate will be paid in part where parents take advantage of the option to work part-time.

Equal pay and equal opportunities

Discrimination

The constitution upholds the equality of all citizens, regardless of birth, sex, language, race, religion or political beliefs. This binds employers to equal treatment of all employees and forbids arbitrary discrimination, for example between blue- and white-collar employees. Discrimination at the workplace on grounds of sex is forbidden by a national law on equality (*Gleichbehandlungsgesetz*). This law forbids discrimination on grounds of sex in the areas of recruitment, the contract of employment, pay setting, payment of social security contributions, training at company level, promotion, general conditions of employment, and termination of contract. Grievances on any of these topics may be taken by the employer, employee or staff representative, to the Equality Commission (*Gleichbehandlungs- kommission*). The commission is run by the Ministry of Social Administration and is made up of eleven members, two from the four main employer and employee representative bodies, and two Ministry officials, with a Ministry official in the chair. If the commission decides that discrimination has taken place, it will issue a written recommendation to the employer on how to comply with the equality legislation. If, within one month, the employer has taken no action, the employee can take the case to the relevant labour court (*Arbeits- und Sozialgericht*). Sanctions for proved discrimination range from sums covering loss of earnings to damages awarded by the court.

Sexual harassment

If sexual harassment of an employee is proved, it is deemed to be discrimination on grounds of sex under the law on equality and the employee may be entitled to a compensatory award.

Retirement

Retirement ages

Retirement age is different for men and women, with the normal retirement age at 65 for men and 60 for women, and early retirement at 60 for men and 55 for women. However, pensionable age for women will be raised gradually, in six-month stages, from 2024 for normal retirement age and from 2019 for early retirement, in order to bring them into line with the normal and early retirement ages for men. Employees are entitled to a full state earnings-related pension if they have 420 contribution months (thirty-five contribution years). In order to take early retirement, the employee must have 420 contribution months (thirty-five contribution years), twenty-four months of which must be in the thirty-six months preceding the retirement date. (Alternatively, the preceding twelve consecutive months must have been contribution months.) In practice, most men and women retire around the age of 57–58, as soon as they have the necessary number of contributions years. Although early retirement age is currently different for men and women, both sexes usually reach their required number of contribution years at around the same time, as women more often take a career break to care for children.

Pensions

The size of the state earnings-related pension paid is calculated according to the number of contribution years and based on the best fifteen years of salary. A pension of 80 per cent of best salary is calculated, up to a ceiling which for 1994 was ASch 32,018 (£1,829) monthly, giving a maximum pension in 1994 of ASch 25,614.40 (£1,433) monthly.

It is not usual practice for companies to provide extra company pensions for their employees. Legislation enabling firms to set up private pension funds in addition to state provision was passed in 1990. However, the take-up has not been as widespread as expected, and it is estimated that these funds manage around ASch 13 billion (£740 million) instead of the ASch 200 billion (£11.4 billion) forecast in 1990. It is estimated that only around 300,000 employees have private pensions, and they are concentrated in industries such as banking and finance.

Individual termination of contract

Resignation

The employment relationship may be terminated by either party at any time. In the case of resignation by the employee, the law differentiates between blue-collar and white-collar workers. For blue-collar workers the statutory minimum period of notice is fourteen days. However, periods of notice are usually regulated by collective agreement, or company agreement in the absence of a collective agreement, and they typically provide for an average one-month period of notice. For white-collar workers, statutory periods of notice range from six weeks to five months, depending on length of service. The Salaried Employees Act states that the date for the termination of the employment relationship must be the end of a quarterly period, which is binding unless a collective or company agreement states otherwise.

Termination by mutual agreement

The parties are free to end the employment relationship by mutual agreement (*einvernehmliche Auflösung*), in which case there is no period of notice, merely an agreed date on which the contract will terminate. However, it must be a genuine agreement between the two parties. All employees have the right to consult their works council before entering into a mutual agreement with the employer to terminate their employment. Mutual agreement to terminate sooner than two days following this consultation is invalid.

Termination by the employer

Summary dismissal   Where sufficiently serious grounds are afforded by the employee's conduct, the employer may terminate employment without notice (*Entlassung*). The statutory grounds for summary dismissal are listed in several pieces of legislation, including the Industrial Code and the Salaried Employees Act. For example, a white-collar employee may be summarily dismissed for disloyalty, for inability to carry out the tasks assigned, for engaging in competition with the employer, or for violence at work. In the case of a blue-collar worker, summary dismissal is possible for incompetence, persistent drunkenness, theft, unauthorised absence, or being ill with a 'serious disease'. In view of the age of these legal provisions, 1859 and 1921 respectively, the courts have built up a body of interpretation more in keeping with currently accepted standards of what constitutes a serious breach. If the employer seeks to impose a summary dismissal which is challenged by the employee, the courts may convert it into dismissal with notice if they consider summary dismissal excessively harsh. For example, case law has established that an employer is not justified in dismissing an employee simply because their work is a little below average; absence from work due to sickness or accident is not grounds for summary dismissal. However, absence due to a custodial sentence would be.

Dismissal with notice (*Kündigung*)   All dismissals with notice must be notified to the works council before being issued. The works council has five days in which to respond. Any notice issued before this deadline is null and void. The reasons for termination do not normally have to be stated when notice is given, but dismissal which either infringes the statutory protection accorded to certain groups of employees (see below) or which is 'socially unwarranted' may be unlawful. In the latter case, the employer needs to demonstrate good cause related to the personal character of the employee or the financial demands of the business.

Dismissal procedures   Most companies have a hierarchy of warnings prior to dismissal, either provided for in the company agreement or of an informal nature. The most common sequence is a verbal warning, followed by one or two written warnings, leading to suspension and/or dismissal.

Terminating executive employment   Managers may have individual contracts of employment and in that case would not be normal employees of the company. Therefore the works council does not need to be informed of the recruitment or termination of managers. Periods of notice and severance payments for managers are regulated by individual contract. The average period of notice is three to six months and the average severance payment is six to twelve months' pay. It may be more if a non-competition clause for a period after the termination of the contract is agreed (see above). In practice, managers do not usually work out their notice, and it is common for the employer to give pay in lieu of notice. However, it is normal for a short period of the notice to be worked in order to effect an orderly hand-over.

Periods of notice

Statutory periods of notice (*Kündigungsfristen*) for white-collar workers are as follows:

- Up to two years' service: six weeks.
- Two to five years' service: two months.
- Five to fifteen years' service: three months.
- Fifteen to twenty-five years' service: four months.
- Over twenty-five years' service: five months.

Length of service means total working years, not length of service with a particular company. Collective and company agreements may improve slightly upon these provisions. The period of notice for blue-collar workers is a statutory fourteen-day period which may be improved upon by collective or company agreement. Employees serving out periods of notice are entitled to eight hours a week paid time to look for a job, or four hours if the employee has resigned. This does not apply to employees leaving to retire.

Severance payments

Employees with at least three years' service are entitled to a statutory severance payment (*Abfertigung*) on termination, with payments increasing in line with seniority as follows:

Length of service	Number of months' pay
3 years	2
3–5 years	3
5–10 years	4
10–15 years	6
15–20 years	9
20–25 years	12

Where the employee terminates employment to take up a normal or early retirement pension, they may still claim the payment but must have at least 10 years' service (reduced to five in some collective agreements).

Provided employees have continuous service with the same employer, they will be awarded severance payments in the following instances:

- Dismissal on economic grounds.
- Unfair dismissal.
- Justified resignation by the employee (constructive dismissal).
- Expiry of a fixed-term contract.
- Termination by mutual agreement.
- Certain cases of individual dismissal by the employee.

Severance provisions may be improved upon by collective or company agreement.

Unfair dismissal

Employees may challenge dismissal with notice (*Kündigung*) on grounds of unjust cause (*verpönte Motive*) or because the dismissal is socially unjustified. In addition, there is a procedure for redress in the event of an unwarranted summary dismissal (*Entlassung*).

Unjust cause is defined by law as any of the following:

- Membership of or activities in a trade union or other representational activity.
- Activities connected with service on conciliation and arbitration boards.
- Call-up for military or community service.
- The sex of the employee.
- Reasonable employee requests concerning equal treatment under the Equality Act (*Gleichbehandlungsgesetz*). The burden of proof lies with the employee.

An employee with six months' service may bring a claim of unfair dismissal if the dismissal is felt to be 'socially unwarranted' – or prejudicial to the 'fundamental interests' of the employee. The burden of proof is then upon the employer to show that the dismissal was due to personal reasons connected with the employee which affected the company detrimentally, or to business conditions which stood in the way of continued employment.

Cases of unfair dismisssal must be taken to the labour and social court (*Arbeits- und Sozialgericht*) within three weeks of the dismissal. Should the employee's case be upheld, they are entitled either to resume employment or to be paid a sum in compensation equal to their earnings between the time of dismissal and the final legal settlement of the case. Any sums earned by the dismissed employee (or saved as a result of not attending the workplace) may be set off against the award. Long-service employees are also entitled to a statutory severance payment (see above). Decisions of the labour and social court may be appealed within four weeks to the district social and labour court (*Oberlandesgericht in Arbeits- und Sozialrechtssachen*). Decisions of the district court may be appealed within four weeks to the High Court (*Oberster Gerichtshof*) if sums of ASch 50,000 (£2,857) or more are involved.

An employee dismissed summarily may also contest the employer's action. If their case is upheld by the courts, they will usually be granted a sum in compensation equal to the pay they would have received had they been allowed to work out their full notice period, subject to any alternative earnings or savings from not attending work except where notice is shorter than three months. Long-service employees may also be entitled to a statutory severance payment (see above).

Collective dismissal

Collective dismissal is defined by law as the dismissal, within thirty days, of:

- At least five employees in firms with twenty to 100 employees.
- At least 5 per cent of employees in firms with 100–600 employees, or
- At least thirty employees in firms with more than 600 employees.

Consultation

Employers must notify the relevant labour authorities (*Arbeitsamt*) in writing of the dismissals at least thirty calendar days before the dismissals take place, giving details of the age, sex and qualifications of the employees concerned. The employer must send a copy of the notification to the works council. If these consultation requirements are not carried out, the dismissals are deemed to be void (*rechtsunwirksam*).

Severance and compensation terms

Statutory and agreed severance payments are as for individual dismissal (see above).

Final formalities

At the end of the employment relationship, employers are required by law to supply any employee who requests it with a written certificate of employment (*Arbeitszeugnis*), stating the duration and nature of the employment. Employees have thirty years in which to request this certificate, under the Civil Code (*Allgemeines Bürgerliches Gesetzbuch*). Employers must pay employees any sums due in compensation for unfair dismissal, pay in lieu of notice, holiday pay and any outstanding bonuses. The employer must erase from company databases all personal data which relate to the employee if the employer has no good reason for keeping them and has no legal duty to do so.

Appendix

Employers' non-wage labour costs and income tax rates

Employer's non-wage labour costs add 20–26 per cent to gross pay, depending on category of employee. Employees must pay around 18 per cent of their salary as social insurance contributions.

Individuals are liable for income tax if they are employed in Austria, have established a home there or been resident for six months or more. Tax is levied on income from all sources, including employment, investment, property, trade or business. Taxable income is arrived at after deducting from gross annual income any non-taxable parts of income and any allowances, which take account of individual circumstances. Thirteenth and fourteenth month salaries are also taxable at a lower rate than basic salary. Tax payable is then calculated according to income tax bands. The 1994 tax rates (on annual income) are:

ASch 0–9,600	0%
ASch 9,600–50,000	10%
ASch 50,000–150,000	22%
ASch 150,000–300,000	32%
ASch 300,000–700,000	42%
above ASch 700,000	50%

The main tax credits are: basic personal allowance (ASch 8,840), employees' allowance (ASch 1,500), commuting (ASch 4,000), sole earner (ASch 5,000), 1st dependent child (ASch 4,200), 2nd dependent child (ASch 6,300), each further child (ASch 8,400), pensioners (ASch 5,500).

Organisations

Labour Ministry
(*Bundesministerium für Arbeit und Sozialordnung*)
Stubenring 1
1010 Vienna
Tel: + 43 1 711 00
Fax: + 43 1 711 00

Federal Chamber of Labour
(*Bundeskammer für Arbeiter und Angestellte*)
Prinz-Eugen-Straße 20–22
1041 Vienna
Tel: + 43 1 50165
Fax: + 43 1 501 65 2230
The Federal Chamber of Labour is the statutory form of representation for employees. It is financed by compulsory levies on employees, and has rights to be consulted on legislative proposals.

Austrian Trade Union Confederation
(*Österreichischer Gewerkschaftsbund*)
Hohenstaufengasse 10
1010 Vienna
Tel: + 43 1 534 44
Fax: + 43 1 533 5293

Austrian Chamber of Trade and Commerce
(*Wirtschaftskammer Österreich*)
Wiedner Hauptstraße 63
Postfach 180
1045 Vienna
Tel: + 43 1 50105
The Chamber of Trade and Commerce is the institution responsible for the statutory form of representation of employers' interests.

Confederation of Austrian Industry
(*Vereinigung Österreichischer*
Industrieller)
Schwarzenbergplatz 4
1031 Vienna
Tel: + 43 1 711 35
Fax: + 43 1 711 35 25 07

Austrian Centre for Productivity and
Efficiency (Personnel management
association)
(*Österreichisches Produktivitäts- und*
Wirtschaftlichkeitszentrum)
1014 Vienna
Rockhgasse 6
Tel: + 43 1 533 8636
Fax: 43 1 533 863618

Main sources

Heinrich Brauner and Günter Stummvoll, *Sozialversicherung für die betriebliche Praxis,* Signum Verlag, Vienna, 1994.

Werner Doralt (ed.), *Kodex des österreichischen Rechts. Arbeitsrecht,* Linde, Vienna, 1990.

Ulrich Runggaldier and Georg Schima, *Manager Dienstverträge,* Manz, Vienna, 1991.

Walter Schwarz and Günther Löschnigg, *Arbeitsrecht,* Verlag des ÖGB, Vienna, 1989.

2
Belgium

Basic rights and labour jurisdiction

The terms of individual contracts of employment are governed by rights enshrined in the constitution, an extensive system of legislation and binding national and industry-wide agreements. Most issues are determined at national level, although a number, such as training and the employment service, now fall within the competence of regional authorities. Moves to devolve powers of labour legislation to the regions have been resisted at national level.

The terms of an individual contract of employment are governed in order of priority by:

- Legislation, in particular the 1978 Law on Contracts of Employment (*Loi relative aux contrats de travail*), together with royal decrees.
- Collective agreements. A nationwide multi-industry collective agreement (*accord interprofessionel*) concluded in the National Labour Council may attain the force of law either totally or in part by royal decree. Collective agreements negotiated at industry level within the joint committees (*commissions paritaires*), on which employers and trade unions are represented equally, are binding on firms belonging to a signatory organisation but can be extended to all firms in a particular industry by royal decree.
- Company-level agreements.
- Contracts of employment.
- Company regulations.
- Custom and practice.
- Verbal agreements.

Basic system of labour jurisdiction

Local employment tribunals (*tribunal de travail*) are made up of professional magistrates and representatives of employers and employees, called *juges sociaux*. Each chamber of the labour tribunal has one president and two social judges, one each representing employers' organisations and trade unions. Candidates for these posts are proposed by the employers' organisation and trade unions through the Ministry of Labour, and are officially appointed by the Crown for a term of five years.

Labour tribunals adjudicate in all matters relating to or arising from employment issues, labour law and social security. This includes matters to do with

45

contracts of employment, collective agreements, vocational training, enterprise closures, works councils, health and safety committees, equal treatment, all aspects of social security, accidents at work, redundancy and dismissal. Cases are referred to the tribunal in the district in which the place of employment is located. Claims are usually made by issuing a summons, although in certain cases (social security, administrative fines and handicapped persons' allowances) they may be made by writing a letter. The parties can appear in person or be represented by a lawyer, by an employers' organisation or by a trade union. All matters decided in a labour tribunal may be taken on appeal to a labour court (*cour de travail*). There are five such courts in Belgium: in Brussels, Ghent, Liège, Antwerp and Mons. They also consist of a mixture of professional magistrates and *juges sociaux*. All rulings of the labour courts can be appealed to the final Court of Appeal (*cour de cassation*).

The application of labour and social legislation at company level is dealt with by the labour inspectorate (*inspection de travail*). Inspectors can enter any establishment where they have reason to believe there are people employed and demand to see all official documentation. Depending on what they discover, they can issue a warning to an employer found to be in breach of legislation, with a given period of time in which to correct this.

Contracts of employment

The law differentiates between two basic categories of employee:

- Blue-collar manual workers (*ouvriers*).
- White-collar employees (*employés*).

Differences mainly concern the frequency of pay, the length of probationary and notice periods, arbitration clauses, holiday pay and sickness entitlement, and some types of bonus payment. A further distinction is drawn for domestic workers and sales representatives under the terms of the 1978 Law on Contracts of Employment. There is no separate legislation governing managers or executives: their terms and conditions are more frequently set by individual negotiation and contract.

Legislation on employment contracts covers all the private sector and employees in the public sector not governed by a specific statute of recruitment, such as some civil servants and ministerial organisations.

According to the 1978 law, a contract of employment may be written or verbal, although certain contracts must be in writing. These include student employment contracts, fixed-term contracts, replacement contracts, part-time contracts and contracts for temporary work. However, the vast majority of contracts are in writing, and Belgium is in the process of enacting into its national law the terms of the EU Directive on Proof of an Employment Contract. The law defines an employment contract as an agreement by which an employee undertakes to carry out certain tasks upon the instruction of the employer in exchange for a certain remuneration (articles 2–3).

Under the terms of the 1978 law, all written contracts must include reference to the probationary period and must normally also cover the:

- Identity of the parties and place of work.
- Starting date, job title and duties.
- Working hours and schedules, including shifts, with reference to other documents, such as collective agreements, where appropriate.
- Rate of pay, method and frequency of payment.
- Health and safety obligations, including issues specific to the job.
- Procedures for terminating the contract.
- Reference to company regulations (see below).

There is no obligation to consult work-force representatives on the terms of new contracts. However, works councils have a statutory right to participate in drawing up and amending company regulations (*règlement de travail*) which are required by law in every company. These include details of hours of work, shift work schedules, the method of payment of wages, periods of notice, procedures for terminating a contract and annual holidays.

Language: French or Flemish?

An employment contract, and all related documentation, must be drawn up in one of the national languages (French or Flemish). In the Brussels region contracts must be drawn up in the usual language of communication of the employee concerned. Companies situated in Flanders and Wallonia must use Flemish or French respectively, although translations may be provided where appropriate for documentation directed to employees.

Contractual terms

A number of general contractual obligations are detailed in section II of the 1978 law. Specifically, employers have a duty to:

- Ensure the provision of work under the agreed terms and conditions, with appropriate equipment, materials and assistance.
- Provide adequate health and safety care, including first-aid facilities.
- Pay employees according to the agreed terms.
- Permit employees to perform religious duties and civic functions as laid down by law.
- Provide induction programmes as necessary.
- Ensure equality of treatment.

- Provide facilities for the safe-keeping of employees' belongings.
- Complete appropriate documents upon termination of the contract.

Employees are required to:

- Work with care, diligence and integrity under the agreed conditions.
- Act in accordance with the employer's instructions.
- Refrain from divulging business secrets or competing unfairly during and after the term of the contract.
- Refrain from any activity harmful to their own, others' or a third party's safety.
- Return any equipment or materials to the employer in good condition.

Types of contract

A contract of employment can be open-ended (*à durée indéterminée*), fixed-term (*à durée déterminée*) or for a specific task (*pour un travail nettement défini*).

Under the Law on Employment Contracts, fixed-term contracts, or contracts for a specific assignment, must be concluded in writing, otherwise they will be deemed to be an open-ended contract. They must be drawn up at the latest on the day on which employment is due to commence – although some collective agreements allow exceptions, as in the case of blue-collar dock workers. The contract must mention the date on which it is to commence and the date on which it is to end or the period for which it is to run. The law states that, in principle, two or more fixed-term contracts concluded without interruption of the work done under their terms are deemed equivalent to an open-ended contract, unless the very nature of the work justifies the use of successive fixed-term contracts. This would, for example, apply to programmes of scientific research. Amendments of the law, introduced in 1994, have clarified and extended the position. Under the new provisions, a maximum of four fixed-term contracts can be signed successively, provided that each contract is for at least three months and the total period does not exceed two years. Upon authorisation by the labour inspectorate, successive fixed-term contracts can be signed for up to three years, provided each is for a period of at least six months.

A fixed-term contract, or a contract for a specific assignment, is automatically terminated at the end of the period, or on completion of the task, for which it was signed and no notice is required. However, if a fixed-term contract is continued without notification that it is to be terminated, it will be deemed to be an open-ended contract. Contracts concluded for a specific assignment are governed by the same regulations as fixed-term contracts but are not covered by the recent amendments.

Part-time employment   Under the 1978 law, contracts covering part-time work must be in writing. They must specify the number of weekly hours to be worked and the agreed scheduling of those hours, or must refer to the appropriate documentation such as collective agreements and company regulations that detail the information. Part-time work must generally amount to at least one-third of normal weekly full-time hours within an establishment, and each period of work may not be less than three hours. These limits are under review. Statute law provides for a number of exemptions: these include staff in emergency and health services, certain teachers and some younger employees. In addition a number of exceptions are made where part-timers are employed on variable schedules (*horaires variables*), in which hours of work may be tailored to the demands of the business. Such employees can average their weekly hours over a three-month period, which may be extended to a twelve-month period by royal decree or collective agreement. Prior notice of the scheduling must be given. The period of notice is usually in accordance with an industry-wide agreement, but must be at least five days.

Temporary work   By law, contracts for temporary work may be concluded only in certain circumstances, including the temporary replacement of a permanent employee, during exceptional increases in the work load, or for a specific and exceptional assignment. Contracts may be concluded directly between an employer and the temporary worker (*contrat de travail temporaire*). Alternatively, a company's need for temporary staff can be met by hiring an employee of a temporary employment agency (*contrat de travail intérimaire*). In that case the temporary worker remains an employee of the agency, not of the hiring company. All temporary contracts must be in writing.

Where a temporary contract is concluded with an employment bureau, it must respect the terms and conditions laid down in the collective agreement covering agency workers. Several industries prohibit the use of agencies, notably certain sectors of the construction and transport industries.

In general, temporary contracts – either direct or via an agency – may run for up to three months. They may be extended to six months for contracts replacing a worker dismissed without notice, and to two years for the replacement of an employee taking a career break. Contracts to cover exceptional increases in work load are concluded for one month initially but can be renewed. In most cases the works council or trade union delegation must be consulted before temporary workers are taken on, and in the event of additional work load the relevant sectoral joint commission must also be notified. The employer must provide the commission with details of the numbers of workers required and the period for which they will be contracted.

Probationary periods

These must be set down in writing, usually among the terms of a contract of employment, before an employee takes up a post. Probationary periods (*période d'essai*) are regulated differently for blue- and white-collar workers. However, for both categories there is a minimum period during which they cannot be dismissed, except for serious misconduct.

Blue-collar workers are entitled to between seven and fourteen days, and where no time limit is specified in the contract of employment it will be set automatically at the seven-day minimum. The contract of employment may not be terminated during the first seven days of the probationary period but thereafter, until the end of the agreed time, may be terminated without notice or compensation.

For white-collar employees the customary probationary period is one to six months, but may extend to twelve months, depending on the level of pay. Those earning over BFr 1,370,000 (£18,950) annually may be set a maximum of twelve months. Where no time limit is stipulated in the contract of employment, the probationary period will be a minimum of one month. During this first month the contract may not be terminated except for serious misconduct. During the rest of the probationary period it may be terminated with seven days' paid notice. If the employee is absent for more than seven consecutive days, owing to sickness or injury, the employer can serve notice without compensation.

Should the contract of employment be temporarily suspended during the probationary period, the period can be extended by a further seven days in the case of blue-collar workers and for a period equal to that of the suspension for white-collar employees.

Restrictive covenants

A restrictive covenant (*clause de non-concurrence*) may be included as a clause of the employment contract or may be a separate written document. It usually prevents the employee, during the period of employment, and for a specified time thereafter, from engaging in any activity, including the communication of commercial or industrial knowledge gained, which could prejudice the employer's business. In the case of employees with an annual income of between BFr 864,000 and BFr 1,728,000 (£14,400–£28,800) the clause affects only certain jobs as laid down in industry-level or company collective agreements. Such a provision is assumed to apply to employees earning above BFr 1,728,000 unless they are specifically exempted by collective agreement.

Workplace discipline

Most disciplinary procedures are set out in company regulations (*règlement de travail*) which are drawn up in consultation with the works council or trade union delegation. Company regulations are governed by a 1965 law which makes them compulsory in all private-sector companies. The law details a number of matters that must be covered in company regulations, including the range of warnings, verbal and written, demotions, suspensions and fines that may be used as part of the disciplinary procedure. The proceeds of any disciplinary fines must be used for the good of the employees as a whole, and details of the uses to which they may be put must be agreed in the company regulations. Such fines may not, by law, exceed one-fifth of daily pay. A record must be kept of all disciplinary measures taken against an employee, with the reason, the date and any fine imposed.

Individual workplace rights

Most grievance procedures are detailed in the company regulations, unless they are covered by statute or by collective agreement. Complaints of sex discrimination may be taken up, on a member's behalf, by a trade union or employers' organisation.

Employment terms and conditions

Hours of work

Although hours of work are extensively regulated by legislation, reforms of the law during the 1980s introduced substantial derogations allowing a large measure of flexibility for operations, provided that official authorisation and the agreement of employee representatives is obtained.

Statutory limits on hours of work are set out in the 1971 Law on Employment Conditions (*Loi sur le travail*), as amended by a number of royal decrees. The law currently states that hours of work may not normally exceed eight per day or forty per week, based on a six-day week. In practice working hours are governed by collective agreement, with an average agreed working week in 1993/94 of thirty-eight hours.

The law provides for some exceptions to these statutory limits. As a general exception, for example, daily hours may be increased to nine where a five-day week is worked, and to ten if the workplace is a long way from the employee's place of residence. Provision is also made for shift workers (*travail par équipes*), who are allowed to work up to eleven hours a day and fifty per week, as long as a weekly average of forty hours is attained over a three-month reference period. Other departures from this rule, such as flexible hours arrangements, require prior authorisation and, typically, must be provided for in a collective agreement.

Under the 1985 Economic Recovery Law arrangements on annual hours may be introduced by collective agreement. The agreement must set out the weekly average to be worked (calculated over a twelve-month period) and a maximum that can be worked, which may not exceed the statutory limit of nine hours per day or forty-five hours per week. The maximum departure from the weekly average is five hours in any direction. This would allow an industry with an average thirty-eight-hour week to vary its hours from thirty-three to forty-three per week, provided the average is maintained within a stated reference period of up to one year. In some instances days off are granted to maintain the average. In the construction industry, for example, six fixed days are allocated.

Further options regarding flexible working patterns were created under a 1987 law on new working hours arrangements. The Act allows private-sector companies to draw up hours of work schedules provided it is done by collective agreement, with the approval of the joint committee which negotiates for the industry in which the firm operates. Arrangements may include Sunday working and work on a public holiday; night work for men (although this has come under fire recently from the European Court of Justice with regard to sexual equality); a twelve-hour working day and the removal of the forty-hour-week limit, provided an average forty hours are worked over a twelve-month period; and an extension of evening work for women and young people.

The 1993 'Global Plan', implemented by the government in the face of deteriorating economic competitiveness, encourages the reorganisation of hours of work to create new jobs (such as more part-time work, overtime limits, career breaks, flexitime) and in return employers may claim reductions in social security contributions.

Weekly rest

Sunday is normally a day off, except where employees are involved in the security of premises, cleaning, repair or maintenance work, accident prevention or other urgent work. Certain industries such as retailing, hotels and catering, transport and health are allowed to work twelve Sundays per year, but not more than four consecutively. Employees working on Sunday are entitled to time off within the following six days. Workers on continuous shifts may work Sundays provided they are granted an eighty-hour period of time off once a week, eighteen hours of which must be on a Sunday.

Employees under 21 are entitled to twelve hours' consecutive break between periods of work. In addition, they must have half an hour's break after every four and a half hours of work.

Annual leave

Full-time employees have a statutory right to four weeks' paid leave per year (twenty-four working days, based on a six-day week). In a few industries collective agreements award additional holiday entitlement for long service, while others give young employees extra days off. However, agreements which award extra holiday for age are relatively rare.

There are ten public holidays (*jours fériés*) per year for which employees are entitled to full pay: New Year's Day, Easter Monday, May Day, Ascension Thursday, Whit Monday, National Day (21 July), Assumption, All Saints, Armistice Day and Christmas Day. It is standard practice for an additional day's holiday to be given when there is one normal working day between a weekend and a public holiday – often called a bridging day (*pont*). In addition, 11 July and 27 September are regional holidays in Flanders and Wallonia respectively. These two are not statutory but most sectoral committees agree to them as paid holidays in the relevant region.

Parental leave

Pregnant women are entitled to fifteen week's paid maternity leave, with payment made by a state fund financed by employer contributions. The first thirty days are paid at 82 per cent of gross pay. After that, payments fall to 75 per cent of gross pay up to a daily ceiling of BFr 3,146.39 (£56.93). By law eight weeks' leave must be taken after the birth, and up to seven weeks may be taken beforehand. If an employee decides to take less than the statutory seven weeks before the birth she may add the amount not taken to her postnatal leave to maintain the fifteen weeks' entitlement.

Under career break arrangements (see below) either parent may take a minimum of twelve weeks' leave after postnatal leave has run out.

Time off

In addition to annual leave and public holidays, workers may be entitled by law to a certain amount of time off for personal reasons (*absences légitimes* or *petits chômages*). Under some circumstances it may be paid time off, and the list is fairly comprehensive. It includes the marriage of the employee (two days) or of a close relative (one day), a death in the family, the ordination of certain relatives, the first Communion of the employee's child, military service induction, jury service and certain political duties. Collective agreements may improve on the statutory minimum, and the majority of industries now have their own agreement on the subject: for example, every worker has a statutory right to two days' leave when getting married, but most workers are awarded three days' by collective agreement.

According to a national agreement signed in 1989, workers are also entitled to unpaid leave of up to ten days for urgent and unforeseen reasons (*congé pour raisons impérieuses*), including a child's illness, the hospitalisation of a member of the family, serious damage to the employee's property and occasions where the employee's attendance is required by the public authorities, e.g. jury service.

Career breaks

Since 1985 workers have enjoyed the right to an unpaid career break lasting from six months to a year on a full-time basis. Employees with at least twelve months' service are eligible, and the employer must consent. If an unemployed person is taken on during the break the employee on leave may receive state benefit (*allocation d'interruption*).

Employees who take a part-time career break (*réductions des prestations de travail*) by reducing the number of hours they work are also entitled to reduced payments. Legislation passed in December 1992 stipulates that employees under 50 are entitled to reduce their hours for a maximum period of sixty months during their career, while there is no limit for the over-50s.

Full-time employees may qualify for paid absence in order to take up an educational course (*congé-education*). A 1985 law encourages employees to follow courses related to their work outside working hours. They are entitled to one hour off work for every fifty minutes of educational activity, without loss of salary, subject to an annual maximum: this is set at 240 hours for vocational courses closely connected with employment or for a mixture of vocational and general courses, and 160 hours for more general courses. The leave is financed through a national fund based on state and employer contributions. Employers are reimbursed 50 per cent of pay and social security contributions for employees on vocational courses, while for general courses they are fully reimbursed.

Individual pay and benefits

Belgium has an extensive system of pay bargaining, backed up by a statutory minimum wage. Pay increases are primarily achieved via the system of wage indexation, which increases pay in line with prices, supplemented by bargaining. Recent statutory incomes policies have intervened to curb real pay growth, though for the most part allowing price increases to be reflected in pay rates through the indexation mechanism; however, this too was modified by the government in 1994 to delay the effect of price rises.

National minimum wage

The 'average monthly minimum guaranteed income' (*revenue minimum mensuel moyen garanti, RMMMG*) was introduced in 1975. It is increased in line with movements in the consumer price index. The minimum guaranteed income is regulated by a binding national collective agreement (No. 43) and provides for two minimum rates, including all normal bonuses. One rate applies to 21 year olds, the other to employees over 21 with six months' service. The national framework agreement signed for 1993/94 provided for a third category: those aged 22 or over with twelve months' service. From 1 September 1993 the rate was worth BFr 40,843 (£680) per month for 21 year olds, BFr 41,969 (£699) for those over 21 with six months' service, and BFr 42,469 (£707) for those over 22 with one year's service.

Minima for young workers are usually expressed as a percentage of the adult rate. Since 1992 youth pay rates have been subject to a 6 per cent reduction for each year under the age of 21, so a 20 year old worker will be entitled to 94 per cent of the adult minimum wage for the private sector, and a 16 year old to 70 per cent. Part-time workers are entitled to a minimum wage, calculated *pro rata* to hours worked.

Industry agreed minima

Binding minima for the majority of workers are set by the relevant industry collective agreement, and negotiated by the joint committee (*commission paritaire*): rates are normally a function of qualification and, for white-collar employees, seniority as well. Since every committee has its own indexation system (see below), some industry minima have in the past slipped slightly below the national minimum wage. A binding national agreement now requires all industry minima to be brought up at least to the level of the national minimum wage.

Pay indexation

Indexation is the most important factor determining pay increases for both blue- and white-collar employees in Belgium. The system is set up by national collective agreement, not by law. It was subject to statutory intervention in the mid-1980s, and in 1989 legislation was passed giving parliament special powers to intervene in the economy, including the pay indexation system, should the country's competitive position be threatened.

These powers were partly invoked, for the first time, at the end of 1993 when the government introduced an austerity package, dubbed the 'Global Plan', aimed at re-establishing Belgium's position *vis-à-vis* its seven main trading competitors. The package was given legislative backing when the 'social partners' (the two sides of industry and the government) failed to come up with a national agreement to implement the measures. The plan included a revision in the price index used for calculating increases in indexed pay, the new index being dubbed the 'health index' (*index santé*) because it excludes such items as tobacco, alcohol and petrol. The introduction of the index was also intended to slow down the pace of indexed pay increases, leading to a partial freeze on automatic pay indexation for 1994. No negotiated pay increases – that is, excluding indexation increases – were to be allowed for 1995 and 1996, freezing real pay, with some exceptions for existing merit pay and profit-linked pay schemes.

In principle pay is indexed in line with national consumer prices, as measured from 1994 by the *index santé*. In practice most individual joint industry committees, covering the vast majority of blue- and white-collar employees in private industry, have devised their own systems through binding national agreements. The mechanics tend to be complex and diverse. However, agreements typically make provision for a 2 per cent increase in pay when the consumer price index rises by 2 per cent (or possibly a lower threshold), though some systems provide for automatic review dates.

Each month, once the official index is published, organisations such as the employers' organisation, the FEB, and the trade unions publish lists detailing which industries' rises have been triggered. Pay components to be indexed may vary, but for the most part actual pay, including supplements and bonuses, rather than basic pay is fully indexed.

The law on pay

The main source of regulation in this area is the law of 12 April 1965 on the protection of remuneration.

Form and frequency   The law states that although in principle wages should be paid in cash, in practice they may be paid either in cash or by other means, provided agreement has been reached with employee representatives or, in their absence, with the consent of the majority of employees. Non-cash payment (cheques or bank/postal transfer) must be agreed to in writing by the employee. Payment must be in Belgian francs.

Legislation defines the scope of permissible types of payment in kind: it includes such items as accommodation, food and lodging, services such as gas and electricity, tools, equipment and clothing. The law includes broad guidelines on how these are to be valued in monetary terms and sets a limit on the proportion of pay which can be in kind. This varies by occupation and may be as much as half for domestic staff, caretakers and apprentices.

Payment must be made at least twice a month, at sixteen-day intervals, with exceptions in the case of:

- White-collar employees, who must be paid at least monthly.
- Commission which is payable quarterly, or according to the rules covering sales representatives.
- Profit-share and similar payments.
- Other arrangements established by a generally binding collective agreement.

Payment must be made no later than the fourth working day following the period of work to which it relates, unless a collective agreement or company regulation prescribes otherwise. In any case the delay may not exceed seven days. Employees must not be forced to travel on a non-work day to collect wages, nor must wages be paid in a canteen or place of entertainment unless workers are employed there.

Deductions   The employer may usually make only authorised deductions in accordance with tax legislation – a pay-as-you-earn scheme exists – and social security legislation. However, deductions are permissible in the following cases:

- Fines imposed as disciplinary measures according to company regulations or for causing damage at the workplace.
- Loans made available by the employer.
- Floats.

Deductions under these four heads may not together amount to more than 20 per cent of pay.

Itemised pay statement   An employer must supply the following information in respect of each regular wage payment:

- Full details of employer and employee.
- Details of the period to which the payment relates, and the basis of payment (hourly, monthly time worked, piecework, task-related).
- Basic pay, bonuses, supplementary payments for overtime and holidays.
- Payments in kind.
- Total gross pay, listing deductions for social security.
- Taxable income, less personal allowance, and any other tax exemptions.
- Net pay.

Levels of pay determination

Collective bargaining takes place at national, industry, regional and company level, and the system remains highly centralised, though in some industries there is extensive scope for local pay negotiation. This can be – and most frequently is – through company agreements, or in some instances (chemicals, engineering) through linked regional agreements. These can relate to highly localised geographical areas. Some 90 per cent of private-sector employees are covered by collective agreements. Most collective agreements are cumulative, that is, they not only build on the agreement at a higher level, but usually add to or amend previous agreements. This explains why a number of sectoral and company agreements may seem to contain few provisions in any one year.

At national level collective agreements are concluded within the bipartite National Labour Council. They are nearly all legally binding and cover issues such as collective dismissal, part-time work and recruitment. Multi-industry agreements (*accords inter-professionels*) may be negotiated between the main employers' organisation and the union confederations outside the framework of the council. Such agreements provide guidelines for industry-level bargaining by the joint committees (*commissions paritaires*). The guidelines are usually valid for two years and cover holiday pay, annual leave, indexation and early retirement. The 1993/94 agreement included a call for wage bargaining to reflect the 'fragile competitiveness position' highlighted in the country's biannual competitiveness report. However, when the government felt that negotiations had not kept in line with this particular guideline there was direct intervention in the form of an austerity package (see above) which modified the pay indexation system and blocked all but indexed increases in 1995 and 1996.

At industry level most agreements are concluded for one or two years. There are some ninety negotiating committees covering ninety per cent of the private sector.

Job evaluation and grading

A clear distinction is drawn in law and in collectively agreed job classification systems between blue-collar workers (*ouvriers*) and white-collar employees (*employés*). Most job classification systems are drawn up by industry agreement within the joint committees and company variations are fitted into these. In small firms, where unionisation is weak, classifications are often imposed unilaterally by management.

Most industry systems covering white-collar staff establish four or five broad categories, detailing job criteria and conditions of access, such as qualifications. A list of posts is attached to each category. Blue-collar systems tend to be divided into very wide categories: trainees, operators, specialist operators, qualified/experienced operators. Within these broad bands tasks are allocated by degree of complexity or technological sophistication, the amount of autonomy and responsibility involved and the level of vocational training/experience. Salary scales are based on the results.

In sectors where job classifications no longer correspond very closely to the actual situation in companies, employers have considerable freedom to implement their own systems. This has happened, in chain stores, insurance and banking, for example. In large companies in the engineering or chemical industries, job classification is customarily a focus of company-level negotiations. In both industries, national agreements set the broad terms, leaving the details to be filled in at regional and, in some cases, at company-level negotiations.

Executives tend to be outside the scope of agreed salary scales and in many companies job evaluation schemes are adapted to cover them, using a simple points system.

Components of basic pay

Blue-collar workers' pay is usually reckoned on an hourly basis, minima being set by industry or sector agreement, with actual pay agreed at company level. Pay progression is commonly based on age. To basic hourly pay can be added shift premiums (an estimated 80 per cent of enterprises operate shift working), including premiums for night work, and overtime payments – with basic rates and supplements set either by statute or by industry agreement – and improvements or additional items such as production bonuses set by the company. Many company agreements specify a *prime syndicale* which is technically a reimbursement of union dues or a supplementary payment for union officials but is often extended to all employees.

White-collar employees' pay is calculated on a monthly basis and salary scales are usually related to age; more rarely, to length of service. The number of age-related increments laid down in industry agreements varies widely. There are as many as thirty-seven increments from age 16 to 63 in the banking sector and for white-collar employees under joint committee No. 218. By contrast, employees reach the top of the incremental scale by the age of 37 in the engineering industry. Annual salary for white-collar staff can be broadly calculated by multiplying one month's pay by 13.85 to include holiday and end-of-year bonuses (see below).

For senior and executive staff, although they are outside the scope of most sectoral agreements, age and length of service play an important role in determining basic salaries, with merit only gradually assuming greater significance.

Overtime

Overtime is normally payable for hours worked in excess of the statutory limit (nine hours daily, forty hours a week) or any other limit set by collective agreement at industry or company level. Overtime hours must be paid at 50 per cent over the normal rate and, under the terms of a royal decree of 1983, must be compensated with time off (*repos compensatoire*) in the thirteen weeks following the overtime worked. The same arrangement applies to overtime on Sundays and public holidays, except that an overtime premium of 100 per cent applies.

Collective agreements may stipulate additional supplements or different methods of reckoning overtime pay. For example, the oil industry pays overtime at double time after the first five hours if it is undertaken from Monday to Friday, or after two hours if worked on Saturday. However, establishments that have introduced flexible working hours in accordance with legislation and collective agreements may be obliged to pay at premium rates only when overtime is worked in excess of five hours above the industry/enterprise norm.

Shift and night work premiums

Shift working is common, affecting some 80 per cent of companies, and rose perceptibly following the implementation of flexible hours of work legislation in 1987.

Night work is defined as work carried out between 23.00 and 06.00, and can be introduced through only a collective agreement. A binding national collective agreement (No. 46) on the regulation of shift work, including night work, provides for financial compensation in the form of premiums. A subsequent agreement, No. 49, concluded in 1991 set this supplement at a minimum level of BFr 31 (60p) per hour (BFr 37 or 71p for those aged over 50) for night work – figures all index-linked. Most industry and company agreements pay supplements which are much higher.

Shift premiums for blue-collar employees are normally expressed as a flat-rate index-linked hourly supplement, with the level of night shift payments being higher. For white-collar staff, shift premiums are usually awarded as a percentage supplement on normal day rates.

Although industry agreements setting minimum rates must be registered, the actual rates are usually agreed at plant level, where there is no such duty to publish. Nevertheless, it has been estimated that in practice companies pay a premium of 7–10 per cent on top of basic rates for discontinuous shifts, 10–25 per cent for semi-continuous shifts and 25–43 per cent for continuous shifts.

Supplements for dirty and dangerous work

Minimum supplements of this type are often determined at industry level, with companies also making their own provision. The construction industry blue-collar pay agreement contains a detailed listing of percentage supplements payable for specified dangerous work, and for dirty, inconvenient and especially for arduous work.

Holiday pay and supplementary holiday pay

Full-time employees are entitled by law to four weeks' annual paid holiday after a year's service, with additional leave granted by agreement. The employer must pay employees for the whole period of leave at the normal single rate (*simple pécule*) plus double rate (*double pécule*) for most of the leave, according to a somewhat complicated formula which differentiates between white- and blue-collar workers as regards the manner of payment. However, in essence three weeks and two days must be paid at double the normal hourly or monthly rate. In addition, the national framework agreement for 1993/94 provided for all workers to be paid an extra sum equivalent to double pay for the third day of the fourth week. So total holiday pay now consists of double pay for three weeks and three days, and single pay for the remainder.

Bonus payments

The practice of paying a bonus equal to a thirteenth month's salary is widespread. Although in most cases it is provided for by industry collective agreement, arrangements can also be made at company level, in an individual contract of employment, via internal works rules or by custom and practice. Often it is awarded as an end-of-year bonus (*prime de fin d'année*) and paid with December's salary. There are differences in the method of calculation and size of bonus as between industries and companies, as well as between blue- and white-collar staff. White-collar employees usually receive a straight additional month's salary. Industry agreements covering blue-collar workers employ formulae such as a percentage of gross annual pay or a multiple of basic hourly pay. Qualifying conditions may apply to the payment of the bonus, such as length of service, all of which are subject to negotiation.

Some executives are covered by collective agreements that stipulate a thirteenth-month payment. Even where such is not the case, however, they are usually awarded a bonus, which may be considerably enhanced as a form of merit payment and thus may be equivalent to a fourteenth, or even fifteenth, month bonus.

Some industry agreements also provide lump-sum payments in respect of length of service.

Financial participation

There is a lack of consensus in this area between the political parties and the social partners as to the merit of financial participation schemes. The legal and tax regimes applying to the various types of scheme remain relatively unfavourable and the social security requirements are unclear. Employers favour such schemes and have been looking to establish a specific legal and fiscal framework. Whilst trade unions have tended to be generally unfavourable towards financial participation, on the grounds that it could increase wage inequalities and income insecurity, attitudes are becoming more pragmatic and schemes are gradually being introduced. However, Belgium has many small family-owned firms which are chary of diluting traditional ownership through forms of employee capital participation. Only around fifty firms, mostly large ones, run schemes. Elsewhere benefits are often restricted to senior and top management. The main forms of participation in company results and capital are set out below.

Share options   This system, regulated by 1984 legislation, involves granting share options to employees, who must have a year's service, on the eventual purchase of shares at a predetermined price. There are equivalent arrangements such as convertible loan schemes where employees make payments to the company in the form of 'loans' to be reclaimed as shares at a price set when the loan is granted. Employees exercising share options are exempt from tax on any eventual capital gain, provided the total value of the options is less than 25 per cent of the previous year's pay of BFr 500,000 (£9,600) and the option is exercised after at least one year but within six years.

This type of scheme is seldom used, and generally only for managerial staff or function heads. There are such schemes at the retailers GB-Inno, for example, and at the motor manufacturer Volvo.

Employee share ownership   This can be effected in a number of ways. A specific legal framework was created in 1991 which entailed reforms in company law and allowed shares to be made available to employees at less than market price. Companies which have declared a dividend to shareholders for two of the previous four years may reserve all or part of the increase in capital for employees of the company, or its subsidiaries, provided this does not exceed 20 per cent of the capital over five years. The maximum discount is 20 per cent. Within certain limits, companies may decide the basis of employee participation, though a company's central works council must be consulted about the plan. Most existing plans involve this form of ownership, which is restricted to companies quoted on the stock market.

Other forms of share ownership, where there is no specific legal framework, include the company purchase of shares for redistribution to employees, the creation of bonus shares for distribution, and company savings plans for eventual investment in shares. These are rare, however.

The 1983 Monory-*bis* law allowed some tax relief on employee share purchases, so giving the introduction of such schemes a boost. Although the tax and social security implications of share ownership schemes remain for the most part unclear, some major companies in financial services and manufacturing have introduced full share ownership schemes. They include UCB, Tessenderlo Chemie and Petrofina.

Profit-sharing   No specific legal framework governs these schemes. Employees are liable to a 25 per cent tax on dividends, rather than the higher rate of income tax, provided certain conditions are met. The social security position for companies is unclear and remains so after a controversial 1991 court ruling, currently under appeal, which required Agfa-Gevaert to pay social security contributions on profit-sharing certificates distributed to employees.

Sick pay and maternity

By law, employers must pay white-collar employees one month's (twenty-eight days') sick pay. Blue-collar workers receive fourteen days' payment from the employer (see below). Two national collective agreements provide for groups to receive sickness benefit so that for the first month of sickness absence they receive the equivalent of their net pay had they been at work. White-collar employees with contracts of less than three months are paid the same as blue-collar workers.

By law, employers are required to pay blue-collar workers their full pay for the first seven days' absence after one waiting day, and 85.88 per cent of pay for the second week. Thereafter, for a further sixteen days, they receive sick pay in two parts: state benefit and a supplement from their employer, taking their income to just over 90 per cent of usual earnings. State benefit is equal to 60 per cent of daily earnings up to a ceiling (in 1994 BFr 3,484.75 or £67 for a six-day week; BFr 4,181.70 or £80 for a five-day week). The employer supplement is equal to 25.88 per cent of earnings up to the daily limit and 85.88 per cent of earnings above this ceiling. The statutory waiting day (*jour de carence*) for blue-collar workers and white-collar employees on contracts of less than three months is paid retrospectively if absence is longer than fourteen days. In a number of collective agreements it may be abolished entirely or paid after a shorter delay:

in the chemical industry, for example, it is paid after seven days' sickness.

White-collar employees receive full pay from their employer for a month. Once statutory sick pay entitlement expires, all employees receive only state benefit at 60 per cent of former daily earnings up to the daily ceiling. Some sectors, however, have collectively agreed sectoral hardship funds (*fonds de sécurité d'existence*) which may make additional payments to employees on longer-term sickness leave. These funds are financed by employer contributions – typically 0.40 per cent to 0.50 per cent of earnings.

Managerial pay

Managerial pay in Belgium is overwhelmingly set by individual negotiation in response to market trends, and executives are not typically covered by collective agreement.

In theory, salary increases in the period 1994–6 are subject to the freeze on non-indexed pay announced in the government's November 1993 'Global Plan'. However, commentators expect that this will be difficult to enforce rigorously as managerial-level payments are less open to scrutiny, and pay increases will be permitted where the nature of the job alters or where extra pay or bonuses are generated through existing merit or profit-related schemes.

The main elements of the executive package consist of a base salary and a cash bonus. According to the 1993/94 Monks Partnership survey *Incentives and Benefits in Europe*, 96 per cent of top managers and 77 per cent of second-tier managers received a cash bonus. However, the proportion of total cash remuneration accounted for by bonus payments was comparatively small, even at very senior levels. For example, some 40 per cent of managing directors received a cash bonus worth 15 per cent or less of base salary. In general, bonuses are tied to job-related indicators rather than profit. Share options are a relatively uncommon benefit, granted to only 50 per cent of top managers and under a third of senior managers. There are no special tax concessions to encourage this form of financial participation.

The principal non-cash benefits awarded are cars and supplementary pensions. Over 95 per cent of top managers and 50 per cent of middle managers receive a company car, with fuel paid for some 80 per cent of top managers. Supplementary pensions were granted to virtually all top and senior managers, reflecting the need to make up for shortfalls in the state system for higher-earning employees. In the past, non-cash benefits were subject to favourable tax treatment, although there has been some shift away from this during the early 1990s.

Equal pay and opportunities

Article 6 of the constitution guarantees equal treatment between men and women as regards access to employment, training and the terms and conditions of employment. This principle was incorporated into legislation through the 1978 Economic Reorientation Law (*Loi de réorientation économique*). Article 119 of the Treaty of Rome on equal pay was enacted into law by a 1975 national collective agreement. Equal treatment is defined as the absence of direct or indirect discrimination on grounds of sex, including reference to family or marital status; special provisions to protect maternity and remove existing inequalities are permissible. Equal treatment must be observed as regards recruitment, contractual terms and conditions of employment, collective agreements, promotion, employee representation, dismissal and pay. The national agreement also bars discrimination in job classification schemes.

A 1987 royal decree aims at promoting equal opportunities in the private sector. It provides for positive action plans (*plans d'égalité de chances*) to remedy existing inequalities or improve women's position and participation at all levels. Such plans may be drawn up at industry or company level in consultation with employee representatives. Plans must specify the objectives in changing the comparative situation of men and women, include a description of the positive action to be taken, and give a date for implementation as well as provide for regular assessments to be carried out by joint bodies of employees and employers. Legislation proposed at the end of 1993 would require companies to draw up annual reports, including a breakdown of the number employed, by sex, of their status as full or part-time employees and of redundancies. The intention would be to submit the reports to the works council for discussion aimed at introducing measures to combat discrimination.

Legislation approved in 1981 outlaws racism in such areas as the provision of goods and services. There is a theoretical requirement for firms employing over twenty people to engage a certain number of disabled people. However, as yet there has been no decree implementing this legislation.

The burden of proof in establishing that discrimination has not taken place falls on the employer. An employee who has lodged a complaint of discrimination – with the labour inspectorate, through company proceedings or before a labour tribunal – may not be dismissed for reasons connected with the claim. In cases where a dismissal is deemed unfair on grounds of discrimination, six months' pay or actual harm suffered may be awarded to the claimant. However, reinstatement is very rare. Criminal sanctions may also be imposed on those infringing equal treatment legislation.

A royal decree issued in 1992 requires employers to include in company regulations a specific condemnation of sexual harassment at the workplace. A specific person must be appointed or a department set up to deal with victims of harassment; there must be a complaints procedure to include guarantees of confidentiality and guidelines in cases where an employee's superior may be involved, and sanctions may be imposed for sexual harassment.

Retirement

Until the end of 1990 the normal retirement age in the state scheme was 60 for women and 65 for men. At the beginning of 1991 a flexible retirement age was introduced, permitting men and women to retire at any time between the ages of 60 and 65. The state scheme covers all manual and white-collar employees in the private sector and most employees in the public sector. Pensions are financed by employer and employee contributions topped up by general taxation.

The state scheme provides a full pension, equivalent to around 60 per cent of assessable earnings after forty-five years of employment for men and forty for women. However, this has led to a number of difficulties. A ruling by the European Court of Justice found that, with the new equal flexible retirement ages for men and women, the differing contribution bases breach the EU's Equal Treatment Directive. Proposals to change the calculation base and overhaul the calculation method were presented to parliament at the beginning of 1994.

A national collective agreement concluded in 1974 established a form of early retirement (*prépension conventionelle*) for older workers who have been made redundant. Schemes are set up on an industry basis by collective agreement and provide for employers to supplement unemployment benefit for male employees up until they can draw their state pension. The provisions have been amended several times, most recently in 1991, when an attempt was made by the social partners to limit access to early retirement. The supplement is equivalent to half the difference between unemployment benefit entitlement and former net earnings, up to a monthly reference ceiling (as of 1 July 1993) of BFr 95,575 (£1,593). It becomes payable once the contract of employment is terminated and after any payments made during the period of notice have ceased.

To be eligible, employees must now have twenty-five years' employment service. Those opting to retire under an agreed scheme from the age of 60 must have ten years' service in the industry over the previous fifteen, or a total of twenty years' employment service in all. Apart from those in financial difficulties, companies in general may not set an early retirement age limit lower than 58 years. Most agreed schemes also cover women from the age of 58. Where lower limits (from 55 years) are agreed, employment service of thirty-eight years is usually required in order to qualify. Employers are obliged to replace departing workers by an unemployed person whenever advantage is taken of one of the industry schemes.

Following the introduction of a flexible retirement age, men who retired under an agreed scheme before 1991 must remain in that scheme until they reach 65. However, employees who retired on sickness or unemployment grounds have the choice of taking a state pension without penalty from the age of sixty or staying in the appropriate sickness or unemployment benefit scheme if that is more advantageous.

Individual termination of contract

Belgian law is weighted in favour of protecting an employee's job, and strict procedures must be followed in connection with termination of contract. Periods of notice are laid down by statute, but are most commonly extended by agreement and the use of generally accepted formulae. Periods of notice must be observed or payment made in lieu. No formal distinction is drawn between individual dismissal on grounds of employee conduct and dismissal on economic grounds. In most cases no consultation is required. A number of employees enjoy special protection and rights. Employers are not normally bound to give reasons for dismissing an individual on an open-ended contract unless a summary dismissal is involved.

Resignation and mutual consent

No obligations are laid down in law when a contract is terminated by mutual consent (*accord mutuel*), though the contract of employment itself may stipulate certain procedures. Either party may give notice or, if both parties are in agreement over the termination of a contract, the period of notice need not be worked out, although it will usually be paid. However, it is always advisable to put the termination details in writing for future reference, should the need for proof of termination procedures arise.

A fixed-term contract is automatically terminated on the expiry of the term, or completion of the task, for which it was signed. Again, no period of notice is required.

Grounds for termination

Either party can terminate an open-ended contract (*contrat de travail à durée indéterminée*) by giving the required notice (see below), or the employer may dismiss an employee summarily. The reasons for termination may be economic or related to the conduct or performance of the employee. Either party can initiate legal proceedings to terminate on the grounds of breach of contract. Clauses on termination in the contract itself may not contravene basic employment rights and may not, for example, adduce marriage, pregnancy or reaching legal retirement age as grounds.

Reaching retirement age does not, in itself, terminate employment. Notice must therefore be given, but the period is shorter than for other dismissals (see below).

Summary dismissal

No period of notice is required for summary dismissal involving a fundamental breach of contract or serious misconduct (*motif grave*). In law the latter involves 'any conduct which immediately and permanently precludes the continuation of a working relationship between the employer and the employee'. It may include theft or persistent unauthorised absence on the part of the employee. The injured party must take action to terminate the contract within three days of the serious incident (or latest in a series of incidents). Methods of notifying the termination are as for normal termination. The notice of dismissal must state the reasons for the dismissal.

Dismissal with notice

Employees may be dismissed with notice for economic or financial reasons, or owing to the conduct or performance of the employee. There is no difference in the termination procedure but disciplinary procedures must be adhered to prior to serving notice where termination is on the grounds of employee conduct (see below). Notice of termination of an open-ended contract must be served in writing upon each individual concerned, by means of a registered letter or a writ from the clerk of the court. It must indicate the date on which the period of notice starts and the length of the notice. An employee may give notice by registered letter, by writ or by handing the letter direct to the employer, who must sign an acknowledgement of receipt.

All employees are entitled to paid leave of up to one day per week for job-hunting. White-collar workers earning over BFr 864,000 (£14,400) a year are entitled to one day per week in the last six months' notice but only half a day per week during the period of notice prior to that.

Disciplinary procedures

Most disciplinary procedures are laid down in company regulations (*règlement de travail*) which are required by statute of every company in the private sector and of some in the public sector. Every employee must be given a copy of the regulations, and another copy must be displayed on the company's premises. Regulations are drawn up in conjunction with the works council, or other employee representatives, and cover a wide range of issues, including discipline. The latter would cover precise details of the use of verbal and written warnings, fines, demotion and relocation. The use to which any fine levied for misconduct may be put has to be mentioned in the regulations; the money is normally employed for the benefit of the work force. No fine may exceed one-fifth of an employee's daily pay.

A record must be kept of all disciplinary measures taken, including details of the employee, the reasons, dates and any fines imposed.

Periods of notice

Periods of notice can be very long and are often not worked out, in effect providing the employee with a form of severance compensation.

Blue-collar workers   For blue-collar workers the period of notice, as set by
statute, starts on the Monday following the week in which notice was served.
The period is twenty-eight days where notice is served by the employer and fourteen days if served by the employee, where the period of employment is less than
twenty years. For workers with more than twenty years' service, the period of
notice is extended to fifty-six days if it is the employer who has served notice
and twenty-eight days if it is the worker. A contract of employment may stipulate that blue-collar workers with less than six months' service are entitled to
only seven days' notice. A royal decree may increase or reduce periods of notice,
affecting entire sectors, while collective agreements (sectoral or company) may
only increase them. In the iron and steel industry agreement for example, blue-
collar workers must be given twenty-eight days' notice after ten years' service;
fifty-six days between ten and twenty years' service; and 112 days after twenty
years' service. If the employee gives notice, it may be less than that required by
statute: fourteen days with less than ten years' service, twenty-one days (between
ten and twenty years) and twenty-eight days (over twenty years).

White-collar workers   For white-collar employees the period of notice takes
effect on the first day of the calendar month following the month in which the
notice was served. Under the terms of the 1978 Law on Contracts of
Employment, all white-collar employees earning less than BFr 864,000
(£14,400) a year are entitled to:

- At least six months' notice for less than five years' service.
- Six months for five to ten years' service.
- A further three months for every additional five-year period of service.

Where notice is given by the employee these periods are halved, with a maximum of three months' notice.

   For employees earning over BFr 864,000, the majority, the period of notice is
subject to negotiation between employer and employee, once the employee has
been informed of the impending termination. It may also be set by the courts,
using one of a number of standard formulas, if no agreement can be reached. In
any case it may not be less than three months per five-year period of service if
served by the employer. For employees earning between BFr 864,000 and BFr
1,728,000 (£14,400–£28,800) maximum notice, served by the employee, is four
and a half months; six months for those earning more than BFr 1,728,000.
Periods of notice for more senior employees and managers are most frequently
determined by the contract of employment, but must respect the legal minima.
During probationary periods white-collar employees are entitled to a standard
seven days' notice.

   In cases where a white-collar employee has found other employment after having been served notice by an employer, the period of notice may be shortened to:

- One month if the employee is earning less than BFr 864,000 per year.
- Two months if earning between BFr 864,000 and BFr 1,728,000.
- Four months, by agreement, if earning over BFr 1,728,000.

Where no agreement can be reached on the length of the period of notice the employer may impose a period which can then be challenged by the employee in the labour courts. Contracts of employment are not automatically terminated when an employee reaches retirement age. Notice must be served, although it will be shorter than under other circumstances: it is set at six months if given by the employer and three months if given by the employee. The period of notice is further reduced by half if the period of employment was less than five years. Since the introduction of flexible retirement (see above) the employer can give notice on the grounds of retirement only at the upper age limit.

Claeys formula   A number of commonly used formulas are often adopted to determine the length of paid notice, which is generally well in excess of the legal minima. The most popular is the Claeys formula, first devised in 1974 from an analysis of court rulings on periods of notice and severance pay. The formula has been amended on a number of occasions since, most recently at the beginning of 1993. All the accepted formulas are based on a variety of factors combining length of service, age, level of responsibility and salary. The Claeys calculation is:

(Length of service × 0.88) + (Age × 0.09) + (Classification × 0.14) + (Salary × 0.0013) − 2.5 = Number of months' paid notice.

Length of service and age are expressed in years and fractions of years, not in months, as follows: one month = 0.08 of a year, two months = 0.16 of a year, three months = 0.25 of a year, etc. Job classification is determined by a five-tier scale, where 1 is the lowest (simple tasks) and 5 the highest (management functions). Salary is taken to be all payments made in the twelve months preceding termination, expressed in units of a thousand Belgian francs. So a salary of BFr 1,500,000 would be expressed as 1,500.

For example, the period of notice for a 37 year old surveyor with fifteen years' service earning BFr 875,000 (£17,500) would be in the region of sixteen months:

(15 × 0.88) + (37 × 0.09) + (4 × 0.14) + (875 × 0.0013) − 2.5 = 15.72

months' paid notice. It should be noted, however, that the formula will provide only an indication of what is deemed a reasonable period of notice. The circumstances of the dismissal may influence the notice period − for example, if an employee is to be dismissed following a series of disciplinary measures that do not, however, warrant summary dismissal, the period will be considerably reduced.

The courts do not officially use the formulas, but they are the most practical guide to periods of notice.

Severance pay

Employees are entitled to a period of paid notice (see above), which in effect serves as severance pay in many cases of termination. Where insufficient notice is given or the procedures of notification are not respected, or either party wishes to terminate the contract immediately, compensation (*indemnité de rupture*) must be paid. It is normally equivalent to the period of notice that should have been given in cases of open-ended contracts. Employers are allowed to pay the compensation in monthly instalments if the company is in financial difficulties. For fixed-term contracts compensation is any pay due for the unexpired portion of the contract, although this cannot be more than double the amount that would have been paid in lieu of notice had it been an open-ended contract. However, there is no other provision in law for additional severance payments in cases of individual economic dismissal, other than by court ruling. There are no special tax concessions for severance payments, which are subject to both tax and social security contributions.

Collective dismissal

Collective dismissal is regulated by two national collective agreements, Nos. 10 and 24, concluded in the National Labour Council, and by a royal decree. These measures detail the information and consultation procedures, as well as the severance payments that may have to be made.

In establishments with twenty or more employees the employer must inform the works council (or the trade union delegation) in writing of the intention to proceed to a collective dismissal. This is defined in law as dismissal taking place over sixty days involving:

- Ten workers from a work force of 20–100 employees.
- Ten per cent of a workforce of 100–300 employees.
- Thirty workers in establishments with more than 300 employees.

The information supplied to employee representatives must state the reason for the dismissals, the number of workers likely to be affected, the period over which the redundancies will take place, and the average number of workers employed in the establishment.

Employers must also inform the National Employment Office (ONEm) of the details of the collective dismissal. The information must include:

- Details of the company (including the number employed).
- The joint committee covering the company.
- The reasons for the dismissals.
- The number to be dismissed, by sex, age, occupation and department.

• Details of work-force consultation.

Employee representatives may submit their views to the ONEm. Formal notices of dismissal may not be issued to individual employees for thirty days after the time of official notification to the ONEm. This period may be shortened by the ONEm or lengthened to sixty days. However, no official authorisation as such is required for the dismissals, and the employer may proceed once the waiting period has elapsed. No criteria are laid down by law for the selection of workers for collective dismissal. The rules may be agreed with the works council as part of the mandatory company regulations. The last in – first out policy is still often adhered to, reflecting the higher costs of dismissing workers with long notice periods.

Periods of notice are as required in the case of individual dismissals. Workers are entitled to an additional payment on top of paid notice in the case of collective dismissal (*indemnité due en cas de licenciement collectif*). This is equal to half the difference between unemployment benefit and net remuneration up to an annually revised ceiling. It is payable for four months following the dismissal. In addition, extra payments may be determined at company level and detailed in the collective agreement. One of the most common ways of making such payments is through the sectoral hardship funds (*fonds de sécurité d'existence*).

Insolvency

When an employer is unable to make a redundancy payment a (national) redundancy fund (*fonds d'indemnisation des travailleurs licenciés en cas de fermeture d'entreprises*), financed by employers' contributions, may make payment on their behalf. Additional sums due when a contract is terminated may be paid from this fund, including payment for the period of notice, accrued holiday pay, wages due when the employee terminates the contract owing to the employer's non-payment, and benefits payable under collective agreements, excluding some early retirement schemes payments.

Final formalities

Employers are required by law to keep an up-to-date register of the personnel they employ. The register contains each individual's personal details and information on wage payments made. In addition, it holds data on schemes to which employees belong for the purposes of holiday pay, accident insurance, family allowances, etc. The employer also has to compile an individual dossier containing personal details, information on wage payments, and the dates of the start and termination of the contract. Once a contract has been terminated, this document must be updated within two months and given to the employee.

Transfer of undertakings

All contractual rights and obligations are fully maintained in the case of a transfer of undertakings. This applies either when a company or establishment is transferred in full, or where a company is merged or partly sold. A change of employer does *not* in itself constitute grounds for dismissal, although it may entail technical, organisational or economic changes leading to dismissal(s). Some company top-ups to social security schemes may be affected by a transfer of undertakings.

Appendix

Social security contributions

Statutory social charges are at the upper end of the scale relative to the rest of Europe. Blue- and white-collar employees pay 13.07 per cent of gross earnings, with no ceiling. The contributions cover pension, sickness or maternity and unemployment. Employers pay into the same funds plus those to cover educational leave, family allowances, workplace accidents and occupational disease. The total contribution varies for blue- and white-collar employees. For white-collar staff it amounts to 26.74 per cent of gross pay. For blue-collar workers it totals 34.74 per cent. In the case of blue-collar workers contributions are levied on 108 per cent of gross pay to take account of the double holiday pay paid from the fund and therefore not subject to deductions for social security.

In addition, employers are liable for charges to finance supplementary unemployment benefit (1.69 per cent in companies with more than ten staff); a 'wage restraint fund' for certain social benefits (7.48 per cent) and the enterprise closure fund (0.22 per cent or 0.33 per cent, depending on size). Some sectors also run funds such as those for long-term sickness, where contributions vary. Under the 1993/94 national agreement, a contribution of 0.30 per cent of the wage bill must be allocated to training. At least 0.10 per cent must go direct to the national training fund, with companies free to allocate the remainder to in-house training if they wish.

Income tax

Taxable income is calculated as gross earnings less social security and a personal allowance (depending on marital status). In addition, certain business expenses and a children's allowance are deducted. Income is taxed progressively in six bands at a rate ranging from 25 per cent to 55 per cent. In addition, a municipal tax is levied on all individuals as a percentage of final tax liability. This varies from 0 per cent to 10 per cent according to place of residence. The most usual rates are between 6 per cent and 8 per cent.

Organisations

ONEm (National Employment Office)
Boulevard de l'Empereur 7, 1000 Brussels
Tel.: + 32 2 510 20 11 (French-speakers),
+ 32 2 513 89 42 (Flemish-speakers)
The National Employment Office deals with
matters relating to unemployment and the
payment of benefits. It used to deal with job
placements, until this service was devolved
to the regions in 1988.

Ministry of Labour
Rue Belliard 53, 1000 Brussels
Tel.: + 32 2 233 41 11
All collective agreements at national and
sectoral level must be registered with the
Ministry. Company agreements do not have
to be registered by law, but frequently are.
Notification of collective agreements is
published in the official gazette, the
Moniteur Belge. Copies of agreements can
be obtained from the Ministry.

Conseil National du Travail (National
Labour Council)
Avenue de la Joyeuse Entrée 17–21, 1040
Brussels
Tel.: + 32 2 233 88 11
The NLC is the bipartite consultative body
on employment and related matters. It has
the power to conclude national collective
agreements, many of which are made generally binding. It has twenty-four members
drawn equally from the three main
employers' organisations and the three
main trade unions. An independent chair is
nominated by the Crown.

Fédération des Entreprises de Belgique
(Federation of Belgian Enterprises)
Rue Ravenstein 4, 1000 Brussels
Tel.: + 32 2 515 08 11
The main employers' organisation at
national level. Enterprises employing some
85 per cent of the private sector work force
are affiliated to the FEB. It is the main
employers' organisation on the NLC.

*Confédération des Syndicats Chrétiens de
Belgique* (Confederation of Christian Trade
Unions)
Rue de la Loi 121, 1040 Brussels
Tel.: + 32 2 237 31 11
The CSC has over a million members and
sits on the NLC. It represents blue- and
white-collar workers across all sections of
industry.

Fédération Générale du Travail de Belgique
(General Confederation of Belgian Labour)
Rue Haute 42, 1000 Brussels
Tel.: + 32 2 506 82 11
The FGTB is the socialist trade union con-
federation, with over a million members
among blue- and white-collar employees.
Like the CSC, it sits on the NLC.

Glossary of terms

National legislation dictates that companies operating in Belgium must use the
language of the region in which they are located for all documentation. Those
operating in Brussels, officially designated as bilingual, must use the language of
employees. On page 74 we give a short glossary of terms in three languages, but
in the text we refer in most cases to the French term where appropriate.

English	Flemish	French
Recruitment	Werving	Recrutement
Works council	Ondernemingsraad	Conseil d'entreprise
Establishment	Technische bedrijfseenheid	Unité d'exploitation
Health and Safety	Comité voor Veiligheid,	Comité de sécurité
Committee	Gezondheid en Verfraaiing	d'hygiène et d'embellissement
	van de Werkplaats	des lieux de travail
National Labour Council	Nationaale Arbeidsraad	Conseil nationale du travail
Open-ended contract	Arbeidsovereenkomst voor	Contrat à durée indéterminée
	onbepaalde tijd	
Trade union delegation	Vakbondsafvaardiging	Délégation syndicale
Blue-collar worker	Arbeider	Ouvrier
Collective agreement	Collectieve arbeidsovereenkomst	Convention collective du travail
Employer	Werkgever	Employeur
Fixed-term contract	Arbeidsovereenkomst voor	Contrat à durée déterminée
	bepaalde tijd	
Joint committee	Paritair comité	Commission paritaire
White-collar employee	Bediende	Employé
Labour tribunal	Arbeidsrechtbank	Tribunal du travail
Mutual agreement	Wederzijds goedvinden	Accord mutuel
Notice	Opzegging	Préavis
Notice period	Opzeggingstermijn	Délai du préavis
Probationary period	Proefbeding	Période d'essai
Restrictive covenant	Concurrentieverbod	Clause de non-concurrence
Summary dismissal	Ontslag op staande voet	Licenciement pour motif grave
Suspension of contract	Schorsing van de overeenkomst	Suspension du contrat
Temporary work	Tijdelijke arbeid	Travail temporaire
Temporary work (agency)	Uitzendarbeid	Travail intérimaire
Termination of contract	Ontslag/Opzegging	Licenciement
Terms and conditions of	Arbeidsvoorwaarden	Conditions de travail
employment		
Works rules	Arbeidsreglement	Règlement du travail
Compensation in lieu of	Opzeggingsvergoeding	Indemnité de rupture
notice		
Compensation for unfair	Ontslagvergoeding	Indemnité de licenciement
dismissal		
Compensation for	Vergoeding wegens collectieve	Indemnité en cas de
collective dismissal	ontslag	licenciement collectif
Hardship funds	Fonds voor bestaanszekerheid	Fonds de sécurité d'existence
Sales representative dismissal	Uitwinningsvergoeding	Indemnité d'éviction
compensation		
Unfair dismissal	Onredelijke ontslag	Licenciement abusif
	Willekeurig ontslag	
Labour court	Arbeidshof	Cour du travail
Labour inspectorate	Arbeidsinspectie	Inspection de travail
Short-term working	Gedeeltelijke werkloosheid	Chômage partiel
Unemployment benefit	Werkloosheidsuitkering	Allocation de chômage

Main sources

Commentaire Social de Poche, Samsom, 1994/95.
Guide de Législation Sociale, Confédération des Syndicats Chrétiens.

Collective agreements for the following industries: chemicals, engineering, foodstuffs, retail, transport; also various national collective agreements supplied by the Conseil National du Travail.

Legislation: 1968 Law on collective agreements (*Loi sur les conventions collectives de travail et les commissions paritaires*); 1971 Law on Employment (*Loi sur le travail*); 1978 Law on contracts of employment (*Loi relative aux contrats de travail*).

3

Denmark

Terms and conditions of employment in Denmark are set primarily by collective or individual agreement within a legal framework which generally gives precedence to collective bargaining in the determination of substantive issues.

Basic rights and labour jurisdiction

The Danish constitution has almost no effect on the relationship between employers and employees. The only important articles in this respect are those which guarantee citizens' right of assembly and grant the freedom to form associations for any lawful purpose. These provide the legal foundation for the operation of trade unions.

General legal framework

Several general laws have some impact on terms and conditions of employment. They include:

- The Contracts Act (*Aftaleloven*), which lays down basic legal principles concerning contracts of employment.
- The Sick Pay Act (*Sygdagpengeloven*).
- The Supplementary Pensions Act (*ATPloven*), which deals with the compulsory supplementary pension scheme.
- The Health and Safety at Work Act (*Arbejdsmiljøloven*).

Legislation which deals directly with the labour market as a whole is limited in comparison with other countries in Western Europe. However, several such laws do exist, covering such areas as leave, holiday and working environment. Perhaps the most important of them is the Salaried Employees Act (*Funktionærloven*), which gives special rights to white-collar workers. Those laws which do make substantive provisions may, in general, be departed from only where it is to the advantage of the employee.

Most other conditions of employment and all pay bargaining are regulated entirely by collective agreements, which are negotiated at central, industry and local level throughout the labour market. Perhaps the most important of these is the *Hovedaftalen* (General Agreement) between the DA, the central employers' organisation and the LO, the blue-collar trade union confederation. This agreement covers all general conditions of employment in the DA/LO sphere and is familiarly known as 'the constitution of the labour market'. (Another volume in this series, *Employee Relations and Collective Bargaining*, deals in detail with negotiating arrangements.)

The lack of substantive legislation has created some areas of difficulty in the enactment of European Union law in Denmark. It has necessitated a shift away from the voluntarist approach – rooted in the extensive coverage of the work force by collective agreements – which has prevailed since the early years of this century.

Labour jurisdiction

The procedural arrangements set up within the context of the General Agreement provide a forum for resolving many issues arising out of collective agreements and their interpretation (see 'Grievances' below).

Any contravention of the statutes named above is dealt with either by the criminal courts, if a breach of public law is involved, or by the civil courts where the issues turn on disputes over contractual terms. There is no separate branch of labour jurisdiction or system of industrial tribunals.

Contracts of employment

Types of employee

There are four main categories of employee:

- Senior manager (*direktør*).
- Salaried (white-collar) employee (*funktionær*).
- Wage-earner (*lønmodtagere*).
- Vocational trainee or apprentice (*elev*).

The concept of senior manager is not expressly defined by law or collective agreement, but is generally recognised as meaning someone with a high degree of autonomy at work who has responsibility for running a business and the power to enter into agreements on behalf of the company. Some Danish laws on conditions of employment are very precise as to exactly which employees they apply to, and senior managers are often deemed to fall outside their scope. For instance, senior managers are not covered by the Holidays Act or the Salaried Employees Act. Nor are they included in collective agreements.

Conditions of employment for a white-collar employee are governed by the Salaried Employees Act (*Funktionærloven*). Section 1 of the Act defines very precisely who is considered to be a salaried employee. The categories are:

- Clerical and office staff.
- Technical and clinical staff.
- Persons whose work consists mainly of the supervision of other employees on their employer's behalf.

The Act applies to those in such positions who work at least fifteen hours a week under the direction and supervision of an employer, and automatically grants the employee various rights. The most important of these are seniority-dependent notice periods and severance pay, and the right to full pay during sickness (see below). However, the Act is not the sole source of employer and employee rights and duties. Pay, for example, is decided by collective or individual agreement.

Apart from the very general provisions laid down in law, the rights and duties of blue-collar employees are overwhelmingly regulated by collective agreement.

Employment conditions for vocational trainees and apprentices are protected by law. However, the law states that pay and conditions should be in accordance with the relevant collective agreement or, if no such agreement exists, those which are 'generally applicable' to the job.

The increasing complexity of jobs carried out by some members of blue-collar unions has given rise to the hybrid concept of *funktionærlignende ansættelse* (literally 'salaried employee-like employment'). Although the concept is not valid in law, collective agreements sometimes contain provisions for the employment of such workers. For instance, the Industrial Agreement (that is, the collective agreement covering manufacturing industry negotiated between the union confederation CO-Industri and the employers' association Dansk Industri) gives these employees the right to the longer period of notice provided by the Salaried Employees Act.

Form of contract

From 1 July 1993 Danish law has required that all employment contracts should be in writing for workers employed for more than one month and working for more than eight hours a week, implementing the EU Directive on Proof of an Employment Contract. Those whose employment commenced before that date have the right to receive a written employment contract within two months upon request.

Owing to the fragmented nature of the rules governing employment, a large number of standard contracts have been agreed between union and employer organisations and are widely used. There is no duty to consult employee representatives about new contracts.

Contents of a contract

In the absence of laws and collective agreements on the employment conditions of senior managers, their contracts have to cover all the details of the employment relationship. The Danish employers' federation (the DA) recommends, in its book *Direktøren – ansættelses- og arbejdsvilkår* (Conditions of Employment for Senior Managers), that the following should be taken into consideration:

- Identification of the parties and a job description.
- The types of employee the manager has the right to hire and dismiss.
- Any agreements on other paid work which the manager may carry out, including whether the manager or the company will receive the fees for such work.
- Hours of work are not generally specified, although the contract should specify the length of annual leave.
- Basic pay and bonus arrangements, pension contributions, other fringe benefits such as cars, telephones and insurance.
- Sickness benefits are not usually specified in senior managers' contracts, although full pay is usually granted.
- Restrictive covenants.
- The period of notice, which is not subject to any legal restriction.
- Contracts may also contain a provision stating that any dispute between the manager and the company should be settled by arbitration, and not through the legal system.

Terms of employment for white-collar employees are subject to the provisions of the Salaried Employees Act, the relevant collective agreement and any locally agreed measures. A typical white-collar contract would therefore contain:

- Personal details, the amount and payment date of salary, with the method of calculation, and cost of living allowances. Companies covered by collective agreements may simply refer the employee to the agreement.
- Weekly working hours, together with any locally agreed variations, such as flexitime.
- Annual leave (usually a statement that the Holidays Act will apply).
- Procedure for notifying sick leave.
- Notice requirements and details of any probationary period.
- Restrictive covenants and copyright rules, where appropriate.

As far as blue-collar employees are concerned, the most important basis of the contract of employment will be a collective agreement or, failing that, the prevailing conditions in the relevant sector. Blue-collar contracts generally contain:

- Personal details (including union affiliation and membership number) and administrative details (time-clock number, etc.).
- Wage rates (by collective agreement, if applicable), payment and tax details.
- Holiday entitlement.
- Record of qualifications, including any apprenticeship completed.

Companies may not employ vocational trainees or apprentices unless they have been approved by the local employer–union trade committee. A vocational training agreement will then be drawn up by a local technical or business school and signed by the employer and the trainee. Periods spent in work experience at the company necessitate a further contract detailing pay, holiday, period of notice, etc.

Types of contract

Contracts may be permanent or fixed-term. Fixed-term contracts may be limited to a certain period of time (*bestemt tid*) or to the performance of a certain task (*bestemt arbejde*). A special term – *midlertidigt arbejde* – is used to describe work lasting less than three months. Where salaried employees are involved, minimum periods of notice may be set by law should either party wish to withdraw during the life of the contract.

Part-time work is defined both by some statute law and, more typically, by collective agreement. The typical range is a lower limit of fifteen hours and an upper limit of thirty. Agreements also customarily regulate employment rights, which must be *pro rata* to full-timers on pay and other conditions.

Most of the labour market is covered by industry-level collective agreements, and many such agreements are supplemented by local agreements. It is usual to specify which agreements affect an individual contract of employment.

Probationary periods

The existence and length of any probationary period are determined by the category of employee. Probationary periods are not usual for blue-collar workers. White-collar workers, on the other hand, commonly undergo probation for up to three months, since the law specifies shorter periods of notice for such employees during this period. Vocational trainees and apprentices have a probation period of three months.

Restrictive covenants and employee inventions

Restrictive covenants (*konkurrenceklausuler*) are generally included only in the contracts of senior managers and some white-collar workers. There are no legal restraints on such covenants as far as senior managers are concerned. However, the validity and duration of covenants is legally restricted in the case of white-collar employees. Legislation recognises covenants for such employees as valid only if the employee occupies 'a position of special trust', and the covenant may not last for more than one year. However, the law states that longer periods may be agreed if employees are compensated financially. The term of the covenant and any compensation should be specified in the employment contract. Restrictive covenants are common in jobs which entail a high degree of managerial responsibility or confidentiality and are legally enforceable.

Clauses regulating employers' rights to employee inventions and copyright entitlements are also common in certain jobs.

Workplace discipline and rights

Under a DA–LO central agreement enterprises with at least thirty-five employees may have a co-operation committee, one of whose tasks is to establish principles governing personnel policy and the working environment. However, companies still have scope to decide their own personnel policies, including internal disciplinary arrangements, as the co-operation committee functions in a purely consultative role. Some internal rules of conduct will arise from statute law – for example, the requirement to wear protective clothing, based on the employer's duties under the Health and Safety at Work Act (*Arbejdsmiljøloven*). Others will tend to arise from the special circumstances of the company or its sector of industry; for instance, it is common for lorry drivers with mobile telephones to be forbidden to use them for personal calls. Employers are free to choose the sanctions they wish to be able to call on to enforce these rules. Sanctions are even occasionally included in sectoral collective agreements. The Industrial Agreement, for example, permits the instant dismissal of anyone working weekend shifts who 'moonlights' during the week. Internal rules would also generally cover such areas as notification procedures in the event of sickness.

Grievances

Grievance procedures are often regulated by collective agreements. Employee grievances will usually be brought to the attention of the shop steward, who will initially try to mediate through the co-operation machinery mentioned above. If agreement cannot be reached at this stage, the nature of the complaint will decide which steps are taken next. If the grievance arises from the terms of a collective agreement, the employee may turn to a trade union for legal assistance and the issue can be subject to the agreed procedures for dealing with collective employment disputes. Should mediation prove unsuccessful and the trade union supports the employee's case it will forward the matter to the labour court on the employee's behalf; in the absence of union support, the employee may pursue the case through the civil courts. However, the labour court has no power to rule on matters solely concerning an individual employment relationship: these must be pursued in the civil courts.

In matters relating to the renewal of a collective agreement, or an attempt to enforce the conclusion of one, industrial action may be resorted to by employers or employees (assuming that an existing collective agreement with its built-in peace obligation has been terminated). Disagreements in connection with the renewal of collective agreements may also be dealt with by an official conciliator (*forligsmand*), who may step in if the social partners fail to reach agreement and call the parties back to negotiations or put forward a mediation proposal.

Disputes about the interpretation of collective agreements are handled according to the Standard Rules for Handling Labour Disputes (*Norm for regler for behandling af faglig strid*) agreed between the DA and the central union confederation, the LO, in 1908. These set out three steps for settling disputes:

- Local negotiation.
- An industrial arbitration court, consisting of two members from each of the parties and an arbitrator, with powers to issue binding rulings.
- If such adjudication fails to gain acceptance the matter passes to the labour court, which considers the case only after the parties have again been obliged to negotiate.

The court has the power to impose fines; its judgements are binding and enforceable by the civil courts, although matters seldom reach that stage: 90 per cent of cases scheduled to appear before the court are resolved by prior mediation.

Data protection

Private employers are bound by the terms of data protection legislation (the 1987 Private Registers Act), which forbids them to collect certain types of information about employees. The law applies to electronically stored files and to manual files if they are maintained systematically, and if there is a reasonable need to protect employees' privacy. The operation of the law is monitored by the Data Surveillance Authority (*Registertilsynet*), which has the right to enter premises and issue orders requiring changes in the management of data. Organisations wishing to hold data must register with the authority. The main provisions of the Act are:

- Employees have a legal right of access to all information held on them in a database, and employers must ensure that access by non-authorised persons is neither possible nor permitted.
- Information of a purely private nature – for example, on a person's race, religion, political views or criminal record – may not be held or communicated without the employee's consent, except where the employer has a legitimate interest, and then only with the permission of the Data Surveillance Authority.
- Different companies' databases on employees may not be linked up, except with the express authorisation of the Data Surveillance Authority.

Databases maintained by private employers may normally contain only information on employees that is essential to the running of the business and personnel administration. This includes, for example, name, address, pay, qualifications, tax details and sickness absence.

Employment terms and conditions

Hours of work

Statutory regulation of working hours is limited to provisions in the Work Environment Act specifying the rest periods to which employees are entitled. The Act states that workers must have a continuous period of rest not less than eleven hours in each twenty-four hour period, calculated from the start of the normal working day. However, this may be reduced to eight hours in certain circumstances for shift workers. Additionally, employees are entitled to twenty-four hours off (on a Sunday, if possible) within each period of seven consecutive days.

Apart from these considerations, hours of work are theoretically unlimited, except for under-18s. In practice they are regulated by collective agreement. The present centrally collectively agreed working week is thirty-seven hours. Agreements typically include detailed provisions on how these hours are to be distributed and allow some degree of local flexibility. For example, the 1993 Industrial Agreement states that working hours should normally fall between 06.00 and 17.00 and that no day should be less than five hours for a five-day week. However, the agreement also gives employers the right, subject to consultation, to introduce changes in these provisions: normal working hours may be moved around (against extra payment) and variable weekly hours may be introduced, provided the agreed figure is attained on average over a reference period.

The length of rest and lunch breaks is sometimes specified in collective agreements, but is often left to local custom and practice. A lunch break of half an hour is the norm.

Shiftwork is regulated by the Joint Arrangement on Shift Work (*Fællesordning for arbejde i holddrift*) agreed between the LO, the blue-collar trade union confederation, and the DA, the central employers' organisation. The most common arrangements are two- and three-shift systems, although other variations are possible: for instance, it is possible, under the Industrial Agreement (see above), for employees to have a working week which consists of two twelve-hour shifts on Saturdays and Sundays. In addition to shift premiums and hours arrangements, the Joint Arrangement also allows scope for local agreements to be struck on working time.

Short-time working or temporary lay-offs (*arbejdsfordeling*) may be introduced with official notification. For periods of less than thirteen weeks, any intention to introduce short-time must be reported to the AF, the State Labour Exchange System, one week before it becomes effective. If short-term working is intended to last more than thirteen weeks, it can only be introduced subject to the AF's approval and must be reported four weeks before introduction. Employees are entitled to unemployment benefit for any hours not worked. In 1994 this was equal to 90 per cent of earnings up to a limit of DKr 509 (£52). In addition, employers are bound to pay an allowance for the first two days of unemployment. This is currently DKr 454 (£46) if more than four working days are lost, and DKr 227 (£23) if fewer than four hours are lost.

Night work and overtime

There are no legal restrictions on night work, with the exception that young people under 18 may not generally work between 20.00 and 06.00. Most collective agreements specify double time for such work.

Any work beyond the collectively agreed thirty-seven hours constitutes overtime and is compensated according to rules quoted in agreements. Compensation usually takes two forms: supplementary payments (*tillæg*) and time off in lieu (*afspadsering*).

Overtime payment schedules are quoted in collective agreements, with amounts varying considerably between sectors. Rates vary between 50 per cent and 100 per cent, depending on the number of hours to be worked and the time of day. Overtime may also be compensated with time off. The freedom of choice between these two varies between agreements. For instance, the collective agreement covering shop and office workers allows free choice, whereas the Industrial Agreement specifies certain types of overtime which can be compensated only by payment. Agreements also stipulate periods of notice for overtime and usually stress that such work should be kept to a minimum: however, there are no formal limits.

Vocational trainees and apprentices may not work more than ten hours per day, but can work overtime within this limit.

Time off

Annual leave

Annual leave as an entitlement is defined by the Holidays Act, which covers all types of private-sector workers except senior managers, domestic servants and agricultural workers. The Act states that all employees are entitled to five weeks' annual paid leave. This is accrued throughout the calendar year according to time worked: each month worked entitles the employee to two and a half days' paid holiday. Any leave earned in a given year must be taken between 2 May that year and 2 May the following calendar year. Employees have the right to take three consecutive weeks' leave during the period 2 May to 30 September.

Holiday pay is equal to 12.5 per cent of pay during the accrual year for blue-collar workers. White-collar employees receive full wages for the holiday period plus a bonus of 1 per cent of salary during the accrual year. This bonus is also payable to vocational trainees and apprentices.

There are ten public holidays in Denmark: Christmas Day, Boxing Day, New Year's Day, Maundy Thursday, Good Friday, Easter Monday, General Prayer

Day (29 April in 1994), Ascension Day, Whit Monday and Constitution Day (5 June). This last, however, is only a half-day.

Maternity, paternity and parental leave

Basic provisions concerning parental leave are contained in law, but may be improved upon in collective agreements. A legislative package providing for a number of new leave opportunities was introduced, for a temporary period, in 1993 (Law 435, 30 June 1993) as a measure intended to help lower unemployment (see below).

Paid maternity leave begins four weeks before the expected date of confinement and continues for fourteen weeks after the birth. Female white-collar employees are also entitled to up to five months' leave on half-pay, beginning up to three months before the estimated date of birth and ending not later than three months after the birth. However, this right can be exercised only if the employee is considered to be unfit to work because of pregnancy. Paternity leave extends for two weeks following the birth.

Parental leave is for the ten weeks following the expiry of maternity leave. It may be divided as required between mother and father, but only one parent may be on leave at any one time.

An employee who adopts a child is legally entitled to twenty-four weeks' leave as long as the authorities require them to be at home in connection with the adoption.

Until the end of 1996 parents are also legally entitled to at least thirteen and at most twenty-six weeks' child care leave, which may be taken at any time before the child reaches eight years of age. A further twenty-six weeks' child care leave may be taken with the employer's consent.

Other time off

The 1993 law which establishes the right to child care leave also gives employees the right to up to fifty-two weeks' educational or sabbatical leave, but only with their employers' consent.

Although there is no legal requirement, most collective agreements now include the right to paid leave for the first day of a child's sickness. In law there is no right to leave for family occasions, although in practice it is usually granted, often by collective agreement, for such reasons as marriage, the death of a close relative or moving house. Workplace safety representatives elected under the Health and Safety Act have the right to time off for carrying out their duties. Shop stewards are usually accorded time off for union business, although collective agreements usually stress that this should not affect working time or production.

Employees are also legally entitled to leave for military service.

Individual pay and benefits

There are no statutes governing general pay determination, nor any provisions on a minimum wage or pay indexation: these matters are left entirely to collective bargaining or individual negotiation. However, collective agreements for the public sector contain a clause which requires that pay rises must be at least 80 per cent of those gained in the private sector.

The frequency and form of payment are similarly unaffected by legal constraints, but are usually specified in collective agreements, where these are applicable. Blue-collar workers are generally paid weekly or fortnightly, white-collar employees monthly. However, agreements usually stress that any variation up to monthly is possible by local agreement. No statutory requirements exist on pay statements, although their form is sometimes specified in agreements. Payment may be either in cash or by bank transfer. Income tax is deducted at source, along with other statutory and collectively agreed contributions.

There is a legally established wage guarantee fund (*Lønmodtagernes Garantifond*), funded by public money, which secures employees' wage claims (up to a ceiling of DKr 75,000, or £7,600) in the event of an employer's insolvency.

Levels of pay determination

Collective agreements cover some 90 per cent of the work force, and pay for the majority of the work force is therefore set mainly by collective bargaining. Although this was previously conducted at central, industry and local level, pay talks are no longer held at the national level. However, the central employer and trade union organisations still fulfil a co-ordinating role in negotiations.

Industry-level negotiations are usually conducted every other year between the unions concerned and an employers' organisation. This has led in recent times to the creation of union and employer 'cartels' which are increasingly involved in pay talks. Indeed, recent moves by both unions and employers have resulted in many tasks previously performed at central level being shifted to these cartels. Since agreements often now specify only a single minimum pay rate, negotiations at company level have become more important in setting actual pay structures and individual salaries (see below).

Pay levels are generally much higher than the minima. For instance, the minimum wage for a skilled mechanic in 1992, the most recent year for which earnings figures were available at the time of going to press, was DKr 66 (£6.70) per hour; in the second quarter of 1992 such an employee working outside Copenhagen earned on average DKr 104 (£10.50), or DKr 114 (£11.50) in the capital.

As there is no provision in law for collective agreements to be extended to cover non-unionised workers, pay-setting for these employees is theoretically a matter entirely for the employer and the employee concerned. In practice, however, the terms of the relevant industry agreement – including pay levels – are usually applied.

White-collar workers outside collective bargaining have the right, according to the Salaried Employees Act, to negotiate individually, in the presence of a lawyer or union official if desired. Collective discussions may also take place involving union officials, although the outcome may be implemented in the form of individual increases. In some companies, white-collar employees may be covered by some collectively agreed provisions, for example on bonus payments or appraisal, although their basic salary will be set individually.

Main payment systems

Pay agreements use two main systems: standard wages (*normalløn*) where a range of pay rates is set by collective agreement for different grades or occupations, and minimum wages (*minimalløn*), where industry-level minima (or a single minimum rate for adult employees) can be supplemented by local-level bargaining.

The number of employees covered by standard wage rates is steadily shrinking. In the sector of the labour market covered by collective agreements signed by organisations affiliated to the main employers' organisation, the DA, and the main union confederation, the LO, the percentage of agreements signed on this basis had declined to around 20 per cent in the 1993 bargaining round, the other 80 per cent being minimum wage agreements.

There are usually lower rates for trainees and apprentices. Any supplements for special types of work, seniority or unsocial hours will also be stated. The rates in standard wage agreements are applicable until the agreement expires; those in minimum wage agreements may be supplemented by local negotiation on an individual basis – usually once a year at most – during the life of the agreement.

In both these types of agreement it is common to find provisions which allow the introduction, subject to local agreement, of various types of incentive-based wage systems such as piecework or productivity agreements.

Job evaluation

The shift from centrally agreed fixed rates to minima and a greater role for local-level negotiations in pay-setting have enhanced the profile of job evaluation schemes as one instrument for securing consistency and equity in a less regulated pay environment. Although there are no laws requiring them to be adopted, many collective agreements specifying minimum rates contain clauses stating that individual pay should be determined with reference to a systematic evaluation of the employee's abilities and responsibilities. Job evaluation is mainly carried out by larger companies, using proprietary systems, although some employer organisations have developed their own procedures for member companies.

Components of basic pay

Basic pay is made up of either a standard rate for the job or an agreed minimum supplemented by local bargaining and, for some white-collar workers, by individual negotiation. Either system may be affected by any locally agreed productivity and bonus schemes, and in some cases these may apply to employees nominally outside collective bargaining.

Standard wage agreements often specify increments based on seniority or the attainment of relevant vocational qualifications, but this is uncommon in minimum wage agreements. However, some of the latter may specify a number of minima. For instance, the agreement covering private-sector shop and office workers in establishments with at least fifteen employees sets out three minima, graded in line with the amount of responsibility the job involves, as defined in some detail in the collective agreement.

Overtime

Overtime pay is generally set by industry-level agreements. Such agreements will also include limits on overtime (see above), periods of notice and provision for time off in lieu. Minimum overtime supplements in the 1993/95 engineering industry agreement for the first and second hours on top of normal working, for which the minimum rate is DKr 68.35 (£6.90), is DKr 22.90 (£2.30); this rises to DKr 36.50 (£3.70) for the third and fourth hours and to DKr 68.30 for each hour thereafter. Weekend and holiday work attracts supplements of DKr 36.50 to DKr 68.30. In shops and offices the first three hours are paid at the hourly rate plus 50 per cent, and thereafter at double time. Weekends and holidays are paid at double time.

Night work, shift and other premiums

Compensation for shift work is subject to a DA–LO agreement (*Fællesordning for arbejde i holddrift*) which is renewed during the bargaining round. This is an unusual example of pay still being set at central level. Hourly supplements in the current agreement are DKr 17.65 (£1.80) for shift work between 17.00 and 22.00 and DKr 19.85 (£2.00) between 22.00 and 06.00. For work between 14.00 on Saturday and all day Sunday, as well as work on public holidays, a supplement of DKr 57.60 (£5.80) is payable. Work between 06.00 and 17.00 attracts no supplement except at weekends. Night work is paid at the same rates as overtime.

Agreements may contain other supplements relevant to the industry. For instance, the Industrial Agreement details tool allowances for woodworkers and coachbuilders as well as extra payments for shipbuilders and foundry workers. The Agricultural Agreement, on the other hand, includes supplements for tractor maintenance and animal husbandry.

Bonuses and financial participation

There is no legal or agreed requirement to pay a Christmas or thirteenth-month bonus, although about half of all senior managers have a bonus clause written into their contracts.

Financial participation is through legally regulated share-based schemes. These must be open to all employees, although compensation levels may vary, and the value of shares granted to an employee must be in reasonable proportion to the employee's income. Two types of scheme are operated:

- *Profit-sharing*, where shares are given to employees. These must be 'frozen' in a recognised financial institution for seven years. Their value is tax-free to employees and tax-deductible for companies, up to a limit of DKr 6,000 (£610).
- *Preferential purchase*, where employees may buy shares for less than the market price. These must be 'frozen' for five years. The price difference is not taxable.

Merit and performance-based pay

Merit systems have generally been on the increase, overwhelmingly for salaried employees. Companies are free, in theory, to introduce such systems, although the Danfoss case (see above 'European Union provisions') has led companies to look more carefully at the sort of elements which might go into determining individual rewards.

Payment-by-results systems are encouraged in some of the major collective agreements. The 1993 Industrial Agreement, for instance, stresses that both parties 'consider it desirable to use such piecework and other productivity-based pay systems as may be adopted at local level to suit the special needs of a particular company'. However, it is also mentioned elsewhere in the agreement that wages should be set on the basis of a 'systematic evaluation'.

For those covered by the DA–LO co-operation agreement, one of the stated aims of the co-operation committee is 'informing employees about proposals for incentive systems of payment, including particulars about their basic structure, effect and application'.

Sick pay

Payment during sickness absence is regulated by the Sickness Benefit Act (*Sygdagpengeloven*), which obliges employers to pay all employees the amount of state benefit (DKr 2,545 or £260 per week in 1994) for the first two weeks of illness. After that period benefit is paid by the local authority.

However, other compensation levels depend upon the category of employee. Blue-collar workers have no legal right to anything other than sickness benefit during illness, although since the 1993 bargaining round most blue-collar collective agreements have clauses requiring employers to pay full wages for up to two weeks in such cases. White-collar employees have a statutory right to full pay during sickness, but the employer may terminate the employment if an employee is sick for more than 120 days in twelve months. Employers must meet the cost in full for the first two weeks, but can then claim the state benefit amount from the local authority.

Maternity pay

Maternity, paternity and parental leave is compensated by an amount equal to state sickness benefit, which is paid by the employer and claimed back from the local authority. Female white-collar employees who take up their right to five months' maternity leave because of incapacity are entitled to half salary. Employers may then claim back an amount equal to state benefit from the local authority.

Child care leave entitles the parent taking leave to 80 per cent of the amount of state sickness benefit, paid by the employer, who can claim the amount back from the local authority.

Managerial pay

Managerial pay is determined according to the customary criteria of company size, responsibility, sector, qualifications and location, with pay in the Copenhagen area typically some 10 per cent above levels in the provinces. As the Danish Institute of Personnel Management (IP) has noted, the strong correlation between company size and executive pay levels creates difficulties for the small and medium-sized firms which form the backbone of the Danish economy and which may find it difficult to attract or retain managerial talent.

In a company with a median turnover of DKr 150 million (£15.2 million), the base salary of the head of a major function is 69 per cent of that of the managing director. However, bonus payments are a considerably greater proportion of the pay package of top management. According to the Monks Partnership 1993–94 survey of incentives and benefits in Europe, all companies covered paid cash bonuses to top management, compared with 75 per cent to other senior board members and heads of major functions. When total earnings are compared, the function head's overall pay falls to 59 per cent of the MD's earnings. Both the incidence and the value of bonuses have continued to grow in recent years: previous Monks Partnership surveys suggest a marked extension of bonus payments to upper and middle management levels. Share options are quite common for top managers, but fall away rapidly below that level.

Comparatively high tax rates in the past tended to lead to some diversion of remuneration into fringe benefits. However, a programme of tax reform – set to run from 1994 to 1998 – will see a general lowering of tax rates, with cuts of some 5 per cent on top rates, partly financed by increased levies on employees to finance employment-related benefits. The main executive benefits are cars and supplementary pensions to top up the state pension, which has an upper limit. However, the incidence of company cars is among the lowest in Europe. According to the Monks Partnership 1993 European Cómpany Car Survey, some 85 per cent of managing directors were provided with a car – a low figure by European standards. Seventy-four per cent of function heads received a car, again virtually the lowest incidence in Europe. Supplementary pensions are provided to over 80 per cent of executives, with a slight preponderance of money purchase over defined benefit schemes. Where they are required, employee contributions average around 4 per cent of salary.

Equal pay and equal opportunities

Discrimination

The Equal Opportunities Act (*Ligebehandlingsloven*) prohibits discrimination on the grounds of gender, pregnancy or matrimonial status. Employers must treat men and women equally in employment, promotion and transfer and must provide equal access to such opportunities as vocational training and retraining. The Act forbids questions about intentions of having children or about pregnancy during recruitment, as also any indication of gender preference in job advertisements. Although there is a government body – the *Ligestillingsrådet* (Equal Opportunities Council) – which oversees the Act, it has no power to take cases to court.

The Equal Pay Act (*Ligelønsloven*) requires employers who have taken on men and women at the same workplace to give them 'equal pay, including equal terms of pay for like work or work of equal value'. 'Pay' is interpreted to mean all forms of compensation granted by an employer. The Act allows individual employees to take legal action through the courts. However, claims based on non-fulfilment of a collective agreement should first be processed by the workplace co-operation machinery (see above). An employer who has entered into a collective agreement with a trade union has a duty to grant all employees working conditions in accordance with the agreement but non-unionised employees cannot bring complaints about a breach of its provisions. Any parts of an agreement which conflict with the Act are deemed invalid.

Sexual harassment

Although there are no specific statutes dealing with sexual harassment, a binding DA–LO agreement on equal opportunities obliges employers to ensure that the workplace is free of 'unwelcome advances of a sexual or gender-based nature'. Since the agreement is a supplement to the Co-operation Agreement, complaints can be dealt with through the workplace co-operation machinery. It should be noted that the only cases in which compensation has been prescribed for sexual harassment have been those which also involved unfair dismissal.

Retirement

Retirement age for both men and women is 67. The flat-rate state retirement pension (*folkepension*) is available to all. However, to obtain the full amount applicants must have been resident in Denmark for forty years. The rate for 1994 was DKr 63,804 a year (£6,457).

All employees working more than ten hours a week are also entitled to the statutory labour market supplementary pension (ATP). The amount of the pension is based not on earnings but on the number of contributions paid in. A person in the scheme from its inception in 1964 and retiring in 1994 would receive DKr 12,408 per year (£1,255).

In addition, many industries now have a collectively agreed labour market pension (*arbejdsmarkedspension*) scheme for blue-collar workers. As such schemes have been in existence only since 1991, payment levels are still unclear. White-collar workers often have their own collectively agreed schemes and have also traditionally been covered by company schemes. Contributions to private pension plans usually form part of senior managers' contract of employment, although any employee is free to take out a private pension and pay their own contributions. Early retirement is possible, at a reduced pension, under most schemes.

The basic state pension is financed through the tax system, whilst ATP and labour market pensions are financed by flat-rate employer and employee contributions. Company schemes usually involve an employee payment of up to a third of the total contribution.

Individual termination of contract

For white-collar employees, apprentices and vocational trainees, termination of contract is governed by law. For blue-collar employees, procedures are specified in the relevant collective agreement. Conditions may also be specified in individual contracts, as is the case with senior managers.

The right to terminate

Employers' right to dismiss salaried employees is restricted by some statutory provisions, but for blue-collar workers the restrictions stem mainly from the provisions of collective agreements.

Contracts for apprentices and vocational trainees are fixed-term. Earlier termination is possible either by mutual consent or by either party. In the latter case, the termination must be due to gross misconduct or because the contract was based on false or misleading information.

The right of employers to dismiss blue-collar workers is constrained mainly by the DA–LO General Agreement, which states that dismissal may not be founded on 'arbitrary considerations'.

According to the Salaried Employees Act, white-collar employees over 18 years of age with one year's unbroken service may be dismissed only because of circumstances 'reasonably based on the employee's or the company's circumstances'.

The right to dismiss senior managers is limited only by the provisions of their individual contracts of employment.

Grounds for termination

Contracts of employment come to an end upon one of the parties giving the agreed notice, except in the case of fixed-term contracts, which end automatically when the agreed duration expires or the assignment is complete.

In cases of dismissal the burden of proof in demonstrating that a termination is not arbitrary rests with the party who wishes to terminate the contract.

Employees may be dismissed on objective grounds, such as lack of work for them to do, for lack of ability to carry out their tasks, for excessive sick leave, or for misconduct, such as theft or violence. Where the offence is minor and correctable the lawfulness of dismissal may turn on whether appropriate and timely warnings have been given. If dismissal is on economic grounds the employer has a right to determine the selection of candidates for redundancy.

The legal and collectively agreed requirements upon employers to justify dismissal have been interpreted as implying that employers have a duty to try to relocate employees before having recourse to dismissal on economic grounds. However, this is not expressly specified in law or in any collective agreement.

Employees may give notice for any reason, but their right to revoke a contract of employment and claim compensation is dependent upon a serious breach of contract by the employer, such as failure to pay wages or major changes in conditions of employment without warning.

Any dismissal hinging upon an employee's membership (or non-membership) of a trade union or involvement in trade union activity is illegal. Such is equally the case when dismissal is prompted by the employee's religious or political affiliation, for women exercising their rights to maternity leave or equal pay, and for those carrying out military service.

Individual termination procedure

Notice to terminate should contain details of the period of notice and the finishing date, and of any leave due. The party wishing to terminate the contract must ensure that the other party is informed in time for the period of notice to run its course. Since subsequent disputes may require proof that notice was given in good time, notice of termination should therefore normally be in writing (although this is a legal requirement only for white-collar employees).

Generally no statutory or collectively agreed consultation proceedings are required before the individual contracts of employees are terminated. Nor is there any difference in procedure between dismissals due to employee conduct and those effected on economic grounds (except for collective dismissal, see below).

Most collective agreements contain rules governing the dismissal of union representatives. It is usually stated that such employees may be dismissed only for 'serious reasons' (*tvingende årsager*). If grounds can be established, it is necessary for employers to negotiate with the relevant trade union before terminating the contract. In addition, supervisors elected to serve as board members who are covered by the *Almindelige Bestemmelser* (General Regulations), an agreement between the DA and supervisors' organisations, cannot be dismissed before their organisation has been notified.

Periods of notice and severance compensation

Periods of notice and compensation vary considerably according to the type of employee and length of service.

For white-collar workers, minimum periods of notice are laid down in the Salaried Employees Act. The requirements are:

- One month's notice during the first five months' employment.
- Three months' notice up to two years and nine months' employment.
- Four months' notice up to five years and eight months' employment.
- Five months' notice up to eight years and seven months' employment.
- Six months' thereafter.

The months used to calculate length of service are calendar months. Employees are always reckoned to have started employment on the 1st of the month; for example, an employee who starts work on 15 January will require a notice period of one month until 31 May. Employees are required to give only one month's notice, regardless of length of service. The Act states that periods of notice should always end on the last day of the month.

If the employee is working a probationary period, the employer period of notice is fourteen days, with no period required for employees (unless the contract of employment states otherwise). Periods of notice for those on fixed-term contracts should be specified in the employment contract, although they may not be less favourable than those in the Act. Employees on short-term contracts of less than three months (*midlertidigt arbejde*) are not entitled to any period of notice, nor do they have to give one, unless otherwise agreed in the employment contract.

There are no general statutes or agreements in Denmark which require redundancy payments of the employer, other than ordinary pay for the notice period. However, the Salaried Employees Act does provide for white-collar employees with twelve, fifteen or eighteen years' service to receive one, two or three months' wages by way of severance payment. The payments are taxable, and are not compulsory if the employee is entitled to a pension from the employer or from the state. Employers are also legally bound to pay employees an allowance for the first two days of unemployment; in 1994 it was a maximum of DKr 454 (£46) per day.

Periods of notice for blue-collar workers are laid down in collective agreements and therefore vary between industries. They are also generally shorter than those for white-collar employees. The 1993 Industrial Agreement between the employers' organisation Dansk Industri and the employee confederation CO-Industri sets the following periods and service requirements for employers:

- After nine months' service, twenty-one days' notice.
- After two years' service, twenty-eight days' notice.
- After three years' service, fifty-six days' notice.
- Over six years' service, seventy days' notice.

Employees over 50 years of age are also entitled:

- After nine years' service, to ninety days' notice.
- Over twelve years' service, to 120 days' notice.

Employee periods of notice are:

- After nine months' service, seven days.
- After three years' service, fourteen days.
- After six years' service, twenty-one days.
- After nine years' service, twenty-eight days.

Special, collectively agreed rules usually apply to worker representatives such as shop stewards. These allow much longer periods of notice for such employees. For instance, the 1993 Industrial Agreement obliges employers to give worker representatives five months' notice rising to six months after five years in the post.

Senior managers' periods of notice are often relatively long, since they are seen as protecting both the manager and the company. Around 75 per cent of senior managers receive six months' to two years' salary in the event of dismissal.

Employers have the right to suspend an employee during the period of notice. Suspension may or may not be conditional upon the employee remaining at the employer's disposal. If no conditions are attached, employees may take up other employment whilst still receiving notice pay. In the case of conditional suspension, the right to notice pay is usually forfeited if the employee takes another job.

Summary dismissal without notice is also possible, although it will be accepted as valid only in the case of serious misconduct and if it occurs immediately after the offence. In more borderline cases a written warning detailing the nature of the misconduct and an explicit statement that repetition will lead to summary dismissal is usually acceptable.

Recourse to law, and compensation

An employee who wishes to contest dismissal will usually turn to a trade union in the first instance. The union will enter into company-level negotiations with a view to mediation. If no agreement can be reached (and the union agrees that the dismissal was unfair), the union may take the case to the civil courts on the employee's behalf or, if the employer is bound by the terms of the DA-LO General Agreement, to the Afskedigelsesnævnet (the Dismissals Arbitration Tribunal) set up under para. 4 of the agreement. Most cases which come before the tribunal are settled by mediation, although it has the power to order reinstatement or compensation. In practice, reinstatement is rare. Compensation payments may be up to the equivalent of fifty-two weeks' wages.

White-collar employees are afforded additional protection by the Salaried Employees Act, which prescribes compensation payments for unfair dismissal. They are based on age and length of service, and range up to the equivalent of six months' wages after fifteen years' employment.

Collective dismissal

Collective dismissal is regulated by the Labour Exchange Activity and Unemployment Benefits Act. The provisions apply where the following numbers of workers are to be made redundant in any period of thirty days:

- At least ten in undertakings which normally employ more than twenty and fewer than 100 workers.
- At least 10 per cent of the work force in undertakings which normally employ at least 100 but fewer than 300 workers.
- At least thirty in undertakings which normally employ 300 or more workers.

Employers wishing to effect redundancies on this scale must inform the work force in writing at least thirty days before notice is to be issued and arrange consultations with workers' representatives. If no means can be found of avoiding the redundancies, notification in writing must be given to the Labour Market Board (Arbejdsmarkednævnet). Dismissals may go ahead thirty days after such notice has been given.

From 1 January 1996 new rules come into force for companies employing over 100 workers that wish to dismiss over half their staff. Consultation with the staff will have to begin at least twenty-one days before any dismissals are notified to the Labour Market Board. Dismissals may then be effected no earlier than eight weeks after such notification has been given.

No special periods of notice or payments are associated with collective dismissal.

Final formalities

White-collar employees have the legal right to a certificate of service (*tjeneste-attest*) detailing length of service, the nature of their work, the remuneration received and the reason why they have been given notice. Under the General Agreement blue-collar employees with nine months' service are entitled to receive written details of the reason for dismissal.

Appendix

Non-wage labour costs and income tax rates

Non-wage labour costs for employers are amongst the lowest in Europe, reflecting a major switch to the financing of the social security system out of general taxation, and in particular indirect taxation, in the 1980s. On average employers pay 4.5 per cent of gross salary for blue-collar workers and 2.5 per cent for white-collar workers to cover supplementary pensions, training and industrial injuries.

Income is subject to both national and local taxes, as well as employee pension contributions. There is a 1 per cent wealth tax on net assets exceeding DKr 1,534,500 (£155,310). Taxable income is arrived at after deducting from gross income social security contributions, a personal allowance and permitted employment expenses, such as travelling, literature and tools of the trade. There is a standard personal allowance equal to 3 per cent of income, subject to an upper limit of DKr 3,900 (£395).

Local taxes are levied on taxable at a flat rate which ranges from 23 to 32 per cent and averages c. 28 per cent. National tax rates are as follows: all taxable income is taxed at 22 per cent; earned and unearned income above Dkr 168,000 (£17,000) is taxed at 6 per cent; income above Dkr 240,000 (£24,300) is taxed at 12 per cent, subject to an overall top marginal tax rate of 68 per cent.

Organisations

Landsorganisationen i Danmark (LO)
(Danish Confederation of Trade Unions)
Rosenørns Allé 12
DK-1634 Copenhagen V
tel. + 45 31 35 35 41
fax + 45 35 37 37 41

Dansk Arbejdsgiverforening (DA)
(Danish Employers' Federation)
Vester Voldgade 113
DK-1790 Copenhagen V
tel. + 45 33 93 40 00
fax + 45 33 12 29 76

CO-Industri
(Industrial unions' bargaining cartel)
Vester Søgade 12,2.
DK-1790 Copenhagen V
tel. + 45 33 15 12 66
fax + 45 33 15 12 66

Dansk Industri
(Industrial employers' federation)
DK-1553 Copenhagen
HC Andersens Boulevard 18
tel. + 45 33 77 33 77
fax + 45 33 77 37 00

Arbejdsministeriet
(Ministry of Labour)
Laksegade 19
DK-1063 Copenhagen K
tel. + 45 33 92 59 00
fax + 45 33 12 13 78

IP
(Danish Institute of Personnel
Management)
Hauser Plads 20
1127 Copenhagen
tel. + 45 33 13 15 70
fax + 45 33 32 51 56

Main sources

Arbejdernes Oplysningsforbund, *Arbejdsmarkedets Håndbog 1994*, Arbejdernes Oplysingsforbund, Copenhagen, 1994.

Dansk Arbejdsgiverforening, *Personalejurahåndbogen*, DA, Copenhagen 1993.

Dansk Arbejdsgiverforening, *Direktøren, ansættelses- og arbejdsvilkår*, DA, Copenhagen, 1990.

Nielsen, Ruth, *Lærebog i arbejdsret*, Jurist- og Økonomforbundets Forlag, Copenhagen, 1990.

DA/LO, *Hovedaftalen* (General Agreement), Copenhagen, 1993.

DA/LO, *Fællesordning for arbejde i holddrift* (Shiftwork Agreement), Copenhagen, 1993.

DA/LO, *Mægling i arbejdsstridigheder* (Disputes Resolution Agreement), Copenhagen, 1991.

Dansk Industri/CO-Industri, *Industriens overenskomst*, (Industrial Agreement), Copenhagen, 1993.

Land- og Skovbrugets Arbejdsgivere/SiD, *Overenskomst for jordbrug* (Agricultural Agreement), Copen- hagen, 1993.

DA/BKA/HK, *Landsoverenskomst* (National White-Collar Agreement), Copen-hagen, 1993.

4

France

Basic rights and labour jurisdiction

Sources of law on employment

Laws regulating employment are extensive and codified into one body of text, the Labour Code (*code du travail*). Legislation governing works councils in individual companies was introduced in 1945, and laws recognising the presence of trade unions at company level were passed in 1968. A further large body of laws, the Auroux laws, was passed in 1981/82, reducing working hours, improving employee rights and strengthening employee representation and collective bargaining, especially at company level.

Hierarchy of legal provisions

The French constitution guarantees certain basic rights which form the basis of individual employment rights, such as the right to work, and to equality of treatment at the workplace, and the freedom to work in the occupation of one's choice.

Specific aspects of the individual employment relationship are regulated in detail by the Labour Code. This extensive legislation covers virtually all aspects of the employment relationship, providing a floor for terms and conditions of employment.

Improvements upon statutory provisions are negotiated at industry level, in the form of collective agreements between employer and trade union representatives in individual industries. By law the parties to the agreement must review the agreement every five years, although there is no obligation to change or amend it. As well as setting out rates of pay and job classification systems for the industry, the agreements cover terms and conditions, such as hours of work, holidays, periods of notice, bonus payments and severance terms. The agreement is binding on all signatory parties. A collective agreement may be extended to non-signatory parties across a sector of industry by the Ministry of Labour, in which case all companies in that sector are bound by its terms.

Companies may negotiate house agreements with the trade union branch at the workplace. Company-level bargaining is, however, traditionally relatively undeveloped. The Auroux laws, passed in 1982, set out to remedy this by requiring companies to negotiate annually on pay, hours of work and work organisation in companies where there is at least one union branch present. However, there is no obligation to reach agreement. (Another volume in this series, *Employee Relations and Collective Bargaining*, deals in greater deal with these aspects.)

Individual contracts of employment may provide for enhanced terms and conditions, particularly in the case of more senior staff. A contract of employment may regulate areas which are not governed by law or by collective or company agreement, such as probationary periods or non-competition clauses.

The system of labour jurisdiction

Conflicts between employers and individual employees which cannot be resolved by discussion or procedures at company level may be taken to an industrial tribunal (*conseil de prud'hommes*). Industrial tribunals are attached to the high court (*tribunal de grande instance*) in each administrative region, or *département*. Each departmental high court will have at least one industrial tribunal; if there is more than one, each tribunal will specialise in a particular field of labour jurisdiction. Industrial tribunals are made up of an equal number of employer and employee representatives. They are divided into five sections: managerial, industry, commercial services, agriculture and miscellaneous. Employer and employee representatives sit on the section most relevant to their own individual area of experience and competence. The sections can be further divided into chambers handling different topics. Each tribunal has a president and vice-president, elected by secret ballot. The posts are occupied alternately by the employer and employee representatives and the mandate is one year. If the president represents the employers' side, the vice-president must be an employee, and vice-versa.

The mandate for counsellors is five years. Counsellors must hold French nationality, be aged 21 or over, be on the electoral register and have experience relevant to the section for which they are standing for election. Lists of employee candidates are drawn up, and companies must give employees paid time off to look at them, either at the town hall or near the place of work. Voting by post is possible, but not on a collective basis. Election is by proportional representation.

Industrial tribunals consist of a conciliation service (*bureau de conciliation*), made up of one employer and one employee counsellor and an arbitration service (*bureau de jugement*), made up of at least two counsellors from each side. The procedure consists of two phases – conciliation and arbitration. The first phase is conciliation, during which both parties are heard in private. Parties should normally appear in person, but in some cases may be represented. They may also be assisted by a colleague, a union representative or a lawyer. Minutes of this meeting are drawn up and a non-binding recommendation is made. If conciliation fails, the case goes to arbitration. Arbitration hearings are public. Both parties are notified by letter and the parties may bring representatives and/or colleagues, as in conciliation. The arbitration service then gives a ruling, which must be unanimous. The decision is notified to the parties in writing. An appeal against the ruling must be lodged within one month with a special division of the appeal court (*cour d'appel*), which is part of the normal system of civil law.

Contracts of employment

Types of employee

Employees are grouped into four main categories:

- Blue-collar workers (*ouvriers*).
- White-collar or clerical workers (*employés*).
- Supervisory staff, technicians and draughtsmen (*techniciens, agents de maîtrise*).
- Managerial staff and engineers (*cadre-ingénieur*).

Each of these categories is divided into job titles which are assigned a position within job classification scales determined by industry agreement, covering a range of occupations from basic blue-collar to upper middle management. Jobs are awarded a number of points, depending on skill and function. The more skilled the job the higher the number of points. The total number of points awarded to each job is called the coefficient (*coefficient hiérarchique*) and is used to calculate basic pay. Managerial staff are generally not covered by the pay-setting arrangements of collective agreements, as most classification scales stop short of managerial positions. Managers also have their own compulsory state supplementary pension scheme (see below). Directors (*dirigeants de sociétés*) and managing directors are not regarded in law as employees of the company, and their terms and conditions are set out in their individual contract. However, the contract must comply with basic statutory terms and conditions.

Form of contract

Employees hired on or after 1 September 1993 are entitled by law to receive a document stating the terms and conditions of their employment within two months of hiring. Employees taken on before that date can request written particulars which the employer must then provide within two months of the request. The document must set out the employee's main terms and conditions in French. Employees whose mother tongue is not French are entitled to a translation. However, under a new Bill under discussion, contracts signed abroad would not be subject to these regulations even if they were executed solely in France.

The document must contain:

- The names of the parties involved.
- The place of employment.
- The job title, grade and job category of the employee.
- The starting date, the length of the contract and expiry date, if applicable.
- Amount of paid holidays.
- Period of notice.
- Rate of pay and method of payment.

- Normal daily or weekly hours of work.
- The name of the relevant industry collective agreement, if any.

These regulations (Labour Code L260-3) bring French law into line with EU Directive 91/533/EEC on proof of an employment contract.

By law, certain basic conditions must be met if a contract of employment is to be valid: the agreement must be freely entered into by the parties; the contract must not be contrary to the law or public morality. Failure to meet one or more of these basic conditions will invalidate it. A clause that is faulty or based on a misunderstanding will not necessarily render the whole contract void. The courts will decide whether the clause forms a fundamental element of the contract; if it is deemed to, the contract will be invalid. Strict regulations govern the employment of minors under the age of 16.

Work-force consultation

Employers are not required by law to consult staff representatives on individual hirings. However, the law does stipulate that they must meet staff representatives once a year to discuss labour turnover and policies for the coming year. If the staff representatives so request, the employer must meet them twice a year (three times a year in companies with over 300 employees) to give a month-by-month breakdown of the employment situation in the company, including all new hirings.

Typical contents of a contract

Express and implied terms Employees have individual rights which are implicit in the signing of a contract. These rights are guaranteed partly by statute and partly by collective agreement. They include:

- The right to receive the contractually agreed salary.
- The right to be treated decently and in the same way as their colleagues.
- The right to maintenance of the conditions set out in the contract of employment. If these are changed substantially – for example, if the place of work is moved so that the employee has a much longer journey or if the nature of the work changes substantially – the employee may bring a claim of unfair dismissal.

Employees also have collective rights, such as:

- The right of free association.
- Freedom of direct and collective expression.
- The right to hold negotiations annually.
- The right to be represented, e.g. by works committees or health and safety committees.

Employees are subject to a duty of fidelity to their employer; they must not reveal confidential information or liaise with competitors. Employees are also bound to 'carry out, diligently and conscientiously' the tasks allotted to them and to take care of their tools and equipment.

Employers must respect these rights and duties, and are under an obligation to pay agreed wages and social security contributions, provide the agreed work and the means of doing it, respect health and safety rules, and issue a certificate of employment to the employee once the contract has terminated.

Variation of terms   If the employer wishes to introduce a reasonable modification of the contract of employment, the employee must be given notice in writing, in the form of an appendix to the existing contract of employment, at least a month beforehand. Case law determines what would and what would not be a reasonable modification of the contract of employment. For example, moving the place of work to somewhere that would mean considerable travel for the employee, a cut in pay or loss of benefits would not be deemed reasonable. In such a case, an employee who refuses to accept the changes may opt to resign. If the changes are found by the courts to be substantial, the resignation is deemed to be dismissal and the employee is entitled to statutory and agreed severance payments (see below).

Types of contract

Fixed-term contracts   Fixed term contracts (*contrats à durée déterminée*) must be written and, by law, may apply to the carrying out of a specific task. They may not be used in order to cover work related to the 'normal and permanent activity of the company'. A fixed-term contract may not be used to replace an employee whose employment contract has been suspended as a result of industrial conflict. Fixed-term contracts have no minimum duration and can be renewed twice for a period not exceeding the initial period. However, the overall term of the contract may not exceed twenty-four months.

Temporary contracts   Temporary working involves a triangular relationship between the temporary employment agency, the employee, who is an employee of the agency, and the client company. Temporary contracts (*travail temporaire*) are strictly regulated. The law limits their use to three broad situations:

- Replacing employees who are absent or providing cover between the departure of an employee and the end of the job.
- Meeting a temporary increase in work load, possibly resulting from a large order or the need to carry out urgent work for health and safety reasons.
- Carrying out tasks of a temporary nature, such as seasonal work.

Temporary workers must be included on the company's personnel register, which must be made available to staff representatives, unions and employment inspectors upon request. Temps are also entitled by law to a wide range of employment rights and conditions, as enjoyed by permanent employees. Employers who have dismissed employees for economic reasons may not cite 'temporary increase in work load' as a reason for using temporary or fixed-term contracts during the six months following the dismissal. Employees on fixed-term and temporary contracts may not be used to carry out dangerous work as listed by the Ministry of Labour.

Part-time contracts   Part-time working is defined by law as hours of work equal to four-fifths or less of the statutory or agreed working week. Works committees or staff representatives must be consulted by the employer before part-time employees are recruited. Part-time contracts must be in writing and must state the agreed working hours. Any changes in hours of work must be communicated to the employee at least seven days before they are due to take effect, although under the 1993 Five-Year Employment Plan the interval may be reduced to three days by company agreement. Part-time workers take priority in consideration for full-time jobs if they express a wish to go on to full-time working. An employee who works part-time has the same rights as a full-time employee, on a *pro rata* basis. In a drive to encourage job creation, as from 1 September 1993 employers who turn full-time contracts into part-time contracts, with a corresponding reduction in pay, and who as a result take on more employees to maintain the hours worked, benefit from reductions in employer social security contributions equal to 30 per cent of payments for sickness, old age, industrial accident and family allowance insurance.

The 1993 Employment Plan has replaced the intermittent contract (*contrat de travail intermittant*) with the concept of annualised part-time working. The definition of annualised part-time contracts is the same as for intermittent contracts: 'a contract concluded in order to carry out permanent work characterised by alternating periods of working and non-working'. However, annual hours worked must be at least one-fifth less than normal statutory or agreed full-time hours. This type of contract is organised directly by the employer, as there is no need for a company or industry agreement. The contract must state either which periods are worked and which not, or periods during which the employee is on call to work. Notice of variation is seven days but can be reduced to three days by company agreement. Call-in notice is seven days. Supplementary hours can be worked up to one-tenth of the contract, by law, or up to one-third of the contract under plant, company or industry agreement. Pay may either be awarded for hours worked or annualised over the year, thus amounting to a monthly salary.

Probationary periods

There is no statutory duty to incorporate a probationary period into a contract of employment, with the exception of contracts for sales representatives ('VRPs') and trainees. However, such a period can be freely agreed between the parties as long as there is no collective agreement expressly forbidding it. During the probationary period either party can terminate the contract without notice, justification or severance compensation, unless otherwise stipulated. The formalities applying to normal dismissal do not have to be observed. However, employees retain the right to seek damages if the termination is patently abusive.

As well as in individual contracts, probationary periods may be stipulated in collective agreements or, in certain occupations, by custom and practice. The length of a probationary period depends principally on agreement between the parties, unless it is prescribed by law or collective agreement. The parties may agree on a shorter, but not on a longer, probationary period than is stipulated in a collective agreement. However, this proviso may be relaxed for senior employees. A probationary period may be renewed provided the employee agrees. However, a renewed probationary period may still not exceed the total probationary period set out in any applicable collective agreement. Thus if the total probationary period allowed is three months, an individual probationary period of one month could be renewed three times. In the chemical industry, for example, agreed probationary periods are as follows: blue-collar employees, fifteen calendar days, up to two months, depending on grade; white-collar/technical employees, up to three months; managers, up to three months.

Restrictive covenants and confidentiality

Restrictive covenants, preventing employees from engaging in competition that might affect the business of their previous employer after the end of the employment, may be included in the individual contract of employment or as part of a collective agreement. However, restrictive covenants may not restrict individuals' freedom to work in their field and must therefore be limited not only in terms of the aspects covered but in duration and geographical scope. (In the event of a dispute, there is a body of case law which sets out what is deemed reasonable.) It must also represent an indispensable and legitimate means of protecting the interests of the employer. A covenant may provide for a payment to the former employee and/or a clause stipulating that the ex-employee must pay a sum to the former employee if the clause is infringed. There is no statutory time limit, and the duration depends on individual agreement. Restrictive covenants may be provided for in sectoral collective agreements. For example, under the national agreement for engineers in the iron and steel industry, restrictive covenants must be set out in writing in the contract of employment, cannot exceed one year and may be renewed only once. As compensation, the employee is paid a monthly sum of 50 per cent of previous monthly earnings, including usual bonuses, for up to a year.

Employee inventions

Statute law draws a distinction between two types of invention. Those which are the work of the employee during the normal course of employment are deemed to be the property of the employer. However, the employee must receive a bonus payment for the invention which, in the absence of an agreement between the parties, is fixed by a conciliation committee or the high court. Some collective agreements provide for the employee's name to be mentioned on the patent application and may provide for lump sums to be paid to the employee if the invention is put to commercial use. Inventions arrived at independently by the employee belong to the employee. However, if the discovery is linked with the employee's work, the employer may have a case for claiming ownership of the invention and all or part of the rights. Disputes can be referred to a conciliation committee. Employers have four months in which to assert title to an invention.

Workplace discipline

The employer may take disciplinary action against an employee on the grounds of the employee's conduct. The law forbids certain disciplinary sanctions, such as withholding normal pay (but not bonuses), fines, and demotion if it is merely a means of cutting pay. Employees may be penalised only on genuine grounds of misconduct and on no other, such as race, sex, trade union membership or industrial action.

Individual workplace rights

Data protection   The type and amount of information which may be stored about an employee is limited by the Civil Code. Information about the employee's private life may be collected and held only if it is considered relevant to the employer's business. The law regulates the collection, storage and distribution of personal information held on computer. Companies wishing to compile a database must inform the National Commission on Rights and Computerised Information. Only next of kin and legal representatives are allowed access to French citizens' personal identity numbers. Employees must be granted access to data stored about them at any time and have the right to insist on inexact data being corrected and unlawfully held data removed.

Right to be informed   The law stipulates that companies with eleven or more employees must have an employee representative and that companies with fifty or more employees must have a works committee. These workplace representatives must be informed by the employer on a number of matters, notably:

- The economic and financial situation of the company.
- The composition of the work force.
- Pay arrangements.
- Hours of work.
- Working conditions.

Smoking   On 1 January 1993 an amendment of the Evin law, No. 91–32, on public health with regard to tobacco and alcohol was passed, limiting smoking at the workplace. It defines two categories of area: indoor communal areas such as reception areas, canteens, meeting and rest rooms, leisure and medical facilities; and group work areas, where two or more employees work. The legislation does not apply to individual work areas. In indoor communal areas, smoking is permitted only in designated places. Every two years employers must consult the health and safety committee or staff representatives on the establishment of these areas, which must be clearly marked and have to comply with minimum statutory ventilation requirements. In group work areas the employer must balance the needs of smokers and of non-smokers without prejudice to the latter. Employers should draw up a plan of smoking arrangements in consultation with staff representatives, identifying which work areas (if any) are to be designated for smokers. Areas must be adequately ventilated, with extractor fans and partitions to separate smokers and non-smokers. Employers are not obliged to grant special smoking breaks.

Employment terms and conditions

Hours of work

Definition of working hours   The statutory working week is defined as hours actually worked, excluding changing or washing-up time, meal or coffee breaks, although some collective agreements may provide for such time to be included in working hours. The law also recognises that certain occupations involve a portion of idle time during the working day (as in the retail trade, catering, hairdressing and hospitals). Where this is the case the law allows a longer period at the workplace to be deemed equivalent to the normal statutory working week of thirty-nine hours.

Statutory and agreed provisions   Since 1982 the statutory normal working week has been set at thirty-nine hours. The maximum average working week is forty-six hours calculated over twelve consecutive weeks, subject to an absolute maximum of forty-eight hours in any one week. In exceptional circumstances these limits can be extended, but not beyond sixty hours a week. A number of derogations permit either longer hours or flexible hours to be worked (see below).

The statutory maximum working day is ten hours, or eight hours for young people and apprentices under 18. During temporary increases in work load, the limit may be increased to twelve hours, subject to the consent of the employee and union representatives, and above twelve hours with the permission of the labour inspectorate. A collective agreement is required if the working day is likely always to exceed ten hours.

Derogations from the statutory working week   The working week can be extended by law, permanently beyond the statutory normal week. However, the extra hours are regarded and remunerated as overtime. Such derogation covers permanent situations where work has to be carried out before or after normal operations, or the case of temporary urgent maintenance.

Daily and weekly rest   There is no statutory provision governing daily rest periods, although by law young workers must not work for more than four and a half uninterrupted hours. Breaks during the daytime are usually covered by collective or company agreement. Lunch breaks are customarily no shorter than forty-five minutes.

By law, each week employees must be allowed a minimum of twenty-four consecutive hours' rest, which should normally fall on a Sunday (see below).

Flexible working hours   The 1987 law on flexible working hours made it possible to offset weekly hours worked in excess of the statutory working week of thirty-nine hours against weeks when fewer than thirty-nine hours are worked within a one-year reference period. Flexibility options must be implemented under an industry or company collective agreement. Any such agreement must not have been opposed by a trade union which won more than 50 per cent of the votes of those registered to elect workplace representatives. Up to a maximum of forty-eight hours a week can be worked without the overtime hours being counted towards the annual overtime quotas for each industry (see below), but employees must be compensated for overtime worked, either by time off in lieu or by overtime payments. Alternatively, up to a maximum of forty-four hours a week may be worked *without* employees receiving compensation for overtime.

A number of major collective agreements have reduced the working week beyond the thirty-nine-hour legal requirements. In the chemical industry, for example, the working week is thirty-eight hours for non-shift workers, thirty-seven hours forty-five minutes for semi-continuous shift workers and thirty-seven hours and thirty minutes for continuous shift workers.

Under the 1993 Five Year Employment Plan (Labour Code L212-2-1), companies may annualise working hours by negotiation if the result is a reduction in hours worked, within existing statutory limits (see above), averaging at an agreed reference figure. Agreements should detail provisions on hours of work and the length of notice employees will be given in the event of changes. If companies reduce working hours by at least 15 per cent, with corresponding reductions in pay, and take on extra staff equivalent to at least 10 per cent of the work force, keeping them on for at least three years, they are entitled to a 40 per cent reduction in social security contributions in the first year and a 30 per cent reduction in the second and third years. Agreements had to be concluded before 31 December 1994. One example is Kodak, at whose Chalon plant employees on semi-continuous shifts work a flexible week of thirty-two to forty hours, with an average of thirty-seven hours.

Flexitime Flexitime (*horaires individualisés*) is permitted by law, provided the work force are in favour of it, the works committee is in agreement, and the labour inspectorate has been informed. Details of how the system functions must be posted up at the workplace. The maximum variation above and below the agreed weekly limit must not be more than three hours. Collective agreements sometimes allow wider margins.

Overtime and weekend work

Overtime working is regulated both by statute law and by industry collective agreement. Employers must consult the works council before instituting overtime arrangements. By law, overtime is worked from the fortieth hour, inclusive, up to an absolute maximum of nine hours in any one week or seven hours a week over a consecutive twelve-week period. However, provision is made for an employer to agree a number of hours of annual overtime per individual employee without requiring the permission of the labour inspectorate. The precise number of hours is decided at industry or sector level through negotiation. In the absence of any agreement there is a nationally agreed annual maximum quota of 130 hours. Annual overtime allocations agreed at industry level vary, from seventy hours in the insurance industry to 130 in chemicals.

Weekend working is allowed after consultation with the works council and trade union representatives at plant level – where they exist – with permission from the labour inspectorate. By law, employers must grant employees one rest day a week (twenty-four consecutive hours' minimum), which should fall on a Sunday. However, there are pemitted exemptions to the rule. They include permanent exemptions which do not require specific authorisation, and where a shut-down would either be technically impossible or against the public interest, as in the case of hotels and restaurants, retail tobacco outlets or hospitals; and exemptions authorised by the departmental prefect after consultation with the local authority, the chamber of commerce and employer and employee organisations. This exemption may be extended to similar businesses in the same area. The 1993 Five Year Employment Plan relaxed restrictions on Sunday working slightly, adding establishments in tourist areas to the list of exemptions. Retail outlets may also open five Sundays a year, with the approval of the local authorities. Manufacturing operations may also agree Sunday working under some circumstances.

Night work

Night work is defined as work done between 22.00 and 05.00. It is generally permitted except for two types of employee: women, and anyone under 18. The ban on night work for bakery workers was lifted by the 1993 Employment Plan. Night working must be compensated for by pay supplements relating to the overtime hours worked. Many collective agreements provide for supplements ranging from 10 per cent to 100 per cent of normal pay.

Recent legislation has somewhat eased the ban on women's night work. By law, hours worked between 22.00 and 05.00 are considered night work. However, after appropriate consultations, and with the permission of the labour inspectorate this consecutive seven-hour period may be put forward or back, allowing women to work during other parts of the prohibited period. The ban is lifted completely for women in commercial establishments and services, such as cleaners. Following two cases referred to the European Court of Justice, dealing with instances in which employers were prosecuted by the French authorities for instituting night work for women, the whole issue of the statutory ban is under review. In both cases the European Court ruled that the ban on night work contravened article 5 of the 1976 EU directive on equal treatment, but referred the matter back to the French courts, recommending that national judges should disallow any national provision which was incompatible with the principles of equal treatment. Discussion of the ban continues. However, there are a number of derogations, such as the provision under the 1987 Flexible Working Law, which permits night work for women when 'because of particularly serious circumstances, it is in the national interest'.

Annual leave and public holidays

All employees are entitled by law to two and a half days' paid holiday per month worked, or thirty working days per year, on the basis of a six-day working week. This amounts to five weeks' actual leave. Employees who take at least one week of holiday outside the summer period (1 May to 31 October) are entitled to two days' extra holiday, and those who take three, four or five days outside this period, to one day extra. Young working mothers under 22 years are entitled to two extra days' holiday a year for each dependent child. Many companies award extra days as holiday if they fall between a public holiday and a weekend, a practice known as bridging holidays (*les ponts*). There are eleven public holidays in France: New Year's Day, Easter Monday, Labour Day (1 May), Victory Day (8 May), Ascension, Whit Monday, Bastille Day (14 July), Assumption (15 August), All Saints' Day (1 November), Armistice Day (11 November) and Christmas Day (25 December). By law, monthly paid employees must receive normal earnings for public holidays, provided they have three months' service with the company and have worked for at least 200 hours during the two months preceding the holiday. Employees who work on 1 May must be paid double time.

Maternity and paternity leave

By law, a pregnant woman is entitled to suspend her contract of employment if she has paid at least ten months' insurance contributions before she goes on leave, for a period normally beginning six weeks before the expected date of confinement and ending ten weeks after the actual date of the birth. If she decides to take less than the full six weeks' leave before the birth, she may add the amount to her postnatal leave entitlement and thereby maintain the total entitlement of sixteen weeks. If the woman's medical condition requires it, and she presents a medical certificate, the entitlement may be extended for up to eight weeks before and up to fourteen weeks after the birth. Maternity leave may be extended to a maximum of ten weeks ante-natal and twenty-two weeks postnatal, depending on the number of children a woman already has and whether it is a multiple birth. Pregnant women also have a statutory entitlement to a temporary change of job during pregnancy with, in most cases, maintenance of previous earnings. Employees returning from maternity leave have the right to re-engagement but not to reinstatement.

Many collective agreements also allow more flexible hours of work for pregnant women, with a reduction of five or more minutes an hour in working time. At Renault, for example, one hour a day's paid leave is allowed from the time a woman presents a medical certificate confirming pregnancy. These hours may be saved up, allowing her to take several hours together, or a whole day, off.

A woman also has a right to ten weeks' adoption leave, the leave to start from the day the child joins the household. Women on maternity leave enjoy protection against dismissal for reasons connected with pregnancy and maternity leave, until four weeks after the end of the leave. Many collective agreements give the right to three days' paternity leave.

Family reasons

Virtually all employees, irrespective of length of service, are entitled by law to paid time off as follows:

- Four days for the employee's own marriage.
- Three days for the birth of a child.
- One day for the marriage of a child.
- Two days for the death of a spouse or child.
- One day for the death of a parent or sibling.

Employees with three months' service have the right to three days for the pre-selection interview for military service and one day for the death of a father-in-law, mother-in-law or sibling. The law specifies that pay must not be deducted for such days off and that they are to be considered as time worked in the calculation of annual holiday entitlement.

Collective agreements may improve on the law. The banking agreement, for example, extends time-off rights for family reasons to ten days off for marriage, two days off for the marriage of a child, five days off for the death of a spouse, and three days off for the death of a parent or a child.

Training leave

Employees must normally have two years' service before they can apply for time off for training (*congé individuel de formation*) – the main exception being young people under 26, who are entitled to 200 hours' job-related training a year after three months' service. Moreover a period of time must have elapsed since applicants obtained their last professional qualification with the company. In companies with 200 or more employees, the employer may postpone an employee's departure on training leave only if 2 per cent of the work force are already absent for the same reason. In companies with fewer than 200 employees, postponement is permissible only if the total number of hours requested for training exceeds 2 per cent of the total number of annual hours worked. Training leave must not exceed a whole year or 1,200 hours in total. The employee receives 80 per cent of previous pay and employers may recoup the cost from a joint fund.

Employee representatives

The law contains detailed provisions on the rights of employee representatives to paid time off to carry out duties related to their function, and for training. Staff representatives (*délégué du personnel*), whose election is mandatory in companies with eleven or more employees, are entitled to fifteen hours a month to carry out their duties. Members of the works council (*comité d'entreprise*), mandatory in companies with fifty or more employees, are entitled to twenty hours a month, rising to forty in some circumstances, and five days for training on appointment. Union delegates (*délégué syndical*) and members of the health and safety committee (*comité d'hygiène, de securité et des conditions de travail*) are entitled to up to twenty hours per month, depending on the size of the company, and up to a further fifteen hours if they are union delegates with negotiating responsibilities.

Sabbatical leave

By law, employees are entitled to suspend their contract of employment for six to eleven months without pay (sabbatical leave), or for one year (which may be extended to two) in order to set up in business. The employee must have over thirty-six months' length of service with the company and a total of six years in employment. Employers may refuse the request if, in companies with under 200 employees, it is agreed by the works council that the absence of the employee would be detrimental to the company. The employee has the right to appeal against such refusal in the local labour court up to fifteen days after being notified of the decision. Employers may also delay sabbatical leave for up to six months in companies with more than 200 employees if more than 2 per cent of the work force are already on leave, or in companies with fewer than 200 employees if more than 1.5 per cent of the work force are on leave.

At the end of sabbatical leave the employee is guaranteed reinstatement in the previous, or a similar, position with no loss of salary.

Military service

The job of an employee is protected when he is called away for reasons connected with military service. An employer must re-employ him in the month following the employee's stated intention of resuming his former job following release from national service. If the job has been abolished in the meantime – for example, in the event of company reorganisation – the employee has priority when applying for vacancies in the company for jobs of a similar type and grade. An employee denied these rights may claim unfair dismissal. The law also specifically protects the rights of an employee during the run-up to military service (for example, whilst attending a selection centre). An employer may not take advantage of such absence to dismiss an employee. A national agreement between employers and unions allows employees three days off for interviews and tests prior to military service.

Promotion and transfer

The law specifies that companies bound by a collective industry agreement should negotiate on measures ensuring equality for men and women on a number of issues, including promotion. Some collective agreements outline procedures to be followed in the event of promotion, as in banking, where lists of candidates are drawn up each year. Employees with five years' service in the same job who have not been put on to a promotion list may lodge a complaint with an internal regulatory body.

The transfer of an employee from one company to another involves the termination of the previous contract and the conclusion of a new one. Employers may lend employees to another company, as long as the situation is temporary and justified, in which case the original contract remains unbroken.

Pay and benefits

Statutory minimum pay

There is a statutory national minimum wage known as Smic (*salaire minimum interprofessionnel de croissance*). It sets the rate below which it is illegal to pay a worker in metropolitan France. It covers all employees except young people under 18 with less than six months' work experience and workers with disabilities, who are subject to other laws. Some 8.5 per cent of the work force are paid at the level of the minimum wage. Smic may be increased in any one of the following ways:

- Annually on 1 July on the advice of the National Collective Bargaining Board.
- By decree of the Council of Ministers (the Cabinet).

• Whenever the national official price index rises 2 per cent or more from the previous reference point Smic will automatically be increased by that amount.

Over the past few years the government has been increasing Smic by more than the minimum required by law, in order to bring it more into line with blue-collar hourly earnings. However, there has been some debate over whether Smic may be contributing to unemployment by pushing labour costs up, especially in low-productivity sectors. In response the government increased Smic only by the statutory minimum amount in 1993 and 1994. Formal pay indexation is expressly forbidden by law.

As of 1 July 1994 Smic stood at FFr 35.56 (£4.11) hourly or FFr 6,009.54 (£695) monthly, based on 169 hours a month.

The law on pay

If the employee wishes, any pay amounting to less than FFr 10,000 (£1,156) monthly must be paid in cash. Salary above this limit may be paid by crossed cheque or bank transfer. An itemised pay slip must also be issued at the time of payment, which in addition to basic employee and pay details must also cite any relevant collective agreement. The pay slip may not contain details of time spent in employee representation meetings or of time spent in industrial action.

Permitted deductions

Employees must pay a variety of social security contributions out of gross earnings. Some of these contributions are payable on earnings up to a regularly adjusted ceiling and others are payable on all earnings. Contribution categories include the CSG (*contribution sociale généralisée*) at a flat rate of 2.4 per cent, social security contributions, supplementary pension insurance, unemployment insurance, training levies, salary tax and transport tax. Employees pay approximately 17–19 per cent of gross earnings in social security contributions and income levies. Fines may not be deducted from pay.

Levels of pay determination

Collective bargaining, at both industry and company level, remained fairly weak until the mid-1970s. An amendment to the 1950 Collective Bargaining Act passed in 1971 (in the wake of the 1968 period of employee militancy) initiated a change. In 1981, legislation (the 'Auroux laws', named after the then Labour Minister) was passed by the incoming Socialist administration. It was intended to foster collective bargaining at industry and company level by introducing an obligation to negotiate (although not necessarily to reach agreement) every five years at industry level and every year at company level. This has provided a spur to bargaining, and in particular has reinforced tendencies towards decentralisation by encouraging company-level negotiations. Trade union density is low, at around 10 per cent of the workforce and less in private industry and services. However, the industry-level bargaining which sets minimum terms and conditions, the results of which may be extended to non-signatory employers, ensures that collective bargaining is more influential in establishing basic terms than a glance at union membership rates might suggest.

Industry level Collective agreements, negotiated at industry level by employers' organisations and unions, set minimum rates of pay for a particular industry. These agreements include job grading scales, in which each job grade or classification is allotted a certain number of points. For example, an unskilled blue-collar worker in the engineering industry is allotted 130 points. Each point has a monetary value, which is renegotiated each year by the signatory parties. The minimum rate for a particular job is then calculated by multiplying the number of points, in this case 130, by the monetary value of the point: if the value of the point was 35, 130 × 35 would give a basic monthly rate of FFr 4,550 (£526). The number of points awarded to each job varies from industry to industry, as does the monetary value of the point. If a calculated minimum rate falls below the statutory minimum wage (Smic), as is often the case at the bottom end of pay scales, the appropriate Smic rate must be paid instead. Many industries have reviewed their collective agreements in recent years to ensure that salaries at the lower end of pay scales are above the level of Smic.

Company level The pay rates set by industry agreement are very much a baseline for the rates which are actually paid by companies. The relevance of the industry agreements on company pay practices varies according to the sector, the job category of the employee and the size of the company. Large companies typically pay well above the industry minima – on average 25 per cent to 30 per cent – and therefore the industry rates bear little relation to the going rate. As long as employers pay above the industry minimum rate they are free to implement their own systems and increases, bargaining with workplace union branches if they exist.

By law, white-collar employees must be paid at least once a month and blue-collar employees at least once a fortnight unless they are covered by a sectoral or company agreement to pay employees monthly (a 'mensualisation' agreement). Travelling sales representatives (*voyageurs et représentants de commerce*) must be paid at least every three months. This law does not apply to the case of home workers, temporary employees, seasonal workers and employees on intermittent contracts.

Job evaluation and grading

As mentioned above, industry collective agreements contain job classification scales, by job function, for determining basic pay. These scales were laid down after the war by government decree (the Parodi decrees). By law, industries must assess their agreements every five years (although they are under no obligation to change them), and many agreements have been amended and new classifications added in order to keep up with technological change and the changing labour market. During the 1970s and 1980s there was a growing trend in industry agreements towards classifying jobs by grade criteria (*critères classants*), that is, using generally applicable criteria such as the initiative and responsibility required in a job and the educational qualifications of the employee. Where there are no guidelines for classifying a post the employer is responsible for deciding the classification and employees may appeal to workplace representatives if they are not happy with the result.

Make-up of the pay package

The pay package consists of a basic salary for the job, plus a variety of bonuses, which may be individual or collective, and which may be awarded unilaterally by the employer or collectively agreed. They are usually counted as an integral part of an employee's wage.

Length of service increments   Most collective agreements provide for service increments (*prime d'ancienneté*) and, in general, these are paid to all groups of employees on monthly pay. (All white-collar employees and the vast majority of blue-collar workers in France receive a monthly salary.) The increment is usually a percentage of the national minimum monthly salary (Smic) or of the guaranteed minimum basic wage as fixed by agreement for each job category. These salaries are generally based on a thirty-nine hour working week, but the amount paid as an increment can vary with the number of hours actually worked. Because service increments are frequently calculated on the basis of minimum basic pay as set by job classification scales, many industries are reluctant to revise their classification systems to bring salaries at the bottom of the scale above the level of Smic, as it automatically causes service increments to rise. Under the engineering agreement for the Ille-et-Vilaine region, for example, the first increment is paid after three years of service and amounts to 3 per cent of the basic wage. The increment then rises by 1 per cent for each subsequent year of service and continues in most industries up to fifteen years of service. In a few industries increments are paid for up to eighteen or twenty years of service and rise in three-year intervals by 3 per cent. Many agreements do not specify which hours not worked are deducted in the assessment of seniority. Some state that periods of illness, redundancy, military service and maternity leave should be deducted. In the late 1980s there was a move towards phasing service increments out.

Travel allowances   Employers in the Paris region must reimburse 50 per cent of commuting costs to employees who come into work by public transport. The law, introduced in 1982, excludes employees who use private means of transport, such as cars, and specifies that the allowance should be based on the cost of a second-class weekly season ticket. The allowance is exempt from social security contributions. Part-time workers count as full-timers if they work at least half the number of hours in the legal working week. If they work fewer hours, they are reimbursed on a *pro rata* basis. Travel allowances are sometimes paid in regions outside Paris, but only under the terms of a collective agreement, not of the law.

Pay increases

Pay increases are negotiated at two levels: industry level and company level. Bargaining at industry level is governed by the 1982 Auroux laws, which impose on employers' associations and unions the duty to bargain annually on pay, although they are not required to come to an agreement. If agreement cannot be reached, as happens with some frequency, an increase will be imposed by the employers. Wage negotiations must also take into consideration the economic and employment situation of the sector, and employers must supply the unions with relevant information at least fifteen days before negotiations begin.

Similarly, employers are under a statutory annual obligation to negotiate on pay, hours of work and work organisation in companies where there is at least one union branch. If an employer has not opened negotiations for more than twelve months, a union can demand their initiation, in which case they must begin within two weeks. In practice, bargaining is fairly weak at company level, mainly on account of the low degree of unionisation, at around 10 per cent of the work force. Employers are therefore relatively free to implement their own payment systems as long as the rates are above the collectively agreed minimum.

Overtime, night work and shift pay

Overtime rates are governed by law. The first eight hours of overtime in any one week must be paid at time and a quarter, and hours worked beyond that at time and a half. Many industries have negotiated annual overtime quotas for individual employees (see above). Overtime which exceeds the negotiated limits requires prior permission from the labour inspectorate and the works council or employee representatives, and must be compensated by thirty minutes' time off for each hour worked.

Shift and night work premiums are governed by collective or company agreement. Rates for shift workers are usually higher than those negotiated for day-workers. In the Renault agreement this additional element is termed the 'daily shift premium' (*prime journalière d'équipe*) and is renegotiated at the time of general pay rises. The same principle applies to night work supplements. At Renault workers who work night shifts for at least five hours between 22.00 and 06.00 are paid a premium to compensate for both shift work and night work (*prime globale d'équipe de nuit*), which is renegotiated in the general pay round. In the chemical industry night work is paid at 120 per cent of usual rates.

Bonuses and supplements

The role of bonuses   Bonuses and supplementary payments are an important aspect of remuneration in France. However, few are directly tied to performance. A survey by the Ministry of Labour showed that in 1992 supplements accounted for on average 6.6 per cent of total earnings, with clear differences between the four categories of employee looked at in the survey: manual, clerical, supervisory and managerial. Regular monthly supplementary payments, such as seniority allowances, accounted for 8.6 per cent of pay for manual workers but only 3.8 per cent for managers, whilst one-off bonus payments, reflecting performance, accounted for 6 per cent of managers' pay but only 2.1 per cent of manual workers' pay. For manual workers the most important supplementary payment is the 'thirteenth month' (see below) which represents between 30 per cent and 50 per cent of all manual workers' bonuses in most sectors, although there are wide differences from industry to industry. After the 'thirteenth month' the most important supplement is that linked with 'individual situation' (age, length of service, etc.), followed by premiums linked with the type of work performed, including 'dirty work' allowances, lunch subsidies and night or shift allowances. The larger the company or plant the greater the contribution of premiums to total earnings.

Clerical employees generally receive a lower proportion of total pay in the form of bonuses than any other category. The 'thirteenth', and any additional, monthly payments make up a larger proportion of annual pay supplements than for manual workers. Extra payments relating to age and length of service remain at roughly the same level as manual workers', but those linked to type of work done are less important.

Bonuses as a proportion of total pay are more important to supervisory and technical employees than to any other category. The 'thirteenth month' payments make up around half of all supplementary payments, and differences between industries are not so wide as for other categories of employee. Seniority payments were higher in the survey than for clerical employees – presumably because of the long service which normally precedes the appointment of a supervisor or foreman – but those linked to company results are lower. Managerial and professional staff rely somewhat less on separately recorded supplementary payments as a proportion of overall pay. The difference is mainly accounted for by the reduced importance attached to length of service payments: long-serving managers are more likely to have such an allowance built into their salary. Premiums based on company results represent a higher proportion of all bonus payments than for other employees, and are particularly common in commerce and in certain branches of industry.

'Thirteenth month' payments   Nearly half the value of supplementary payments is accounted for by thirteenth-month payments – that is, an extra month's salary paid over and above the annual rate. Over two-thirds of the French work force receive such bonuses, some of whom receive fourteenth, fifteenth and – sometimes – even sixteenth-month bonuses. The timing of payments varies from industry to industry. In banking, for example, fourteen and a half monthly salaries are paid annually: one additional month is paid at the end of the year, one at an agreed time and half at the beginning of the summer holiday.

Pay for performance

Merit pay (*individualisation*) was the subject of a good deal of discussion in France in the 1980s when performance-related pay increases became more wide-spread. However, there is some evidence that the trend may be slowing. It is estimated that some 36 per cent of companies award some element of individualised pay. In larger companies the practice of mixed increases is very common, with around 90 per cent of companies with 500 or more employees giving general and individual increases. Pay increases which are solely general awards are quite rare in companies of this size. Pure merit awards tend to be much more common in companies with up to fifty employees, partly because such companies tend to be owner-managed and without formal structures for employee representation.

Managers' pay

Managers (*cadres*) are generally not covered by the salary scales of industry agreements. However, in some industries, notably engineering, there are separate agreed salary scales. This particular agreement has a number of minimum rates depending on seniority and job category. However, these very much represent a minimum; company-level salaries will either be individually negotiated or dealt with via a domestic salary and benefits structure.

In addition to customary factors like company size, region and industrial branch, levels of management remuneration in France are heavily determined by educational background, with the graduates of the *grandes écoles* often enjoying a premium of up to 30 per cent more than graduates of universities (although this partly reflects the higher grade and status of job into which they are recruited). Salaries in the Paris region tend to be 5–10 per cent above those for the provinces, and the highest salaries by industry are paid in financial services and 'high-tech' sectors such as computing.

Cash bonuses, typically involving performance of individual tasks and possibly a measure of profit, are almost universal for top management and paid to 85–90 per cent of second-tier management, according to the Monks Partnership survey of *Incentives and Benefits in Europe*. The amount of pay at risk for top managers tends to be below 20 per cent, and was less than 15 per cent for around a third of managing directors. The trend in recent years, reinforced by the recession of the early 1990s, has been to make more use of non-consolidated cash bonuses in place of general salary increases.

Bonuses are also supplemented by payouts under statutory profit-sharing arrangements. Share options are uncommon in French companies, but much more prevalent in foreign-owned firms. Overall, around 60 per cent of top managers were granted share options, falling off rapidly below that level. The extensive state pension scheme – now in serious financial difficulties – has deterred the establishment of company schemes. However, around half of all managers are in receipt of some form of supplementary company scheme to enable all their earnings to be covered.

Financial participation

In France the subject of financial participation is a complex one, governed by a network of laws and regulations. In October 1986 legislation was passed on profit-sharing and shareholding which simplified and harmonised rather than radically changed existing fiscal and legal regulations, specifically to encourage and facilitate the extension of profit-sharing. Since then, the growth of such schemes, especially of immediate profit-sharing (*intéressement*), has been rapid and legislation was passed at the end of 1990 to limit them. In early 1994 a Bill was introduced with the aim of easing restrictions on profit-sharing, as the number of schemes had fallen, partly in response to restrictive legislation and partly owing to the economic recession and reduced company profits.

Profit-sharing

There are two basic types of profit-sharing scheme: deferred profit-sharing (*participation*) and immediate profit-sharing (*intéressement*).

Deferred profit-sharing   This type of scheme, under which there must be no pay-out to employees for at least three years, is compulsory under legislation passed in 1990 in companies with over fifty employees (previously the threshold was 100) and optional in smaller firms. A law passed in April 1994 offers incentives for small companies to adopt profit-sharing schemes. Employees have the right to a proportion of a firm's after-tax profits according to a prescribed formula, although a collective agreement may employ any alternative method of calculation. A special profit-sharing reserve (*reserve spéciale de participation*, or RSP) is established each year, as a function of taxable profits, with provision for a deduction of a 5 per cent return on capital. Profits in the form of cash deposits in blocked current accounts, shares or quasi-equity are distributed to the work force in proportion to employee's earnings up to certain ceilings, though a company agreement may take other criteria into account.

   Deferred profit-sharing schemes benefit from privileged tax arrangements, subject to the funds being blocked for a period. Neither the company nor its employees have to pay tax or social security contributions on amounts payable through this type of profit-sharing scheme, provided profits are not distributed from the special fund for five years. The 1986 legislation reduced the limit to three years, subject to the existence of a company agreement to that effect, in which case half the tax advantage to the company and employee would be forfeited. Where there is no company agreement on deferred profit-sharing the proceeds may not be distributed for eight years, with the company losing some of the tax benefits which would normally accrue. The April 1994 legislation allows pay-outs to employees before the expiry of the three-year period for the purchase of certain items such as new cars or property-related expenses.

As well as basic scheme rules on profit distribution, a profit-sharing agreement must also set out how funds are to be invested and make provision for information disclosure to employees. A copy of the profit-sharing agreement must be deposited with the labour authorities in the relevant *département*.

At the end of December 1992 some 16,901 companies had set up such profit-sharing schemes, involving over 4.9 million employees, and up a fifth on the previous year, mainly as a result of legislation passed in 1990 lowering the threshold for compulsory schemes from 100 employees to 50. Average annual pay-outs from these schemes are FFr 5,000 (£578) per employee.

Immediate profit-sharing   This type of scheme (*intéressement*) yields an annual pay-out after the end of each financial year, dependent on positive company financial results. Schemes are voluntary but must be agreed with the trade unions. In contrast to deferred schemes, voluntary profit-sharing schemes do not have to cover the whole work force. They may be set up for specific categories of employee (e.g. managers) and/or individual work units and – in multi-plant companies – for individual establishments. Agreements inaugurating voluntary schemes are concluded (and terminated) in exactly the same way as deferred schemes (see above) for three financial years.

Formerly, the total sum paid out in profit-sharing could not exceed 15 per cent of the company's wage bill, reduced to 10 per cent of the wage bill for companies with no in-house pay agreement. In April 1994 a Bill was passed raising the ceiling to a uniform 20 per cent of the wage bill for schemes concluded on or after 1 October 1994. The ceiling for pay-outs to individual employees (in schemes agreed or updated after 11 November 1990) is set at half the ceiling for which social security is payable: in 1994 this stood at FFr 76,560 (£8,850).

The average amount paid out under profit-share schemes in 1992 was 2.9 per cent the wage bill, although larger pay-outs of up to 20 per cent of the wage bill are sometimes given to senior executives in small companies. By sector, the percentage of the pay bill awarded in pay-outs ranged from 4.6 per cent in the food industry, just over 3 per cent in consumer and intermediate goods, and 3.3 per cent in services, to 2.6 per cent in finance.

Company savings schemes   A company savings scheme (*plan d'épargne d'entreprise*), may be set up by any firm under legislation passed in 1967 (Labour Code L 443 1–15). Significant tax advantages and social security exemptions accrue to employees who put the proceeds from a deferred or an immediate profit-sharing scheme into such a fund. Employees may also opt to pay voluntary contributions into the savings scheme. Firms may pay in further contributions within certain limits. Savings scheme funds may be used to purchase shares in the company as well as to acquire other financial assets.

Share options   A law passed on 31 December 1970 and amended in 1984 and 1987 provides for income and corporation tax relief on share options granted to employees, provided certain conditions are met. The employees must have a minimum of five years in which to exercise their option and the discount must not exceed 20 per cent. Income tax relief on the gain is available provided the employees retain their shares for at least five years after the date on which the option was granted, and for at least one year after the shares have been acquired.

An employer can offer share options to all employees and certain kinds of managers, including directors and others who do not have a formal contract of employment with the company. Employees holding more than 10 per cent of the capital of the company may not participate in such a scheme. Corporation tax relief is available on the costs incurred in running discounted share schemes.

Sick pay

Sickness benefit   Sickness benefit is available to all employees from the fourth day of sickness absence. It is paid at a rate of 50 per cent of basic assessable earnings, with a daily minimum in 1994 of FFr 44.74 (£5.17) and a daily maximum of FFr 211.33 (£24.43). After thirty days of sickness the rate increases to two-thirds of earnings for employees with three or more dependent children, up to a maximum of FFr 281.77 (£32.57) per day. The benefit may be reduced in certain circumstances where the employee is hospitalised. Benefit is payable for a maximum of 360 days over a three-year period.

Sick pay   A national agreement on sick pay was signed by employers and unions in December 1977 and subsequently extended to all employees by decree. Under the agreement, all monthly paid employees with at least three years' service are entitled to continued payment of a proportion of salary. The employee must notify the employer within forty-eight hours and provide proof of sickness. For the first thirty days employees receive 90 per cent of the gross pay they would have received had they continued to work. For the following thirty days the rate is reduced to two-thirds. These periods are increased by ten days for each five years of service, up to a maximum of ninety days. Sick pay is payable from the first day of absence in the case of an accident at work or industrial disease, and from the fourth day in all other cases. Sick pay is limited within a twelve-month period to the employee's total entitlement on grounds of length of service.

These legal provisions on sick pay are often considerably improved under the terms of collective agreements signed at industry or company level. Most collective agreements, for example, provide sick pay from the first day of absence for illness from whatever cause.

Maternity pay

During maternity leave 84 per cent of salary is paid by social security up to the level of the social security ceiling. However, many collective agreements guarantee the maintenance of full salary, with the employer making up the rest sometimes, provided the employee has one year's service. In some cases other benefits are provided as well: for example, a woman may receive a lump sum on the birth of a baby.

Main benefits

Benefits in France tend to take the form of cash rather than fringe benefits, such as company cars, assisted house purchase or discount on own-company products, reflecting the country's relatively heavy indirect taxes by international standards. Although nearly universal for top management, the incidence of cars for middle-managers is well below the European average.

Equal pay and equal opportunities

Legal framework

Equality of pay for men and women is a statutory requirement, and breaches of the principle are punishable by fine or imprisonment. Provided the same job is performed by men and women, all items which make up the pay packet must be calculated using the same standards for women as for men. The law of 13 July 1983 on equality in the workplace aims to improve women's conditions by defining 'work of equal value'. It states that jobs are of equal value if they are broadly comparable in terms of the professional skills and experience required, the responsibility involved and the mental or physical effort. As well as affirming the principle of non-discrimination in all areas of work – apart from temporary positive discrimination in favour of women – the law enables representative trade unions within a company to take legal action on an employee's behalf in cases of discrimination and introduces measures to help women catch up with men. All companies with fifty or more employees must draw up an annual report on the comparative situation of men and women in the company, covering such areas as recruitment, training, promotion, qualification, job grades, employment conditions and pay. Details must also be given of measures taken during the previous year to ensure equality, and the steps planned for the coming year. This report is submitted to the works council or, where none exists, to the employee representatives and is sent to the local labour inspectorate.

Sexual harassment

A law (No. 92-1179) on sexual harassment at the workplace was passed on 2 November 1992, defining sexual harassment as 'the behaviour of an employer or a superior who, abusing their position of authority, puts pressure on an employee in order to obtain favours of a sexual nature'. The legislation forbids all discrimination in the areas of recruitment, and renders void penalties and dismissal concerning a person who has been the victim of, or witness to, sexual harassment. The law also provides for health and safety committees to provide information on sexual harassment and suggest ways of preventing it. On 1 September 1993 these provisions on general sexual harassment were made part of the criminal law (article 225-2), entailing fines of FFr 100,000 (£11,560) and up to a year's imprisonment. Industrial tribunals have the power to impose these penalties in cases of sexual harassment at the workplace if they are deemed appropriate.

Discrimination in the case of HIV+ employees and AIDS

There are at present no statutory guidelines or collective agreements on the subject of discrimination in the case of AIDS and HIV. However, some companies, mainly large corporations, are now pursuing a policy of informing their employees about how the virus can and cannot be transmitted at the workplace, holding general education seminars and displaying information posters. Companies which have a policy on this subject include the car maker Renault, the bank BNP, the computer company IBM and the engineering firm Thomson. There is now a body of case law building up on the subject of unfair dismissal in the case of AIDS and HIV.

Retirement

Retirement ages

The normal retirement age for both men and women is 60 years. Employees who retire at the age of 60 are entitled to receive a full pension under the state scheme (*régime général*), amounting to 50 per cent of former annual earnings. In addition to the basic pension, all employees are also members of compulsory, jointly managed supplementary schemes, funded by employer and employee contributions. These typically provide an average 20 per cent of former earnings, in addition to the 50 per cent received from the state scheme. There are two compulsory supplementary pension schemes, one for non-managers, ARRCO, covering some 16 million blue- and white-collar employees, and one for managers, AGIRC, covering almost 2 million managerial employees.

The size of the pension is based on the number of contribution years in the state pension scheme and is calculated according to a number of years of best salary. The rules for the calculation of the state pension were changed in 1993 under general pension reforms. Although the principle of retirement at age 60 remains unchanged, the number of contribution years required to qualify for a full pension will be increased in stages from the current 37.5 to 40 between January 1994 and December 2002. The reference period for calculating the size of the pension will rise from the current provision of the best ten years to the best twenty-five, at the rate of one extra year per year from 1994 to 2008.

Early retirement

Companies may retire an employee gradually if there is provision for doing so in a collective agreement and the works council is consulted. The contract of employment is changed to a part-time contract of 40–50 per cent of former working hours. In order to qualify for early retirement, employees must be between 55–65, have ten years' contributions into the state retirement fund, and have one year's seniority in the company. The employee will receive salary for the reduced hours worked plus 30 per cent of their reference salary up to the social security ceiling and 25 per cent of the reference salary between one and four times the social security ceiling.

Full early retirement can be introduced by companies in economic difficulty for employees aged at least 57 years and threatened with redundancy. These employees must also have ten years' contributions into the state pension fund. The employer must conclude an agreement with the state and consult the works committee. The employees receive 65 per cent of former salary up to the social security ceiling plus 50 per cent of salary between one and four times the Social Security ceiling, paid by the unemployment fund Assedic.

Company provision

Because the state provision is so comprehensive, companies only rarely provide extra schemes for their employees, and then primarily for senior staff. However, there is on-going debate about the funding of state pension schemes, which owing to high unemployment and demographic changes, are in deficit. There has been recent debate over proposals to bring forward legislation which would encourage the setting up of private pension funds.

Individual termination of contract

Resignation

Unlike dismissal and redundancy – which are subject to a strict legal framework – resignation does not, legally, entail any particular procedure. (However, certain collective agreements lay down that resignation must be notified by registered letter and that any other means – word of mouth or ordinary letter – is invalid.) Since a period of notice (*délai-congé*) begins when an employer receives such notification, employees are always advised to send in their resignation by registered letter. The decision to resign must have been arrived at freely and without pressure, and be expressed unambiguously.

An employee who resigns is required to abide by the period of notice fixed by collective agreement or by custom and practice for a job or profession (Labour Code L122-5). If there is no agreement, custom and practice often allow a week for blue-collar workers, a month for white-collar workers and three months for managerial and supervisory staff. Employees who suddenly break the employment contract without observing the period of notice laid down by agreement or custom and practice risk losing to the employer a sum in lieu of notice (*une indemnité de brusque rupture*) equal to the earnings they would have received during the period of notice had it been served out. However, pregnant women may resign, if they wish, without having to serve notice and without having to pay a sum in lieu.

An employer must allow an employee who is resigning to serve out the period of notice by doing exactly the same kind of work as before. Any attempt by the employer to alter working conditions unilaterally – or to prevent the employee from serving the notice period – gives the employee the right to claim payment in lieu of notice (*indemnité compensatrice*).

Constructive dismissal

If a court finds that an employee has resigned as a result of employer pressure or threat, the resignation is treated as dismissal and appropriate payments, such as severance pay, must be made by the employer.

Termination by mutual agreement

The Civil Code permits employers and employees to negotiate the termination of a contract of employment by mutual consent. Any such agreement must be in writing and must entail genuine concessions on both sides. For example, the renunciation by the employee of the right to claim unfair dismissal, and the employer in turn waiving a charge of misconduct, would constitute reasonable mutual accommodation. In contrast, an employer's agreeing to pay a sum of money equal to or less than the amount which would in any case be due to the employee would not be valid.

Case law has determined that mutual termination of contract may be agreed at any point, before the formal notification of dismissal, during the interview prior to formal notification of dismissal or during the period of notice. Termination by mutual consent must not be based on error, coercion or threat of force. The employee should therefore be fully informed of all matters relevant to the situation and should be given a period of time for reflection. In the event of a dispute the burden of proof is on the employee to show that an agreement has been signed in any of the above circumstances. It is advisable for employers to indicate clearly that any agreement to terminate the contract by mutual consent is acknowledged as such, refer to the relevant articles of the Civil Code and make sure that the documentation is signed, dated and in duplicate.

Grounds for dismissal

There are two major grounds for termination of contract. The first is some non-economic reason, to do with the conduct and person of the employee, where the responsibility or fault is the employee's (*la faute du salarié*), such as misconduct. The second is some economic reason. The procedure in the second case differs from that in the first in that it involves wide-ranging consultation not only with the employees concerned but also with their workplace representatives and the labour inspectorate.

However, by law the employer must give real and well-founded reasons (*causes réelles et sérieuses*) for all dismissals, irrespective of whether they are for economic or non-economic reasons (Labour Code L122-14-2).

Dismissal with notice and summary dismissal

There are three basic grounds of dismissal for non-economic reasons: flagrant misconduct (*faute lourde*), gross misconduct (*faute grave*) and any other cause related to the person of the employee (*causes liées à la personne même du salarié*). In cases of flagrant misconduct and gross misconduct the employer may summarily dismiss the employee, who loses the right to notice and severance pay (and to holiday pay in the case of flagrant misconduct). In all other cases, notice is given and severance and holiday pay are awarded.

Summary dismissal on grounds of employee conduct   Flagrant misconduct is defined as intolerable behaviour on the part of an employee which has particularly serious consequences for the company and as such represents a fundamental breach of the contract of employment. This would typically include fraud, industrial espionage, theft or violence in the workplace, instances of employees causing damage to stock during industrial disputes, assaulting supervisors, threatening employers and so on.

Gross misconduct is defined as behaviour which precludes the continued presence of the employee in the company, such as insubordination, jeopardising the security or interests of the company, and behaving in such a way as to lose the trust of the employer.

Dismissal with notice   Employees can be dismissed, with notice, and upon payment of severance compensation and holiday pay, for the following reasons related to the conduct or person of the individual concerned: loss of confidence in the employee following acts of dishonesty, or prosecution through the courts; unacceptable behaviour on the part of the employee, such as aggression or even sheer incompatibility of temperament. Illness may not in itself be cause for dismissal. However, frequent or lengthy absence as a result of illness which disrupts work organisation may in some cases suffice. An illness lasting six months or more may warrant dismissal, but under special circumstances the courts may accept a shorter period. Under some collective agreements an employee rendered unable to work at their current post because of illness may be entitled to a transfer with no loss of pay.

An employee may be dismissed for professional reasons (*motifs professionels*), which include incompetence, negligence and, in some cases, poor productivity or sub-standard work. The treatment of poor performance may be governed by collective agreement. For example, the banking agreement requires that the causes of poor performance should be investigated, and opportunities sought for a transfer to work more suited to the employee's abilities. Where incompetence may be culpable employees are dealt with via disciplinary procedures (see below).

Disciplinary procedures

Dismissal on grounds of the employee's conduct requires disciplinary procedures, which may be regulated by collective agreement at industry or company level, to be properly observed. The most common disciplinary procedures are a verbal warning, a reprimand, suspension and ultimately dismissal. Withholding normal pay (but not bonuses) or fining employees is forbidden by law. Employees may be demoted, provided that it is a genuine change of job and not merely a means of cutting pay.

The collective agreement for the banking industry, for example, contains the following gradation of disciplinary procedures: for first-degree instances of misconduct, such as minor lapses of discipline, employees may be subject to a written warning, a reprimand, or a reduction in thirteenth-month salary of up to 10 per cent; second-degree instances, entailing more serious lapses, are punishable by cuts in bonus entitlement, demotion or dismissal. Disciplinary sanctions are deemed to be spent after an agreed period, which may not be more than five years.

Dismissal procedures

An employer who wishes to dismiss an employee for non-economic reasons must send the employee a registered letter, or put a letter into the employee's hand, requesting their attendance at an interview. The employee may be accompanied by a person of their choice, who must be someone employed by the company. At the ensuing interview the employer explains to the employee the grounds of the dismissal. The employee has an opportunity to explain their point of view. There is no statutory time limit within which the interview should be held, except in the case of companies where there are no staff representatives, when the interview must be held within five working days of the letter being sent. After a period of time to think things over – at least one full day after the interview, and a maximum of one month – the employer must send the employee a registered letter confirming the dismissal and the reasons for it. Dismissal may be adjudged void if the grounds for it are not expressly stated in the letter notifying dismissal.

There are a number of employee groups, such as employee representatives, those carrying out civic duties, pregnant women and recent mothers, who are protected from dismissal for all but gross misconduct.

Economic dismissal

Dismissal for economic reasons, or redundancy, is defined by law as 'dismissal by an employer for a reason or reasons, unrelated to the person or the workers concerned, resulting from the disappearance or restructuring of employment or a substantial modification of the employment contract as a result of economic difficulties or technical change'. The employer is under no obligation to consult the works council or staff representatives about individual redundancies. As with dismissal for non-economic reasons, the employee is requested to attend an interview at which they may be offered a retraining contract (*convention de conversion*) if they have two years' service with the company, are physically capable of work and are under 56 years 2 months. Retraining contracts are intended to enable employees to learn new skills and gain further qualifications. The scheme is jointly managed and financed by the state, by the unemployment insurance organisation Assedic and by companies. An employee has twenty-one calendar days in which to decide whether or not to take up the offer. An employer who fails to offer an eligible employee a retraining contract must pay Assedic the equivalent of one month's salary. A registered letter confirming the redundancy must be then sent to the employee during the twenty-one days following the interview, but no earlier than seven days after the date of the interview. If the employee does not reply to the offer of a retraining contract during the twenty-one days the offer is taken to have been declined. The employer must inform the local labour inspectorate of the redundancy, in writing, within eight days of sending the letter notifying redundancy. Employees made redundant have priority claim to reinstatement for a period of one year from the termination of their contract, provided that they make the wish to be considered known to the employer within four months of the termination of their contract. The courts have found that this right applies even in cases where the employee has found other employment.

Terminating executive employment

Individual dismissal of managerial and supervisory staff (*cadres*) follows the same procedures as that of other employees (see above) except that a wider range of definitions of flagrant or gross misconduct is acceptable. For example, disloyalty, breach of confidence or loss of trust may, in the appropriate circumstances, be reason for fair dismissal. Dismissal on economic grounds also follows the same procedure as that for other employees. However, companies with fifty or more employees must inform – but need not consult – the works council of the redundancy. Fifteen days must then elapse before the employer may apply to the labour inspectorate for authorisation to go ahead with dismissal.

Periods of notice

There is no statutory period of notice in the event of resignation by the employee. Notice in such a case is determined either by collective agreement or by custom and practice. The most common notice periods are:

* One week for blue-collar employees.
* One month for white-collar employees.
* Three months for managers.
* Six months for senior managers.

If the employer terminates the employment relationship, employees have a statutory right to periods of notice if they have at least six months' continuous service with the employer and have not been summarily dismissed. Periods of notice are graduated by service as follows:

* Up to six months: custom and practice.
* Six months to two years: one month.
* Over two years: two months.

It is usual for statutory notice periods to be improved upon by collective agreement. For example, the agreement covering the engineering industry in the Paris region specifies notice periods of between two weeks and three months, according to length of service.

Severance payments

Employees have a statutory entitlement to severance payments if they have at least two years' continuous service with the same employer, are not being summarily dismissed and have a permanent employment contract. Statutory minimum severance payments are one-tenth of a month's salary per year of service for monthly paid employees, or twenty hours' salary per year of service for hourly paid employees, plus an additional payment of one-fifteenth of a month's salary for each additional year of service over ten years. Severance payments are exempt from tax and from social security contributions. Collective agreements usually improve upon these minimum statutory provisions. For example, in the chemical industry, employees with at least two years' service receive three-tenths of a month's salary for each year of service, with higher payments for older workers aged 50 and 55.

Holiday compensation payments

Employees also have a statutory right to payments in compensation for holidays lost through dismissal. The sum paid must be equal to either one-tenth of total annual earnings between 1 June and 31 May or earnings which the employee would have received during their holiday period, whichever is the more favourable. If the employee has already received some holiday pay for the year, the payment upon dismissal must be equal to the difference between that sum and the total payable.

Unfair dismissal

An employer dismissing an employee for non-economic reasons must give well founded reasons for dismissal (*causes réelles et sérieuses*). A dismissed employee who has two years' service, has worked in a company with eleven or more employees and is of the opinion that the reasons for the dismissal are not well founded can take a claim of unfair dismissal to the labour tribunal (*le tribunal*). If the tribunal upholds the employee's claim reinstatement may be recommended, but if either of the parties objects it cannot be enforced, and a sum in compensation must be paid by the employer. The amount must not be lower than a sum equal to six months' gross earnings. In addition the employer must reimburse the state for any unemployment benefit claimed by the employee between the date of dismissal and the date of the tribunal's judgement.

In addition the employer may be liable for compensation payments to the employee of up to one month's wages if the employee is found to have been dismissed for just cause but the employer has failed to follow the correct procedures.

Employees who have less than two years' service and/or are employed in companies with fewer than eleven employees, and therefore are not covered by unfair dismissal legislation, are not entitled to compensation or reinstatement by law. However, they may bring a civil action against the employer where appropriate, and the court would be likely to award compensation equivalent to six months' earnings if the claim of unfair dismissal were upheld.

Collective dismissal

Definition of collective dismissal

Collective dismissal is defined in law as the dismissal of two or more employees on economic grounds. The law distinguishes between the dismissal of fewer than ten employees over a thirty-day period and the dismissal of ten or more employees over a thirty-day period.

Statutory requirements on consultation

Dismissal of two to nine employees over thirty days Employers must by law inform staff representatives (or works councils in companies with fifty or more employees) of the dismissal of two to nine employees for economic reasons. At the meeting the employer should outline the exact details of and reasons for the proposed dismissals and the supplementary measures it is proposed to take, such as the offer of retraining contracts. The employer must then send each employee facing dismissal a registered letter requesting attendance at an interview. At the interview the employer explains the reasons for dismissal and offers eligible employees a retraining contract. The employer must then issue notice of termination no earlier than seven calendar days after the interview. In the case of a manager the period is extended to fifteen days. No prior authorisation is required from the labour inspectorate for the dismissal of under ten employees. However, the employer must inform the labour inspectorate of the dismissals within eight days of the notice of termination being sent out. The dismissals should also be recorded on the monthly employment return (in companies with over fifty employees) and in the firm's register of employees.

Dismissal of ten or more employees over thirty days Employers must inform and consult workplace representatives before the dismissal for economic reasons of ten or more employees. There is an obligation upon firms with fifty or more employees to hold two consecutive consultation meetings at intervals of between fourteen and twenty-eight days, depending on the extent of the dismissals. Detailed information on the proposed redundancies must be supplied to employee representatives in advance of the first or only meeting. The works council (in companies with fifty or more employees) may appoint an accountant, at the employer's expense, who has twenty to twenty-two days in which to produce a report. In the interval between the first and, where applicable, the second meeting, the employer must consider and respond to suggestions put forward by the works council. Although works councils must be informed and consulted about proposed redundancies and suggest ways of limiting or preventing the redundancies, they have no power of veto at all and the employer is also under no statutory obligation to take on board any suggestions made.

The employer must notify the labour inspectorate of the proposed redundancies one day after the first (or only) meeting with employee representatives. After the second (or only) meeting the employer sends exact details of the redundancies to the labour inspectorate, which checks that the employer has complied fully with the statutory information and consultation procedures and that the reasons given for the redundancies are valid. The labour inspectorate has between twenty-one and thirty-five days to respond to the information, depending on the scale of the redundancy. The employer may formally notify employees of redundancy after the expiry of time limits ranging from thirty days to sixty days (depending on the scale of the redundancy) after the labour inspectorate has been notified.

In firms or establishments with fifty or more employees a 'social plan' (*plan social*) must be drawn up setting out all the supplementary measures which might be taken with the aim of retraining the work force, offering alternative employment or facilitating employees' withdrawal from employment. The social plan does not deal with severance compensation (see below). There are two compulsory elements in a social plan. The first is the offer of early retirement to all affected employees aged over 56 years 2 months. The second is the offer of a retraining contract to those eligible.

Severance and compensation terms

Statutory and agreed severance terms for collective dismissal are as those for individual dismissal. The statutory minimum payment of one-tenth of a month's salary per year of service after two years' service is often improved upon by collective agreement (see above).

Transfer of undertakings

Under the Labour Code (article 432-1), the employer must consult staff representatives or, where appropriate, a works committee before making any change in the economic or legal organisation of the company, including mergers, acquisitions, sale of a subsidiary or other significant change in the organisation of production. Contracts of employment which are valid at the time of the change remain in force, although the (new) employer is entitled to proceed with dismissals on grounds of rationalisation or reorganisation without any waiting period. Variations in terms may be proposed by the employer, with the risk of termination if the employee rejects a reasonable change.

Final formalities

Once an employment contract has expired, for whatever reason, the employer must comply with a number of statutory formalities. Former employees must be issued with an employment certificate (*certificat du travail*), containing details of their employment with the company, including the starting and finishing dates. The employer must pay all outstanding sums due, such as salary, bonuses, any payment in lieu of notice, and so on. As a safeguard against further demands from the employee, the employer should ask for a receipt for all payments due (*un reçu pour solde de tout compte*). If the employee wishes, the employer must provide a proof of employment document (*attestation d'emploi*), containing all relevant information concerning the employee's contract and its termination. As soon as the employment relationship has ended, the employer must give the employee a document confirming the position with regard to unemployment benefit, which the employee can then use in support of a claim.

Appendix

Non-wage labour costs and income tax

Average employer social contribution rates for white-collar non-managerial employees of firms located outside the Paris region and employing over ten persons are approximately 42.5 per cent of gross earnings. Social contributions break down into eight categories for employers:

- Social security.
- Supplementary pension insurance.
- Unemployment insurance.
- Construction and housing fund.
- Apprentice training tax.
- Continuous vocational training fund.
- Salary tax.
- Transport tax (Paris region).

There are various government-initiated job creation incentives consisting of the waiving of social charges if employers hire certain types of employee such as the long-term unemployed and young people with no qualifications.

Liability to income tax is assessed on the basis of residence in France, defined as one of the following:

- Having a home where the contributor's family normally resides.
- Spending 183 or more days a year in the country.
- Being employed or pursuing a professional activity.
- Organising a centre of vital economic interest.

Income tax is progressive, with rates from 5 per cent to 56.8 per cent, arranged in seven bands according to income. The head of household is assessed on aggregate total household income. Taxable income is calculated by deducting standard allowances. The total household taxable income is then divided into parts which correspond to the number of dependants and marital status of the head of the household. For example, a childless married couple would be two parts, with an additional half part for each of the first two children and an extra part for each subsequent child. Tax rates are then set against each individual part, so taxpayers benefit from lower tax rates through income splitting.

Organisations

Ministry of Labour
127 rue de Grenelle, 75700 Paris
Tel. + 33 1 40 56 60 00;
Fax + 33 1 40 56 67 24

Agence Nationale pour l'Emploi (ANPE)
(national employment agency)
23 rue Galilei, 93198 Noisy-le-Grand
Cedex
Tel. + 33 1 49 31 74 00;
Fax + 33 1 43 05 67 96

Association pour l'Emploi des Cadres
(APEC)
(state managerial employment agency)
51 boulevard Brune, 75689 Paris Cedex 14
Tel. + 33 1 40 52 20 00;
Fax + 33 1 40 45 40 94

Conseil National du Patronat Français
(national employers' organisation)
31 rue Pierre 1er de Serbie, 75016 Paris
Tel. + 33 1 40 69 44 44;
Fax + 33 1 47 23 47 32

British Chamber of Commerce
41 rue du Tyren, 75003 Paris
Tel. + 33 1 44 59 25 20;
Fax + 33 1 44 59 25 45

*Commission Nationale de l'Informatique
et des Libertés* (National Commission on
Rights and Computerised Information)
21 rue St Guillaume, 75340 Paris Cedex
07
Tel. + 33 1 45 48 39 39
Fax + 33 1 45 49 04 55

Main sources

Liaisons Sociales, *Legislation Sociale*, various issues.
Liaisons Sociales, *Bref Sociale*, various issues.
Lamy S. A., *La Semaine Sociale Lamy*, Juridiques et Techniques, various issues.
Mémento Practique Social, Francis Lefebvre, Paris, 1993.
Code de Travail, Dalloz, 55th edition, Paris, 1993.
Ministry of Labour national collective agreements for: chemicals, banking,
metalworking (Paris region), road haulage.

5

Germany

Basic rights and labour jurisdiction

Sources of law on employment

The legal regulation of terms and conditions of employment in Germany is derived from a number of constitutional principles, particularly in the area of collective rights, and a large number of uncodified individual pieces of legislation. Some of these, such as the Civil Code, the Industrial Code and the Commercial Code, date back to the nineteenth century, although all have been subject to numerous amendments since. Most legislation in the employment field is introduced at federal level, although in theory the Federal Republic's constituent states, the *Länder*, can also claim competence in this field. Apart from laws on educational leave, little *Land* legislation affects employment relations.

Basic rights in employment are those granted via the Basic Law (*Grundgesetz*), the founding constitution of the Federal Republic of Germany, promulgated in 1949. Although there are few explicit employment elements, the clauses guaranteeing the inviolability of the individual, freedom of association for employees and employers, the regulation of employment for established civil servants, and the ban on Sunday working, have all been either developed via case law or incorporated into substantive legislation.

Employment legislation embraces some forty individual statutes, including relevant sections of the Civil Code, with their associated orders and regulations. The most important for the regulation of the individual employment relationship are:

- The Civil Code (*Bürgerliches Gesetzbuch*), which sets out underlying provisions on contracts of employment, periods of notice, equality, transfer of undertakings and employee liability.
- Works Constitution Act (*Betriebsverfassungsgesetz*) 1972, which underpins many individual as well as collective workplace employee rights.
- Protection against Dismissal Act (*Kündigungsschutzgesetz*) 1969, which provides general protection against unfair dismissal for eligible employees, and the Employment Promotion Act 1985 (amended in 1994), which regulates non-standard forms of employment.
- Working Time Act (*Arbeitszeitgesetz*) 1994, which replaces the 1938 Working Time Ordinance, as well as extensive legislation on workplace health and safety.

- Laws on sick pay and holiday pay, minimum holiday entitlement, maternity protection and parental leave.
- Laws on employee inventions and on data protection.

Collective agreements, which are binding and legally enforceable between the contracting parties, represent a crucial area of employment regulation, and create the basis of pay, terms and conditions for 80–90 per cent of employees. In general, collective agreements – in the main concluded at industry level – either improve on statute law or create new binding regulations in areas such as pay, where there is no statute law. However, in one or two areas, most notably periods of notice, collective agreements may include provisions which are poorer than the statutory minimum or which deviate from statutory terms. (Another volume in this series, *Employee Relations and Collective Bargaining*, deals in detail with collective agreements.)

Works agreements, concluded between individual employers and works councils elected by employees, regulate employment issues at workplace level. As well as providing the vehicle for enshrining local agreements on a wide variety of subjects, works agreements also play a role in the system of workplace co-determination in that works councils have the right to insist on negotiating and reaching agreement on some basic issues, such as the organisation of working hours at workplace level, pay arrangements (but not level), and schemes for compensating employees in the event of dismissal for economic reasons (see below). Should the employer refuse, or if no agreement can be reached, works councils have a legal right of recourse to arbitration, the outcome of which will be binding. Works agreements are also legally enforceable, but they are subsidiary to collective agreements in a number of respects. In the first place, they may not regulate pay or any conditions of employment normally set by collective agreement unless the collective agreement expressly allows it. Secondly, and in contrast to collective agreements, they may be terminated by the employer at three months' notice, although their provisions will continue in force until superseded by a fresh agreement.

Case law has played a major role in the development of employment regulation in Germany, not only through the interpretation of statute law but also by elaborating areas of regulation where there is effectively no substantive statutory provision. This applies, in particular, to the law relating to industrial action (see *Employee Relations and Collective Bargaining* in this series). In the deliberations of judges, and in debates on employment issues, frequent reference is made to 'prevailing legal opinion' in the writings or formal legal opinions of leading academics and judges. Court rulings may also be shaped, in the absence of written law, by custom and practice as evidence of elements of the employment relationship which have tacitly become part of the individual contract of employment.

European Union law has been especially influential, for two reasons. Firstly, a number of precedent-setting cases which have come before the European Court of Justice had their origins in disputes in the German courts. They include important cases on indirect sex discrimination and on gender bias in job evaluation schemes. Rulings of the European Court have also required changes in German statute law and procedures. For example, in spring 1994 the law on sick pay was amended to remove a qualifying hours threshold which excluded some part-timers and therefore constituted indirect sex discrimination. The Court also found that the official placement monopoly of the Federal Employment Authority was contrary to EU law where it involved executives, paving the way for subsequent deregulation.

Labour jurisdiction

Germany has a separate branch of labour jurisdiction, with its own courts at local level (*Arbeitsgericht*), at the level of each constituent *Land* of the Federal Republic (*Landesarbeitsgericht*), and with a Federal Labour Court at the apex of the structure (*Bundesarbeitsgericht*). The first and second-instance courts consist of both professional judges and lay assessors nominated by employers' associations and trade unions. Cases and existing legislation can be taken on appeal to the Federal Constitutional Court (*Bundesverfassungsgericht*) where issues of fundamental principle are involved, and this has proved important in some areas. In 1990, for example, the Constitutional Court found that unequal periods of notice for blue- and white-collar employees violated the constitutional principle of equality before the law. In consequence the government – after some delay – introduced legislation, effective from October 1993, equalising statutory minimum periods of notice for all employees.

The system is intended to offer speedy resolution of differences, especially at first-instance level and in the case of contested dismissal. There are constraints on the right of appeal, based on the amount at issue, intended to limit the work load of the higher courts and encourage settlement at the first instance unless the case is of fundamental legal importance. In all, some 350,000 cases come before the local labour courts each year in west Germany, with around 15,000 going on to appeal, of which 600–700 end up at federal level.

Labour courts reach two types of resolution: rulings and judgements. Rulings are primarily concerned with the operation of the works council system and the system of board-level employee representation. No court fees are charged in such cases. In the case of judgements, which may be issued on individual litigation or on cases arising out of the enforcement of collective agreements, there is a scale of court fees offering a much cheaper system of justice than in other types of case. Lawyers' fees too are kept low by limiting the amount in dispute to a quarter of the individual's annual salary in cases of contested dismissal, irrespective of the ultimate award.

Contracts of employment

The contract of employment (*Arbeitsvertrag*) is one form of contract of service (*Dienstvertrag*), and contrasts with a contract for services (*Werkvertrag*), which involves the supply of finished goods or the rendering of a service. In a dispute over whether a contract establishes an employment relationship the courts will be guided by the substance of the contract, not by how the parties choose to represent it. Following revelations of abuses of contracts for services with companies based in Eastern Europe, the government decided in 1993 to exercise greater control over work permits and pay levels.

Types of employee

The status of 'employee' confers rights and duties *vis-à-vis* the employer and brings the individual under the jurisdiction of the labour courts. There are two basic categories of employee: manual, or blue-collar (*Arbeiter*), and white-collar (*Angestellte*). Within the white-collar group, 'executives' (*leitende Angestellte*) are covered by separate provisions on termination, and do not count as employees under the law on works councils. Executives are defined as employees who have the power to hire and fire, the authority to conduct business and work free of direct instruction, and responsibility for major business areas. Where there is uncertainty, an employee may be classed as an executive if they are paid a salary typical of other executives in the enterprise or at least three times the social security calculations base (in 1994 DM 141,120, or £56,000).

Managing directors or managing partners, generically termed 'registered managers' (*Geschäftsführer*), occupy a special position in limited liability companies (GmbH) and limited partnerships (GmbH & Co. KG). They represent the company legally and are responsible for seeing that the business is conducted in accordance with the law, the articles of association and shareholders' instructions. A GmbH may have several registered managers who share this responsibility and exercise specific business functions. They may also partly own the company. The employment, social security and legal rights and obligations of *Geschäftsführer* will vary, depending on whether they are part-owners or work wholly under contracts of service.

The contracts of *Geschäftsführer* will consist of the same basic elements as those of other senior staff but the responsibilities may be more closely defined and their activities more tightly circumscribed. Moreover, because they are not covered by some protective legislation and are often on fixed-term contracts, periods of notice and severance arrangements need to be more closely governed by the individual contract (see below, 'Termination of executive employment').

Harmonisation

Despite the almost complete elimination of differences in terms and conditions between blue- and white-collar employees, the social insurance system still requires individuals to be formally allocated to one category or the other. No entirely unambiguous or statutory definitions exist, and borderline or controversial cases still occasionally come before the courts. Single-status pay agreements are increasing in number, but are still fairly rare. One major example is in the chemical industry.

Form of contract

Except in the case of trainees, contracts of employment do not have to take any particular form and may be oral, in writing, explicit or implied. However, restrictive covenants must be in writing. Collective agreements too may require written contracts. At the time of writing the government had prepared draft legislation to implement EU directive 91/533/EEC on proof of an employment contract.

A contract may be null and void if one of the parties has misrepresented anything central to the transaction or has engaged in deception or threats, if the contract is not in the required form or if it is in breach of the law or is unduly onerous or is intended for an illegal purpose. In general, the Civil Code allows employers and employees freedom to settle the terms of their contract subject to any statutory provisions (for example, on hours of work). Since collective agreements (*Tarifverträge*) and works agreements (*Betriebsvereinbarungen*) have the force of law, individual contracts must also conform with these where appropriate. Any divergence must be in the employee's favour. Employers may not arbitrarily discriminate between employees on terms and conditions, nor may they treat employees more or less favourably because of sex, or employee status.

Rights and duties under the employment contract

Section 611 of the Civil Code obliges the employee to render 'the services promised' in the contract of employment, and the employer to pay 'the agreed remuneration'. Where the contract is not specific, the employee's duties can be determined by the employer exercising the right of direction, so long as they are lawful and reasonable. The courts have upheld employees' right to refuse certain types of work if it conflicts with their conscience, and have required employers to make alternative work available.

Employees owe a duty of fidelity to their employer and employers have a duty of care towards employees. This requires employers to ensure, for example, that workrooms, equipment and the organisation of work do not constitute a hazard to the employee's life or health. Employers are also responsible for the safety of employees' property, and for providing secure areas where belongings may be kept during working hours.

The obligation extends to the employee's rights as an individual. For example, employers may not bug employees' telephones or secretly observe them with videos, and must safeguard confidential information about them. Equipment intended to monitor employee performance cannot be introduced without works council agreement.

Employees may take on other employment provided that this is not expressly ruled out in the contract of employment, does not involve unfair competition with the employer, does not prejudice the employees' ability to work for their first employer, and does not mean exceeding the statutory maximum working week of forty-eight hours. Employees are forbidden to divulge commercial secrets for the purposes of competition, for their own gain or with intent to harm the interests of their employer.

Confidentiality

There is a broad requirement of confidentiality covering trade and business matters such as pricing, a company's credit rating, technical know-how and financial information. However, once employment has terminated employees may, within reason, use any knowledge and experience honestly acquired in the course of their employment to further their career. Information acquired unlawfully or in breach of 'good morals' may not be used in this way. The area remains one of legal controversy.

Under the Unfair Competition Act employees may not divulge trade secrets, expressly denoted as secret by the employer, for the purposes of competition, for their own gain or with intent to harm the interests of their employer. There is also a general principle of confidentiality on matters such as price lists, technical know-how and financial information which, although not technically trade secrets, would be seen as commercially sensitive. Members of works councils are bound to secrecy on trade and business secrets which they have access to in the exercise of their responsibilities.

Employee liability

Until 1994 employees were held liable for damage due to their negligence unless the work could be seen as 'predisposed to damage or danger'. However, a 1993 court ruling determined that employee liability should be limited in all situations, except where there is demonstrable malice or gross negligence.

Restrictive covenants

During employment employees may not engage in activities which compete directly with their employer. More specific arrangements could be set out in an agreement, especially in the case of senior managers, and a breach of such an agreement would constitute grounds for summary dismissal. A restrictive covenant to cover the period *after* employment is subject to a number of conditions. Firstly, the restraint must serve a legitimate business interest of the previous employer, must be in writing and may not unreasonably obstruct the career advancement of the employee. Secondly, former employees must be compensated during the period of the restraint, the sum to be not less than 50 per cent of their former remuneration. The compensation may be reduced by earnings from any subsequent employment, depending on their level.

The restraint may not, in general, last for more than two years. Both the geographical extent and the scope of the restraint must be specified. (Often they are inversely related.) All three aspects must be fair and reasonable, allowing for the interests of both parties and the nature of the business. A 'socially unwarranted dismissal' (see below) or constructive dismissal could release an employee from any obligation under a restraint.

Around a third of top German executives are estimated to be bound by restrictive covenants of this type. Restrictive covenants are both enforceable and sometimes enforced in Germany, although some consultants argue that their inclusion in a contract may convey a negative impression when a new employee is being appointed.

Employee inventions and copyright

Employee discoveries are governed by the 1957 Employee Inventions Act, which deals both with genuine patentable inventions and with technical improvements. It differentiates between 'free inventions', which are the work of the employee wholly outside the context of the employment relationship, and 'service inventions', which are the result of direct instruction or experience gained in the workplace. Free inventions must be notified to the employer, and in certain circumstances offered in part to them. Service inventions must be notified to the employer, who ultimately determines whether and how to make use of the invention. The employer must pay the employee 'appropriate remuneration' related to the employee's status and the commercial value of the invention. The law provides for conciliation machinery in the event of a dispute.

Variation of terms

An employer may not transfer an employee to lower-paid work unless the contract expressly allows it. An employer who wishes to change an employee's basic terms of employment must go through the procedure for conditional termination of employment in order to change the terms of the contract. This entails the termination of the existing contract and an offer of employment on fresh terms. Employees may accept the change, with continuity of employment guaranteed, or they can follow the procedure for contesting dismissal (see below). The offer may also be accepted but with the reservation, which must be expressed within three weeks, that the new terms are 'socially unwarranted'. This allows the employee to continue in employment without implicitly accepting the new conditions. If the employee cannot prove such a case, the employer's offer will be upheld. The works council must be notified of any termination to vary a contract, and no such change is valid without its consent or a court ruling if it is not forthcoming. In establishments with twenty or more employees transfers must be notified to the works council.

Probationary period

This can take the form either of a fixed-term contract prior to engagement (see below) or a conventional period of probation. Unless there is an agreed provision the length of probationary periods is governed by general principles set by the courts. They might entail a period of one to three months for simple tasks, and up to six months for more complex ones. The period may not exceed six months (the length of service at which dismissal protection legislation becomes operative and the employer must cite grounds for termination). Pay during a probationary period may be lower than for an inducted employee. Collectively agreed probationary periods are common. For example, the framework agreement for the engineering industry in the North Württemberg/North Baden region sets an eight-week probationary period for manual workers and a three-month period for white-collar workers, extendable to six months in some cases with the consent of the works council. A probationary period may be terminated subject to the minimum statutory provision of two weeks.

Types of contract

Indefinite contract of employment   The most common form of contract of employment is that concluded for an indefinite term, possibly after a probationary period. In 1992 just over 90 per cent of all contracts in west Germany and 85 per cent in east Germany (the ex-GDR) were open-ended.

Fixed-term contract   Fixed-term contracts may be concluded only for a 'material reason', such as probationary employment, a specific task or project limited in time (or subject to finite funding), as a stand-in for an absent employee on maternity leave, or at the employee's request. The duration of a fixed-term contract is governed by case law rulings on appropriateness. In the case of a probationary contract it is set at six months. In the case of scientific or technical staff on long-term projects, up to four years might be agreed. Fixed-term contracts may be renewed repeatedly only if there are telling 'material reasons'.

A fixed-term agreement can be concluded *once* for up to eighteen months without a 'material reason' in the case of a new employee or after training if no permanent post is available. A series of such contracts can be concluded so long as four months elapse between the end of one contract and the beginning of the next and there is 'no close material relation' between the successive periods of employment. This eighteen-month period can be extended to two years if the employer started business less than six months previously or employs ten or fewer employees, excluding trainees.

Contracts for registered managers (*Geschäftsführer*), who are not covered by dismissal protection legislation, are commonly on a fixed-term basis. A fixed-term contract may also be agreed with a manager who is covered by the Protection against Dismissal Act, provided the contract includes a sum in compensation on termination.

Part-time contract   Part-time employment, which accounts for 16 per cent of the German labour force, is defined as hours of work which are shorter than those worked by full-time employees in the same establishment. Some collective agreements specify minimum periods for part-time work. Collective agreements may also specify further terms applicable to part-timers, such as preferential treatment when applying for full-time posts. Part-timers who work less than fifteen hours a week and earn less than DM 560 or £224 a month (in east Germany DM 440 or £176) do not qualify for social security contributions and benefits. Part-timers who work fewer than nineteen hours are excluded from unemployment insurance and benefits. Employees who work less than ten hours a week or forty-five hours a month do not count towards the minimum number of employees required to bring an establishment within the scope of the Protection against Dismissal Act. Employers are liable for all the social insurance contributions of employees earning less than DM 610 or £244 per month (in east Germany DM 450 or £180).

Part-timers may not be treated differently from full-time employees without material reason. Any differential treatment must not constitute indirect sex discrimination. For example, part-time workers must not be denied sick pay (full pay for the first six weeks' illness). Statute law, which holds otherwise, has been invalidated by rulings of the European Court and the Federal Labour Court.

In 1994 the government mounted a campaign to promote part-time working as a way of mitigating unemployment. Although there were no major new incentives, part-time employees now enjoy better access to unemployment benefits than they used to. This follows moves to encourage part-time working in several collective agreements signed in 1993/94, reflecting a more positive view from the trade union side and greater readiness to explore part-time options on the part of employers.

'Zero hours' contracts (work on call)   This type of contract, known as 'capacity-oriented variable working hours' (KAPOVAZ), or 'work on call', requires employees to work when requested to do so by the employer. Such arrangements have been termed 'zero hours contracts' in the UK, although this is a slight misnomer in the German context. Contracts must specify the length of the working week. If hours are not specified a minimum period of ten hours applies, for which the employer is liable to pay the employee. Weekly working hours may be averaged over a year, although there is still some uncertainty about how the law should be interpreted. Employers must give at least four days' notice of call-in and, unless there is a specific agreement on the number of daily hours, the minimum period for which an employee can be employed per day is three hours in succession. Such arrangements need prior agreement with the works council (with a right of appeal to conciliation machinery).

Job-sharing   Under a job-sharing contract the partners are each required to specify the period of work for which they are responsible. Contracts may not require that the post should be constantly occupied – that is, that one partner should deputise for the other in the event of absence, although there may be agreement to deputise in the event of 'serious operating exigencies'.

Workplace issues

Data protection   The treatment of personal data in private-sector workplaces is primarily regulated by the federal Data Protection Act, most recently amended in 1990. This sets out general principles which apply to all organisations holding such data, in either computerised or manual form, and contains a number of special provisions relating to data about employees.

A Data Protection Officer must be appointed by the employer to ensure compliance with the law, oversee data-processing activities and inform employees. Works councils also have a statutory duty to ensure that the law, and any relevant collective agreements, are applied. Employers are required to register with the federal data protection authority.

Collection and storage of data must be undertaken legally, and whatever is stored must not prejudice employee rights to protection and confidentiality. Any measures which allow data to be communicated externally in an anonymous form must remove or disguise details which would allow employees to be identified. They have a right of access to all personal data held about them and a right to request that inaccurate, irrelevant, illegally compiled or incomplete records are rectified or deleted. They can also attach their own comments to records.

Smoking   Non-smokers have a statutory right to a smoke-free environment in rooms set aside for breaks or during waiting periods (when the working day includes times of inactivity). There is also an obligation to provide adequate ventilation in work areas. The courts have determined that the employer must take appropriate measures to protect non-smokers from the effects of smoke, including (if necessary) partial smoking bans. (Blanket smoking bans are more problematic, but the interests of smokers may be met by smoking zones.) Employers who fail to make provisions may be liable for civil damages if a non-smoker can establish a detriment to health and the employer failed in their duty of care. Any smoking bans must be agreed with the employee representatives (works councils) under the provisions of the 1972 Works Constitution Act.

Bullying at work   Bullying by colleagues or superiors, or the loss of support from fellow workers (dubbed 'mobbing'), has become something of an issue in recent years, featuring large in personnel management and trade union literature. According to specialists in the field, 3–5 per cent of employees are estimated to be victims at any one time. The outcome in severe instances ranges from chronic anxiety conditions, through physical illness induced by stress, to suicide.

Employment terms and conditions

Hours of work

Statutory and agreed provisions   During the 1980s and early 1990s, the length of the working week was a major focus of collective bargaining and, in 1994, of legislative activity. The trade unions regard cuts in working hours as a priority in efforts to stem unemployment and improve the quality of working life. A number of major industries, notably engineering, will move to a thirty-five-hour week for all employees from 1995. For employers the pursuit of flexibility in hours of work has been a prime concern for a decade. Recent settlements include both aspects. For its part the government has been seeking to bring German law into line with European directives and to overhaul a body of legislation that dates back to 1938, as well as to foster flexibility and encourage non-standard forms of employment, such as part-time work, whilst preserving a protective framework. On 1 July 1994 new legislation, the Working Time Act (*Arbeitszeitgesetz*), came into force, with changes in health protection for shift workers, with new scope for collective bargaining, and with scope for greater flexibility. In particular, the statutory ban on women's night work, found to be unconstitutional, has been removed (see below).

Against the background of the statutory framework, hours of work for most employees are set by collective agreements typically negotiated at industry level. Such agreements specify the length of the working week, shift arrangements, and any provisions on annual hours or other forms of flexibility. The implementation of agreed provisions at workplace level is often settled between management and works councils, which have statutory rights to conclude agreements on the start and finish of the working day, breaks, and any temporary increase (overtime) or cut in working hours.

Statutory daily and weekly hours of work   Under the 1994 Working Time Act the working day should not generally exceed eight hours, over six work days, yielding a maximum forty-eight hours a week. However, daily hours may be extended to ten, provided the eight-hour average (i.e. the forty-eight hours a week maximum) is adhered to over a reference period of twenty-four weeks. (This may be lengthened by collective agreement to enhance flexibility.)

Shop opening hours   Shops must close on Sundays and public holidays, and between 18.30 and 07.00 on Mondays to Fridays. (Shops at railway stations and airports are exempted.) They may remain open until 20.30 on Thursdays. On Saturdays shops open between 07.00 and 14.00 except on the first Saturday of the month, the so-called 'long Saturday', when they may open until 16.00 during the months April–September, and until 18.00 on the four Saturdays before Christmas Eve. Arrangements must be agreed with works councils.

Sunday and weekend working   Some 4 per cent of employees regularly work on a Sunday in Germany, compared with 10 per cent in the European Union. Under the constitution there is a general ban on Sunday work, and the trade unions and Churches have campaigned heavily against the prospect of Sunday working becoming general in industry. Apart from cafés and restaurants, public transport, music and the arts, working on a Sunday is illegal except in emergencies or to meet the 'daily needs of the population', for essential cleaning and maintenance purposes, to prevent the deterioration of raw materials or defective output, or where for technical reasons operations must not be interrupted. Seasonal work may also be exempted. Under the 1994 Working Time Act, several new technical grounds for Sunday working were allowed, such as the need to operate computer and data networks.

The Act for the first time also allows Sunday working on economic grounds ('to secure employment'):

- By statutory instrument if it is deemed likely to benefit the general good.
- With the permission of the regulatory authorities if the employer can demonstrate that foreign competitors enjoy an advantage through being able to run their plant longer and that employment in Germany would be safeguarded by Sunday working.

Where Sunday working is undertaken, the individual employee must have at least 15 Sundays in each year free. Employees must also have a compensating day of rest within two weeks, to be taken in conjunction with the normal 11-hour rest period to yield at least 35 hours off.

Hours of work in collective agreements   The terms of collective agreements have long overtaken the law as a basis for regulating most aspects of working time, including annual leave. The 1994 Working Time Act allows some derogation from statutory provisions by collective agreement (not simply by works agreement) within certain prescribed limits. For example, the statutory start for night work of 23.00 can be put back or brought forward one hour. Collective agreements can also set a longer reference period for the achievement of the average normal working week without a maximum limit, allowing for project-related activities or fully annualised hours, as in the three-year period permitted in the chemical industry agreement. By collective agreement, up to 10 hours a day may be worked on 60 days a year without any compensatory time-off – in addition to the theoretical quota of hours based on normal weekly maxima. This provision may prove to be incompatible with the EU Working Time Directive.

The main elelemts of collective bargaining over the past decade or so have been:

- A steady trend towards a shorter working week, from some forty hours in the mid 1980s to thirty-six or thirty-seven by 1994. A further reduction to thirty-five hours has been agreed in several sectors, together employing some 4.8 million workers. The most significant are the steel and printing industries (both from May 1995) and the engineering industry (from October 1995).
- A trade union emphasis on the job creation aspect of cuts in working hours, which also informed the union bargaining agenda in the 1994 negotiating round.
- Greater flexibility in the organisation of working time. This has taken various forms, details of which are set out below (see 'Flexibility').

In 1993, according to a survey of collective agreements conducted by the Ministry of Labour, average agreed hours were 37.7 in western Germany (a fall from 38.1 in 1992). Hours of work continue to be longer in the *Länder* which make up eastern Germany: they stood at 39.97 in 1993, a slight fall from the previous year's 40.12.

Overtime   On average, employees work some 1.5 hours a week overtime. That the figure is considerably lower than in the UK is partly attributable to limits in collective agreements and flexible working time arrangements. Following the removal of statutory limits on overtime under the 1994 act, overtime is effectively regulated by collective agreements, which may set annual limits beyond normal agreed hours and specify time off in lieu. For example, under the engineering industry agreement for North Württemberg/North Baden, up to ten hours a week and twenty hours a month overtime can be worked by agreement with the works council. By a formal works agreement, overtime of more than twenty hours per month may be worked by individuals or groups of employees. Such agreements must be renewed every eight weeks.

Some groups, such as young people, people with disabilities, mothers-to-be and part-time workers, are exempt from the overall injunction on employees to work overtime if requested. Works councils must be consulted, and have a right of co-determination.

Breaks   Employees must have a minimum 11-hour rest period between shifts, which may be reduced to 10 hours in hotels and public houses, transport, hospitals and other institutions for providing care, on the condition that the individual employee is granted a compensating period of time off within four weeks, which must be added to another rest period to yield a minimum break of 12 hours. There is a normal weekly break of 24 hours on Sundays, with compensating time off where this is worked.

Employees working more than six hours must have at least half an hour's unpaid break, increased to forty-five minutes where the period of work exceeds nine hours.

Additional breaks may also be arranged by collective agreement, and collective agreements may also re-arrange the statutory minimum break periods in the case of shiftworkers. In the *metalworking* industry in North Württemberg/North Baden, workers on payment by results or on assembly lines receive personal needs time of three minutes per hour, plus five minutes per hour recovery break in addition to other statutory breaks. In one or two instances, most notably at a new plant planned for Mercedes Benz, some relaxation of these provisions has been negotiated in return for other concessions.

Shift work   Single-shift working is still common in medium sized manufacturing firms, with two shifts in larger firms and more capital-intensive industries. According to a 1989 survey by the national engineering trades employers' confederation Gesamtmetall, 50 per cent of surveyed members operated shift systems covering, in all, 25 per cent of their employees. A 1991 survey by the Fraunhofer Institute found that alternating double day shifts were by far the most common system, followed by alternating three-shift systems. Round-the-clock working is uncommon, and confined to industries such chemicals, paper, and iron and steel.

Night work   The 1994 Working Time Act introduced a number of changes in the regulation of night work. The principal novelty was the abolition of the statutory ban on night work for female blue-collar workers, and the introduction of a number of health and safety measures for all night workers. The law also introduced a statutory definition of night work as the time between 23.00 and 06.00, although this can be varied by up to an hour either way by collective agreement.

Under the 1994 Act, employers must give due weight to the ergonomic considerations in setting the pattern and duration of night work (such as those published by the Dublin-based EU Foundation for the Improvement of Living and Working Conditions). The working day should not exceed an average of eight hours, which may be reckoned over a period of four weeks. By law night workers are entitled to a medical examination before starting on night shifts and at three-yearly intervals, with the right to switch to days should they experience any health problems. Employees aged over 50 have a right to ask for an annual examination. The same right can be claimed by night workers with family responsibilities. Night workers also have a statutory right to a certain number of additional paid days off and to pay supplements, unless these are already provided for by collective agreement.

Flexibility   The steady reduction in working hours over the past decade has prompted the introduction of various forms of flexible working in manufacturing. Flexitime (*Gleitzeit*) has been in use since the 1960s for office employees, either with flexible starting and finishing times pure and simple or with the option of building up time credits and debits. Around 20–5 per cent of employees are now thought to be covered by flexitime arrangements. Introducing such a system requires works council agreement. The statutory reference period of two weeks for taking debit/credit hours, subject to a maximum working day of ten hours, may be altered by collective agreement. A typical provision might be one month with ±16 hours. At Drägerwerk, an engineering company based in Lübeck, executives may transfer up to fifteen days a year of their annual leave to a 'long-term time credit' which can be accumulated into longer blocks and used for a sabbatical, a spell of part-time work (for example, following the birth of a child) or earlier retirement. Some companies have taken their executives out of flexitime systems entirely in favour of greater task orientation.

Forms of **annualised hours**, or averaging over a six-month reference period, have emerged since the mid 1980s as a corollary to the progressive shortening of overall working hours. In the engineering industry, for example, the (1994/95) working week of thirty-six hours may be attained over a twelve-month reference period, subject to legal limits on the length of the working week. The agreement in the chemical industry also allows annualised hours, with the option of extending the reference period to three years for project-related activities, subject to works council consent.

Systems of **time-banking**, developed in parallel with cuts in working hours, are also common in manufacturing industry. Companies continue to work the previous forty hours, with the time in excess of the agreed norm accumulated and taken as days (or shifts) off in addition to regular annual leavel.

Longer hours for selected employees. In the engineering industry companies may offer up to 18 per cent of their work forces hours in excess of the agreed norm. Employees may work up to forty hours a week without incurring overtime. According to a study carried out by the engineering workers' union IG Metall, some 18 per cent of firms have taken advantage of this option, covering in all 7.5 per cent of their work forces but only 2.23 per cent of employees paid under the terms of collective agreements. The remainder were 'exempt employees' (*AT-Angestellten*). Eighty per cent of those working forty hours were white-collar employees, primarily middle and first-line management. Most blue-collar employees covered were engaged on maintenance and repair work.

Protected groups

Pregnant women and nursing mothers may not work overtime, or between 20.00 and 06.00, or on Sundays. (Overtime in this context is defined as any work beyond eight and a half hours per day for women over 18 (or ninety hours over two weeks), or eight hours per day (eighty hours over two weeks) for women under 18.) There are some exemptions for women employed in catering and public services.

Employees with a disability may be entitled to longer annual leave by collective agreement. Collective agreements may also provide for shorter working hours for older employers, and shorter hours or longer holidays for shift workers.

Time off

Annual leave   There is a statutory minimum entitlement under the 1994 Act of twenty-four working days as from 1 January 1995, based on a six-day week, with a longer entitlement for young workers. In practice, leave is regulated by collective agreement. Most major manufacturing and service industries in western Germany provide six weeks for all adult employees, and in 1993 the average holiday entitlement across all sectors was twenty-nine days, with some 80 per cent entitled to six weeks' holiday. Entitlement is less in eastern Germany but converging rapidly with the west: the average agreed basic provision stood at twenty-seven days in 1993, with just over a third of all employees having six weeks. In some industries an extra one to three days are granted if the leave is taken between 1 October and 31 March.

Public holidays   There are ten national public holidays with a further four applying only in some or all of the predominantly Catholic federal states. The national holidays are: Christmas Day, Boxing Day, New Year's Day, Good Friday, Easter Monday, May Day, Whitsun, Ascension Day, German Unity Day (3 October) and the Day of Prayer and Penitence (in November). Regional holidays include: Epiphany, Assumption, Corpus Christi and All Saints' Day. Following agreement on a universal scheme of care insurance (*Pflegeversicherung*), to be financed by levies on employees and employers, one public holiday in each state will be dropped as from 1995 to offset the employer contribution.

Sick leave and sick pay   Employees are entitled to full pay from their employer for the first six weeks of illness. Sick pay and sick leave arrangements are also secured and often improved by collective agreement, and sick pay for around 85 per cent of employees is guaranteed by collective agreement as well as by law. After six weeks employees receive sickness benefit from their sickness insurance fund. This is equivalent to 80 per cent of regular earnings, subject to an upper limit, but may not exceed net earnings. Benefit is payable for up to seventy-eight weeks in a three-year period for the same illness. Under some collective agreements the employer makes up the difference between sickness benefit and normal net pay, for a period determined by length of service, once entitlement to sick pay has expired. Companies may add to this, either unilaterally or by works agreement, with some firms paying up to two years for senior employees, depending on length of service and the likelihood of a full recovery.

  In 1994 the limits on part-timers' access to guaranteed sick pay were abolished.

Maternity and parental leave   Female employees are entitled to six weeks' leave before the expected date of confinement and to eight weeks' leave after the birth (twelve weeks in the case of premature or multiple births). Maternity benefit, paid from the relevant sickness insurance fund, is equivalent to net earnings up to a maximum of DM 25 (£10) per day. The employer makes this up to the full amount of net pay.

Either parent is entitled to three years' leave once statutory maternity leave has expired. Parents can alternate up to three times during the overall period of leave. Parents are protected against dismissal during parental leave, except in special circumstances.

Parental benefit, which is tax-free, is payable for twenty-four months during parental leave. The basic rate is DM 600 (£240) a month, with reductions according to household income. Employees must give three months' notice of their intention to return to work.

Additional provision for career breaks may be granted at industry or company level. Larger companies are also exploring a number of methods of offering child care, in conjunction with local authorities.

Personal needs and family occasions   Parents insured through the statutory health insurance system are entitled to ten days off work on sickness benefit to remain at home with a child under 13 years of age on medical grounds. A lone parent is entitled to twenty days off. The maximum annual allowance is twenty-five days. Some collective agreements require sickness benefit to be topped up to usual net pay for some part of this entitlement, typically five days.

Additional paid leave may be stipulated in collective agreements for family occasions such as births, deaths or marriages. Typical provisions are from one to three days for each. At Siemens employees may take up to a year's unpaid leave to take care of a member of the family.

Educational leave   Educational leave, usually one week per year, is provided for by law in most western *Länder*. Certain basic criteria of civic or occupational relevance must be met, and employers may have recourse to the courts if courses stray beyond these bounds.

Works council and trade union duties   Works councils, which may be elected by employees in establishments with five or more employees, meet during normal working hours and works councillors (elected directly by the work force) are released from their usual duties to attend meetings. In large workplaces some may be released from work entirely to carry out works council duties full time. Plant-based lay trades union representatives (*Vertrauensleute*, shop stewards) have no statutory right to paid time off but may be granted time off to attend training courses under some agreements.

Military service   Employment does not cease for military service (twelve months, or fifteen months for the alternative of community service) and employees cannot under normal circumstances be dismissed on ground of absence for military service alone.

Pay and benefits

Minimum wages

There is no national statutory or agreed minimum wage, and there is strong emphasis on the primacy of collective bargaining in pay-setting. Minimum pay levels are set on an industry basis by collective agreements which are not only legally binding on signatory employers but can also be extended to apply to non-signatory parties. There are, therefore, a number of legally binding minima, varying according to industry and region. Minimum agreed pay in the *Länder* of the old East Germany has risen rapidly since unification in 1990. There has been full convergence in a small number of industries, but for the most part agreed minima in 1994 were running at 70–85 per cent of comparable western rates, with annual earnings trailing because agreed bonus payments tend to be lower in the east. Full convergence on agreed minima will take place in a number of major industries in 1995/96. Although originally agreed for April 1994, convergence in the engineering industry was delayed until 1 July 1996 after the employers' side took the rare step of withdrawing from the agreement on grounds of serious economic distress.

The courts have a theoretical right to raise pay rates if existing levels 'violate good morals'. This rarely happens. In addition, legislation on the statute book since 1952 gives the state reserve powers to set minimum working conditions. It has never been used. However, a recent court decision did rule that youth rates could not fall more than a certain percentage below adult rates.

The law on pay

The payment of salaries and wages is governed by the Civil Code (*Bürgerliches Gesetzbuch*), the Industrial Code (*Gewerbeordnung*), collective agreements, works agreements involving the participation of works councils, individual contracts of employment and company handbooks.

In establishments with a works council the employer must reach agreement or submit the question to a conciliation committee for a binding ruling on the following issues:

- The time of payment.
- The place of payment.
- The form of payment.
- Pay arrangements at the workplace, in terms of general principles, the introduction and application of new remuneration methods and any modification of existing methods.

Form of payment   Payment is generally calculated and denominated in monetary terms, although in some industries – such as merchant shipping and hotels – payment in kind is allowed (including accommodation or the provision of products made by the employer). Payment for industrial workers, technical white-collar employees and miners must be calculated in Deutschmarks and paid in cash. The employer is forbidden to sell goods to the employee on credit, unless these are common objects of use manufactured or distributed by the employer, and for which repayments do not exceed 10 per cent of the employee's net pay.

Cashless pay   may not be imposed unilaterally by the employer. Any such provision must be either in a collective agreement, often subject to works council veto, or by direct agreement with the works council. Most employees are in fact paid by credit transfer, and only an estimated 5 per cent are still paid in cash.

Form and frequency   Payment must be made after the performance of the service. Where payment is measured in discrete periods of time, payment should follow once that time has elapsed. That is, monthly payment takes place at the end of the current month. Most collective agreements provide for payment once a month in arrears, with the details subject to agreement with the works council. Many blue-collar workers are now paid a regular monthly wage (*Monatslohn*), with supplements for performance and with any overtime paid one month in arrears in addition to the agreed basic. (See pages 158–9.)

Deductions   Deductions from pay are permissible for income tax under the German PAYE system (*Lohnsteuer*), for church tax in the case of members of a religious denomination, and for social insurance contributions (pensions, health, unemployment benefit). Employers are liable to the tax authorities for employees' tax due. Collective agreements may sanction the deduction of employee contributions to pension, holiday or other benefit funds, as in the construction industry (where the provisions are generally extended beyond the signatory companies).

Attachment of earnings   Attachment of earnings requires an order to be issued by the local district court (*Amtsgericht*). However, certain components of pay may not be subject to an attachment order, or only to a limited degree: travel expenses, other reimbursed expenses for costs deemed necessary if the employee is to continue in employment, and half of any overtime remuneration. Employees must be guaranteed a minimum level of net pay sufficient for subsistence.

Pay statements   Employers in establishments with at least twenty employees must provide an itemised pay slip, and case law has ruled that all employees are entitled to a written pay statement. Other details may be governed by collective agreement.

Employer's insolvency   For any pay due for the three months prior to insolvency proceedings employees not only have the right to apply to the liquidator but also to claim reimbursement from the Federal Employment Institute (*Bundesanstalt für Arbeit*). This benefit, financed by employer contributions, makes up the difference between any wages paid and net pay outstanding, together with unpaid social insurance contributions. The sums are reclaimed from the company's assets. Any claims for payment of wages which are less than six months old have first priority among the bankrupt company's liabilities. Claims extending back between six months and a year are accorded lesser priority, and those over a year are classified as normal debtors. There are limits on the claims of employees under a 'social plan' in the event of redundancies.

Levels of pay determination

For the vast majority of employees minimum pay levels are set through the system of industry-level collective bargaining, mostly on a regional basis, which also determines allowances and premium pay. This system of collective bargaining, which embraces 80–90 per cent of the non-managerial work force, is complemented by a second tier of pay-setting at company level. In larger concerns this typically involves discussions and negotiations with elected employee works councils. In smaller organisations, unilateral management decisions may prevail. Where works councils have been elected they enjoy a statutory right of codetermination on a number of issues connected with pay, although their right to negotiate on basic pay or grading is circumscribed by industry collective agreements, which take legal precedence.

Although collective bargaining between trade unions and employers' associations or individual employers has legal primacy and establishes the context in which establishment-level bargaining takes place, both levels are integral to the overall mechanism of pay-setting and works councils. There is, in practice, a dual structure for the determination of contractual pay, with works councils exercising formal rights under the law, powers granted under collective agreements, and some bargaining strength depending on the level of unionisation and the state of the local job market. Collective agreements often require interpretation at plant level, enhancing the scope for works councils to engage in unofficial forms of pay negotiation. There is both wage and grade drift when labour markets are tight, evidenced in the accumulated differences between minimum and actual rates of pay (see below). The 1993/94 pay rounds saw a widespread effort by companies to rein in company-level pay and benefits, in part by cancelling existing arrangements but also by various devices to reduce the impact of increases in agreed minima, which must be paid, on actual company-level pay rates, which may be held constant.

Formal collective bargaining at company level is estimated to cover only 6 per cent of the work force. Volkswagen and the oil companies are the main examples of private-sector company bargaining. Major companies such as Ford, General

Motors (Opel), Siemens, BASF, Bayer and Hoechst are covered by their respective industry agreements.

There is no scope for plant-by-plant bargaining over minimum pay by employers locked into industry agreements, but minima may vary between plants in a multi-plant firm if the plants are in different collective bargaining regions of the industry. The relationship between agreed minimum industry rates and company pay varies by sector, company size, long-run performance and work-force organisation. In the engineering and chemical industries company pay can make up 25–30 per cent of the individual pay packet. In banking and commerce, company supplements add only an estimated 5–7 per cent to the industry minima.

According to a 1993 study of supplements to agreed minima carried out by the employers' research body the Institut der deutschen Wirtschaft, the average wage gap (the difference between agreed minimum and contractual pay) stood at 7.7 per cent for skilled manual workers, 10.7 per cent for administrative white-collar workers and 10.9 per cent for technicians. There was a marked correlation with company size, and substantial regional variations, were evident.

In practice, collective agreements apply to all employees in an industry who are employed by companies that belong to a signatory employers' organisation, irrespective of union membership. An employer may seek to avoid the terms of a collective agreement by leaving or not joining an employers' organisation. Few do so to pay below agreed rates. Companies outside the scope of collective agreements often pay above industry minima but may not wish to be bound by the agreed hours of work or they may simply have a 'non-union' policy. However, withdrawing from an employers' association does not mean that an employer is no longer bound by a collective agreement. Any collective agreement to which the employer was party continues in force until replaced by other agreed arrangements. IBM, for example, which withdrew from some collective agreements negotiated with the engineering workers' union IG Metall, concluded a company-level agreement with another (non-DGB affiliated) union, the independent white-collar union Deutsche Angestellten-Gewerkschaft.

An employee's terms and conditions of employment may diverge from collectively agreed provisions only if they are more favourable to the employee.

An industry agreement may be applied by official regulation to employers who are not members of signatory employers' associations and who have no company agreement with a trade union. In all, some 4.4 million employees are covered by agreements thus extended, although only about 700,000 of these are covered by wage provisions.

Employees outside collective bargaining

Collective agreements will usually cover all blue- and white-collar workers in an establishment, but with a number of exceptions. Young people under 18 may be subject to special provisions. Senior white-collar workers and executives may be subject to a company pay structure which builds on top of the collectively agreed structure, or is entirely individually determined. Collectively agreed pay scales extend some way up the managerial/specialist ladder in Germany, and frequently cover employees earning DM 80–90,000 (£32–36,000) per year.

Managers and specialists outside the scope of collective bargaining (known as *außertarifliche Angestellten* or 'AT' employees) are estimated to make up around 2 per cent of the work force in private industry, ranging from 3.5 per cent in chemicals to 1.7 per cent in engineering. There are several convergent statutory definitions of who is exempt from collectively agreed pay. The 1972 Works Constitution Act, amended on this issue in 1989, offers a definition of 'executive' for the purpose of elections to works councils. Collective agreements usually also contain a line of demarcation either by level of responsibility (or prospective responsibility in the case of management trainees) or by salary: for example, some agreements rule that employees are not counted as falling within the scope of an agreement if, on average, they earn more than a set percentage – typically 15–25 per cent – above the highest agreed grade. Definitions of responsibility are often ascertained at plant level through job evaluation, and exclusions agreed with works councils.

Pay for this group may be negotiated individually, although in larger concerns this is unlikely to be the case. In many companies pay scales for AT employees, often determined by job evaluation, are added on to the collectively agreed rates, albeit with a larger salary range and with the individual's position due to appraisal rather than seniority. The variable element of pay is also likely to begin to grow at this level. The grades may be set out in a formal agreement with works councils. There is some legal debate as to the entitlement of this group to regular pay reviews, and employer discretion in making differential awards. An employer may not treat employees differently without a material reason: a merit system would be justified, provided the objectives were clearly identifiable. In theory, however, a cost-of-living increase could not be awarded to one AT employee and denied to others.

Main payment systems

In manufacturing industry blue-collar workers are employed either on time rates or on one of two systems of payment by results:

• Piecework (*Akkord*), with the option of money- time- or straight output-based systems.
• A bonus system (*Prämienlohn*), in which earnings are tied to a variety of objectives, including output, savings on material or waste, quality, and use of equipment.

Bonus rates must usually be agreed locally, as most industry agreements contain only very general provisions. Piecework is still fairly widespread: some 60 per cent of employees in a union survey carried out in 1989 in the engineering industry, for example, were on piecework, 25 per cent on time rates and 9 per cent on bonus rates, with a residual 6 per cent who could not readily be classified.

In order to compensate for the lack of incentives for workers on time rates, collective agreements in manufacturing allow scope for a merit or performance allowance (*Leistungszulage*). The total sum available for distribution is usually defined as a percentage of the total agreed basic pay for all employees and ranges from 13 per cent to 16 per cent. It is distributed either to all employees equally – often where local unions are strong at workplace level – or as individual payments following a performance appraisal by supervisors: under some agreements there is an agreed analytical evaluation procedure.

White-collar workers are paid a regular monthly salary, and in some industries also receive an agreed merit allowance (typically 10 per cent of the relevant pay-bill is available for distribution).

Job evaluation and grading

Grading structures are typically agreed between the trade unions and employers' organisations at industry level. In a number of sectors, grading agreements set out the procedure to be followed in applying job evaluation methods, including detailed weightings for skill, knowledge, responsibility and factors in the work environment (dust, gases, noise, vibration, etc.). The choice of job evaluation technique is often devolved to workplace level. There are the beginnings of a move to 'skill-based pay', with negotiations currently in progress in the engineering industry in which both sides have agreed on the need to reflect skill acquisition and employee potential in the grading structure.

The allocation of jobs to grades at company level is usually a matter for the employer alone, unless the relevant collective agreement provides for a joint procedure. However, works councils have a right of co-determination in the grading, regrading and transfer of employees. In addition, several collective agreements provide for the setting up of joint grading commissions in the workplace with responsibility for implementing the industry structure at plant level, agreeing individual grades and resolving differences.

Employees have a right to object to their grading under collective agreements, under the Works Constitution Act or, if neither applies in the workplace, under civil law to the labour courts. Employees who alongside their normal duties do work which would normally be more highly paid are entitled to be put on a higher grade.

Some collective agreements place limits on the number of grades an employee may be moved downward, and also provide for retraining and earnings protection in the event of regrading.

Make-up of the pay package

Pay at company level will consist of the agreed minimum wage or salary, plus any agreed incentive element. A company may offer additional payments, through higher basic rates, bonuses or additional merit pay. As well as regular monthly/weekly pay, employees' annual earnings are boosted by the payment of a 'thirteenth month's' salary, which usually consists of an agreed end-of-year or Christmas bonus and a bonus paid when the employee goes on holiday. It may or may not add up to exactly one month's pay (see below). The relationship between agreed minima and actual pay varies according to sector, as noted above.

When applying a binding increase in minimum agreed rates companies may, under certain specific circumstances, impose a total or partial freeze on their employees' overall contractual pay by squeezing the gap between agreed minima and company-level pay. There were numerous instances in the 1993/94 pay round, giving rise to a period of 'negative wage drift' in which agreed industry minima rose faster than company pay.

Service increments   Service increments are common for white-collar employees under many collective agreements. Companies may also build a structure of pay progression on top of any agreed rates, with extra increments for each grade or faster movement through the structure.

Child and social allowances   In some industries and regions, employees receive extra pay if they have children or are married. The sums are usually fairly small, ranging from DM 25 (£10) per month for one child for which the employee has responsibility to DM 40–50 (£16.50–£20) for two or more children, paid until the child's eighteenth birthday, up to age 25 if the dependent child is still at school or in vocational training, and indefinitely if the child is physically or mentally disabled. Sectors which pay such supplements include banking, insurance, in some regions the textile, chemical and engineering industries (white-collar only), and the utilities.

Regional pay differences   Agreed allowances for higher local living costs are virtually unknown. In the private sector the dominant system of regional collective bargaining allows some adjustment of pay levels to local labour market or cost conditions, but this is reflected in regional differences in agreed minima rather than in a separate and identifiable cost-of-living addition. Companies usually also negotiate locally on bonuses or offer additional premium pay, and this is reflected in higher earnings in high-cost regions or cities, with marked variation in accumulated wage drift between regions. Employers with a national pay structure, as in banking, can also grade employees more generously in regions affected by labour market or cost pressures, or, in the final analysis, offer individual higher salaries.

Official statistics on pay, which give a breakdown by *Land*, allow some comparisons between regions. However, they can be misleading. For example, the city of Hamburg is both a large city with a concentration of high-paying industries and a constituent *Land* of the Federal Republic: its pay levels appear to be consistently higher than those of other *Länder*. In contrast, there are no separate pay figures for high-cost cities such as Munich or Frankfurt which are located in *Länder* with a rural hinterland. Average earnings for blue-collar workers in Hamburg are around 10 per cent higher and blue-collar earnings in Bavaria 8 per cent lower than the national average. Average earnings in the *Länder* of the old East Germany stood at about 70 per cent of earnings in western Germany in 1993, with rapid convergence on both basic pay and earnings since unification.

Managerial pay appears to vary by region more than blue- or white-collar pay. However, differences in disposable income are more heavily influenced by large regional variations in the level of rents.

Bonuses

Agreed annual bonuses The so-called 'thirteenth month' received by most employees is usually made up of two components: a holiday bonus and an end-of-year or Christmas bonus. In most cases the bonuses are regulated by collective agreement but frequently topped up at company level with extra amounts sometimes related to company performance. Because collective agreements are legally binding, companies must pay the agreed amounts. However, as evidenced during the 1992–94 recession, many organisations used the legal scope for varying company-level supplements to renegotiate, or impose, changes in bonuses.

Holiday bonus In 1993, 94 per cent of employees covered by collective bargaining in west Germany and 72 per cent in east Germany received additional holiday pay (*Urlaubsgeld*), according to a Labour Ministry review of agreements. This can take the form of a percentage of basic holiday pay, a lump sum or a fixed daily rate. Typically, expressed as a lump sum, the bonus was worth DM 945 (£378) in the west and DM 634 (£254) in the east.

End-of-year bonus Nearly all employees covered by collective agreements receive a Christmas or end-of-year bonus which may be calculated as a fixed lump sum, as a percentage of the agreed monthly minimum or as a percentage of earnings. The level may vary according to seniority and may also be topped up at company level. In some companies it may be tied to a performance indicator. For example, following a review of company-level pay and benefits in 1993, Opel, the German subsidiary of General Motors, decided to link the supplement which it paid on top of the agreed bonus to a reduction in the absence rate.

Overtime, night work and shift pay In practice, premium rates for overtime, night work, shift and weekend work are regulated by collective agreement. Typical provisions in the engineering industry, for example, require the first ten hours of overtime in one week to be at an extra 25 per cent of the hourly rate, with additional overtime attracting a supplement of 50 per cent of the hourly rate.

A number of collective agreements include provision for overtime to be compensated for by time off, but with the overtime premium element paid as cash.

Shift premiums are laid down by collective agreement, and vary considerably according to the type of shift working, the duty roster of the employee (for example, permanent early shift working or rotating shifts) and when the shift is worked (night time, weekends and public holidays attract higher premiums). The engineering agreement for North Württemberg/North Baden provides for a supplement of 20 per cent for each hour worked between 12.00 and 19.00 provided that regular hours of work begin after 12.00 and finish after 19.00. Night work between 19.00 and 06.00 attracts a supplement of 30 per cent. In the chemical industry manual workers are paid a 15 per cent supplement for night work, with additional supplements for weekend work. In addition, workers on fully continuous processes receive a supplement of 10 per cent of their basic pay; workers on semi-continuous operations get an extra 6 per cent.

Work on Sundays and holidays is also governed by collective agreement. In the chemical industry employees get a 60 per cent supplement for work on Sundays, and 150 per cent for work on major public holidays.

The premium element of pay for night work and work on Sundays and public holidays does not count as taxable income, provided the supplement is granted under a law or a collective agreement, and does not exceed 25 per cent for nights, 50 per cent for work on Sundays, 125–50 per cent for work on public holidays (depending on which holiday).

Merit pay

Companies may develop systems of merit pay as a means of adding to agreed minima, for employees covered by collective agreement, or of regulating pay increases – in addition to cost-of-living payments – for employees outside the scope of collective bargaining (see above). In addition, a number of collective agreements include systems of merit or performance allowances, with performance appraisal, for both blue- and white-collar employees. In the engineering industry, for example, 16 per cent of the pay bill is set aside for such payments. Implementation at workplace level varies. In some companies, employees will get differing sums, depending on appraisal by a supervisor. In others, particularly where there is greater workplace union strength, all employees may end up getting the same amount, with no effective appraisal.

In a survey of variable remuneration carried out on behalf of the German Personnel Management Association (DGFP) in September 1992 variable remuneration was found to be effectively confined to the top three levels of management on a possible seven-scale hierarchy (see also 'Management pay', below).

Management pay

Collective agreements often provide for minimum salaries, or more typically salary ranges, for senior white-collar workers, technical specialists and middle management (such as those heading a sub-department), even on salaries up to DM 6,500–7,000 per month or DM 91,000 a year (£36,400). As with other employees, a thirteenth month's salary is almost universal. Company-level supplements, possibly awarded on an individual merit basis, could add a further 15 per cent to these minima. Above this level, pay will either be located on a company scale – sometimes built on top of an industry scale – or entirely set individually.

The past decade or so has seen a greater emphasis on the variable element of senior and top management remuneration, and over 90 per cent of senior and middle management are now eligible for cash bonuses. In European comparison, the proportion of pay at risk is about average – although the survey evidence is not entirely consistent. According to the Monks Partnership survey *Incentives and Benefits in Europe*, some 50 per cent of top managers had a cash bonus worth 20 per cent or more of their base pay. The most common measures at this level of management were spread between profit and job-related systems. The incidence of variable pay may have been encouraged by the recession, in which base pay increases were either below or at inflation.

Regional pay differences are not marked within west Germany, despite the high cost of living in cities such as Munich and Frankfurt. Managerial pay in east Germany is steadily converging with that in the west, and is currently hovering around 50–70 per cent of western levels, in line with the increase in productivity of those enterprises which survived the dramatic shake-out following unification. Companies seeking to recruit western managers still typically have to pay a premium, in view of the perceived lower quality of life in many eastern urban centres.

Executive share options are not a highly developed form of benefit, and are mostly confined to the upper tiers of management. International companies may offer shares in the parent company as part of internationally operating benefit schemes. Under German tax law, exercising an option is deemed to be a taxable event, with the gain to the employee treated as normal compensation. Neither the structure of the equity market nor the tax regime is especially favourable to this form of financial participation.

The main management benefit, in terms of cost to the employer, is the company pension scheme, which makes up for the shortfall of post-retirement income above the maximum pension paid out under the state system. These are available to all employees in the bulk of medium-sized and large companies, but often only to senior staff in smaller concerns (see also 'Retirement' below). Most company schemes aim to replace 10–20 per cent of income up to the statutory assessment limit, and 40–60 per cent above that – which applies to most executives. Although the statutory vesting period of 10 years is long, companies negotiating with an incoming senior manager may agree to add in extra years to ensure continuity of cover. Following the recession, and combined with extensive reviews of employee benefits carried out in 1993/94, employers have been looking more closely at pensions. In contrast to the UK, few pensions are provided via a fund; instead, they are often financed from book reserves, with pension guarantee insurance to protect payments in the event of insolvency.

Cars have become a standard benefit for top and senior management, and German managers in general have one of the highest levels of provision in Europe: 90–95 per cent of top managers and 70–80 per cent of senior managers are eligible. Cars are most commonly taxed to the employee at 1 per cent per month of their list price, plus a cash value on their use for commuting based on distance. Employees also receive a tax allowance intended to reflect commuting costs.

Employees with an income above DM 68,400 (£27,360) in west Germany (or somewhat lower in east Germany) may opt to leave the state system of health insurance and take out a private policy for which employers usually pay half the contributions.

Financial participation: profit-sharing and equity-sharing

There are a number of schemes under which employees can acquire a capital stake in their employer's firm, or enjoy tax-advantageous saving. The Capital Participation Act of 31 December 1986, as amended from 1 January 1994, includes two concessions designed to encourage employee saving and share ownership:

- Provisions under which regular payments from employers may be used on a tax-favourable basis for savings or to acquire other assets, known as 'Capital formation' (*Vermögensbildung*).
- Preferential tax treatment for the acquisition by employees of various forms of interest (equities or debentures) in companies.

Capital formation schemes   Under capital formation schemes, governed by a statute generally known as the 'DM 936' law, employers make regular (usually monthly) payments to employees for savings or investment, typically under terms collectively agreed. Such benefits are treated favourably for tax purposes. The contributions must be used to acquire a specified range of assets, such as quoted equities, shares in the employer's own company, debentures and convertible debentures. The law was amended as from 1 January 1994 to exclude certain types of assets which the authorities decided were too risky or potentially disadvantageous for employees. Employees may also use the payments for a savings account, for buying a house or an ordinary savings account. In addition to the employer payment, the government adds a 'savings premium' (*Arbeitnehmer-Sparzulage*) of 10 per cent. Although employer payments count as taxable income for the employee, the 'savings premium' does not, and nor does it attract social security contributions. Under normal circumstances, the assets or savings may not be touched for at least six years.

The maximum payment which can qualify for beneficial tax treatment is DM 936 (£375) per year, equivalent to DM 78 (£31) per month. This amount may be contributed wholly by the employer, wholly by the employee, or partly by each. Nearly 95 per cent of employees were entitled to a collectively agreed capital formation payment from their employer in 1993, with an average payment of DM 535 (£214) a year in western Germany, and of DM 204 (£82) in eastern Germany, where schemes are still in the relatively early stages.

To qualify, the employee must:

- Be covered by a collective, company or individual agreement with the employer providing for payment of the premium.
- Save the required amount.
- Have a taxable income below a certain threshold. This is currently DM 27,000 (£10,800) for a single person and DM 54,000 (£21,600) for a married couple assessed jointly. ('Taxable income' in Germany is about 20 percent below 'gross income' in the United Kingdom.)

Share grants   Under section 19(a) of the Income Tax Act, tax concessions are available where employers offer shares, debentures or profit certificates to employees at a concessionary price. As noted above, the employee may also use funds accumulated under the capital formation legislation to acquire shares, with preferential tax treatment. In order to gain the tax benefit the employee must retain the shares for at least six years and the value of the concession must not exceed half the value of the shares, with a maximum of DM 300 (£120) per year. Companies may deduct the concessionary element of the share award from taxable profits and are exempt from social security contributions on the concessionary element.

Main benefits: cars, insurance, health care   The main benefits for non-managerial employees, in terms of average cost to the employer, are company pensions (which cover around 50–60 per cent of the workforce) and profit-sharing bonuses. Subsidised canteens and health and safety measures are the next most significant. Although many other individual benefits are in themselves fairly cheap, the range is large and cumulatively expensive. Such cash and non-cash extras include anniversary payments, rest cures, employee suggestion schemes, removal expenses, clothing allowances, travel to work subsidies and housing subsidies.

Equal pay and equal opportunities

Legal framework and practice

Under the 1949 Basic Law, the federal constitution, no one may be disadvantaged on the grounds of their sex, origin, race, language, home, creed or religious and political beliefs. As noted above, similar provisions apply through the Works Constitution Act, under which appointments require works council agreement.

Article 3 (2) of the Basic Law states that 'Men and women shall have equal rights'. Germany has also ratified ILO Conventions 100 and 111, which provide for equal pay and equal treatment at work. Under the 1980 European Community Adjustment Act, the Federal German Civil Code was amended to incorporate EC directives on equal treatment. Article 611a of the Civil Code forbids discrimination against an employee in the sphere of appointments, promotion or dismissal, except where the gender of the prospective employee is directly relevant to the activity in question. The burden of proof rests with the employer. Article 611b of the Civil Code requires employers to refrain from issuing job descriptions or job advertisements which specify a particular gender, unless this is an indispensable prerequisite.

Before 1984, German courts paid only actual damages to an individual denied a job on grounds of their sex, typically the immediate expenses incurred during the application. Following a European Court ruling in 1984, national courts had to ensure that any such award constituted an effective deterrent to employers. Many German courts interpreted this by awarding six months' pay in the prospective post. However, in the absence of a statute, uncertainties continued, and some courts went on paying lesser amounts. The 1994 Equal Treatment Act, in force from 1 September 1994, limits awards in such situations to three months' salary, or 12 months in all if many applicants are involved.

Extensive case-law on indirect sex discrimination affects the terms and conditions of part-time employees (see below).

Sexual harassment

Sexual harassment has been dealt with in Germany under a variety of legal provisions. In the first instance, acts of sexual harassment potentially fall under a number of criminal charges, including rape, 'sexual coercion' and insults of a sexual character – which may be an insult to the person via an unwanted action of a sexual character. In contract and employment law, as embodied in the Civil Code, employers have a duty of care, which has been interpreted as requiring them to take appropriate measures to protect employees from sexual harassment. The Civil Code also provides for an individual to seek damages if their life, body, health, freedom, property or 'any other right' is unlawfully damaged by another person: this clause has frequently been used to obtain damages in rape cases. In practice, most cases of proven sexual harassment have been dealt with by the criminal courts, with only a handful of cases – mostly concerning dismissal – coming before the labour courts.

In 1994 a new single statute dealing with sexual harassment was introduced. The 1994 Employee Protection Act (*Beschäftigtenschutzgesetz*) brings together existing employment law provisions on sexual harassment into a single framework and offers a statutory definition, most aspects of which are already subject to criminal penalties. Under the employer's duty of care, they must protect employees from sexual harassment, and take preventive action if needed. Employees have a right to refuse to work – with no loss of pay – should the employer fail to protect them or respond to a complaint. Although not really adding to existing law in the field, the formulation of a single statute is expected to raise awareness of the issue.

Retirement

State pensions

The normal retirement age in Germany is 65 for both men and women, although reaching this age does not automatically terminate employment. Entitlement to a state pension (*Regelaltersrente*) begins at age 65, provided the individual has a minimum qualifying period of five years. This five-year period does not have to consist of years of employment but may include periods in which contributions are deemed to have been made, such as during unemployment, and up to three years' child care. There is no limit on additional earnings, except for those taking early retirement.

The state pension usually yields some 40–5 per cent of final earnings, subject to the assessment ceiling.

Company pension schemes

Company pension plans pay between 10 per cent and 20 per cent of pay to those wholly covered by the state system and between 40 per cent and 60 per cent of pay beyond that level (relevant for high earners). This brings the total amount of pension for employees covered by such schemes to between 60 per cent and 70 per cent of final gross earnings. Around 40 per cent of employees belong to company schemes, which have a coverage of 66 per cent in industry and 28 per cent in commerce, according to a 1993 survey of company pension provision by the Munich-based research institute ifo. The incidence of company pensions appears to have been static for several years, and may be declining.

Just over half of company pensions are financed direct via book reserves, with supplementary insurance against insolvency. Such reserves are compulsory for any pension commitment made after 1 January 1987, unless the pension is backed by direct insurance, a support fund or a private pension fund. The choice of financing arrangement lies with the employer. There is a statutory vesting period of ten years.

The majority of schemes are non-contributory for employees and cost, on average, about 7.5–8 per cent of salary. By law, company pensions must be reviewed every three years.

Separate provision is usually made for senior executives (*leitende Angestellten*) who are covered by special employment contracts and who may be able to negotiate some relaxation of statutory vesting regulations when moving from one company to another.

Early retirement

There are a number of early retirement options under the state scheme, many of which will be curtailed over the next fifteen years as the general retirement age is harmonised at 65 for all under the 1992 Pension Reform Act. For example, the long-term insured may retire at 63 provided they have been insured for thirty-five years, with limits on additional earnings up to the age of 65. From 2001 the minimum age for claiming this pension will be raised in steps until the provision is ended by 2005. Women with sufficient contributions may retire at 60. This concession will be removed in stages by 2012.

Unemployed men may retire at 60 provided they have been insured for at least fifteen years, have paid pension contributions for at least eight of the previous ten years, and have been unemployed for twelve of the previous eighteen months. This concession will also be removed in stages by 2012. The provision under which employees with a disability may retire at 60, provided they have been insured for thirty-five years, will continue, although with limits on additional earnings up to the age of 65.

From 2001 early retirement of up to three years before the specified age limit will be possible on a reduced pension, with the entitlement cut by 0.3 per cent per month (3.6 per cent for each year) of earlier retirement. From 1992, should an employee opt for a delayed pension, entitlement is increased by 6 per cent for each year. Company schemes, which top up the state scheme, may make supplementary provision for early retirement.

The early retirement option for unemployed men is used particularly often, as it enables companies to terminate employment and then allows the employee to move into retirement. In some cases, companies will top up normal unemployment benefit (see below), paid at 60–67 per cent of previous earnings, depending on family circumstances, to 80–90 per cent of previous earnings. However, as a deterrent to firms using this is as a form of early retirement, employers must repay unemployment benefit to the labour authorities under certain circumstances.

Individual termination of contract

Termination procedures can be complex and may require a good deal of time because of the consultation requirements, protective legislation and practical and legal complications with periods of notice. It has been estimated that up to one-third of attempted terminations breach some statutory or agreed provision.

Dismissal on non-economic grounds

Depending on the reasons which prompt the dismissal, a contract of employment may be terminated either by 'ordinary dismissal' with notice or by summary dismissal. Dismissal must be warranted by factors related to the employee's character or conduct, or by 'urgent operational reasons' (see below, 'Economic dismissal'). In general, the longer the individual's employment the more serious the reasons warranting dismissal need to be. Personal factors might include:

- *Basic unsuitability* and inability to acquire requisite skills.
- *Illness*, if persistent, frequent and unlikely to be cured. The employer must show that continuing employment would place an unreasonable economic burden on the establishment and that the balance of interest lies with the employer. Some companies may offer voluntary severance to chronically or repeatedly ill employees to avoid the possibility of being taken to court.
- *Age*. Reaching 65 – the normal age of retirement – is not itself grounds for termination. Under the 1992 Pension Reform Act employees have a choice of when to retire and may continue to work beyond 65. Contracts of employment should, therefore, specify that employment will end at 65 if that is the intention. A number of collective agreements also protect employees above a certain age (usually 50 or 55) from ordinary dismissal.

Employee conduct which might be considered grounds for ordinary termination includes: refusal to carry out duties, unexcused absence, taking leave without permission, unpunctuality, breaking company rules on the consumption of alcohol or smoking, fighting, threats and insults. Breaches of broader contractual obligations may also be cited. Dismissal is permissible on grounds of poor performance, inadequate exercise of management skills or failure to meet agreed targets.

Where employees' conduct or performance may provide grounds for termination, the employer must ensure that they have been given adequate written warning and opportunities for the problem to be remedied. Employees have the right to add their version of events to their file, to demand the removal of any inaccurate material, and to have warnings removed after a reasonable period.

Summary dismissal   An employer or employee may terminate employment without notice for 'an important reason', that is, a breach of contract sufficiently serious to make continuation of employment unreasonable for the party seeking to withdraw. Summary dismissal must take place within two weeks of the relevant incident.

Notification requirements for dismissal on non-economic grounds   Works councils must be notified and given the reasons for all dismissals before notice can be issued. Any notice of dismissal issued without consulting the works council is null and void. Works councils have a week in which to respond in the case of dismissal with notice and three days in the case of summary dismissal, either of which deadlines may be extended by mutual agreement. Works councils can respond in one of three ways:

- Agree to the dismissal.
- Object within the time limits set out above.
- In the case of ordinary dismissal only, usually in the event of redundancy, object on the grounds that the dismissal breaches agreed guidelines or has not taken account of factors which might allow continuing employment.

Works councils' objections do not stop the employer from issuing notice. However, if the works council objects to an ordinary dismissal and the employee has initiated proceedings in a labour court within three weeks of the notice, then the employer must continue to employ that person if the employee requests it until final legal settlement of the case (see below, 'Unfair dismissal').

Dismissal on economic grounds (individual redundancy)

Dismissal on the grounds of 'urgent operating reasons' would include factors outside the control of the establishment (such as a fall in orders) or a proposed change in the establishment's work organisation (rationalisation, closure of all or parts of an establishment) which mean that employment cannot be sustained at its existing level. Employers are free to adopt such measures provided they are not unreasonable or arbitrary. Dismissal should constitute a measure of last resort: employers must consider whether redundancy could be avoided by short-time working, reducing overtime, internal transfers, or other measures (most of which require consultation with the works council at some stage). Under some collective agreements concluded in 1994, notably in the engineering industry, employers may be required to examine the option of a general cut in hours, possibly accompanied by the demand from works councils for an agreement banning compulsory redundancies for a period.

Employers must ensure that employees dismissed are those least affected 'socially'. Factors to be taken into account include: length of service, age, family status, number and incomes of dependants, health, occupational disability, membership of a protected group (see below), and prospects in the labour market. Works councils and employers may agree a set of criteria and/or a points system for selection. Employee performance, in general, may not play a role in selection for redundancy. The employer must select from all employees doing 'comparable work' in the establishment as a whole. Employers can plead against using 'social criteria' where 'operational, economic or other legitimate requirements' justify it.

Employees may not be dismissed if there is a possibility of continued employment either after retraining or under changed conditions of employment. An employee offered such an alternative may object that the change is not 'socially warranted' and can resort to law. Should the court find in the employee's favour the employee must be reinstated on their original terms, with compensation for any loss.

Notification and consultation procedures depend on the number of proposed redundancies and the size of the establishment. Works councils must be notified according to the procedure set out for dismissal on non-economic grounds irrespective of the number of redundancies. Again, as before, the works council can express reservations about the proposed dismissal, agree to it (implicitly by not responding to the proposal within the required period) or object to it.

The works council can object to an individual dismissal on the grounds that:

- The employer has not observed social criteria or has breached an agreed selection guideline. (In workplaces with more than 1,000 employees works councils can demand the setting of 'selection criteria' to be applied in the case of appointments, transfers and dismissals. In smaller establishments any criteria proposed by the employer require the approval of the works council.)
- The employee can be employed elsewhere in the company, if necessary after a reasonable period of training or retraining.
- The employee could continue in employment under changed contractual conditions to which the employee had agreed.

There is no statutory duty to pay redundancy compensation in the event of an individual termination, but collective agreements may provide for compensation payments which would be payable in individual instances (see below).

Terminating executive employment

The most common form of termination for executives is mutual agreement. Most managers fall under the scope of general dismissal protection legislation but with a number of important limitations. Firstly, registered managers with powers to represent the company in legal terms are not covered by the 1969 Protection against Dismissal Act. Secondly, executives, heads of department and 'similar senior white-collar employees' who are empowered to hire and dismiss employees have no right of recourse to the works council. In addition, an executive who is unfairly dismissed has no right to reinstatement.

Although executives are not covered by the 1972 Works Constitution Act, works councils must still be informed of any managerial dismissals. Moreover, where an Executive Representation Committee' has been elected under legislation passed in 1988, the committee must be consulted. Failure to do so will render termination null and void. The employer must also report to the committee any proposed changes to the running of the business which might have disadvantageous consequences for executives, and discuss ways of compensating for or mitigating such disadvantages.

Registered managers with board-level responsibilities (*Geschäftsführer*) are frequently employed on fixed-term contracts, during which termination is possible only for an 'important reason' warranting immediate dismissal. The length of contract may vary, but typically will be at least a year initially and probably three, with renewal up to five years. Severance compensation in the event of a cessation of employment before the due date, typically by mutual agreement, will be negotiable according to how long the contract had still to run. Severance terms may be agreed in the event of non-renewal, with a typical minimum of a month's pay for each year of service.

Periods of notice

Periods of notice for blue- and white-collar employees were equalised by law in 1993. Under the new law all employees have a minimum statutory notice period of four weeks, either to the fifteenth or to the end of a calendar month. The same statutory notice also applies in the case of termination by the employee. Where notice is given by the employer, the minimum period increases with length of service, with notice running only to the end of the month (Table 1). Any agreed period of notice above the minimum for the employee may not exceed that for the employer. In all cases, only service completed after the employee's twenty-fifth birthday is counted towards eligibility for a longer period of notice.

Table 1   Minimum notice to be given by employer

Years of service	Length of notice (months) to the end of a calendar month
2	1
5	2
8	3
10	4
12	5
15	6
20	7

During an agreed probationary period, which may not exceed six months, notice of two weeks can be given by either party.

For many employees length of notice is governed in reality by binding collective agreement. The law allows collective agreements to stipulate longer or shorter periods of notice than those laid down by statute. But these must now either offer equal periods of notice to white-collar and blue-collar employees or give a material reason for any differential treatment. However, if an agreement merely repeats the wording of the old law, or states that 'the statutory provisions shall apply', then the new law supervenes. If individually agreed periods of notice are less generous than the new law, they will be superseded: in contrast to collective agreements, individual contracts cannot reduce statutory provisions. If they offer longer periods of notice the old provisions may continue in force. In some cases this may require notice to run to the end of a calendar quarter, as under previous statute law.

Shorter minimum periods of notice may be agreed under an individual employment contract in two circumstances:

- Where an employee is engaged as temporary help for less than three months.
- Where the employer has fewer than twenty employees, excluding trainees, working at least ten hours a week, provided a minimum of four weeks is adhered to.

Termination by mutual agreement

Termination by mutual agreement, with the payment of a sum in compensation, is a common way of ending the employment relationship, especially for senior staff. It offers the employee tax advantages and figures large in voluntary redundancy arrangements. Mutually agreed termination releases the employer from any obligations under the contract of employment and obviates the threat of legal challenge. In addition, severance payments are free of statutory social insurance charges.

An agreement to terminate (*Aufhebungsvertrag*) will normally specify when the employment will cease and the reason. The employee must agree to:

- Allow employment to end before the expiry of notice.
- Provisions on the level of compensation to be paid and any other financial elements reflecting loss of benefits.
- A provision for time off to find another post.
- Any restrictive covenants where appropriate.
- A 'settlement clause' stating that the employee discharges the employer from all obligations under the contract of employment, with the employee relinquishing the right to take legal action over the dismissal.

Individual severance payments

There is no statutory severance payment for a fair individual dismissal. However, in the event of collective redundancies, works councils may have an enforceable right to negotiate a 'social compensation plan' (*Sozialplan*) which includes severance compensation (see below, 'Collective dismissal').

Levels of individual severance compensation paid voluntarily by firms – or as part of a termination by mutual agreement – vary widely. Under the Protection against Dismissal Act (sections 9–10) the courts can award compensation of up to one year's pay, with higher amounts for older employees, in the event of unfair dismissal (see also below) and these awards often serve as a general guideline for ordinary severance compensation. According to a study by Wyatt Data Services (*Wirtschaftswoche*, 23 July 1993), the average amount of severance compensation for a manager ranged from ten times monthly salary for someone aged 40 with five years' service to fifteen times monthly salary for a 50 year old manager with ten years' service, and up to twenty-one times monthly salary where the employee had accumulated twenty years of service.

Top managers will not receive a severance payment as such but rather will be paid to the end of their fixed-term contract.

Many collective agreements also offer earnings guarantees and redundancy protection for older employees, as well as compensatory payments for employees who are transferred or who lose their job.

Severance payments up to certain limits are entirely free of income tax. The limits are:

- DM 24,000 (£9,600) for all employees.
- DM 30,000 (£12,000) for employees aged at least 50 with a minimum of fifteen years.
- DM 36,000 (£14,400) for employees aged at least 55 with twenty years' service.

Severance payments are taxable above these limits, but the rate due can be halved on individual application to the tax authorities.

Unemployment benefit may be partially reduced by a proportion of the severance payment. In some circumstances, employers may be liable to repay the cost of unemployment benefit where they use early retirement as a way of reducing work-force numbers.

Protected employees

Some types of employee enjoy special protection against ordinary and, under certain circumstances, summary dismissal. The categories are:

- Conscripts (protected against ordinary but not summary dismissal).
- Pregnant women and nursing mothers (protected against both ordinary and summary dismissal during pregnancy, provided the employer is informed of the pregnancy or is so within two weeks of notice being given, and for four months after confinement).
- Parents on parental leave. (The right can be withdrawn with the permission of the *Land* labour office under exceptional circumstances such as the closure or relocation of the establishment.)
- Employees with a disability. (Either ordinary or summary dismissal of a disabled employee requires prior notification in writing to the Central Disabled Workers' Office.)
- Apprentices/trainees (summary dismissal only).

- Members of works councils (protected against ordinary dismissal during their period of office and for one year after leaving office, although summary dismissal is possible with works council permission).
- Candidates for works council office are also protected against ordinary dismissal from the date of their nomination until six months after the results of the election have been declared.
- 'Older employees', usually over 53/55, with a minimum length of service are protected from all but summary dismissal under several collective agreements.

Unfair dismissal

Employees are protected from 'socially unwarranted' dismissal under the 1969 Protection against Dismissal Act. This applies only:

- In establishments employing six or more employees, excluding trainees.
- To employees with at least six months' service.

Dismissal will be unwarranted if:

- It is unconnected with the character or conduct of the employee.
- It contravenes a guideline laid down in the Works Constitution Act.
- The employee could be offered alternative employment under different conditions.
- The works council has objected.

In addition, dismissal will be socially unwarranted in cases of redundancy if the selection of candidates has failed to take due account of social factors (see above).

Employees seeking to contest notice of dismissal must notify their works council within a week. If the works council decides to back the employee it must first attempt to resolve the differences between employer and employee. If no resolution is achieved, the employee may appeal to the local labour court for a ruling. Before a case can proceed to a full hearing, an attempt must be made at an amicable resolution.

Employees have a right to continued employment – that is, actual work at the workplace – where the works council objected to an ordinary dismissal within the prescribed period and the employee has initiated proceedings before a labour court. The right extends to the point at which a final legal decision is handed down. The employer can be released from this obligation if the action brought by the employee is unlikely to succeed or appears abusive or if continuing the employment relation would impose an unreasonable burden. Between the expiry of notice and the first-instance hearing the balance of 'justified interest' lies with the employer. The employer does not have to provide employment in this period unless the conditions outlined above are met. However, should the labour court of first instance rule in favour of the employee, and should the employer appeal, then the balance of justified interest is held to move to the employee. The employee must be offered actual work between the first- and second-instance hearings.

Reinstatement and compensation

If a labour court upholds an employee's appeal, and the employer takes no further steps to seek to have the decision reversed, the employee has a right to reinstatement with full pay for the period between the expiry of notice and the date of reinstatement. Reinstatement is rare, however. Employers may apply to the courts to terminate employment in return for a compensation payment to the employee if they can argue that continued co-operation is impossible. In the case of managers and executives, the employer can refuse reinstatement without stating reasons. The maximum sum payable in compensation is twelve months' pay, increased to fifteen times monthly pay for employees aged 50 with at least fifteen years' service, and up to eighteen times monthly pay for employees aged 55 and over with at least twenty years' service.

Collective dismissal

Employers must notify the local employment authorities if they envisage any changes in the running of the business which might lead to collective redundancies within the coming twelve months, adding any views expressed by the works council. In establishments with more than twenty employees the employer must inform the works council of any major changes which may be to the disadvantage of the work force. Any dismissals which would count as collective (see below) must be notified to the works council. Employers and works councils are required to examine ways in which redundancies might be avoided or reduced and their consequences mitigated. Collective redundancy is defined as the dismissal on economic grounds within thirty calendar days of:

- More than five employees in an establishment employing more than twenty but fewer than sixty employees.
- More than twenty-five employees or 10 per cent of those regularly employed in establishments with at least sixty and fewer than 500 employees.
- At least thirty employees in an establishment employing more than 500 employees.

Following notification of the works council, the employer must notify the authorities of details of the business and the proposed dismissals. There is a normal minimum of one month between the submission of the notification and the date from which dismissals can be effective. Although dismissals do not need official authorisation, failure to notify will render any notice of dismissal invalid.

Provision for redundancy compensation is customarily made via a social compensation plan (*Sozialplan*) agreed between the employer and the works council. If the employer and works council cannot agree, either party may apply to the authorities for mediation, and ultimately the matter may be settled by binding arbitration. Works councils cannot enforce agreement on a social plan by resort to arbitration in any enterprise in the first four years after its establishment.

Social plans can make provision in a variety of areas, including severance payments, out-placement, time off and fares for finding a new job, and in cases of hardship. Payments are exempt from income tax, subject to the limits set out above.

Final formalities

If the dismissal is not contested, on the expiry of the legal or contractual period of notice the employer is required to give the employee all the documents relevant to the employment, completed and up-to-date: that is, tax documents, social security record, a final pay statement, and holiday records. The employee may also ask the employer to provide a written statement of the nature and length of the employment, including details of the employee's conduct and performance. Employers must notify the appropriate sickness insurance fund (*Krankenkasse*) within six weeks of the end of employment that they are no longer liable for the employee's contributions.

Transfer of undertakings

The transfer of ownership of undertakings is regulated by Section 613(a) of the Civil Code, intended to give effect to EU Directive 77/187 on acquired rights. Workforce consultation is not provided for in the Civil Code. However, the Works Constitution Act 1972 (Section 111) already requires works councils in establishments with more than 20 employees to be informed of any changes with possible disadvantageous consequences for the workforce. Section 106 of the same Act (which applies in undertakings with more than 100 employees) provides for extensive information to be provided on any plans which might impinge on the interests of the workforce.

The German Basic Law also provides for the individual employee to exercise a right of objection to the new employer, and to choose to continue to be employed by their former employer – albeit at risk of redundancy. In order for this right to be realised, the transferor is obliged, and specifically in the absence of a works council, to inform employees of the proposed change, in line with the consultation requirements of Article 6 of the EU Directive.

No regulations have been issued to clarify how the EU law and German law are to be put into effect, and this has caused problems in the interpretation of the provisions. Specifically, the law requires that:

- In the event of a transfer, the transferor assumes the rights and obligations arising out of the employment relationships existing at the time of the transfer. If these rights and obligations are regulated by a collective or works agreement, then these provisions become part of employees' individual contracts of employment and may not be altered to the disadvantage of the employees until a year has elapsed. This does not apply, however, if the rights and norms of employees at the new employer are regulated by a different collective agreement or works agreement.
- The transfer may not be used in itself as grounds for termination (even for employees who would otherwise not be covered by dismissals protection legislation, such as those in small firms or with less than six months' service). However, termination on other grounds, such as genuine redundancy, is not precluded. There is a substantial body of case law determining where the transfer itself provides the principal motive for dismissal, and identifying instances in which employers have sought to circumvent the law.

Appendix

Non-wage labour costs and income tax

Statutory social insurance contributions typically amount to around 21 per cent for the employer, with a further 15–20 per cent for company pensions, statutory sick pay and other customary or agreed benefits. Employees pay about 19 per cent, excluding contributions to company pensions. From 1 January 1995, employers and employees will each pay an additional 0.5 per cent to finance the new system of care insurance.

Taxable income is arrived at after deducting from gross annual income i) personal and basic allowances, and any non-taxable income (such as severance payments, employee discounts), ii) employment-related expenses (commuting, fees to unions or professional associations), and iii) other allowable expenses (such as social insurance contributions, premiums for life assurance, child care costs for lone parents). Tax rates are progressive, beginning at 19 per cent and rising to 53 per cent. From 1 January 1995 taxpayers will also have an additional liability of 7.5 per cent of their due tax as a 'solidarity surcharge', to help meet the costs of unification. Members of religious denominations also pay 8–9 per cent of their tax liability as 'church tax', although this sum can be deducted from gross income as an allowable expense.

Organisations

Federal Ministry of Labour
Postfach 14 02 80, Rochustraße 1,
5300 Bonn 1
Tel. + 49 228 5271

Bundesanstalt für Arbeit, (BfA) (Federal
Employment Institute)
Regensburgerstraße 104,
8500 Nuremberg 30
Tel. + 49 911 170; fax + 49 911 17 21 23

*Deutsche Gesellschaft für
Personalführung* (DGFP) (German
Personnel Management Society)
Niederkasseler Lohweg 16,
4000 Düsseldorf 1
Tel. + 49 211 59 78 0; fax + 49 211 5978
505

*Bundesverband Deutscher
Unternehmensberater* (BDU) (Federal
Association of German Management
Consultants)
Friedrich-Wilhelm-Straße 2,
5300 Bonn 1
Tel. + 49 228 23 80 55; fax + 49 228 23 06
25

*Bundesvereinigung der Deutschen
Arbeitgeberverbände* (BDA)
(Confederation of German Employers'
Associations)
Gustav Heinemann Ufer 72,
5000 Cologne 51
Tel. + 49 221 37950; fax + 49 221 37 95
235

Bundesverband Zeitarbeit (BZA)
Federation of Temporary Work Agencies
Bachstraße 1–3,
5300 Bonn 1
Tel. + 49 228 63 24 50

Schutzgemeinschaft Zeitarbeit eV
(Confederation of Temporary Work
Agencies)
Hainer Weg 50,
6000 Frankfurt/Main 70
Tel. + 49 69 61 80 68; fax + 49 69 603
1287

Main sources

Ministry of Labour, *Bundesarbeitsblatt*, various issues.
Fraunhofer Institut für Arbeitswirtschaft und Organisation, *Flexible Arbeitszeiten im Trend*, Stuttgart, 1991.
Michael Kittner, *Arbeits- und Sozialordnung*, Bund Verlag, Cologne, 1994.
DGFP, *Personalführung*, various issues.
Claus Schnabel, *Die übertarifliche Bezahlung*, Deutscher Instituts-Verlag, Cologne, 1994.
Personal, Special issue 'Betriebliche Sozialleistungen', Wirtschaftsverlag Bachem, Issue 3, 1994.

6

Greece

The sources of law on employment in Greece are the constitution, international labour conventions ratified by parliament, EC directives and statute law, including the Civil Code. Article 22 of the 1975 constitution provides for the right and freedom to work and for equal pay for work of equal value. Article 23 safeguards collective rights of association. Labour legislation covers all employees, regardless of the size of the employing organisation. However, certain categories of employees are excluded from the provisions of labour law: these include seamen, agricultural and fisheries workers, domestic servants and home workers.

Terms and conditions of employment are governed both by statute and by case law, which can prove decisive in determining the outcome of a contested dismissal, for example. The main pieces of legislation governing terms and conditions include the Civil Code (articles 645–80), laws 2656/53 and 763/70, which regulate the organisation and control of the labour market and the hiring of employees, laws 2112/20 and 3198/55 on termination, and law 1387/83 on collective dismissal. Emergency law 539/45, legislative decree 4504/66 and law 1364/83 regulate leave allowance. Law 1483/84 makes provisions for leave for employees with family responsibilities. Law 1876/90 established a voluntary system of collective conciliation, mediation and arbitration by an independent agency. Rights conciliation on individual issues is offered by the Ministry of Labour. In-house regulations in the form of company handbooks are another source of labour law. Under order-in-council 3789/57 such regulations are compulsory in firms employing more than seventy employees.

Minimum pay is settled by the National General Collective Agreement (EGSSE) negotiated between the central trade union confederation, the GSEE, and the main employers' organisations, although individual employers often improve substantially on the agreed provisions. This agreement also determines hours of work, and may set other binding terms, such as entitlement to time off (see below). The terms of central agreements are binding on all employers following a declaration to that effect by the Ministry of Labour. Other collective agreements or arbitration awards, which have equal force, regulate pay and benefits in individual industries and occupations.

Contracts of employment

Types of employee

According to statute law and Supreme Court rulings, employees are categorised as either blue-collar (*ergates*) or white-collar (*hipaleli*) on the basis of the tasks

179

they perform, not the manner of payment: a blue-collar worker carries out manual labour while a white-collar worker does non-manual, clerical or administrative work. Further criteria may be established by collective agreement and there is a body of case law on the subject.

Some multinational companies classify all their employees as clerical, both to facilitate flexibility and as a form of benefit: the main practical difference between the two categories is the fact that clerical employees enjoy a substantially larger severance indemnity on dismissal or retirement (see below).

Managerial employees, in as much as they are deemed to be the direct representative of the employing organisation, 'decisively influence the direction and progression of the enterprise' and exercise authority over hiring and dismissing personnel, are exempt from labour legislation on working hours (including Sunday and holiday work), on payment for overtime and on holiday leave. Supervisors, branch managers, department heads, chief accountants, and company directors who sit on executive boards but without voting rights, have all been categorised by the courts as non-managerial employees.

Form of contract

Contracts of employment may be, but do not have to be, in writing. An oral agreement is acceptable as an open-ended contract of employment. Larger – and in particular multinational – companies use written contracts for all grades of employees. Such contracts may vary considerably in length and detail but usually take the form of a simple 'agreement upon engagement'. The contract could serve as proof – if needed – of the basic terms of employment and pay.

In the event of a dispute between the parties as to the substance of a contract, the burden of proof lies with the party seeking to assert their rights. What counts as the substance will be, in general, the basic facts of the employment relationship: pay, hours and other benefits. Most of these elements are either derived from collective agreements or a matter of record (from the tax and social insurance authorities, for example).

A contract of employment between a member of the executive board and the company has to be approved in advance by a general meeting of shareholders (law 2112/20, article 23a). A contract of employment with a minor below the age specified for that employment (generally 15) will be null and void, irrespective of parental consent (Civil Code, articles 127, 136). Contracts with minors above 15 are permissible with parental consent.

Any term in a collective agreement or individual contract of employment which conflicts with the provisions of the 1984 Sex Equality Act will be null and void (see below).

Types of contract

Fixed-term contracts may be agreed, either for short-term or for specific tasks, such as seasonal work or sales campaigns, provided their use is justified by the nature of the business. Otherwise they could be deemed by the courts to be open-ended. If in writing, such contracts must specify the proposed period and assignment (articles 669-74 of the Civil Code). There is no statutory provision governing the renewal of fixed-term contracts. However, the courts may hold that an employment contract has become open-ended if the employee can demonstrate that it entails covering the regular, not temporary, needs of the employing firm. This could be shown either by reference to the nature of the tasks, or by repeated renewal without a justifying cause.

Under article 671 of the Civil Code a fixed-term contract could be held to have been renewed indefinitely if after the expiry date the employee continues to be employed without objection from the employer. Under certain circumstances an open-ended contract may be converted into a fixed-term one. The duration of a fixed-term contract may also be tied to an age limit. **Part-time** contracts of employment are subject to the provisions of law 1892/90 and presidential decree 410/88 and have to be in writing (see also below).

Varying the terms of employment can be problematic where the change involves not solely or necessarily pay or material benefits but also any diminution of the employee's status within an enterprise. Such a change, without the employee's consent, or without a change in business conditions that would justify it, can be successfully contested in the courts. Where an employment relationship is also covered by collective agreements, the most favourable provision (individual contract; enterprise, sectoral or occupational agreement) will prevail, with enterprise and sectoral agreements taking precedence over occupational agreements.

Part-time employment

According to OECD figures, part-time work accounted for some 4 per cent of total employment in 1991: some 63 per cent of part-timers were women. Law 1892/90 forms the current legal basis of part-time work, and social security coverage in particular. Part-time work is defined as work for fewer than forty hours a week, or for less than the agreed full-time week in the industry, company or profession concerned.

The law requires part-timers to be paid on *pro rata* basis, with *pro rata* entitlement to holidays and other benefits. This provision was extended and clarified in the 1993 General Collective Agreement, which covers all private-sector employers, to include access to training and development and to company social benefits, such as transport. Part-timers may not be required to work beyond the agreed number of hours per week if this would clash with other responsibilities, such as family responsibilities or other employment. When full-time vacancies arise, part-timers have a right to priority application.

Hourly rates for part-time work are calculated by dividing the monthly salary by 25 (the number of working days in a month), multiplying the quotient by 6 (the working days in a week), and dividing by 40 (working hours per week). That is, monthly salary multiplied by 0.006. Similarly, the monthly salary is calculated as: monthly salary = hourly rate $\times$ hours of employment per week x 4.1666.

Temporary employment

Temporary employment, including seasonal work, is covered by the same provisions as regular employment. Seasonal employment is extensive in tourism and the manufacture of seasonal products. Employees doing casual work for the same employer for a period of twelve months or more are entitled to one-twelfth of the customary annual leave for every twenty-five days of actual employment. Temporary agency employment has no legal standing at present. However, agencies supplying staff to render office or industrial services, such as security or cleaning, are allowed to operate. Where this happens, the staff concerned are employees of the agency, and the general principles of employment law apply.

Probationary periods

A probationary period is often agreed for managerial positions, although it is not common practice for ordinary white- and blue-collar positions. The two parties may agree to a probationary period of, typically, a few months, extended to as much as a year, after which a permanent post will be offered subject to satisfactory performance. The initial period may be designated a fixed-term contract. However, if the employer does not indicate in writing the intention of dismissing the employee, the contract will be deemed open-ended. The length of the probation may not exceed the time needed by the employer, acting in good faith, to assess the knowledge and capability of the employee. Alternatively, an indefinite contract may be agreed immediately but with a performance review before two months have elapsed, after which statutory indemnity payments become due in the event of dismissal.

Restrictive covenants and confidentiality

Restrictive covenants, imposing constraints on employment after resignation, would not be recognised by the courts and are therefore of little juridical importance. However, a company operating in a specialised area of the labour market might ask an employee to agree, in writing, to a provision under which the employee would undertake not to work for a direct competitor or set up in competition for a specified period. Although ultimately unenforceable, the agreement would have moral and practical force for executives interested in preserving their reputation.

Internal company regulations

In-house regulations are mandatory for firms employing more than seventy people. Under the 1988 Works Councils Act, which applies to all companies

with at least fifty employees, company handbooks setting out disciplinary procedures must be agreed jointly.

Employment terms and conditions

Hours of work

The statutory normal working week under the national collective agreement is
forty hours. The maximum legal working week is forty-eight hours. Employers
violating hours of employment are liable to a fine and/or imprisonment for a
period that may extend from ten days to six months.

In practice, most of industry works a forty-hour week, with thirty-eight or
thirty-nine hours in some service industries, and thirty-seven hours in banks.
Under the 1990 Development Law (law 1892, article 47), normal working hours
can be extended to nine hours per day and forty-eight hours per week for a
period of three months by collective agreement, provided hours are reduced in
the following three months to ensure that the forty-hour norm is observed over a
reference period which may not exceed six months. During this period, pay will
remain constant, and additional hours will not count as overtime.

The same law also allows employees to be hired to work at weekends solely
for two shifts of twelve hours a day. The total remuneration for twenty-four
hours' work, including overtime, Sunday and night work, is equal to the remuneration for a full forty hours (unless a shorter number of hours is normally
worked per week), and social insurance cover is provided as if for full-time
employees.

Double-day shift working is quite common in industry. Flexible working
hours (usually starting at 7:30–8:30 and finishing at 15:30-16:30) are widely
adopted by large and multinational employers, but the practice of carrying over
hours' debits or credits in a full flexible-time system is limited.

In general employees, with the notable exception of small retailers, do not take
long lunchtime breaks or a siesta. Lunch breaks are often paid, or at least part-
paid, by companies – and tend to be up to forty-five minutes.

Overtime and night work

Any hours worked between the agreed normal forty and the permitted maximum
of forty-eight per week are termed 'excess' or 'supplementary working', and
must by law be paid at time-and-a-quarter. The nine-hour maximum day and
five-day working week yield a practical limit to 'supplementary working' of five
hours a week. True 'overtime' – that is, over and above forty-eight hours –
requires the permission of the Ministry of Labour. Minimum supplements
payable are on a sliding scale: 25 per cent for overtime up to sixty hours a year,

50 per cent between sixty and 120 hours and 75 per cent for over 120 hours. (legislative decree 435/76, article 1). Rates for the first sixty hours of overtime are increased for certain categories of employee; for example, to 30 per cent for white-collar workers in non-industrial enterprises, and to 50 per cent for employees in the textile industry.

Unless official permission is obtained, overtime will be deemed 'illegal' and must be paid at double time plus compensation. Frequently companies simply opt to pay double time for all 'excess' and 'overtime' hours in order to avoid the formalities and achieve flexibility at enterprise level. The Ministry of Labour has powers to set overtime limits by occupation and by industry, and they are reviewed every six months. For the second half of 1993, for example, most industries were allowed thirty hours. However, for the first six months of 1994 no normal overtime was allowed, in order to contribute to curbing levels of unemployment. Daily and weekly limits may be exceeded in industry in emergencies, to carry out urgent work to meet social needs, repairs and transport, and where necessitated by acts of God.

Night work, that is, work between 22.00 and 06.00, must be paid at time-and-a-quarter. Since 25 February 1993 it has ceased to be prohibited for women but remains illegal for young people up to 17 in industrial enterprises.

Time off

Annual leave

Any employee with one year of service with the same employer is entitled to annual paid leave plus a holiday bonus for half salary, or thirteen days' pay for daily-paid workers. Holiday entitlement starts at twenty days after the first year and rises to twenty-two days for three or more years' service. Employees with twenty-five years of employment in all are entitled to twenty-three days' leave in the first year of employment with a new employer, rising to twenty-five days after three years' service or more. This entitlement is often increased in company agreements or by unilateral company decision, with additional holiday according to grade and length of service. Many companies have an annual shutdown, usually in August.

Leave has to be granted and taken within one calendar year, regardless of the availability of a substitute, and cannot be transferred to the next year. It is normally regarded as continuous, but may be allowed bit by bit in exceptional business circumstances, or at the justified wish of the employee, and subject to approval by the local administrator of the Ministry of Labour. Where this happens, the first portion of the leave has to be at least six days. At least half of all employees have to be given leave between 1 May and 30 September. Parental, maternity, sick or other non-paid leave entitlement is excluded from the annual leave.

Employees in 'intermittent employment' with twelve months of contractual employment (not actual service) with the same employer are entitled to one-twelfth of the leave of comparable full-time employees for each twenty-five days of actual employment. Leave must be granted on days during which they would normally be at work. Employees in part-time work are also entitled to *pro rata* leave and benefit.

Public holidays

In the private sector there are obligatory public holidays on 25 March (Independence Day), Easter Monday, 1 May, 15 August (Assumption) and Christmas Day. In addition, there are customary public holidays on 28 October (National Day) and the 'half-holiday' of Good Friday (start at 11:00 a.m.). Banks, public enterprises and civil service departments also take New Year's Day, Epiphany, the first Monday in Lent, Good Friday, Easter Saturday, the Day of the Holy Spirit (Pentecost), 17 November and Boxing Day. In addition, there may be one or two local holidays per year.

Maternity leave

Maternity leave is sixteen weeks (eight weeks before the due date and eight after the birth). For two years after the birth a mother can be granted one hour's paid leave at the beginning of, during or at the end of each working day for nursing (regardless of whether she actually nurses the baby). Nursing leave can be taken by the father if the mother does not wish to use it, or may be changed to two hours per day for one year. Employees on maternity leave are entitled to full pay, half of which can be reclaimed by the employer from the state social security fund.

Parental leave

Under law 1483/84 and the 1993 General Collective Agreement parents of either sex with responsibility for dependent children may apply for a period of unpaid parental leave lasting no longer than three and a half months, subject to one year's service. The provision applies only in companies employing at least fifty workers, and no more than 8 per cent of a company's work force are entitled to the leave in any one calendar year. The parent not applying for leave must also be working outside the household. The leave may be taken following on from maternity leave for up to two and a half years from the birth. During the period of leave, employees continue to be responsible for paying social insurance con-tributions. Workers are entitled to return to the same or a similar, but not an infe-rior, position. Larger companies usually allow unilaterally extended maternity and parental leave.

Leave for marriage or the birth of a child

Under the 1993 General Collective Agreement employees who marry are entitled to five days' paid leave, exclusive of their annual leave. In the case of a birth the father is entitled to one day's paid leave per child.

Leave for workers with family responsibilities

Under law 1483 employees in the private sector with dependent children are also entitled to apply for unpaid leave of up to six days per year to look after a sick child or spouse. The leave may be extended for up to ten working days where the employee has more than two dependent children. Parents of children with a chronic disability working in enterprises employing at least fifty workers may also apply for a reduction of one hour per day in their normal working hours, subject to a corresponding reduction in pay. Parental leave of up to four working days per calendar year may also be taken for visits to the schools of children below the age of 16 years. Larger companies may also provide, either through agreement or on a unilateral basis, leave for other family reasons, such as the death of a close relative.

Sick leave

Under law 4558/30 absence through certificated illness for a relatively short period of time is permissible without prejudice to the employee's contract of employment. The period ranges from absence of one month for employees with up to four years of service to three months for those with four to ten years, four months for ten to fifteen years and six months for more than fifteen years of service. These periods of absence are not set against annual leave; however, any extra sick leave is deducted. Obligatory sick leave is available to women who wish to terminate a pregnancy. Maternity leave is also sometimes extended by adding a period of sick leave and the employee's annual leave entitlement.

Sickness benefit is paid out by the state scheme (IKA) for employees with qualifying length of service. The rate is equal to 50 per cent of normal earnings, plus 10 per cent of that sum for each dependant, up to a maximum of four. Benefit is reduced by one-third where there are no dependants. Benefit is initially payable for 180 days for the same illness, rising to 720 days, depending on the length of qualifying service. Under article 658 of the Civil Code the employer must pay the difference between the daily rate of the state benefit and the usual daily wage for a period of fifteen days for employees with more than ten days' but less than one year's service, and up to twenty-six days for employees with at least one year's service. There are three waiting days before the state benefit is paid, although the employer is obliged to pay half the daily wage during that period. On 1 July 1993 the maximum amount of sickness benefit became Dr 2,450 (£6.60) for the first fifteen days and Dr 4,550 (£12.20) per day thereafter.

Educational leave

Employees aged under 25 undertaking an educational course may take fourteen days' non-paid leave a year in order to sit examinations. Benefit for this period is payable by the state Manpower and Employment Organisation (OAED).

Trade unionists

Under law 1264/82 employers must grant unpaid leave of absence to any employee who is a member of the executive board of a trade union, or a delegate to a different tier of a trade union, to enable them to carry out their duties. The amount of paid leave to be granted varies according to the size and status of the trade union. For example, officials of representative national trade union organisations (the so-called 'third tier') may take paid leave of absence for the whole of their period of office. The president and the general secretary of federations with more than 30,000 members are entitled to paid leave of six days per month and other union officials to three days per month. If the federation has under 10,000 members, leave is reduced to four and two days, respectively. Officials of smaller unions which, because they are workplace unions, may have fewer than 2,000 members get one or two days per month off.

Paid leave lasting no longer than fourteen days per year is also granted to employees, so that they may participate in trade union education programmes, provided that no more than 1 per cent of a company's work force is affected.

Union officials are entitled to unpaid time off to attend trade union congresses for the duration of the congress. Members of the executive committee of a union are also granted varying amounts of unpaid time off, depending on the precise office and the size of the trade union. Leave on union business is regarded as employment for the purpose of qualifying for all entitlements arising out of employment, or for fulfilling the qualifying period for benefits paid under social insurance. (However, the trade union itself is responsible for covering the social contributions of any of its officials on leave of absence.)

Pay and benefits

Statutory pay determination

There is a legally binding minimum wage which is negotiated nationally and embodied in the national General Collective Agreement between the main union confederation, the GSEE, the Federation of Greek Industries (SEB), the General Confederation of Artisans and Handicrafts of Greece (GSEBEE) and the Federation of Commercial Associations of Greece (EESE). The national agreement is directly binding on all private-sector employers. In addition, the Ministry of Labour can intervene to extend sectoral or occupational agreements to cover non-signatory employers, either on its own initiative or by application, provided that the agreement to be extended already covers 51 per cent of the relevant work force. This minimum applies in the private sector, in public sector enterprises and in local government.

Separate national minimum rates are specified for salaried employees and wage-earners, with additional amounts according to marital status and years of employment in the same occupation. For example, the additions are 10 per cent for salaried employees and 5 per cent for wage-earners for every three years of experience, up to nine years and 10 per cent 'marriage benefit', all based on the basic rate. As from 1 July 1994, for example, a blue-collar employee, married and with no previous experience, is entitled to a daily minimum of Dr 5,428 (£14.60). A white-collar employee in the same position is entitled to a monthly minimum of Dr 121,248 (£327.70). Married employees with nine years' service or more are entitled to Dr 6,169 per day (£16.70) in the case of blue-collar workers, and to Dr 154,316 per month (£417) in the case of white-collar workers. In practice all these minima are substantially exceeded in most companies for all but the most inexperienced or unskilled workers.

Pay indexation

The statutory system of pay indexation for the public sector was abolished in 1991. However, two recent two-year national collective agreements for the private sector have included an indexation mechanism to deal with any consumer price inflation above the forecast amount allowed for in the settlement. For example, according to the 1994–95 General Collective Agreement, should the consumer price index rise by more than 11.5 per cent between December 1993 and December 1994, basic rates will be increased, as from 1 July 1995, by the amount in excess of 11.5 per cent up to a maximum of 20 per cent above the highest excess rate. If actual consumer price inflation exceeds this limit, the two sides will meet to determine a possible corrective adjustment, taking into consideration the general state of the economy.

In 1995 minimum salary and wage rates will be augmented by a rate equivalent to the increase in consumer prices forecast in the state budget. Again there is an indexation element, with automatic compensation up to a 30 per cent margin above the forecast figure.

The law on pay

Payment for employees working and residing in Greece must be denominated and paid in drachmas and cannot be linked to any foreign currency (law 362/45). Law 1082/80 requires employees to be given a fully itemised pay statement. Employees have first priority as creditors in the event of bankruptcy, under law 1545/85. Under law 1914/90 employees can lodge a claim for any back pay due with the Manpower Employment Organisation (OAED) if there are insufficient assets to meet employee claims.

Pay determination

All private-sector employees are covered by the national collective agreement. How pay is determined at company level will depend on whether the company is covered by a sectoral and an occupational agreement, and whether it negotiates or sets pay unilaterally at enterprise level.

Pay set by collective agreement continues to play a major role for blue-collar and lower-level clerical employees in the private sector: above those grades, company policy becomes the prime determinant. (A detailed presentation of the different levels and pattern of bargaining will be found in the volume in this series on *Employee Relations and Collective Bargaining*.) Large and multinational employers pay all their grades well above the minimum levels set by national or sectoral collective agreements and in practice do not negotiate on pay with an enterprise union, where such exists. A firm offering pay in the top quadrant of the market will usually pay an average of about 150 per cent across the board above the minimum sectoral pay level.

Companies can determine their own pay structure and practices to a considerable extent, with more discretion the greater the divergence between company rates and collectively bargained rates. For example, local firms paying nearer the agreed minima are much more subject to the complexities and of being covered by several agreements, including occupational agreements for some employees which can cut across company grades.

There is little public domain information about pay levels and increases at company level. Salary clubs are virtually non-existent, although informal exchange and market surveys do take place and are influential in guiding the approaches of multinational firms in particular. Comparability of positions tends to be a problem because of the lack of formal job evaluation. Both Hay and the Greek Personnel Managers' Association (see appendix) produce local surveys. One practitioner noted that pay setting and the transmission of market signals often took place via 'osmosis' rather than explicit orientation to known market trends.

In some cases, high rates of inflation have led companies to institute two reviews a year, with a general plus merit increase as from 1 January and the balance of the general increase paid from 1 June. Recently some large companies have opted to pay a general increase at the beginning of the year, before a national agreement has been concluded, reflecting the lack of linkage in some cases between high-paying multinational firms and national collective bargaining. More typically, rates are adjusted following the national agreement, with supplements where firms can afford them. There have been efforts to restore differentials in the private sector, following a period in the 1980s when they were compressed.

Payment systems

Most blue-collar workers work on time rates. Incentive pay systems remain, as yet, fairly undeveloped and performance monitoring can present problems. Systems for white-collar employees are tending to shift from individual informal systems to greater formality and comparability. Job evaluation can be difficult to introduce because of the existence of occupational agreements based on seniority. In general, there is much greater freedom to introduce job evaluation at company level for managerial employees. However, practice tends not to be systematic, and the norm for pay setting at this level remains either unilateral management decision and/or individual negotiation.

Make-up of pay

Pay is built up on the base of the national minimum, or any applicable occupational or sectoral minima. Most companies in developed sectors will be paying considerably above this level, as noted above, and have the scope to structure company-based supplements either unilaterally or in negotiation with enterprise unions.

In addition to basic pay, employees also receive a plethora of allowances. Many large companies have consolidated these into basic pay in order to simplify pay structures.

Service increments are an important element of pay, a fact reflected in the service-related nature of the statutory minimum wage. Industry agreements provide for a series of increments encompassing the employee's whole working life, with a total range of up to 40 per cent of the starting minimum for employees in the same grade. In addition, many companies also pay loyalty bonuses every three years or so, which are consolidated into basic pay.

Other common benefits and allowances include family, marriage and children's allowances, staff Christmas parties and presents for employees' children, subsidised meals and presents upon marriage (usually a lump sum) and on the birth of a child (such as jewellery and flowers). Some firms also organise free weekend trips for employees' families and provide low-interest or interest-free loans.

A certain number of bonuses are also payable by law, as set out separately below.

Family allowances

Several collective agreements and individual employers provide for the payment of an allowance to married or divorced individuals and parents. Typically, an extra 10 per cent of minimum salary is paid to married individuals, including divorced or widowed individuals and single mothers with custody of children, and extra allowances are paid for each child, either as a percentage of basic salary or as an annual lump sum.

In the 1991 survey of benefits carried out by the Greek Personnel Management Association, 26 per cent of companies covered expenses for nursery schools, and 19 per cent for summer camps. Bonuses to top-performing students were paid by 14 per cent of surveyed firms, and 13 per cent provided student allowances for the children of their employees.

Overtime, holiday and night-work pay

Any hours worked between the agreed forty and the legal maximum of forty-eight hours are termed 'excess' or 'supplementary' work, and must be paid at time-and-a-quarter. Work beyond this is termed 'overtime' and payment is on a variable scale. Permission must be obtained from the Ministry of Labour, otherwise the rate payable is automatically double time. Some companies choose to pay double time for all 'supplementary' work and 'overtime' in order to avoid having to get official permission, whilst others pay time-and-three-quarters for 'supplementary' work, and then double time for true overtime. Holiday work and Sunday work are payable at time-and-three-quarters. Night work between 22.00 and 06.00 must be paid at time-and-a-quarter by law, with double time for any night work on Sundays or at weekends.

Bonuses

The law (1082/80 and ministerial decree 19040/81) provides for certain annual bonuses to be paid to all employees, leading effectively to salaries being paid fourteen times a year. These include:

- *Christmas bonus*, equal to one additional month's salary (or twenty-five days' pay), paid in full to all employed continuously between 1 May and 31 December. Those who have worked for only part of this period are entitled to a bonus equal to two twenty-fifths of each month's salary (or two days' wages for every nineteen days worked).
- *Easter bonus*, equal to half a month's salary (or fifteen days' pay), paid in full to all staff employed continuously between 1 January and 30 April. Those who have worked for only part of this period are entitled to a *pro rata* bonus.
- *Holiday bonus* equal to half a month's salary (or thirteen days' wages), paid when the employee takes the annual holiday (see also above).

The granting of bonuses in general must not be discriminatory as between employees, unless the employer can cite good grounds for differential treatment. There can be problems with the withdrawal of bonuses, if they are deemed to be part of customary remuneration, unless the employer has expressly indicated in the contract of employment that the payment is revocable.

General and unspecified bonuses can be seen as an alternative to consolidated merit increases and present particular problems in this respect. Bonuses tied to

specific targets, such as profits, are easier to withdraw should company performance slacken: however, they could entail extensive disclosure of financial
information to trade union negotiators. (Under law 1876/90 employees are in any
event entitled to 'comprehensive and precise information' relevant to collective
bargaining, including information on the financial situation, business position
and personnel policy of the employer.)

Any bonus greater than three months' usual pay paid to an employee with at
least ten years' service may be divided into three, with one-third taxable in the
current year and the other two-thirds taxable in the preceding two years.

Pay for performance

The element of seniority in Greek pay structures, and the employee expecta-
tions deriving from them, raise a number of difficulties in the implementation
of merit pay. Such schemes are much easier to introduce where pay levels are
well above agreed minima, enhancing employer discretion. This applies particularly in multinational firms, which enjoy this structural advantage as well as
being able to recruit suitably motivated staff by virtue of their reputation and
above-average working conditions and pay. Local practitioners working in
such enterprises indicated that performance-related pay and individually based
reviews have gained acceptance among employees. Successful schemes have
been based on close consultation and training. In some pioneering cases, merit
reviews are being extended to blue-collar employees, although this is still a
novelty.

The problems of building a merit element into normal salary progression have
been solved in some cases through the expedient of moving above-average performers more rapidly through the seniority structure, with average performers
going up one increment a year.

Managerial pay

The most important criteria in determining managerial pay are organisational
size and business sector. Fast-moving consumer goods and financial services
provide higher earnings and faster pay growth than traditional sectors. The skills
regarded as important tend to reflect this, with marketing skills continuing to be
in demand. According to the 1993-94 Monks Partnership survey *Management
Remuneration in Europe*, the highest-paid function was finance, followed by
sales and marketing, with approximately 67 per cent and 65 per cent of chief
executive's pay respectively. Production, and admin. and personnel, lagged some
way behind, with 47–50 per cent of the top manager's total earnings.

Location is important in as much as it reflects the availability or non-availability
of skills. The concentration of skilled employees (as well as about a third of the
total population of the country) in the Athens area means that, in contrast to many
capital cities or conurbations, employers do not have to pay an 'Athens premium'.

Rather, employers must offer an incentive to transfer to the provinces, and pay more for scarce skills.

According to Monks Partnership, cash bonuses are paid to virtually all chief executives and functional heads, tailing off markedly below that level. Share options are much less frequent, being available to only just over 60 per cent of top managers and just under 30 per cent of functional heads. The value of cash bonuses is highly dispersed, but some 40 per cent of top managers receive a bonus worth 30 per cent of base pay or more.

The survey of employee benefits conducted by the Greek Personnel Management Association in 1991 found that 46 per cent of surveyed companies offered bonuses to senior managers and 35 per cent offered them to middle managers, 19 per cent offered them to white-collar employees, 9 per cent to blue-collar employees and 30 per cent to all. According to the SSDP survey, in 35 per cent of the companies bonuses are tied to individual performance, in 33 per cent to meeting targets and in 30 per cent to company profits. Multinational firms may have a broader range of quantitative and qualitative objectives.

Other prevalent benefits include life assurance, medical insurance (often for all employees, see below), and cars (see below).

Cars have become a familiar and tax-effective benefit. The high cost of executive-range cars, because of road duties (second only to Denmark in the EU), increases the attractiveness of using cheaper company finance to buy vehicles and make them available to senior employees. All expenses incurred by the employer can be treated as business expenses and are not taxed as income of the employee. According to Monks Partnership, cars were provided to all top and senior management in the firms surveyed, and in over 80 per cent of cases fuel was also included in the benefit.

The provision of housing, either rent-free plus an option to buy, or through subsidised mortgage, is also a factor in the market for senior executives. In the Greek Personnel Management Association survey 14 per cent of the companies provided employees with housing loans.

Financial participation

The legal framework for employee participation in either company results or the employer's capital developed considerably in the late 1980s. Profit-sharing schemes allow companies to distribute a proportion of profits to employees as cash, subject to the requirement that no more than 15 per cent of annual net profits may be distributed and that profits may not exceed 25 per cent of an employee's gross annual remuneration. Profits enjoy favourable tax treatment for both employer and employee, and are exempt from social insurance contributions.

Employee share ownership is regulated by law 1731/87, supplemented by two subsequent pieces of legislation. The law provides, firstly, for the acquisition by companies of their own shares for sale to employees at concessionary rates, subject to shareholder approval. Options must be exercised within five years, and no more than 10 per cent of the company's total share capital may be made available for this purpose. If a firm uses part of its profits to increase its Greek equity, and distribute the shares to employees, no income tax is due on the value of the shares. However, as noted above, executive stock options are rare in Greek-owned companies, reflecting the thinness of the stock market. Share option plans in multinationals usually entail an offer of parent-company stock.

Pay for trainees

Trainees aged between 15 and 18 years are paid in accordance with youth pay rates as laid down in the national collective agreement: that is, 50 per cent of the national minimum wage in the first six months, increasing in stages to 100 per cent in the sixth. They also have full medical and hospital insurance, the whole cost of which is covered initially by the OAED (in the first year) and subsequently by the employer.

Main benefits

Provision of health insurance is regarded as an important benefit, reflecting problems in the state system. In some companies, two schemes may operate: the first will be non-contributory for employees and will offer life insurance, doctors' fees and prescription charges; the second, covering full hospitalisation costs, involves an employee contribution. According to the 1991 benefits survey carried out by the Greek Personnel Management Association, 94 per cent of firms provided employees with life/permanent disability insurance, 83 per cent provided medical plans, 49 per cent loss of income insurance and 41 per cent travel insurance.

Supplementary payments, in addition to the statutory minimum severance, are made by many companies to employees on retirement, often simply double the statutory termination indemnity (see below). Auxiliary pensions, usually financed via an insurance company, were offered by just under half the companies in the Greek Personnel Management Association benefits survey.

Equal pay and equal opportunities

Legal framework and practice

Sex equality in employment is provided for under the 1975 constitution, and by law (46/75 and 1414/84). Law 1414/84 forbids any discrimination on grounds of sex or marital status in relation to access to, the content of and the implementation of programmes and systems of career guidance, vocational training, apprenticeships, further training, retraining, training for a change of occupation, open retraining courses, refresher courses and information for workers. It guarantees access to all branches and levels of employment, irrespective of sex and marital status, as well as equal pay for work of equal value. It also forbids termination of employment for reasons relating to sex and specifies fines for employers.

Under the 1984 Act a department of the Ministry of Labour was established to monitor equality issues and compile statistics. The General Secretariat for Equality, established by law in 1982, and with enhanced responsibilities under 1985 legislation, is an autonomous department within the Ministry to the Presidency and is entrusted with 'promoting and achieving the legal and substantive equality of men and women in Greece'. The secretariat also compiles statistics on pay.

Discrimination

Despite the lack of Equal Opportunities practices, women have entered management at senior and middle level, and certain professions (such as the law, computing and personnel management) have a high proportion of female practitioners. However, equal opportunities and pay are generally not a live issue. There is little awareness of the role of Equal Opportunities strategies, and no advertisement in the Greek press will identify a company as 'an Equal Opportunities employer' (including multinational employers). Sex is often stipulated in advertisements for blue-collar employees, or for single-sex-dominated occupations.

Individual termination of contract

Individual termination of contract in Greece does not require any distinction to be drawn between dismissal for factors related to the employee's person or conduct, or dismissal on economic grounds or for reorganisation and rationalisation.

The law distinguishes three types of termination:

- Termination of an open-ended contract, after due notice, known as 'regular termination'.
- Termination of an open-ended contract, without due notice, known as 'irregular termination'.
- Termination of a fixed-term contract for a serious reason and before the expiry of the contract, known as 'exceptional termination'.

Although statute law makes provision for periods of notice, broadly speaking employees *can* be dismissed without notice in return for payment of an indemnity or with the notice period set out in law for a reduced indemnity. The length of notice and levels of severance indemnity are set out in Table 2. Severance indemnities are payable in all instances of dismissal, for whatever reason, including poor performance, except where the employee is potentially guilty of criminal misconduct and the employer chooses to take the matter to court.

Table 2   Notice periods and severance payments in Greece (salaried employees)

Service (years)	Months of notice or salary in compensation
2 months to 1 year	1
1–4	2
4–6	3
6–8	4
8–10	5
10 and over	6

All dismissals must be notified in writing to the employee (unless the duration of service is under two months) and also – within eight days – to OAED, the official employment service.

Periods of notice and levels of indemnity vary according to whether the employee is white-collar or blue-collar. Dismissal of white-collar employees is regulated by law 2112/20 and of blue-collar employees by royal decree 16/18.7.20. Under these provisions an employer can terminate the contract of employment of a salaried employee subject to the notice periods or levels of indemnity in Table 2.

Beyond this, thirty days' notice or salary is due for each additional year up to a maximum of twenty-four months, attainable after twenty-eight years of service. The full amount of indemnity is payable where the employee is dismissed without notice: half the stated indemnity is paid where the appropriate notice is given.

In the case of wage-earners the contract can again be terminated with or without notice, together with payment of an indemnity, according to the schedule in Table 3, which reflects the enhancements introduced by the 1994–95 national General Collective Agreement. The indemnity is calculated by the formula: daily pay = usual daily wage $\times$ 25 $\times$ 14/25 $\times$ 12. Where notice is given, the indemnity is halved.

Table 3   Notice periods and termination indemnities in Greece (wage earners)

Service (years)	Notice (days)	Indemnity (days' pay)
2 months to 1 year	5	5
1–2	8	7
2–5	15	13
5–10	30	26
10–15	60	52
15–20	60	78
20 and over	60	91

If the amount of indemnity payable exceeds six months' salary, the employer may pay any sums in excess of the six months in three-monthly instalments, each of which may not be less than three months' pay. Failure to pay the indemnity or an instalment may render the termination invalid. The amount of indemnity is boosted by Christmas, Easter and holiday bonuses and calculated by multiplying the usual monthly salary by 14 and then dividing the total by 12.

In all cases the indemnity is a tax-deductible expense for the employer. Should the employer decide to pay above the statutory indemnity, either on dismissal or on retirement, the tax-deductibility remains. The indemnity is tax-free for blue-collar employees but taxable for white-collar employees at a rate of 10 per cent for the amount between Dr 60,000 and Dr 1,000,000 per month and of 15 per cent for higher amounts, collected via a withholding tax deducted by the employer. In the event of employer insolvency, employees are entitled to any outstanding indemnity pay, and claims have a high priority (see above).

Grounds for dismissal and company discipline

The reason for the dismissal does not have to be given at the moment of dismissal, unless required by the individual contract of employment. However, it must be stated should the employee wish to challenge the termination in the courts. In broad terms, dismissal must be on 'objective' grounds, and not 'abusive'. Notice of dismissal must be in writing and delivered to the employee (or their legal representative) in person.

Dismissal on grounds of poor performance or persistent misconduct should be preceded by adequate warning to the employee. In the case of poor performance, it could take the form of appraisals signed and accepted by the employee. In companies with over seventy employees the law requires a personnel handbook, setting out company rules and employee rights and obligations, to be agreed with enterprise union representatives. A breach of agreed rules may constitute grounds for dismissal, but this has to be the last resort, and be preceded by:

- An oral warning.
- A written warning.
- Deductions from pay not exceeding a quarter of a day's pay.
- Suspension for a period without pay.

Protected employees

Notice of termination must not be issued to:

- Any employee on leave.
- Pregnant women or women on maternity leave up to a year after the birth or while they are on sick leave related to maternity.

- Trade union officials or health and safety representatives, depending on the particular office, both during office and for a period afterwards.
- Employees studying in certain vocational schools.

Unfair dismissal, appeal and reinstatement

Dismissal may be deemed void if it:

- Constitutes discrimination.
- Constitutes an act of retribution by the employer.
- Violates the proper procedures (non-payment of severance pay or failure to report the termination to the labour authorities).
- Is on grounds of trade union or political activity.

A resignation prompted by a prejudicial variation of contract, such as transfer or assignment to an inferior position not related to economic reorganisation, may also be ruled unfair. The employer can plead economic circumstances as a justifying factor, but in that case the employee may still be entitled to seek termination (with the appropriate indemnity).

Appeal is via the civil courts, although the first step by an employee might be to contact the local representatives of the Ministry of Labour to seek mediation.

If a dismissal is found to be unfair, a court can order reinstatement should the employee wish. Where this takes place, the employee must repay the severance indemnity but is entitled to any remuneration due from the time of dismissal to the court ruling, plus interest. However, an employer can immediately re-dismiss an employee, with the appropriate indemnity. In practice such protracted disputes are rare, and in most instances the parties will come to a settlement involving a higher than statutory indemnity payment to allow the contract to be terminated by mutual consent. Employees may agree to relinquish their right to appeal on termination of employment.

Collective dismissal

Without formal permission from the Ministry of Labour, according to law 1387/83, no enterprise with more than twenty and fewer than fifty employees can dismiss more than five employees in a month; those with more than fifty employees cannot dismiss more than 2 to 3 per cent of the work force (up to a maximum of thirty). The law does not apply to enterprise or plant shutdowns or to liquidations.

In such cases the employer has to consult employee representatives (as defined in 1988 legislation on works councils) and inform them in writing, stating the reasons for the dismissals, the exact number by gender, age and occupation, and the current number of employees.

If employer and employee representatives agree, dismissals may take place within ten days after the authorities have received notification and given approval.

If the employer and employee representatives cannot reach agreement within the ten-day period of notice, the local prefecture or the Minister of Labour can extend the consultation period for a further twenty days. Should the parties still fail to agree the authorities can set limits on the number of dismissals. Failure to comply will render the terminations null and void.

Severance arrangements are as for individual termination.

Appendix

Non-wage labour costs

Benefits and contributions to sickness funds, pensions and to the official employment service (for unemployment benefit and training) are based on computable daily pay, according to category of employee. There are twenty-eight categories in all. Contributions are subject to an earnings ceiling (Dr 4,481,515 in 1993, approximately £14,670). Total employer contributions are some 27 per cent of earnings, with employees paying about 16 per cent. An additional 1–2 per cent may be payable in some dangerous or unhealthy occupations.

Organisations

Official Manpower and Placement Agency
(OAED)
Thrakis 8, 16610 Glyfada
Tel. + 30 1 993 2589; fax + 30 1 993 7301

Ministry of Labour
40 Piraeus Street, Athens
Tel. + 30 1 523 2110

General Secretariat for Equality
2 Mousseou Street, Plaka, Athens
Tel. + 30 1 321 2094

Federation of Greek Industries
5 Xenofontos Street, 10557 Athens
Tel. + 30 1 323 7325

Greek Personnel Management Association
3 Karitsi Street, 10561 Athens
Tel. + 30 1 322 5704

British–Hellenic Chamber of Commerce
25 Vas. Sofias, 10674 Athens
Tel. + 30 1 721 0361; fax + 30 1 721 8571

General Confederation of Greek Labour
(GSEE)
Patision and Pipinou 27, 11251 Athens
Tel. + 30 1 883 4611; fax + 30 1 822 9802

Organisation for Mediation and Arbitration
89 Patision Street, 10434 Athens
Tel. + 30 1 881 4922; fax + 30 1 881 5393

Main sources

Deltion Ergatikis Nomothesias (Index of Employment Law), Athens, various issues.
Harilaos Goutos and George Leventis, *Ergatiki Nomothesia* (Labour Legislation),

seventh edition, Deltion Ergatikis Nomothesias, Athens, 1988.

General Collective Agreement, various years.

Greek Personnel Management Association, *Survey of Employee Benefits* (in Greek), Athens, 1991.

Irish Republic

The Irish constitution lays down basic rights for employees, particularly freedom of association and (by implication) non-association. The Irish system of industrial relations is basically of a voluntarist nature, with the emphasis on the individual parties concerned negotiating mutual agreements. However, there is a basic framework of protective legislation affecting terms and conditions, such as provisions on redundancy, minimum notice, minimum leave entitlement, equality and termination of employment. Moreover, pay increases have been subject to a series of tripartite agreements since 1987.

Labour jurisdiction

The system of labour jurisdiction is characterised by a complex set of institutions, with some overlapping responsibilities for both individual and collective labour law. A major change was initiated with the 1990 Industrial Relations Act, which created a new body, the Labour Relations Commission, and reassigned and redefined the roles of existing institutions. (The role of the Labour Relations Commission in industrial conciliation is dealt with in another volume in this series, *Employee Relations and Collective Bargaining*.) Decisions of lower-level bodies (such as the Employment Appeals Tribunal) specifically established to determine employment law issues, may be appealed to the civil courts. In some circumstances, and specifically in the case of contested dismissal, an employee may have the choice either of pursuing the case through the ordinary civil courts where the matter involves a breach of the employment contract (such as non-adherence to an agreed period of notice) or of using the specific machinery for employment disputes created by statute.

The Labour Court

The Labour Court, set up in 1946, is not a conventional court or industrial tribunal. Rather, it was established as a bipartite institution with independent representation 'to promote harmonious relations between employers and workers' and – with some exceptions – has served primarily as a forum for resolving collective disputes. However, it also operates as the supervisory body for minimum wage-setting machinery (see below), as an arbitrator in industrial disputes in certain instances, and more recently as a tribunal specifically in the field of sex equality. Under the 1990 Industrial Relations Act the Labour Court was divested of its functions in industrial conciliation, which were assumed by the newly created Labour Relations Commission. Cases may be referred on to the Labour Court if no resolution is possible before the commission, or directly in some exceptional circumstances.

Rights Commissioners

Individual disputes or any collective disputes which are not connected with rates of pay, hours of work or holidays, may be taken initially to a Rights Commissioner. There are five Rights Commissioners in the Irish Republic, appointed by the Minister for Enterprise and Employment. A Rights Commissioner will hear evidence from both parties at an informal hearing and issue a non-binding recommendation. If either of the parties wishes to appeal, they must do so to the Labour Court (see below) within six weeks of the recommendation. The decisions of the Labour Court on appeals under the Industrial Relations Acts are binding. Rights Commissioners also hear cases under the Unfair Dismissals Acts, the Maternity Protection of Employees Act (1981) and the Payment of Wages Act (1991). Recommendations under these Acts may be appealed to the Employment Appeals Tribunal. Rights Commissioners or the Labour Relations Commission are often cited as the first external stage in company grievance procedures.

Complaints on issues related to equal pay and sex discrimination may be taken directly, or via the Employment Equality Agency, to an Equality Officer of the Labour Relations Commission, who may issue a recommendation. Appeal may be had from there to the Labour Court (see below). Appeal is possible from the Labour Court to the High Court on matters of law. The Employment Equality Agency, set up under the 1977 Employment Equality Act, may, at its discretion, assist individuals in bringing cases to Equality Officers or the Labour Court.

The Employment Appeals Tribunal

The Employment Appeals Tribunal (EAT) is intended to offer a swift and informal forum for resolving disputes over individual employment rights. It consists of an equal number of employee and employer representatives and an independent, legally qualified chair. The EAT hears disputes relating to redundancy, minimum notice, unfair dismissal and maternity protection. It issues binding decisions on redundancy or minimum notice, which are only appealable to the High Court on a point of law. Parties may appeal to the civil courts against an EAT determination on unfair dismissal or maternity protection in writing and within six weeks.

Contracts of employment

The law of contract in the Irish Republic is based on the common law traditions of the British judicial system. This tradition continues but is subject to the influence both of the Irish Constitution and statute law on the contract of employment, especially in fields such as dismissal, equality and maternity protection. In developing case law the Irish courts and legal authorities would take into account rights under the Constitution and previous rulings of the courts. They may also refer to precedents from other jurisdictions, particularly the United Kingdom.

The determination of whether the provision of labour services constitutes a contract of service, allowing the worker concerned to be classified as an employee and hence to enjoy some forms of statutory protection, is a matter which has been developed by the courts, applying a number of complementary tests.

Types of employee

There is no legal differentiation between categories of employee, although company agreements tend to grade employees into manuals, clerical employees, specialists and managerial staff. Manual employees tend to be paid weekly and clerical employees monthly, although there is a growing trend towards monthly pay for all employees.

Form of contract

There is no statutory requirement for contracts of employment to be in writing. However, under the Employment (Information) Act, 1994, all employees working eight hours or more a week and who have one month's service are entitled to receive from their employer, within two months of the commencement of employment, a written statement of their terms and conditions of employment, including details of any collective agreements which affect the person's employment. A copy of the document must be kept by the employer for a period of one year after the expiry of the contract. This legislation implements EU Directive 91/533/EEC on Proof of an Employment Contract. In practice, contracts for the vast majority of employees are written, with the exception of some manual employees.

There is no statutory requirement for employers to consult work-force representatives on new hirings, although if a union is present in a firm it would be customary for the employer to inform the union about new employees.

Express and implied terms

Those terms of a contract which have been agreed, either in writing or verbally, between the parties – the express terms – are also subject to common law and to statutory constraints which imply further terms. For example, employers are under an obligation to:

- Maintain the employment relationship.
- Pay agreed wages.
- Provide a safe working environment.
- Treat an employee with respect.

For their part, employees must obey any reasonable instruction from the employer, be professionally loyal and treat the employer's property and tools of work with care.

Types of contract

Part-time contracts   There is no statutory definition of part-time work. However, under the Worker Protection (Regular Part-time Employees) Act, 1991, employees working eight or more hours a week who have thirteen weeks' service are entitled, on a *pro rata* basis, to the benefits enjoyed by full-time staff, such as holidays, workplace health and safety, notice of dismissal, redundancy payments and redress for unfair dismissal.

Fixed-term contracts   There is no statutory definition of a fixed-term contract, nor do employers have to justify recourse to such contracts. There is no automatic right for employees on fixed-term contracts to enjoy the same benefits and rights as comparable permanent employees. Although the right to bring a claim of unfair dismissal does not apply to employees with less than one year's service, under the Unfair Dismissals (Amendment) Act, 1993, people who have been employed on two or more successive fixed-term contracts, each of less than a year, may bring such a claim. Any ruling on the issue would be a matter for an individual determination by the EAT or a civil court in the light of all the circumstances.

Temporary agency employment

As in the United Kingdom, and in contrast to most other EU member states, the employment status of temporary agency workers is not unambiguously resolved. Although some agencies, in particular the leading ones, provide holiday pay, sick pay and maternity pay for their staff, and take on the responsibility of employers, some case law has ruled that agency employees are neither employees of the agency nor of the user company, with difficulties in enforcing rights against either. However, under recent legislation (the Unfair Dismissals (Amendment) Act, 1993) temporary workers may bring a complaint of unfair dismissal against the user company.

Restrictive covenants and confidentiality

Restrictive covenants may be agreed as part of the contract of employment, provided they are restricted by geographical area, duration and subject matter, and do not unreasonably restrict employees in the exercise of their profession. Employers are also entitled to protect trade secrets and confidential information, and, under the implied terms of a contract, the employee has a duty of fidelity to the employer, encompassing non-disclosure of confidential information. Some companies, particularly in the high-tech sector, require technical specialists to sign confidentiality agreements.

Employee inventions

The Patents Act, 1946, governs inventions made by the employee, and although it does not expressly state whom such inventions belong to, rulings have shown that they usually belong to the employer. This is because most inventions are produced in working time and at the workplace. It is usual for ownership to be stated in the contract of employment. Disputes are taken to the Controller of Patents or the High Court.

Workplace discipline

Under the Unfair Dismissals Act, 1977, employers must give details of their own dismissal procedure, within twenty-eight days of hiring, to all new employees. Any amendments to the procedure must also be notified within twenty-eight days. Procedures must meet general criteria of fairness, such as the right to know the reason(s) for the dismissal, the right to be represented, and the right to a fair and impartial hearing. Although the lack of formal procedures will not render a dismissal automatically unfair, it could make it more difficult for the employer to demonstrate that their conduct had been fair. (See also 'Individual termination' below.)

Individual workplace rights

Grievances   There is no statutory provision on grievance procedures, although there is a Labour Relations Commission code of practice with guidelines for establishing procedures for both collective and individual disputes. Practice varies according to the degree of unionisation and state of workplace trade unionism, and the existence of other company-level consultative mechanisms, such as Company Councils. Agreed grievance procedures typically provide for initial recourse to first-line managers, the involvement of staff or union representatives, and referral to senior management: companies may indicate time limits by which they hope to achieve a resolution. External reference usually begins with a referral to senior management: companies may indicate time limits by which they hope to achieve a resolution. External reference usually begins with a referral to a Rights Commissioner or, in the event of a collective dispute, the Labour Relations Commission. Thereafter the parties can take the case to the Employee Appeals tribunal. Equality issues are dealt with via the Employment

Equality Agency, which may bring cases to the Labour Court (see above).

Data protection   Under the Data Protection Act, 1988, employees are allowed access to personal data stored on computer, and have a right to have inaccurate data amended or deleted. The employer, in the person of the company officers responsible, must ensure that automated data are accurate, up-to-date and kept for lawful purposes. Data may not be disclosed for reasons unrelated to the purpose for which they are stored; for example, personnel records should not be used for direct mail, unless it is clearly stated that such will be the case. Organisations which hold sensitive data, such as those on personal details or political opinions, physical and mental health, or an individual's private life, must register with the Data Protection Commissioner. However, ordinary employment data, including absence records, are not deemed sensitive and there is no obligation to register where this applies.

Smoking   There is a voluntary code of practice on smoking in the workplace, issued by the Department of Health. It recommends that employers should develop a policy which ensures that employees are protected from passive smoking, ideally by instituting non-smoking in the workplace, but in any event by ensuring that public areas are smoke-free and that vulnerable employees are protected. Employers should consult employees and their representatives in the formulation and implementation of a smoking policy, taking care to introduce policies which are sufficiently flexible to accommodate changes to statutory requirements and other needs of the organisation.

Employment terms and conditions

Hours of work

The Conditions of Employment Acts, 1936 and 1944, limit the working week in industry to forty-eight hours and the working day to nine hours. Dayworkers may not work beyond 20.00 on an ordinary day or beyond 13.00 on a half-day. Young workers may not work before 08.00 or after 20.00, nor must they work more than eight hours a day or forty hours in a week. Different regulations apply to retail and wholesale shops, hotels, restaurants and cafés, which are governed by the Shops (Conditions of Employment) Acts, 1938 and 1942. These Acts limit the maximum working day to eleven hours, the maximum working week to fifty-six hours in hotels or forty-eight hours in shops and set absolute limits in hotels of sixty-six hours weekly, 244 hours monthly and 2,900 annually.

Actual working hours are mainly decided at company level and tend to be around thirty-nine hours weekly, on average.

A framework for reducing weekly working hours from forty to thirty-nine was part of the 1987–90 Programme for National Recovery (see below). Most companies implemented the cut, typically by granting one hour off on Friday afternoon. There have been moves towards more flexible working patterns, principally in the context of avoiding reduncancies.

Annual leave and public holidays

Employees are entitled to paid annual leave of three working weeks under the Holidays (Employees) Act, 1977, if they have worked for the same employer for 1,400 hours in the agreed leave year (1,300 hours if the employee is under 18). Other employees are entitled to one-twelfth of the statutory period for each full month (defined as 120 hours) worked. On average companies grant twenty days' paid leave a year, with higher entitlements in some cases for long service.

There are nine public holidays: 1 January, St Patrick's Day, Easter Monday, the first Monday in May, the first Monday in June, the first Monday in August, the last Monday in October, Christmas Day and Boxing Day (St Stephen's Day). Employers are not obliged to grant the actual day of the public holiday to the employee, and may choose either a paid day off on that day, a paid day off within a month, an extra day's annual leave, the closest Church holiday before or after the day, or an extra day's pay.

Maternity and paternity leave

All permanent female employees working at least eight hours a week are entitled to a minimum of fourteen weeks' maternity leave under the Maternity Protection of Employees Acts, 1981 and 1991. There is no length of service requirement for full-time workers but part-timers must work at least eight hours a week and have thirteen weeks' service. The leave must begin at least four weeks before the end of the expected week of confinement and end no sooner than four weeks after that week. Women on maternity leave receive state benefit of 70 per cent of their earnings in the relevant tax year, subject to minimum and maximum rates, from July 1994, of Ir£74.20 and Ir£158.90 weekly. Employees may take an additional four weeks' unpaid leave if they wish and are entitled to paid time off for ante- and post-natal check-ups and care.

Employees on maternity leave are guaranteed the right to return to work in the same position under the same contract of employment. Written notice of return must be given at least four weeks in advance. Not giving notice four weeks prior to return has been found in the court to be a fair reason for dismissal. There is no statutory provision for parental leave. Nor is there any statutory provision for educational leave, although some companies will allow their employees unpaid career breaks.

A draft Bill on adoptive leave was put before the Senate in October 1993 and could become law by the end of 1994. It contains provisions for a minimum of ten weeks' unpaid adoptive leave, beginning on the day a child joins the home. An adopting parent would be entitled to take an additional period of up to four weeks' leave, also unpaid, after the initial ten-week period, or before it, in the case of the adoption of a foreign child. The provisions cover adopting mothers and sole male adopters.

Individual pay and benefits

There is no statutory minimum wage in the Irish Republic. However, there are mechanisms for setting binding minimum rates and conditions in some industries. Joint Labour Committees (JLCs) may be established to set minimum rates in industries where pay is traditionally low and union organisation weak. Such committees cover some fifteen sectors, including hairdressing, hotels, catering and textiles, employing an estimated 88,000 people in 1992. JLC awards are legally binding. The Labour Court may set up a JLC in any industry if it deems that rates of pay or wage-setting mechanisms warrant a JLC, or that a JLC is desired by employers and employees. The rates of pay set by a JLC represent a floor and are usually lower than actual average earnings in an industry. Sectors with a higher degree of union organisation but with low pay are regulated by Joint Industrial Councils (JICs), independent bodies set up by government with the aim of promoting good industrial relations. There are three registered JICs and eleven unregistered JICs covering some 83,000 employees in total. They operate under the jurisdiction of the Labour Relations Commission and issue regulations termed Registered Employment Agreements, setting minimum pay and conditions for a particular sector.

There is no statutory system of pay indexation.

The law on pay

The payment of wages is governed by the Payment of Wages Act, 1991, which came into force on 1 January 1992 and covers all employees, including temporary workers and apprentices. It sets out permitted methods of paying wages in addition to any designated by the Labour Ministry. They include: cash, draft or bill of exchange, credit transfer, postal, money or paying order or bankers' draft. All employees paid in cash prior to 1 January 1992 have a right to continue to be paid in that way unless agreement is reached otherwise. In practice there has been a marked movement away from payment in cash over a number of years.

Pay slips must be itemised, showing the gross amount and details of all deductions. Deductions must be authorised by statute, the contract of employment or the consent of the employee. Employees must be given at least one week's written notice of a deduction and the deduction should be made within six months of the notice. This does not apply to deductions in order to recover overpayment, deductions as a result of disciplinary or court proceedings, income tax and social security deductions, agreed deductions such as check-off arrangements, and deductions as a result of taking part in industrial action.

Employees may complain to a Rights Commissioner if they feel that there has been an illegal deduction from their wages.

Employer insolvency

The Protection of Employees (Employer's Insolvency) Act, 1984, guarantees debts owed to employees by insolvent employers. The Ministry of Labour will reimburse employees up to eight weeks' pay, with an upper limit of Ir£300 weekly (from 1 May 1994) together with up to eight weeks' holiday pay, up to eight weeks' sick pay, provided a company sick pay scheme exists, notice pay and any outstanding unfair dismissal awards or equal pay arrears. Employees may take grievances in this area to the Employment Appeals Tribunal within six weeks of the Ministry's decision. EAT decisions may be contested in this matter only on a point of law.

Pay determination

Pay is determined predominantly at company level, in some industries – with historically low pay rates – subject to binding minima set by joint bodies with statutory backing. This represents a marked devolution of pay setting from the industry-led rounds of the 1960s. Since 1987 pay increases at company level have been determined within the framework of three successive national tripartite pay agreements which have limited percentage increases but provided for flat-rate minimum rises for basic pay. Although they are not legally binding, the vast majority of companies (well over 90 per cent) have kept to the agreed pay provisions, at least for non-managerial grades. A number of foreign companies traditionally remain outside the national pact and trade union bargaining culture. Rates of pay in these companies tend to be higher than the average, and in some cases increases have exceeded the national guidelines.

The agreement which ran from 1990 to 1993 included a further optional increase of up to 3 per cent, to be negotiated at company level and intended to reflect business performance and productivity improvements. The clause proved controversial in as much as union bargainers expected the additional increase to be paid, whilst employers were reluctant to concede it as a matter of course. The clause generated a large number of grievances, many of which ended up before the Labour Relations Commission (see above). According to trade union research, around 45 per cent of settlements included the extra increase.

The current tripartite agreement, the 'Programme for Competitiveness and Work', runs from 1994 to 1996, and is phased in as the individual company agreements under the previous agreement expire. In contrast to the 1990–93 agreement, the 1994–96 programme is based solely on flat-rate increases and does not provide scope for local bargaining. The agreed increases are for 2 per cent in the first year, 2.5 per cent in the second, and in the third year 2.5 per cent for the first six months and 1 per cent for the final six months.

Implementation of national pay agreements is via local negotiation. Under the 1994–96 programme, companies may pay below the agreed rates of increase, provided that they give employees an increase of at least Ir£3.50 in years 2 and 3 of the programme. Companies tend to negotiate on an annual basis, usually in the first three months of the year. The actual rate of earnings growth nationally tends to be above the provisions of the national pact, as the pact does not cover additional bonuses and promotions.

Main payment systems

Blue-collar pay is usually calculated on an hourly rate and paid weekly. White-collar employees' and managers' pay is normally an annual salary paid monthly. According to an employer survey, over 90 per cent of companies paid their blue-collar workers on a weekly basis; just under 60 per cent of companies paid white-collar employees monthly.

During the 1970s and 1980s many Irish companies established incremental pay scales as a means of retaining employees in a period in which unemployment was comparatively low and inflation high. Annual increments of around 4 per cent, quite apart from cost-of-living increases, were not considered excessive with inflation at 15 per cent or more. In recent years there has been some shift away from incremental pay scales towards performance-related pay systems, largely on grounds of cost, against a background of lower inflation (about 2 per cent) and the search for ways of making employees more effective and less mobile. Clustering of employees at the top of incremental scales has raised costs, and reportedly fostered employee frustration. In addition, new technology has served to broaden and merge areas of responsibility, requiring wider responsibilities and a more flexible approach to tasks. Performance-related pay systems have acquired a particularly high profile in the banking and finance sectors. The Bank of Ireland, for example, has introduced performance-related pay for managers and executives and, on a voluntary basis, for lower-grade bank assistants. Similarly, at the insurance company Irish Life, employees voted to replace increments with performance-related pay.

Job evaluation and grading

Standardised grading systems are quite well developed in the public sector and civil service. In the private sector, in the absence of national guidelines, job evaluation systems and grading structures tend to be set up according to individual companies' needs. They may be imposed by management or negotiated with staff or union representatives.

Overtime, night work and shift pay

Overtime   Any overtime worked beyond forty-eight hours weekly must by law be paid at the rate of at least time and a quarter. Companies tend to pay overtime supplements for hours worked beyond the agreed working week, which is usually within the range of thirty-five to forty hours. The most common form of payment is time and a half; some companies pay double time after the first four overtime hours worked per day and double time after midnight. Saturday working is usually paid at time and a half and double time after the first few hours; Sunday working and work on public holidays are normally paid at double time, with some companies awarding time off in lieu in addition, or triple time. It is not usual for companies to pay overtime supplements to managers and professionals.

Shift pay   There is no statutory provision guaranteeing enhanced pay or time off for shift work. Compensation is governed by company agreement, and an employer survey found that the average shift payment in 1993 was 16 per cent of normal pay for day-shift and 30 per cent for night-shift working.

Holiday pay   Employees are guaranteed a minimum of three weeks' paid leave annually under the Holidays (Employees) Act, 1973. The average company holiday entitlement tends to be twenty days a year. If employees are paid on time rates, weekly holiday pay should equal the average weekly payment for normal working hours in the preceding quarter.

Bonuses

There is no statutory provision for bonus payments, but the awarding of bonuses is common practice. According to an employer survey, some 40 per cent of companies award Christmas bonuses to white-collar workers and 44 per cent to blue-collar workers. Holiday bonuses are awarded to both blue- and white-collar workers by around 7 per cent of companies. Average bonus payments tend to be between Ir£37 and Ir£44 for blue-collar workers, paid on a monthly basis, and Ir£1,000 to Ir£1,350 for white-collar workers, paid annually.

Pay for performance

The element of pay related to performance, either through bonuses or merit pay, is an important element of the remuneration package for managers and specialists. According to the Irish Management Institute's 1993 survey of executive salaries, performance-related bonuses accounted for an average of 22 per cent of salary for chief executives, 11 per cent for senior managers reporting to heads of function, and 7 per cent to 8 per cent for first-line and middle managers. (See also 'Main payment systems' above.) It is common practice in high-tech industry to award attendance incentives, typically six days' pay for a perfect year's attendance, diminishing by one day's pay for each day of absence.

Managers' pay

The national agreements which have governed pay-setting since 1987 do not expressly provide for managerial pay. Although the guidelines set in the agreements would serve as a basis, a survey conducted by the Irish Management Institute found that less than 50 per cent of the companies it surveyed adhered to the national pay guidelines when setting managerial pay. It is common for managers' pay to be set and revised individually, outside the company's collective bargaining process.

Financial participation

Share options   Under the Finance Act, 1986, there is favourable tax treatment for share options granted under schemes approved by the Revenue Commissioners. There is no requirement for employers to offer schemes to all employees, and many schemes are restricted to senior management. If approval has been obtained, the granting and exercise of an option incur no income tax liability provided the option price is not less than the market price when the option was granted. Companies normally set an upper limit on the amount of shares an employee may buy.

Profit-sharing   There has been statutory provision for approved share-based profit-sharing schemes since the 1982 Finance Act. Under approved schemes, companies must use profits to acquire shares and hold them in a trust fund for at least two years before releasing them to employees. If employees retain the shares for seven years in all, they are entitled to full tax relief, reduced if shares are sold before then. There is a maximum of Ir£5,000 worth of shares per employee per year.

Sick pay

Statutory sickness benefit, known as *disability benefit*, is payable from the fourth day of absence from work due to illness, on production of a medical certificate. Rates are graduated according to earnings, with the standard rate for an employee earning over Ir£70 per week standing at Ir£55.60 in 1994: there is a further sum payable for adult and child dependants. From the fourteenth day of absence a state pay-related supplement may be added. Employers are not required to provide sick pay. However, the majority of companies offer schemes in addition to state provision, ranging from full normal salary to a fixed-rate flat payment. The majority of schemes operate from the first day of absence due to sickness. According to an employer survey of companies in the Dublin region, some 66 per cent of companies had schemes in place for blue-collar workers and 75 per cent for white-collar workers. The employer usually deducts the amount of state sickness benefit to which the employee is entitled from the amount of company sick pay due. Some companies have an attendance-related scheme, with perfect attendance over the previous twelve months giving 100 per cent of salary for a pre-specified period which varies by length of service.

Equal pay and opportunities

Legal framework

Under the Anti-Discrimination (Pay) Act, 1974, there is a statutory requirement of equal pay for like work. Men and women are entitled to receive equal rates of pay for carrying out the same tasks, tasks of a similar nature or tasks which are of equal value in terms of responsibility, physical or mental effort, skill and working conditions. Equal pay claims are referred to an Equality Officer, directly by the complainant, by the employer or via the Employment Equality Agency (see too below). Should either party reject the Equality Officer's recommendation, or if the recommendation is not implemented, appeal is possible to the Labour Court, with a right of further appeal to the High Court on points of law.

The Employment Equality Act, 1977, provides for equal treatment as regards training, promotion and conditions of employment. It protects employees against dismissal for taking legal action to secure the right to equal pay and opportunities. Disputes are referred to the Employment Equality Agency, which has investigative powers and can issue a non-discrimination notice. There is a right of appeal to the Labour Court, and from there to the civil courts on points of law. If discrimination is proved, the employer may be liable to pay compensation of up to 104 weeks' pay. If the discrimination has resulted in dismissal, the employer may be liable for compensation of up to two years' pay, a fine of up to Ir£100 for failure to follow a course of action recommended by the court, and Ir£10 for each day the offence continues. The burden of proof is on the claimant. In the event of dismissal on discriminatory grounds, or on the grounds that the employee was seeking to assert their rights under the Act, the Labour Court can order reinstatement, re-engagement or an award of damages of up to two years' pay. Failure to comply with a Labour Court order is a criminal offence and can involve the complainant in further damages.

There are proposals in the pipeline to consolidate the two separate equality Acts into a single statute.

AIDS- and HIV-related discrimination

There is no legislation dealing with discrimination in the case of employees who are HIV+ or who have AIDS. However, the employers' organisation IBEC has issued guidelines for companies in drawing up a policy in this area. Policies should contain the following main points:

- A commitment to treat infected individuals fairly, with compassion and in the same way as any other employees with a serious illness.
- A commitment to confidentiality.
- The provision of information on the means by which HIV is spread and how it can be avoided.
- The provision of training for persons responsible for first aid and the adoption of safe procedures for dealing with cuts and blood spillages. More general training on HIV awareness for management personnel might also be considered.
- The provision of counselling or information on counselling to employees who are concerned about or affected by the HIV virus.

Sexual harassment

Following a ruling by the Labour Court in the mid-1980s, sexual harassment is deemed to constitute an act of sex discrimination under the 1977 Employment Equality Act. Subsequent court decisions have taken a broad view of sexual harassment, including a ruling that acts outside the workplace involving employees could constitute harassment. There is no statutory definition of sexual harassment. Forty-nine cases of sexual harassment have been brought since 1990 – one of them by a male employee – but the Minister for Equality and Law Reform stressed that these figures do not accurately reflect the incidence of harassment, much of which is either not reported or resolved directly with the employer or with the help of a trade union or the Employment Appeals Tribunal.

Retirement

The statutory retirement age is 65 years for men and women. There is no state provision for early retirement, and research has shown that the majority of people of both sexes tend to work right up to the age of 65. The state pension scheme provides a flat-rate benefit (Ir£71 weekly in 1994), some 25 per cent of the average industrial wage, with a higher rate paid to the over-80s (Ir£75.70 weekly in 1994). Entitlement to benefit is based on contributions during employment. Although there is no statutory requirement for companies to top pensions up, the majority of firms offer employees an additional occupational scheme, usually entailing employee contributions.

Occupational pension schemes are now regulated under the provisions of the Pensions Act, 1990, which established a Pensions Board to monitor compliance with the Act, issue guidelines and codes of practice for trustees, and advise the government. In addition to the creation of the Pensions Board, the 1990 Act improved and protected employees' rights to pension benefits, and notably the right to a preserved benefit after five years' service or the right to transfer when leaving schemes.

Individual termination of contract

Resignation and constructive dismissal

Employees may tender their resignation at any time during the contract of employment and are subject to the agreed period of notice. There is a statutory definition of constructive dismissal in the Unfair Dismissals Act, 1977, allowing cases to be brought where 'because of the conduct of the employer, the employee was or would have been entitled or it was or would have been reasonable for the employee to terminate the contract of employment without giving prior notice'. If a case of constructive dismissal is brought before an Employment Appeals tribunal, and the employer maintains that the employee has not been dismissed, the burden of proof rests with the employee.

Termination by mutual agreement

The parties to the contract of employment may agree to end the contract at any time. There is no statutory requirement for the agreement to be in writing. An employee who comes to a mutual agreement with the employer that the contract should be terminated automatically loses the right of redress under the Unfair Dismissals Act, the Minimum Notice and Terms of Employment Act and the Redundancy Act.

Grounds for dismissal

Under the Unfair Dismissals Act, 1977, dismissal on the following grounds may be fair:

- The capability, competence or qualifications of the employee.
- The conduct of the employee.
- Redundancy.
- The employee's continuation in employment would have resulted in contravention of statutory provisions.
- The expiry of a fixed-term or temporary contract.

If so requested by the employee, the employer must supply written details of the grounds within fourteen days of the dismissal.

Dismissal with notice and summary dismissal

Employees working eight or more hours weekly and with thirteen weeks' continuous service are entitled to a period of notice dependent on length of service (see below). In cases of serious misconduct, employees may be summarily dismissed and therefore lose their right to a period of notice. There is no statutory definition of misconduct, although case law has ruled that it must be of 'a deliberate or positive kind', rather than due to neglect, incompetence or absenteeism.

Dismissal on grounds of employee conduct

Dismissal resulting wholly or partially from an employee's lack of ability, competence or skills is deemed to be fair. In case law, repeated absence due to illness has been found to be a fair reason for dismissal on grounds of incapacity to do the job. However, it might not be upheld if the employee could have been put on to lighter duties. Failure to meet reasonable targets set by the employer would constitute grounds for dismissal, subject to judicial interpretation. For example, the dismissal of a sales representative following failure to meet an excessively increased sales target was deemed unfair. Moreover, poor performance may be held to be insufficient grounds for dismissal in the absence of clear objectives and guidance from the employer.

The lawfulness of dismissal resulting from employee misconduct is determined largely by case law. It is generally held that conduct which justifies dismissal is that which undermines the relationship of trust necessary for the employment relationship to continue. It may be an employee's refusal to carry out tasks they were engaged to do or required to do by implication. Misconduct may be a single act, a single breach of discipline or a series of acts following a number of warnings. There is no statutorily prescribed disciplinary procedure or series of warnings to be followed by employers, although it is generally held that a warning should be issued prior to dismissal in order to give the employee an opportunity to improve in order for a dismissal to be fair. Under the Unfair Dismissals Act, employees must be informed within twenty-eight days of the start of employment of any disciplinary procedures which would apply to them. Failure by the employer to adhere to an agreed disciplinary procedure could in itself render a dismissal unfair. Common practice is a verbal warning, a written warning and a final written warning, followed by suspension or dismissal. The employers' organisation IBEC recommends that if an employee's record subsequently remains clear for at least one year the individual should revert to the previous stage of the warning procedure in the event of any further breach.

Dismissal on economic grounds

There is a statutory definition of dismissal on economic grounds (redundancy) under the Redundancy Payments Acts, 1967–91. It embraces:

- Cessation or relocation of the employer's business.
- Diminution of the needs of the business for the employee's work.
- A decision by the employer to reduce the work force, or to have work done by other, more suitably qualified, employees.

Failure to make a fair selection, or to abide by an agreed redundancy procedure, may open the employer to a claim of unfair dismissal.

Under the Redundancy Payments Acts, 1967–91, employers wishing to make individuals redundant must inform them in writing at least two weeks before the proposed date of dismissal (even though an agreed or statutory notice period is usually longer). A copy of the notice must be lodged with the Department of Labour. Employers failing to comply with this provision are liable to a fine of up to Ir£50. Employees made redundant are entitled to a period of notice and to severance payments (see below). If the employee has at least 104 weeks' service the employer must provide a certificate of redundancy on the date of dismissal, or be liable to a fine of up to Ir£300.

Periods of notice

The Minimum Notice and Terms of Employment Act, 1973, regulates minimum notice periods for employees with thirteen weeks' continuous service as follows:

- Thirteen weeks to two years' service: one week's notice.
- Two to five years' service: two weeks' notice.
- Five to ten years' service: four weeks' notice.
- Ten to fifteen years' service: six weeks' notice.
- Fifteen years' service or more: eight weeks' notice.

Individual contracts or company-level agreements may provide for longer periods of notice, which are binding unless mutual agreement is otherwise reached. Periods of notice for executives range, on average, from three to six months. Notice periods may be waived if payment is offered in lieu.

Severance payments

Severance payments for redundancy are governed by the Redundancy Payments Acts, 1967–91, and are payable to employees with at least two years' service. Minimum payments are: one week's pay, plus half a week's pay for each year of continuous employment between the ages of 16 and 41 years, plus one week's pay for each year of continuous employment over the age of 41 years, all these figures subject to an upper limit of Ir£15,600 per year as from 1 May 1994. The calculation of weekly pay is based on normal weekly remuneration, including average overtime, commission and other varied bonuses. Severance payments are tax-free. Employers are usually reimbursed by the Redundancy Fund for 60 per cent of the statutory payments to employees. However, reimbursement may be reduced to 40 per cent if the employer has not complied fully with the provisions regarding notice. Trade unions often negotiate higher severance payments with employers. Payments may range from the statutory minimum only to six weeks' pay per year of service in addition to the statutory minimum. No rebate can be claimed by the employer for any redundancy lump-sum payments above the statutory amount.

Unfair dismissal

Protection against unfair dismissal under the Unfair Dismissals Act, 1977 (amended in 1993), extends to all private-sector employees aged under 65, working eight hours a week or more, and with one year's continuous service. In 1993 the provisions of the law were extended to agency workers, who for the purposes of the Act are deemed to be employees of the hiring company. The 1993 amendment also extended protection to employees on fixed-term contracts which expire before one year's service where it can be established that the contracts are intended to thwart the intention of the Act.

Dismissal will be deemed unfair if it is wholly or mainly attributable to or occasioned by:

- Race, colour or sexual orientation.
- The age of the employee.
- Membership of a trade union.
- Membership of the travelling community.
- The employee's religious or political opinions.
- Civil or criminal proceedings against the employer, or in which the employee is a party or a witness.
- The exercise of maternity rights.
- Unfair selection for redundancy.
- Selective dismissals following industrial action.

Claims of unfair dismissal are heard by Rights Commissioners who make a recommendation. Claims must be submitted within six months, but this deadline may be extended to twelve months in exceptional circumstances. The burden of proof lies with the employer, except where the claim involves trade union membership or pregnancy and the exercise of maternity rights, or where the employee claims constructive dismissal.

If either party objects to the case being heard by the Rights Commissioner, it can be taken straight to the Employment Appeals Tribunal. Appeals against a Rights Commissioner's recommendation are taken to the EAT and must be lodged within six weeks of the recommendation. The EAT will then issue a determination. Appeals against an EAT determination must be taken to the circuit court within six weeks. An appeal may be lodged by either party, or the Minister of Labour may decide to proceed against an employer for non-compliance with a determination of the EAT, in which case a binding order will be issued.

If unfair dismissal is proved, one of the following courses of action may be recommended:

- Reinstatement, with arrears of pay from the date of dismissal and any improvements in terms and conditions agreed during the period since dismissal.

- Re-engagement in the same or a similar position on conditions specified by the Rights Commissioner, the EAT or the court.
- Compensation by the employer, up to a maximum of 104 weeks' pay.

In practice, most contested dismissals end in the payment of compensation, with reinstatement ordered only where the employee contributed in no material way to the dismissal. The average compensation payment in 1991 was Ir£2,660.

Collective dismissal

Collective dismissal is defined as the dismissal within thirty days of:

- At least five employees in companies with twenty-one to forty-nine employees.
- At least ten employees in companies with fifty to ninety-nine employees.
- At least 10 per cent of employees in companies with 100–299 employees.
- At least thirty employees in companies with 300 or more employees.

Statutory requirements on consultation

Under the Protection of Employment Act, 1977, employers in companies with at least twenty employees must consult work-force representatives and notify the Ministry of Labour of the details of the dismissals thirty days prior to effecting collective dismissal. Employee representatives should be consulted on the reasons for the redundancies, the number to be made redundant, the selection criteria for redundancy and ways of avoiding or reducing the impact of the redundancies. Severance payment arrangements are as those for individual redundancies (see above).

Transfer of undertakings

Employee rights in the event of the transfer of an undertaking are protected by the European Communities (Safeguarding of Employees' Rights on Transfer of Undertakings) Regulations, 1980. The statute covers all employers and all employees, and provides for the transfer of all employee rights and obligations and for workforce consultation. Terms and conditions set out in a collective agreement must be observed until they are replaced by a new agreement or upon the expiry of the old provisions.

Employees must be informed of:

- The reasons for the transfer.
- Its legal, social and economic implications for employees.
- Any measures envisaged in relation to the employees.

Information must be provided 'in good time' by both the original and the new employer. Where there are no employee representatives, the employer must inform each employee individually in writing and through notices at the place of work. Dismissals are permissible on economic, technical or organisational grounds, but not solely by virtue of the transfer.

Final formalities

Employees are normally under an obligation to work out any period of notice agreed. However, upon mutual agreement, the employee may leave before the end of the period. An employer should grant the employee 'reasonable' paid time off, during the last two weeks of the notice period, in order to find new employment. Employers must honour obligations with regard to the payments of wages, holiday pay and sick pay.

Appendix

Non-wage labour costs and income tax rates

Average employer contributions for social welfare (pay-related social insurance contributions, PRSI) are 9 per cent for earnings up to Ir£9,000 per year and 12.2 per cent on earnings between Ir£9,000 and Ir£25,800. Employees pay 5.5 per cent for earnings up to Ir£9,000 and 7.75 on additional earnings up to Ir£20,900, with 2.25 per cent due on remaining earnings.

There are two rates of income tax: 27 per cent and 48 per cent. The low threshold at which the higher rate starts – Ir£8,200 taxable income in 1994 for individuals – means that levels of taxation are high in international terms. Tax evasion has led to periodic amnesties, during which outstanding liabilities are levied at a reduced rate.

Organisations

Department of Labour
Mespil Road, Dublin 4
Tel. + 353 1 6765861; fax + 353 1 6769047

Training and Employment Authority (FAS)
27–33 Upper Baggot Street, Dublin 4
Tel. + 353 1 6685777; fax + 353 1 6682691

Irish Business and Employers' Confederation (IBEC)
84–6 Lower Baggot Street, Dublin 2
Tel. + 353 1 6601011; fax + 353 1 6601717

Irish Congress of Trade Unions (ICTU)
19 Raglan Road, Dublin 4
Tel. + 353 1 6680641; fax + 353 1 6609027

Association of Management Consulting
Organisations (AMCO)
Confederation House
Kildare Street, Dublin 2
Tel. + 353 1 6779801; fax + 353 1
6777823

Irish Institute of Personnel Management
35–9 Shelbourne Road, Ballsbridge,
Dublin 4
Tel. + 353 1 6686244; fax + 353 1
6608030

Labour Relations Commission
Tom Johnson House, Haddington Road,
Dublin 4
Tel. + 353 1 6609662; fax + 353 1
6685069

Industrial Relations News
121–123 Ranelagh Road, Dublin 6
Tel. + 353 1 4972711; fax + 353 1
4972779

Irish Management Institute
Sandyford Road, Dublin 16
Tel. + 353 1 2956911; fax + 353 1

Main sources

Industrial Relations News, IRM Publishing, Dublin, various issues.

Fennell, Caroline, and Lynch, Irene, *Labour Law in Ireland*, Gill & Macmillan, Dublin, 1993.

Federation of Irish Employers (now IBEC, see above), *A Guide to Employment Legislation*, fifth edition, Dublin, 1991, supplemented by original statutes in the case of subsequent amendments.

Irish Business and Employers' Confederation, *IR Data Bank*, IR Publications Ltd, Dublin, various issues.

Irish Management Institute, *Executive Salaries in Ireland*, Irish Management Institute in association with the Irish Times, Dublin, 1993.

Department of Enterprise and Employment, explanatory circulars on employment legislation.

Department of Social Welfare, circulars on PRSI contributions and social welfare payments.

8
Italy

Basic rights and labour jurisdiction

Sources of law on employment: hierarchy of legal provisions

Economic relations constitute an important part of the Italian constitution, with corresponding emphasis being put on the protection of employee rights. The constitution guarantees all employees the basic rights: to work, to be paid for that work, to enjoy a weekly rest day and annual holidays, to receive social welfare and benefits; and the right to freedom of association. Within this broad framework a body of protective legislation and legally enforceable collective agreements has evolved, covering most industries and many categories of employee, including managers. Some constitutional provisions, for example article 36 on the notion of 'fair pay', have also had a direct effect on the regulation of terms and conditions; based on this clause, the courts have declared industry collective agreements generally binding on all employers.

Terms and conditions of employment in the private sector are governed by a pattern of collective agreements which are binding on the whole of the sector which they cover. Individual employment contracts are established within the general legal framework underpinned by the Civil Code. Collective and individual rights on issues such as termination are both rooted in constitutional principles and the Workers' Statute, passed in 1970 following the upsurge in industrial militancy in the late 1960s. Termination procedures are lengthy, and a major amendment of the legislation in this field in 1990 extended protection against unfair dismissal to all employees.

Labour jurisdiction

There is a special system of court proceedings applying to individual labour disputes which is considerably speedier than ordinary civil proceedings and which confers greater powers of investigation on the inquiring judge. The court's findings are immediately enforceable.

Under this system, the court of first instance to which a dispute will be referred is the *pretore del lavoro*, which involves a single magistrate. The *tribunale del lavoro* is the court of second instance and the highest specific instance for employment matters: it consists of three judges who will hear appeals brought against the rulings of the *pretore*.

The *corte di cassazione* is the national supreme court, which can test decisions of the lower courts for legitimacy. The *corte costituzionale* examines the legality of laws passed by parliament to see if they accord with the constitution.

Contracts of employment

Types of employee

There are four legally differentiated categories of employee:

- *Operai*, blue-collar workers.
- *Impiegati*, white-collar workers.
- *Quadri*, senior technical and supervisory staff.
- *Dirigenti*, managers.

Managers are covered by their own collective agreements, with separate agreements for managers in industry (*dirigenti industriali*) and in commerce (*dirigenti commerciali*). The other three categories of employee are covered by the single-status *dipendente* agreement for their particular industry.

Form of contract

Generally, there is no legal requirement for contracts to be in writing except in specific cases. It is sufficient for the parties – the employer (*datore di lavoro*) and the employee (*lavoratore*) – to have given a verbal undertaking for the agreement to be binding. In practice so many collective agreements stipulate that a contract of employment must be in writing that verbal agreements really apply only to blue-collar workers in certain industries.

By law the following types of contract must be in writing:

- Fixed-term contracts.
- Part-time contracts.
- Training and work experience contracts.
- Reinstatement contracts.

In addition, particular types of contractual clauses must be in writing: these include clauses specifying the length of probationary periods and restrictive covenants following termination of contract. EU Directive 91/533/EEC on proof of an employment contract has not been implemented yet.

Express terms

In industrial companies a verbal agreement is generally sufficient for blue-collar employees, except for fixed-term contracts or if a collective agreement requires a written contract. For example, the agreement covering the engineering industry states that the company must communicate in writing to all employees upon engagement: the date upon which the contract begins, the exact location of work, the grade and professional qualifications required, the rate of pay, any particular regulations applicable, the length of the probationary period and any other conditions which have been agreed.

Contracts for sales representatives and commercial travellers should, in addition, specify the scope and limits of their functions, the sales area for which they are responsible, the minimum period in the year during which the company undertakes to keep them on the road and any duties which may be assigned to them when they are off the road (provided these are compatible with the job grade). For managers, a written statement must be provided on engagement or promotion setting out details of duties, pay and any terms and conditions more favourable than those contained in the relevant national collective agreement.

In commercial companies, managers must be given a written statement on engagement or promotion, giving the date of engagement, the duration of the probationary period, the initial place of work, recognition of the current national industry agreement and any possible future changes in the agreement, details of duties, responsibilities, remuneration and the possibility of transfer. For all other employees in commercial companies the contract must be in writing and should register the date of recruitment, the duration of the probationary period, grade and remuneration.

Implied terms

Article 2094 of the Civil Code defines a 'subordinate employee' (*prestatore di lavoro subordinato*) as one who 'undertakes, for remuneration, to collaborate within the enterprise, by providing his own labour, intellectual or manual, as an employee under the direction of the employer'.

The concepts of 'dependence' and 'subordination' lie at the core of the employment relation in Italy and confer on the employer both a hierarchical responsibility for, and authority over, the employee. The employer has the right to manage and direct the enterprise and the power to discipline its employees, together with a duty of care towards them. Employees have a reciprocal duty of obedience, loyalty and diligence within the limits of their assigned function.

Internal transfer

If the issue of transfer is not covered by company rules or collective agreement, and if no specific limitations have been placed on it by the agreement of the parties, the employer is generally held to have the right to transfer employees within reasonable bounds according to their function and the locations in question. However, trade union officials and employee representatives on works committees (*consigli di fabbrica*) may not be transferred during or for one year following the cessation of their duties without the written authorisation of the relevant union at district level.

Grading

Article 96 of the Civil Code states that employers should inform employees when they start work which grade and category of employment their job falls into.

Responsibilities

Employees can be required to accept only those responsibilities which fall within their own job grade or within the grade to which they have been promoted or equivalent responsibility without loss of pay. Where employees undertake a job above their own grade for a period longer than three months (or for longer than a period specified by collective agreement) the job becomes permanent. An employee may not be transferred from one unit of production to another without proven technical, organisational or production-related reasons. All other agreements are null and void. This, however, does not apply where the employee is acting as a replacement for another employee who is on temporary extended leave.

Types of contract

Employment contracts which are not permanent and full-time are considered to be atypical: for example, only 5 per cent of the labour force works part-time. Such employment contracts are governed by separate legislation in each case. The number of permitted forms of non-typical employment has been extended as a result of the recession, with new types of 'solidarity' contract (see below) intended to conserve employment. The main types, together with their requirements, are as follows:

- *Apprenticeships.* Applicants must appear on a special list at state job placement offices. There are a limited number of apprenticeships at each company, and authorisation from the labour inspectorate is required. Apprentices may not be younger than 15 or older than 20, and the maximum duration of the contract is five years. Piecework is not permitted.
- *Part-time contracts.* These must be in writing and must stipulate the job to be done, the distribution of working time over hours, days, weeks or years (as appropriate) and must be registered with the provincial labour inspectorate. Collective agreements can establish the percentage of the work force on part-time contracts, and the permitted range of tasks, as well as patterns of working hours. Overtime working is not permitted unless stipulated in an industry agreement, and pay and all benefits must be *pro rata* to those of full-time employees.

Some industry and company agreements may stipulate that the employer must consult work-force representatives on part-time contracts. In such cases the Law on Part-Time Working states that agreement should be reached on the percentage of part-time employees relative to full-time, the jobs to be undertaken by part-time employees and the hours of work of part-time workers.

- *Solidarity contracts* are intended for periods of business difficulty and were strengthened by statute in July 1993. They are essentially work-sharing contracts whereby part of, or sometimes the whole, work force works reduced hours. The reduction in hours can be daily, weekly, monthly or annual. Compensation for lost earnings is provided by the national social security institution, INPS (*Istituto Nazionale della Previdenza Sociale*). Employees receive 75 per cent of the payment for hours not worked, with the remaining 25 per cent going to the company. In addition, the company pays reduced social charges on the hours worked. Not all companies qualify for the full financial benefits outlined above, though most are permitted to use this type of contract.
- *Re-employment contracts.* These are aimed at recruiting workers who have been in receipt of special unemployment benefit (*trattamento di disoccupazione speciale*) for at least twelve months and attract social security reductions for the employer. They must be in writing and must be copied to both the provincial labour inspectorate and the provincial office of INPS. No employer may use this type of contract who has been responsible for any economic dismissals during the previous twelve-month period.
- *Training and work experience contracts.* Applicants should be aged between 15 and 29 years. The maximum duration of the contract is twenty-four months. The employer benefits from reduced social charges. There are limits on the use on these contracts to prevent employers abusing the incentives they attract.
- *Fixed-term contracts* are permitted where necessitated by the inherent nature of the work involved, when cover is required for an individual on leave (e.g. maternity, military service), or to accomplish a specific task. The contract must be in writing and a copy must be sent to the employee. It is renewable only once and for a term no longer than the original. Pay and benefits should be *pro rata* those of full-time employees.
- *Contracts for managers* (*dirigenti*). The special nature of this type of contract embraces enhanced powers and responsibilities within and on behalf of the enterprise; rights of supervision over other employees; exclusion from social legislation such as the duty to sign on at the official job placement office and to carry an employment record (*libretto di lavoro*); exclusion from legislation on hours of work and on fixed-term working. However, *dirigenti* are covered by their own collective agreements setting minimum pay levels.

There are no specific regulations on the relationship between collective agreements and individual contracts. Individual contracts however, normally conform to the appropriate industry agreement.

Probationary periods

In general, probationary periods must be specified in writing. (One exception would be where an enterprise has a clear code of practice set out in its personnel handbook.) Either party can terminate the contract of employment at the end of this period without giving notice and without payment, except for services already rendered by the employee. Should the probationary period be completed satisfactorily, it is added to the employee's length of service once the contract has been made permanent.

Restrictive covenants

Article 2125 of the Civil Code rules that a restrictive covenant (*patto di non concorrenza*), preventing the employee from competing with the former employer, will be null and void unless certain conditions are met:

- The agreement must be in writing.
- It must contain compensatory provision for the employee.
- It must specify limits on the purpose, period and scope of the agreement.
- It cannot be valid for more than five years in the case of executives or for more than three years in that of other employees.

Employee inventions and copyright

If an invention is made as a result of work undertaken as part of the employment contract then employees are not entitled to additional compensation.

Workplace discipline: the 1970 Statute

Under the 1970 Workers' Statute (1970), any disciplinary procedures which discriminate against a person's union affiliation or activity, their participation in a strike, their political opinions or their religious faith are null and void.

Disciplinary procedures and sanctions must be posted up where all employees can see them and should reflect collective agreements where these exist or the employer's disciplinary code where they do not, especially where misconduct could lead to dismissal. All procedures must conform to the Workers' Statute. Employers may not proceed to discipline employees without first informing them as to the reason and without first listening to their defence. Employees have a right to be assisted by the representative of a trade union. Disciplinary measures must not amount to a permanent change in terms of employment. Fines cannot exceed a sum equal to four hours' basic pay, and suspension from work or pay must not exceed ten days. In any event, disciplinary measures beyond a verbal warning may only be implemented five days after communication in writing, whereupon employees have the right to appeal within twenty days to a conciliation and arbitration panel (*collegio di arbitrato e conciliazione*). Alternatively either party has the right to approach a judicial authority instead of a panel.

The engineering industry agreement, for example, states that individual grievances or disputes will be dealt with by management and workplace representatives. Failure to agree means that matters will be referred to their respective central organisations. In addition it lays down a basic framework for conduct within the organisation which includes undertakings such as:

- Mutual courtesy and correctness.
- Superiors to encourage co-operative relations between themselves and subordinates.
- The organisation to ensure that no employee is placed in an 'equivocal position' regarding anyone, including their immediate superior, whom an employee might need to turn to for help or instructions.

Workplace discipline

Absences, lateness and disciplinary measures are governed by collective agreements but must conform with the Workers' Statute. In industrial undertakings most collective agreements require employees to justify absence on the day following the beginning of a period of absence except where this is not possible for good reason. Unjustified, prolonged or repeated absence can give rise to disciplinary measures (fines or suspension) or to dismissal, though this is very rare.

In commercial undertakings all absences must be notified immediately and justified in writing within forty-eight hours unless the employee can show good reason for not doing so. Unjustified absences are punishable by fines or by dismissal if they exceed three days in any one calendar year.

Lateness is punishable by fines or by dismissal if unauthorised more than five times in a calendar year. The dismissal must follow the procedure laid down in the collective agreement.

Individual workplace rights

Individual workplace rights such as rights concerning information, grievances, data protection and access to management are dealt with by collective agreement or by custom and practice.

Workplace issues

Matters such as smoking at work, sexual harassment and drug or alcohol abuse are dealt with either by industry agreement or by local agreement. Employees will be supported where necessary by their union representatives. Those with addiction problems are entitled to have their job kept open for the period stated in the industry agreement (three years in some cases), provided they can furnish evidence that they are receiving suitable treatment. Some companies provide the services of a resident counsellor.

Employment terms

Hours of work

The statutory maximum working day is eight hours, with a maximum working week of forty-eight hours based on a nominal six-day working week. These maxima were established by decree 692 (15 March 1923) and became statute law with law 473 (17 April 1925). In practice, hours of work are governed by collective agreement. In 1992 average agreed weekly hours in manufacturing stood at forty a week, or 1,722 on an annual basis. A large number of collective agreements either express or manage hours of work on an annualised basis, with cuts in hours in recent years generally taken in the form of additional days off rather than a shorter working week.

This applies, for example, in the engineering industry. Under the terms of the current agreement the basic week is fixed at forty hours, but with sixteen hours off the working year from 1987, and a further sixteen-hour reduction agreed in 1991. Agreed annual hours in 1992 were 1,709. In the private-sector chemical industry the basic working week is forty hours for dayworkers and thirty-seven and a half hours for shift workers. To cater for flexible hours of work arrangements, the normal working week may, with the consent of the works council, be arrived at by averaging out the total number of hours worked weekly over a reference period to be agreed at company or plant level. Hours worked above the statutory maximum week as part of these flexible arrangements are paid at rates higher than normal.

Annual leave

The constitution guarantees workers the right to paid annual holidays (*ferie annuali*), which they may not surrender (though no penalties are laid down for infringement). If, in exceptional circumstances, employees have to work during their leave they are entitled to double time. Entitlement to leave is acquired following the successful completion of a probationary period. If an employee falls ill while on leave the holiday entitlement may be suspended for the period of illness. There are currently no general legal provisions relating to the length of annual leave, which is determined by collective agreement. Agreements may link holiday entitlement with job grade – and, more often, with length of service. (However, from November 1996 the EU's working time directive will require three weeks paid leave, rising to four from 1999.)

Basic leave entitlement ranges from four to six weeks a year. The bulk is almost always taken during August, when most factories in manufacturing, for example, shut down. Industry-level agreements usually provide for a basic annual leave entitlement of four weeks, but an additional week is often given to compensate for the abolition in 1977 of five state and religious holidays.

In engineering a basic annual entitlement of four weeks is increased by one day for employees with between ten and eighteen years' service and by six days (calculated on the basis of a six-day working week) for those with nineteen years' service or more. The number of weeks taken off together may not exceed three, unless a company-level agreement provides otherwise. Companies may improve on the agreed arrangements. Fiat, for example, adds five days to be taken individually to offset the past cut in public holidays. Moreover, any Christmas shutdown is not taken out of employees' holiday entitlement.

Public holidays

There are ten public holidays (*giorni festivi*). In addition to the national holidays local saints' days are also observed as public holidays in certain cities (such as 24 June in Turin and 7 December in Milan). Employers are obliged to pay normal pay on a public holiday – that is, what employees would have earned had they been at work. Article 2 of law 90 (31 March 1954) requires the employer to pay even if the employee would have been off work in any case – because of illness, injury, maternity leave, annual holiday, etc. Where an employee has to work over a public holiday (*lavoro festivo*) – for example, on shift work or some other agreed exception – collective agreements lay down special supplements in addition to a day off in lieu.

Maternity leave

Mothers are forbidden to work during the statutory period of maternity leave (*sospensione obbligatoria*) which runs from two months before the expected date of the birth to three months after the actual date. In certain jobs – laid down by ministerial decree – this period begins three months before the expected date of birth.

Maternity benefit during statutory maternity leave is equal to 80 per cent of normal pay. The cost of the benefit is borne by the social security organisation. Maternity benefit is payable to the employee, with the first month's salary or wage following resumption of work. However, the employer must pay an amount in advance which is normally laid down by collective agreement, but which in any case may not be less than half of previous monthly pay. Some collective agreements provide for maternity pay at 100 per cent of normal pay, payable on a monthly basis during the period of leave.

The law also prohibits women from doing dangerous, unhealthy or heavy work from the beginning of pregnancy until the seventh month after the birth.

During this period a woman normally on such work has to be assigned to other duties without loss of pay.

Time off for breast-feeding

During the first year of a baby's life the employer must allow the mother two special breaks during the day (one break if her working hours are less than six) to breast-feed her baby. These breaks must each be of one hour's duration (half an hour if the mother has the use of a room for the purpose, or of a crèche provided on the premises by the employer). The breaks are counted as normal working time and are paid.

Optional parental leave

In addition to maternity leave, a woman may choose to take a further six months' leave during the first year of the baby's life. Her job is protected until the baby is one year old. She is entitled to payments from the sickness benefit fund equivalent to about 30 per cent of normal salary. Payment is made by the employer, who recovers the amount by offsetting it against social security contributions.

A woman is also entitled by law to time off in order to nurse a sick child if the child is under 3 years old. She must present a medical certificate to her employer. This leave is normally unpaid.

Rights to special leave can also be exercised by the father should he replace the mother or have primary responsibility for the child.

Periods of optional absence from work are counted as periods of employment for the purpose of calculating length of service.

Other time off

Educational leave   The Worker's Statute gave all employees in companies employing more than fifteen people certain rights to facilitate study. Article 10 distinguishes between employees attending university (where attendance at lectures is not compulsory) and workers enrolled and regularly attending classes at primary, secondary or vocational schools which are public, state-approved or authorised to award legally recognised qualifications. The latter – but not the former – are entitled to have their hours of work arranged to facilitate attendance at classes and preparation for examinations. In addition, they may not be compelled to work overtime or during weekly rest periods.

All employees, including university students, are entitled to paid leave in order to sit examinations.

Many collective agreements contain additional provisions on study leave. The pace-setting agreement in this field was the national engineering agreement of 1973, which specified that workers wishing to attend certain schools (that is, state or other schools agreed by employers and unions) were entitled to total paid leave of up to 150 hours over a period of three years. (The leave could be used up in one year by any individual employee.) This allowance was subsequently increased to 250 hours for workers attending primary and middle school courses (that is, completing their basic education under the Italian system). There are certain limitations on the use of study leave under the engineering agreement. The total cost to the employer must not exceed 0.5 per cent of the payroll; student workers must produce a school certificate demonstrating their attendance for a number of hours two-thirds greater than the number paid for by the employer; no more than 2 per cent of the work force can be simultaneously absent from work for study reasons; and absence from work for study reasons must not hamper normal production. In addition the agreement provides for 120 hours of unpaid leave per annum for all workers provided that it can be scheduled to take account of the company's organisational and production needs.

Similar agreements exist in most sectors, although the number of hours' leave and the limitations may vary slightly from sector to sector. Sector-level agreements along these lines are aimed at improving the educational standard of workers in general. Other provisions may exist at company level, or may be worked out on an informal basis for individual workers following courses other than the approved ones.

Trade union activities   Under section 3 of the Workers' Statute all employees are entitled to ten paid hours' time off per year to attend trade union meetings in the workplace. Trade union delegates are also entitled to paid leave of absence for the performance of their duties. Entitlement is usually at least eight hours per month. The number of delegates entitled to leave of absence depends on the size of the company (see the volume in this series on *Employee Relations and Collective Bargaining*).

Trade union officials are also entitled to unpaid leave of up to eight days a year in connection with union responsibilities. Collective agreements may improve on the law's provisions.

Employees elected to trade union office at national or provincial level are entitled to unpaid leave of absence at any time during, or for the entire duration of, their term of office.

Family leave   Most industry-level collective agreements provide for employees to take paid leave if they get married. Entitlements range from ten to thirty days, starting on the wedding day. All white-collar employees are entitled by law to at least fifteen days.

Many collective agreements provide for a short period of leave to be allowed on the death of a close relative, for attending funerals or for other family reasons. A typical allowance would be up to twenty-four hours, or three working days, per year. Many companies also grant short spells of leave for personal reasons on an informal basis.

Military service Employees called upon to perform compulsory military service are entitled to have their job protected for the duration of the service – that is, to unpaid leave (for the army and airforce, service lasts twelve months; in the navy, it lasts eighteen months). On completion of military service the employee must present himself for work within thirty days, otherwise the employment contract may be terminated automatically. In the case of recall to the reserve for any reason an employee is entitled to paid leave. The amount of pay or benefit is laid down by special laws or may be determined by collective agreement.

Leave for public duties Under the Workers' Statute an employee elected as a member of the national parliament, of a regional parliament or to other public office is entitled to unpaid leave at any time during, or for the entire period of, his term of office. The period of elected office must, if the employee so requests, be taken into account for the purposes of calculating pension rights. Employees elected to public office who do not wish to be granted unpaid leave are entitled, upon their request, to leave of absence with full pay for the time strictly necessary to carry out their official functions.

An employee who is elected mayor or deputy mayor, chairman or vice-chairman of the provincial council is likewise entitled to unpaid leave not exceeding thirty hours a month.

Employees who are carrying out election duties are entitled to three days' paid leave over and above their normal leave entitlement.

Individual pay and benefits

Statutory pay determination

Statutory minimum wage There is no single statutory minimum wage. Binding minimum pay rates for various levels and categories of employee are set by national industry-level agreements. These apply to all employers in an industry, on the basis of a number of legal principles and administrative practices outlined below (see 'Extension procedures'). Industry agreements set out rates for all employees, from blue-collar workers to executives, although at higher levels the minimum wage represents a diminishing proportion of total remuneration. There are no other mechanisms for setting minimum pay levels.

Extension procedures Though there are no formal procedures for extending collective agreements to other parties there is provision for this under the constitution. However, national industry agreements are held to be binding on all employers in the industry, even though they may not be members of signatory organisations, through the effect of various legal principles and administrative practices. An employer who implements one term of an agreement is deemed to have accepted all its terms. Moreover the Italian constitution provides that all employees are entitled to a level of payment commensurate with the 'quantity and quality' of their work, a level which must be sufficient to ensure a 'free and dignified existence' for the worker and their family: the courts have typically interpreted this as meaning the agreed rate in the industry. Finally, the state social insurance fund INPS requires employers to indicate which collective agreement applies to them when submitting social insurance returns.

Employers are therefore obliged to pay the agreed minimum rates even if they themselves are not party to the agreement. The courts have also interpreted this 'basic rate' to include thirteenth-month payments, which are now virtually universal.

Pay indexation   Pay indexation, which had been a major feature of pay determination for forty-five years, was abolished in July 1992. Indexation payments plus agreed minimum rates had accounted for around 90 per cent of the pay packet in some cases. Frozen indexation payments still appear in employees' pay packets but cost-of-living increases will now be negotiated, in accordance with the principles set out in the July 1993 accord between the government, unions and employers (see below).

The law on pay

Form and frequency   There are no laws regulating the frequency of payments, which is laid down by collective agreement and is generally weekly, fortnightly or most commonly monthly. Article 2099 of the Civil Code stipulates that the form of payment must be in accordance with the custom and practice of the place where the work is undertaken. Law 45/53 states that employers must provide most categories of employee with an itemised pay slip.

Permitted deductions   Employers may deduct all social security contributions and income tax at source, provided they are clearly identified in the pay slip (see appendix. The law (the Workers' Statute, 1970) also sanctions the right to deduct trade union contributions at source if employees wish. The way union dues are collected must be laid down by collective agreement, with the aim of ensuring confidentiality regarding employees' choice of union. This measure is intended to prevent employers discriminating against employees on the grounds of political or trade union affiliation.

Levels of pay determination

Private-sector bargaining can take place at three levels: national, industry, and company or plant.

National agreements are occasionally negotiated between the national employers' confederation, Confindustria, and the three main union confederations (CGIL, CISL, UIL). Examples include the agreement of 25 January 1975 which reformed the wage indexation system and the agreement of 26 January 1977 on labour costs and productivity. Very occasionally tripartite agreements are also negotiated between Confindustria, the union confederations and the government. The most recent examples of such agreements were concluded in July 1992 and July 1993, abolishing pay indexation, reforming the industrial relations system and agreeing guidelines for the future conduct of pay bargaining.

Agreements signed at national industry level are legally binding on all employers in a sector, irrespective of whether they are members of a signatory organisation. It is at this level that basic minimum rates of pay are set, according to category of employee. Company or plant-level agreements, which improve upon the basic provisions of industry agreements, also have the force of law once negotiated. There is no obligation to bargain at either company or industry level.

The system means that all employees in the work force are covered by a national industry agreement governing minimum pay and conditions, but only employees in larger, more profitable firms tend to be covered by company or plant agreements. Agreements cover either *dipendenti* (dependent employees), i.e. blue- and white-collar workers, or *dirigenti* (executives).

At industry level, employer associations, such as Federmeccanica, and industry unions, such as Fiom, Fim and Uilm (see above) in engineering, negotiate industry-wide agreements which establish minimum wage rates and agreed bonus provisions for the industry, with supplementary payments and/or benefits agreed at company level with workers' representative bodies such as the *rappresentanze sindacali unitarie*. The importance of these levels to the various components of pay depends on the category of employee. For unskilled blue-collar grades by far the largest components of the pay packet are frozen indexation payments and the industry minimum rate, which together can add up to over 90 per cent of pay. The element of company, plant or individual pay (often known as the *superminimo*) is usually no more than 5 per cent of total pay for blue-collar workers, though it rises to 35–40 per cent for white-collar and managerial employees. Recent pay rounds have seen some innovation in company bargaining, with experiments in performance-related bonuses and bonuses tied to targets such as quality objectives.

For managerial employees mainly, increases at industry level can be offset against company pay. This sometimes happens when employers make advance awards and industry settlements are delayed.

The structure of public-sector bargaining has been changed recently to reflect that of the private sector. Salaries are negotiated between a government agency and trade unions and must be pegged to inflation forecasts.

Pay agreements

Under the terms of the July 1993 national framework agreement, industry agreements will now be negotiated for a four-year period, with the pay clauses valid for two. Pay increases must be 'compatible' with projected inflation. Company and plant bargaining will follow a four-year cycle.

Employees outside collective bargaining

Officially, no employees are outside collective bargaining except those in the 'black' economy. The importance of collectively agreed pay, however, varies according to job category. As a rule it is far more important for blue-collar workers than for managerial staff.

Main payment systems

The main payment system for blue-collar workers is a standard monthly rate for the job which is adjusted occasionally for overtime. Piecework systems, which existed until the 1970s, are now extremely rare. White-collar employees are paid monthly. Both blue-collar and white-collar employees are paid thirteen-monthly salaries a year, with an additional payment at Christmas, and in some cases a further month's pay in July.

Job evaluation and grading

Formal job evaluation is not very widespread. Grading structures are determined by collective bargaining and usually yield about seven basic grades, with detailed specification of which jobs fit into the agreed grades. The various levels of the grading structure correspond to particular jobs, skill levels, qualifications and levels of responsibility. For pay purposes the basic rate for each grade is expressed as a percentage of the lowest grade. These grade points or parameters (*parametri*) vary from industry to industry and also evolve, as a result of negotiation, over time.

The regrading of existing personnel and grading of new personnel are usually agreed locally, with practice depending on the status and influence of work-force representatives. Local management can adapt the national grading structure locally, provided individuals are not graded at a lower level than is explicit in the national agreement. The national grading structure is sometimes adapted at local level, using job evaluation systems to include new jobs not already accounted for.

Single-status pay

There are separate national agreements for executive employees (*dirigenti*) and for blue- and white-collar workers (*dipendenti*) which cover the four legally recognised categories of employees: blue-collar workers (*operai*), white-collar workers (*impiegati*), senior white-collar workers (*quadri*) and managers (*dirigenti*).

The first three groups are included in the single grading system (*inquadramento unico*) which – with small variance of detail from industry to industry – operates throughout the Italian economy. *Dirigenti* are not graded. Although their basic pay and conditions are negotiated, they receive additional pay and some benefits, often on an individual basis and outside any negotiated framework. There are two national executive agreements, one for industrial executives and another for executives in retailing, distribution and services.

Earnings protection

Employees must be paid at the rate for the job they were taken on to do, or to which they have been assigned. They may not be moved to a job at a lower level of the grading structure save in exceptional circumstances, such as when regrading is the only alternative to being permanently laid off.

Make-up of the pay package

The average pay packet is made up of a number of components – agreed minimum pay under national industry agreements, frozen indexation payments from the period prior to 1992, agreed bonuses – such as seniority increments and production bonuses – and any supplements paid under company agreements, some of which may have a performance element.

Service increments are very common for both blue- and white-collar employees and managers in most sectors. They have been criticised as a further element of 'automaticity' in Italian pay determination, which makes it difficult for individual employers to control their labour costs. Typically, incremental scales for blue- and white-collar workers have five points for each grade, with movement up the scale every two years. Around 4.7 per cent of a skilled blue-collar worker's average monthly earnings are accounted for by seniority payments. For managers, flat-rate seniority payments are also triggered every two years, up to a maximum twenty years' seniority.

Children's or social allowances

State family allowances (*l'assegno per il nucleo familiare*) are payable to eligible employees through their employer with their monthly pay packet. The level of the family allowance varies according to the number of dependants and family income.

Regional pay differences

There are no regional differences in basic minimum pay, since it is agreed at national level for a whole industry or sector. There may be regional differences in pay agreed or received at company level, which may take account of local labour market conditions. However, there is no statutory or agreed system for paying local cost-of-living allowances. The inflexibility of the system of national bargaining has been seen as a problem in that it imposes a cost burden on the south, depriving that region of a possible comparative advantage.

Overtime, night work and shift pay

Premium rates for overtime, night work, etc., are usually calculated on the basis of the employee's agreed minimum, plus any merit elements, service increments and frozen cost-of-living payments.

Overtime   The law regulating overtime working dates from 1923, although, as with many other issues, statutory provision has long since been overtaken by collective agreement.

Article 5 of law 692 (15 March 1923) lays down the maximum amount of overtime which an employee may work at two hours per day and twelve hours per week, provided that agreement has been reached between the parties. However, as article 1 of the same law defines the standard working week as forty-eight hours, the restriction takes effect only above this limit, unless a collective agreement establishes a lower threshold based on the normal working week, the most common practice. Overtime must be paid at not less than 10 per cent above the normal basic rate. In practice, agreed overtime rates for work beyond the agreed working week exceed the minimum: in engineering, for example, overtime is paid at 25 per cent above basic pay for the first two hours, and 30 per cent thereafter.

Statutory overtime in excess of the forty-eight-hour standard week may be worked only on an occasional basis, and in any case the appropriate labour inspectorate must be informed twenty-five hours before it is due to begin. The employer must pay a sum equal to 15 per cent of the employee's overtime earnings (that is, basic plus overtime rates) into the unemployment fund. Fines payable upon contravention of the law are equal to L 10,000 (£4.10) a day per employee affected, but are doubled in cases of subsequent conviction.

Night work and shift premiums   Collective agreements – especially at company and plant level – tend to regulate shift working in some detail, and many lay down additional payments for shift workers for work done outside normal working hours: in many agreements there are no additional rates for shift work as such, with shift workers receiving premium pay rates for portions of shifts worked at night, which attract a 15 per cent supplement, or at other unsocial times. However, the definition of night work may be widened to ensure that a shift, say from 24.00 to 08.00, is all paid at night work rates, although night work normally extends only to 06.00. Shift workers also often enjoy shorter annual working hours.

The Civil Code states that night work must be compensated for by special premiums, in practice set by collective agreement. The national engineering agreement, for example, establishes that night work is payable at a 20 per cent premium for usual dayworkers up to 22.00 and 30 per cent thereafter, with overtime rates for night work ranging between 55 and 75 per cent, depending on whether the overtime is worked on a normal working day, a Sunday or a public holiday.

Production bonuses   Production bonuses (*premi di produzione*) may be laid down under collective agreement either at national or at company level and take the form of collective rather than individual payments. While originally intended as a form of incentive payment, production bonuses have now become an item of basic pay. In engineering they make up around 2 per cent of a salaried workers' pay, rising to about 11 per cent (but now frozen) in the chemical industry.

Other types of allowance, e.g. for attendance (linked to the number of hours worked, excluding overtime), dirt or danger, and canteen allowances, are often found in company agreements. Sometimes a company will combine several of these smaller items of pay to make one larger supplementary payment.

Bonuses

Holiday pay and bonuses   All employees have a non-forfeitable right under the constitution to an annual holiday and are entitled to be paid at the normal basic rate during their leave. Some agreements provide for a holiday bonus, payable prior to annual holiday leave. Others provide for the payment of company supplemental pay (*superminimi*) in two lump sums, prior to annual holiday leave and then before the Christmas break.

Annual or other bonuses   A thirteenth-month bonus is universal. It is normally paid in December. Some agreements provide for fourteenth- and sometimes fifteenth-month bonuses. Collectively agreed length of service bonuses may also be paid in some industries.

Pay for performance

Performance/merit pay can exist for all grades of employee. Although the proportion of pay accounted for by individually determined elements increases markedly at senior levels, and may account for half of total annual remuneration at the highest levels, it remains rare for ordinary grades. The way performance/merit pay is allocated depends on company policy. Some companies may use a performance appraisal system, others a management by objectives scheme.

In recent years there has been an attempt to award performance pay on a collective basis. Several company agreements in the 1988 pay round made a break with the usual practice of awarding a fixed level of company pay by varying payments in line with indicators of corporate performance. Around 400,000 employees were estimated to be covered by variable, performance-related, elements of pay under the 1988/89 agreements. In some cases the chosen indicator was the company's declared profit; in others, an index of competitiveness *vis-à-vis* other firms; in yet others, declared profit and productivity. The new performance-related pay increase either replaced the previous element of company pay known as the *superminimo* or *terzo elemento* or was awarded in addition. These incentive arrangements are usually agreed with trade unions at local level, and are set to become more common following the July 1993 framework agreement, which stipulates that company pay awards must be linked with some agreed target.

Managers' pay

As noted above, Italy is unusual in that senior positions are covered by industry-level collective agreements, providing for minimum pay levels, extensive seniority payments and a special pay indexation system (now abolished) which, from 1983, updated minima once a year on 1 July. However, these agreed minima make up only a proportion of most executives' total remuneration, with companies paying essentially in line with market rates.

Executive pay is therefore made up of agreed minima such as a basic industry minimum, agreed seniority increments (see below), frozen indexation payments plus agreed bonuses and any company-level performance-related bonuses or merit pay, which make up around 20–30 per cent of total remuneration. Profit-sharing and stock option schemes are not common, except in the largest local or international companies.

The most significant fringe benefits are company cars, personal pension schemes and medical plans as well as, more recently, portable telephones. According to the 1993/94 Monks Partnership survey *Incentives and Benefits in Europe*, 90–5 per cent of surveyed companies provided the most senior-level managers with a car, around 75 per cent offering middle managers one. Provision of fuel ranged from 40 per cent for middle managers to 62 per cent at chief executive level.

The state pension system, which covers senior managers, has, as yet, left relatively little scope for private pension schemes, even for high earners. For example, according to the Monks Partnership survey, only 33 per cent of top managers were in a company pension scheme, compared with nearly 90 per cent in Germany.

Financial participation

There is no specific legislation on the granting of share options or offering a special tax regime for employee profit-sharing. However, there was reported growth in employee shareholdings in the late 1980s, much of it attributed to the long upward movement of the Italian stock market. Studies have found, however, that shares distributed to employees rarely exceeded 5 per cent of the employer's total share capital, and were often non-voting. Where shares are allocated to employees, and held in trust for two years, the employee is not taxed on them. Nor is capital gains tax payable if shares are acquired at below market price and then disposed of, provided the shares do not exceed a threshold value of the total share capital (2 per cent of a listed company and 5 per cent of a private company). No capital gains tax is payable if shares are held for at least five years. Fully fledged share option schemes are a rarity, however.

Similarly, employer-financed savings schemes are unusual. The national agreement for managers in retailing, distribution and services does provide for a provident fund, the Fondo Mario Negri, which is financed mainly by the employer.

Sick pay

By law, all employees are covered by the state sick pay scheme. Entitlement to state sickness benefit does not begin until after three 'waiting days', during which payment is customarily made by employers under collectively agreed provisions, and is not payable for more than 180 days in the calendar year. The amount of benefit received depends on the particular scheme, but for blue-collar workers and white-collar workers in retailing, distribution and services it represents 50 per cent of average gross pay for each of the first twenty days of illness and 66.66 per cent for each subsequent day.

Employees who are entitled to sickness benefit receive it from their employer, who may then offset it against their social contributions. The benefit must be included in the pay which employees receive for the period in which they first resume work, unless a collective agreement makes provision for advance payment. By law, this benefit may not be less than 50 per cent of the previous month's pay.

Most collective agreements improve significantly on the law's provisions. The employer usually makes up 100 per cent of normal pay for all employees. The length of time for which full sick pay is due varies from industry to industry and is often determined by length of service. For example, an employee in the private-sector chemical industry with three to six years' service qualifies for normal net pay for four months and 50 per cent for a further six months.

Maternity pay

Female employees are legally entitled, during the five-month statutory period of maternity leave, to maternity benefit equal to 80 per cent of their normal pay. The cost of the benefit is borne by the social security organisations and is administered by them. They are also entitled to payments equal to about 30 per cent of their normal salary during the optional period of maternity leave, which lasts for a further six months. Some collective agreements make up maternity pay to 100 per cent of normal pay.

Short-time/lay-off pay

This is covered by a scheme known as the *cassa ordinaria per l'integrazione dei guadagni*, or 'ordinary CIG' for short. This fund should not be confused with the 'special CIG' aimed at dealing with longer-term crises in which employment may have to be reduced (see below, 'Collective dismissal'). The CIG is regulated by law and permission for its use must be sought from the Ministry of Labour. Under the scheme, workers are guaranteed 80 per cent of their basic earnings up to a given ceiling. There are no agreed provisions on lay-off pay to maintain earnings if there is a temporary stoppage.

Main benefits

Car, travel and subsistence allowance

Such allowances are not common, since they are taxed as ordinary income (with the exception of meal vouchers, which are tax-exempt). Companies therefore tend to reimburse employee expenses directly. Some collective agreements – for example, the national agreement for industrial managers – provide an entitlement equal to a proportion of the manager's basic minimum pay for every night the manager spends away from home on company business.

Housing allowance

Generally speaking, only expatriates qualify for housing allowances. Occasionally, when employees relocate and incur a higher rent, they may qualify for an allowance up to a certain limit, for a given period (usually eighteen months).

Occupational/company pensions

Given the generosity of statutory pension schemes for all employees, including high earnings coverage for managers, occupational/company pensions are not common. Given recent changes, however, which reduce the value of the state pension, there is pressure to set up private plans. As yet the requisite legislation has not been passed. Some companies may provide additional personal pension schemes for their executives.

Cars

Cars solely or predominantly for business use are not taxable: a tax charge is imposed on private use, and may be set, for example, at two-sevenths of the annual cost to the company (reflecting weekend use), which is added to the employee's taxable income each month. Although the incidence of company cars is above 90 per cent for top management posts, according to the Monks Partnership *European Company Car Survey* Italian senior managers (head of function) are about half-way down the European league, with about 60 per cent of posts entitled to a car.

Life and sickness insurance and medical benefits

Most employees are covered by statutory provision. The national agreements for industrial managers and for those in retailing, distribution and services provide supplementary medical plans, as well as life insurance, in addition to state provision. Very few companies provide extra life insurance cover for other categories of employee. Executives in industry are covered by the INPDAI fund for life insurance and a survivor's pension, and by the FASI medical plan. Similarly, executives in retailing, distribution and services are covered by the FPDAC and PREVIR plans for life insurance and survivor's pension, and by the FSDAC medical plan.

Equal pay and equal opportunities

Women

Article 37 of the constitution declares that 'the female worker shall have all the rights and, in the same job, the same pay due to the male worker'.

Equality of pay and opportunity is enshrined in law 903 of 9 December 1977, which appeared in the Official Gazette on 17 December 1977. The first sentence of the first article reads: 'It shall not be lawful to practise any form of discrimination based on sex as regards access to employment at any level of responsibility, irrespective of the conditions in which the person is recruited and of the sector or branch of activity.'

Discrimination is also prohibited if practised in relation to the person's marital status, family circumstances or pregnancy, or if practised indirectly, for example through pre-selection procedures or publicity indicating that candidates must be of one sex or the other as an occupational requirement. These prohibitions cover the allocation of skills, jobs and promotion, and admission to schemes for vocational guidance, training and further training. Exceptions are allowed only for arduous jobs, as specified by collective agreement, for work in the fashion trade or for artistic performances when essential to the nature of the work under consideration.

On equal pay, article 2 of this law reads: 'Female workers shall be entitled to the same remuneration as a male worker if the services required are equal or of equal value . . . Occupational classification systems applied for the purpose of determining remuneration shall adopt common criteria for men and women.'

Since 1979 – when many industry agreements provided for greater disclosure of information – consultation and report-back on equal opportunities have been the responsibility of the works council (*consiglio di fabbrica*). Because the 1977 legislation had remained largely a dead letter a new law, No. 125, was passed in 1992 to promote positive action to implement equality between men and women in the workplace. This legislation was achieved through cross-party co-operation among women's groups in parliament.

The most important points of the new legislation are the regulations governing:

• Positive action and the definition of discrimination.
• The burden of proof to rest on the employer against whom a case is brought.
• Powers for an Equality Counsellor at regional level to bring a case against an employer for an alleged act of collective discrimination.
• Requirement to provide regular data on the breakdown of the work force by gender.

One innovation under this law was that it granted working fathers the right to paid leave and time off after the birth of a child, instead of the mother or where she becomes gravely ill or dies.

Although many industry agreements contain clauses prohibiting sexual harassment few company policies are in operation.

Disabled workers

The legislation on recruitment procedures where the state has the sole right to place individuals in jobs is aimed, among other things, at providing rights of access to employment for people with disabilities. Under the legislation any organisation, public or private, which employs more than thirty-five people is required to recruit a work force at least 15 per cent of which has some form of disability. Enforcement of the law is patchy; although employers can buy themselves out of the responsibility, they are rarely called to account anyway.

Ethnic minorities

Law 943/86 aims at regulating the recruitment and treatment of workers from outside the European Union, and controlling the flow of illegal immigrants into Italy. The law states that all non-EU community workers resident in Italy should enjoy rights and treatment equal to those of other workers. It also made provision for a *consulta* (council) to be set up under the auspices of the Ministry of Labour which would deal with the problems faced by non-EU nationals and their families.

Retirement

The official retirement age is 61, rising to 65 in 2002 for males and 56 rising to 60 in 2002 for females. Women can opt to work until the age of 60 provided they inform their employer three months before the date on which they would qualify for an old-age pension.

Despite recent changes the state social security system still provides comparatively generous old-age pensions. Private company pension schemes are relatively rare, although pressure is mounting for their introduction. Covered earnings are high, and in 1988 the upper earnings limit under the state scheme was abolished in both industry and commerce, leaving little scope for private supplementary pensions for managers. INPS (*Istituto Nazionale della Previdenza Sociale* or National Social Insurance Institute) is the basic scheme which provides old-age, disability and survivors' pensions for blue- and white-collar workers in industry and commerce and for executives in commerce. Contributions must be paid into this scheme for virtually all employees. INPDAI (*Istituto Nazionale per la Previdenza dei Dirigenti di Aziende Industriali*) provides old-age, disability and survivors' pensions for executives in industry.

To qualify for an INPS pension employees must be retired and aged 61 (if male) or 56 (if female) and must have paid sixteen years' contributions; or they can be any age provided they have paid thirty-five years' contributions and have retired. To qualify for an INPDAI pension, industrial executives must be aged 65 (males) or 60 (females) with fifteen years' contributions. This arrangement normally replaces INPS. Executives in industry also benefit from a supplementary pension scheme called PREVINDAI.

Early retirement under INPS with no reduction in benefit may be taken provided the employee has thirty-five years of contributions. Executives can retire at any time provided they have paid thirty years' contributions: benefits are reduced by 1 per cent for each year of early retirement before the usual retirement age. There is an incentive scheme – usually brought into use where job losses are required – under which the government may sanction retirement five years before the normal retirement age where the employee has made fifteen years' contributions.

Individual termination of contract

Resignation and constructive dismissal

There are no legal restrictions on withdrawal from the contract by the employee through resignation, although the Civil Code stipulates that periods of notice laid down in collective agreements must be adhered to.

Termination by mutual agreement

Again there are no legal restrictions on termination by mutual agreement but the appropriate periods of notice would apply, unless otherwise agreed.

Grounds for dismissal

The main circumstances under which an individual contract may be terminated are:

- When the contract expires (in the case of fixed-term contracts) or when the task to which the contract relates is complete.
- If the company ceases trading entirely.
- By mutual consent.
- *Force majeure*, including the total incapacity of the employee.
- By one party withdrawing from the contract, with or without notice (see below).
- If one of the parties fails to fulfil or breaches the contract.

Termination by the employer is warranted in two main situations, explained in more detail below.

- Summarily, for a very serious reason – 'just cause' (*giusta causa*).
- Instances where a legitimate reason is required – termed 'justified motive' (*giustificato motivo*).

Dismissal is not permitted, except for 'just cause' – that is, for a very serious reason – or where the company has ceased to trade, in the following circumstances:

- For one year following a female employee's marriage.
- During pregnancy or for one year after a woman has given birth.
- Following an accident or an occupationally caused illness.
- On grounds of sickness (where the permitted duration of sickness is usually governed by collective agreement).
- Military service.
- For a year following service on employee representative bodies.
- Following election to public service bodies.
- Where employees take part in industrial action.

Dismissal with notice and summary dismissal

Individual dismissal is regulated by two main pieces of legislation, law 604/66 and the Workers' Statute, 1970. Law 604 was amended in May 1990: the change resolved some of the previous conflicts between different legislation on termination, and extended protection against dismissal to all employees. It states that employees cannot be dismissed except for 'just cause', as defined by article 2119 of the Civil Code, or for 'justified motive'. The burden of proof lies with the employer.

'Just cause' is defined as very serious misconduct or an omission which constitutes a fundamental and irredeemable breach of contract. It entitles the employer to dismiss the employee without notice, and allows the employee also to withdraw without notice. Omission on the part of the employee could relate to behaviour which endangers the health and safety of other employees or violence at work. On the part of the employer it could relate to the obligation to pay the employee or to grant leave. An employer committing such a breach of contract will face penalties set out below.

Dismissal on grounds of employee conduct

An employer may dismiss an employee so long as 'justified motive' can be proved and the correct procedures have been followed (see 'Workplace discipline' above).

'Justified motive' is defined as arising from the evident failure of the employee to fulfil their contractual obligations. It may lie in factors inherent in the production process, the organisation of work or the smooth running of the undertaking. That is, it covers dismissal owing to the conduct of the employee (termed 'subjective' grounds, such as repeatedly being caught smoking where it is not permitted, failure to undertake work as requested, unauthorised absences, persistent lateness) and economic dismissal or termination due to protracted ill health (termed 'objective' grounds). Most industry agreements guarantee that a person's job will be kept open for them for a certain length of time in cases of prolonged illness. The period ranges from one year (in textiles) to three (in chemicals).

Dismissal on grounds of poor performance can be difficult to prove and is rare.

Economic dismissal (individual redundancy)

Individual dismissal on economic grounds is accorded no special legal treatment, nor is there any separate legislation providing for compensation payments to employees dismissed on economic grounds. All organisations, including those which are not companies, are covered by law 108 on individual dismissals.

Under this law dismissal with notice may be considered to be dismissal for 'justified motive' if it is 'for reasons inherent in the production process, the organisation of work, or the smooth running of the undertaking'. In such a case the employee will be entitled to notice and statutory, as well as agreed, severance payments in accordance with law 198 and any relevant collective agreements.

If the dismissal is found to have been unfair, then, depending on the size of the company, the provisions which apply will be, either those of article 18 of the Workers' Statute with regard to reinstatement or those laid down by law 108, which entail severance compensation.

Dismissal of executives

Executives are not covered by the provisions either of law 604/66 or of law 108/90. In strict terms, therefore, their dismissal is governed by articles 2118 and 2119 of the Civil Code, which permit unilateral withdrawal from the contract by either party with or without notice, depending on the circumstances.

Protection from unfair dismissal, however, can be found in binding national industry agreements which affect the bulk of executives. If an executive is found to have been dismissed without 'just cause' or 'justified motive', or the correct procedures were not followed, the employer may be liable to the (often severe) penalties laid down in the agreement.

Both national agreements which cover executives state that withdrawal from the contract for whatever reason must be communicated in writing and that, in the case of the employer, the reasons must be stated. In most cases a period of written notice will also be required. The executive may appeal against the termination to a college of arbitration set up under the terms of the national industry agreements. The appeal must be notified to the regional office of the relevant professional federation (FENDAI or FENDAC) within thirty days of receipt of written communication of termination. Failure to observe the procedures renders the termination null and void. In practice, apart from cases of serious misconduct, an executive is highly likely to appeal against termination.

However, there is no obligation to reinstate an executive. Settlements in the event of a finding of unfair dismissal of an executive are in the region of two years' salary plus the statutory severance payment (*trattamento di fine rapporto*) – see below.

Periods of notice

Under article 2118 of the Civil Code either party may terminate the contract of employment by giving the requisite notice in the manner specified by regulations in force or by custom and practice or according to equity. Should either party fail to give the required notice they become liable to a payment equal to the remuneration which would have been paid during the period of notice. The employer must also make such a payment in lieu of notice where the employer dies in service. The length of periods of notice is governed largely by national collective agreement at industry level and varies according to sector, category of employee and, often, length of service. The range of notice periods is very large.

For example, an executive in industry with less than two years' service is entitled to a period of eight months' notice, which rises by an additional half a month with every extra year of service up to an overall maximum of twelve months. In contrast, an ordinary employee in commerce with ten or more years' service is entitled only to a period of twenty calendar days' notice. Under the agreement, periods of notice are the same for employer and employee, and failure to give notice on either side renders the party liable to a sum equivalent to salary during the period of notice.

Severance payments

In addition to a statutory pension, all employees are entitled to a termination payment (*trattamento di fine rapporto*) when, and, for whatever reason, their contract of employment ends, including resignation. The payment is based on length of service, and in general employees receive one month's pay for each year of service, although collective agreements may provide otherwise. A special fund guarantees payments in the event of insolvency. Within certain limits, employees with eight years' service in a company may draw up to 70 per cent of their entitlement for 'a serious purpose' (such as buying a first home). This benefit passes on in full to the next of kin in the event of death. It is taxed at a rate which is effectively lower than income tax.

Unfair dismissal, appeals, compensation and remedies

Where dismissal is considered unfair it must be challenged in writing within sixty days of receipt of notice of dismissal. Penalties for unfair dismissal vary according to company size and structure.

Employers with more than fifteen employees in each establishment, branch, office or separate department; employers with more than fifteen employees in the same commune (local authority area) even if they are working in smaller production units; and employers employing more than sixty workers, wherever located, are liable to:

- Reinstatement of the employee and payment of damages equal to a minimum of five months' pay.
- Damages equal to fifteen months' pay should the employee refuse reinstatement.
- If the employer invites the employee to return to work and the offer is not taken up within thirty days, then the contract is automatically terminated.

The limit on employee numbers is lowered to five in the case of agricultural establishments.

Employers who refuse reinstatement can be required by the courts to continue paying the employee at the full normal rate until they comply.

In smaller establishments employing up to fifteen people in each production unit (or up to five if they are in agriculture) and where an employer employs up to sixty people wherever they are located:

- The case cannot be heard by a magistrate unless conciliation has been requested beforehand under collectively agreed procedures or as laid down in the Civil Code.
- If attempts at conciliation fail, either party can request within twenty days that the matter should be brought before a college of arbitration (*collegio arbitrale*).
- If the matter is still unresolved and the court finds against the dismissal the employer must reinstate the employee within three days or pay damages of at least two and a half months' up to a maximum of fourteen months' pay.

The following maximum damages apply: up to six months' pay, depending on the number employed, length of service and the behaviour and circumstances of each party, but up to ten months' pay if the employee has more than ten years' service and the employer employs more than fifteen workers. If the employee has more than twenty years' service, damages can extend up to fourteen months' pay.

Final formalities

On termination the employer must:

- Pay all sums due to the employee, including all indemnities, remuneration and other benefits or entitlements. Where there is a dispute over the amount to be paid, the employer must pay any sums that are not in dispute. Compromise settlements are not allowed.
- Return all documents to the employee promptly at the proper time and make all the necessary entries in the employee's employment record (*libretto di lavoro*).
- Where employment documents are not obligatory, provide a certificate stating the duration of the employee's employment with the firm and the nature of their duties.
- Provide the employee with a copy of the income declaration form which has been sent to the National Social Insurance Institute (INPS).
- Notify all the relevant official bodies. These include the local employment office (within five days), INPS and the relevant sickness benefit fund.

Collective dismissal

Definition of collective dismissal

Collective dismissal is defined in law 223/91, which also implemented, after some delay, the provisions of the 1975 EU directive on collective dismissal. It applies to all employees except managers (*dirigenti*) in firms employing more than fifteen people. All dismissals in firms with fewer than fifteen employees are governed by the laws relating to individual dismissal even if they take place together.

Collective dismissal is defined as a change in employment levels caused by a reduction in, or change of, activity involving five or more employees in a single unit of production over a period of 120 days, or five employees in several units belonging to a single employer within one province. The law also embraces job losses in firms which cease trading entirely.

Procedure

When confronted by the need for economic dismissals, larger employers will often simultaneously open proceedings to put surplus workers on to the special support fund, the *cassa integrazione*, to avoid or delay termination of contract. Employees drawing payments from the *cassa*, which is financed by employer contributions topped up by the state, have not terminated their employment with the original employer.

In the past the *cassa integrazione* was widely used as a means of avoiding economic dismissals and offering employees threatened with redundancy some form of continuing financial support. There is no universal system of state unemployment benefit in Italy.

Reforms intended to tackle abuses of the *cassa*, by shortening the period of entitlement, and changes in the law on dismissal have now made it possible to move more quickly to redundancies: however, the path can still be fraught with political and procedural difficulties.

Statutory requirements on consultation

The legislation stipulates that, to initiate redundancy procedures, companies must inform employee representatives and the appropriate industry union in writing of their intentions. Where there are no local representatives, the company must notify full-time officials of the relevant union(s). At the same time the company must also inform the labour authorities (local, regional or national, depending on the scale and spread of the dismissals). Within seven days of union representatives being informed the parties must conduct a joint examination (*esame congiunto*) on:

- The reasons for the surplus labour and the proposed dismissals.
- The scope for redeployment, the use of 'solidarity contracts' or the introduction of flexible working hours to forestall dismissals.

These discussions may last up to forty-five days from the receipt of the initial communication by employee representatives. This period may be halved if fewer than ten jobs are at risk. If no agreement can be reached, the labour authority will accept conciliation.

Following attempts to mitigate the impact of dismissals, the company and employee representatives will move to conclude an agreement on measures to help those faced with redundancy. In larger firms this will almost invariably involve the labour authorities, as continuing payments to the unemployed under specific agreements are met by the state. Costs to the employer are reduced where an agreement with a union has been concluded (see below).

Severance agreements may contain:

- Selection criteria for the employees to be dismissed (see below).
- Decision to use 'solidarity contracts' offering shorter hours for less pay but with compensation paid by the national social security organisation, INPS.
- Provisions for use of the *cassa integrazione*, retraining, out-placement and early retirement.
- Arrangements for dismissed employees to receive special continuing redundancy payments (termed 'mobility payments') – see below.

Once agreement has been reached, or the procedure has been exhausted, the employer may move to terminate employment. Notification of termination of employment must be communicated in writing to individual workers, who must be given the appropriate period of notice.

Compensation payments

Employees whose employment is terminated enjoy a special status, termed 'mobility' (*mobilità*), for subsequent job search through the state placement system and may receive continuing payments in addition to the statutory severance payment to all employees on termination of employment, whatever the grounds (*trattamento di fine rapporto*). The new mobility benefits, which equal 100 per cent of previous agreed pay, subject to an upper limit, are paid by the state social security institution INPS.

Some workers on 'mobility' receive payments for between twelve and thirty-six months, depending on age; all enjoy priority as regards rehiring by the same employer (which may be on special fixed-term contracts not exceeding one year), and become a priority category for recruitment. Should workers on 'mobility' payments be reinstated before the period of their entitlement to payments has expired (for example, because selection criteria have been violated), the company is entitled to dismiss an equal number of workers in their place without having to start the procedure afresh, provided the correct criteria have been applied and the workers' representatives informed.

Costs to the employer

Employers are required to contribute to the cost of financing the *cassa integrazione* and 'mobility' payments. In the case of mobility payments, the rules require the employer to pay for each employee: one month's mobility payment × 3 if the employer has concluded a redundancy agreement, or one month's mobility payment × 9 if no agreement has been reached. Small companies do not pay into this fund, and their employees are not entitled to the benefit.

Selection criteria for dismissal

Workers can be made redundant only for technical, production or organisational reasons and according to criteria laid down by collective agreement. Where no agreement exists the following criteria must be used, though the law does not specify which takes precedence:

- Number of dependants.
- Length of service.
- Technical, production and organisational demands.

In addition the law specifies that companies should not take more than seventy-five days to complete the redundancy procedure.

Dismissal will be null and void if the correct procedures and criteria have not been followed, and the employees affected will be entitled to reinstatement. This penalty contrasts sharply with those laid down by most other EU states, where compensation is normally paid. In addition the lack of clarity over the order of precedence of dismissal criteria gives rise to a great deal of uncertainty and could leave substantial scope for interpretation by the courts. It also makes recourse to the *cassa integrazione* a more attractive proposition, despite efforts to curb its use.

Appendix

Social security contributions and income tax

The Italian social security system levies differential contributions according to job category, sector and the size of the company. Contributions are payable as a percentage of total gross pay. They range between 9.69 per cent and 9.99 per cent for the employee and between 39.41 per cent and 45.96 per cent for the employer. (The picture is more complex with executives.) Although the figures are nominally high, the picture is mitigated somewhat by the existence of an income threshold. The lower limit at which contributions are payable is daily income of L 57,223 (£23.50), except for executives, where daily income of L 157,240 (£64.57) applies. There is no upper limit except for one or two funds which have only a marginal effect on the total contribution.

Taxation

Tax on employment income is subject to personal income tax (IRPEF). Income tax is progressive, the rates ranging from 10 per cent to 51 per cent, and the incomes of husband and wife are assessed separately. Tax on employment income is deducted at source by the employer and employees must complete a tax return only if they have other sources of income or deductible expenses. Taxable salary includes all compensation and emoluments in cash or in kind, however received.

Organisations

Employers' organisations

Confindustria (Confederazione Generale dell'Industria Italiana)
Viale dell'Astronomia 30, 00100 Rome
Tel. + 39 6 59031

Confindustria, which was established in 1910, is the main employers' organisation in the private sector, with more than 100,000 companies employing about 3 million people. As well as co-ordinating employers' action at local and regional level, Confindustria represents private-sector industry in national talks with the unions and with government. It has a special internal body representing the interests of smaller companies.
President: Luigi Abete.

Intersind
Via Cristoforo Colombo 98, 00147 Rome
Tel. + 39 6 51751

Intersind is the employers' organisation representing publicly owned companies in the engineering industry. It was set up in 1958 following a government directive providing for separate employer representation in the public and private sectors. President: Agostino Paci.

Federmeccanica (Federazione dell'Industria Metalmeccanica Italiana)
Piazza Benito Juarez 14, 00144 Rome
Tel. + 39 6 59 25 44 6

Federmeccanica represents employers in the private sector of the engineering industry. It is the largest employers' federation belonging to Confindustria. It represents over 10,000 companies employing around 1.2 million people.
President: Luigi Lang.

Confapi
Via della Colonna Antonina 52, Rome
Tel. + 39 6 67 82 44 1

Confapi represents small and medium-sized companies in the private sector (although Confindustria also does this). It was set up following the creation during the 1950s of a provincial organisation representing small employers.
President: Gianantonio Vaccaro.

Trade unions   The traditional political alliances of Italy's three main trade union confederations were shaken by the general election of 1994, which saw the virtual disappearance of the Socialist Party and the breakup of the Christian Democrats. At the same time, the Northern Leagues and neo-fascist MSI/National Alliance have developed their own union confederations, although these have little influence over collective bargaining.

Confederazione Generale Italiana del Lavoro (CGIL)
Corso d'Italia 25, 00198 Rome
Tel. + 39 6 84761

The CGIL, which claimed some 5 million members in 1991, is the largest of the three main confederations. It has had close relationships with the Communist Party (now the Party of the Democratic Left, PDS), though a significant minority of its membership is socialist: by tradition the Deputy General Secretary was a socialist, although this practice ceased after the 1994 elections in which the Socialist Party was eliminated as an electoral force. Following the reorganisation of the CP as the PDS, a number of the CGIL's industrial militants joined the Rifondazione Comunista, which maintains a more orthodox communist tradition. CGIL influence is centred in engineering and heavy industry. General Secretary: Sergio Cofferati.

Confederazione Italiana Sindacati Lavoratori (CSIL)
Via Po 21, 00198 Rome
Tel. + 39 6 84731

The CISL, with 3.6 million members in 1991 (1.2 million of them pensioners), had close links with the old Christian Democrat Party. General Secretary: Sergio D'Antoni.

Unione Italiana del Lavoro (Uil)
Via Lucullo 6, 00187 Rome
Tel. + 39 6 49731

The Uil had close links with the Socialist Party. It had approximately 1.7 million members in 1991, and tends to recruit from the higher grades in industry. General Secretary: Pietro Larizza.

Both the Lombard League (Lega Lombarda) and the right-wing MSI (Movimento Sociale Italiano) have a union organisation, the SAL.

Federazione Nazionale Dirigenti Aziende Industriali (FNDAI)
Via Palermo 12, 00184 Rome
Tel. + 39 6 47 40 35 1/2/3/4

FNDAI is the largest association negotiating for Italy's estimated 120,000 industrial managers. It claims a membership of around 50,000, represents industrial managers across all sectors, and negotiates with employers' organisations in both the private and the public sectors. General Secretary: Bruno Losito.

Federazione Nazionale Dirigenti di Aziende Commerciali
Via Nazionale 163, 00184 Rome
Tel. + 39 6 67 81 49 8

The FNDAC negotiates on behalf of Italian commercial managers. In 1990 it claimed 18,426 members, of which 2,388 were pensioners. President: Francesco Colucci.

Organisations representing senior white-collar staff (*quadri*) Senior white-collar staff with technical and managerial responsibilities were for long unrecognised as a separate category of employee under Italian law. However, after much parliamentary lobbying, legal recognition was finally accorded through an amendment to article 2095 of the Italian Civil Code passed by the Senate on 23 April 1985. Under the amendment employers are required to establish, through collective bargaining, which of their employees fall into this category. This was to take place within one year of the amendment's appearance in the Official

Gazette. Although Italy's 700,000 or so *quadri* now enjoy legal recognition, the national organisations which represent many of them have still not been given legal bargaining rights. These organisations do, however, act as pressure groups and have some influence on the bargaining practices of the unions.

Official bodies

Ministero del Lavoro e della Previdenza Sociale
Via Flavia 6, 00187 Rome
Tel. + 39 6 4683

The Ministry of Labour is responsible for policy formulation on all employment and social security issues. It may also intervene in industrial disputes, and its powers of mediation and arbitration are regularly used. The Ministry is also responsible for questions relating to sex equality at work.

Main sources

Collective agreements, including: *Contratto di lavoro, industria metalmeccanica privata* (engineering); *Contratto collettivo nazionale di lavoro – industria chimica* (chemicals); *Contratto collettivo nazionale di lavoro – industria tessile* (textiles); *Contratto collettivo nazionale di lavoro per i dipendenti da aziende del terziario: distribuzione e servizi* (commerce and services); *Contratto collettivo nazionale di lavoro per i dirigenti di aziende commerciali* (commercial managers); *La contrattazione sindacale collettiva per i dirigenti di aziende industriali* (managers in industry).

Bruno Durante and Camillo Filadoro, *Enciclopedia dei diritti dei lavoratori*, Nicola Teti Editore, Milan, 1991.

Codice civile a leggi complementari, Maggioli Editore, Rimini, 1991.

Franco Volpini (ed.), *Agenda per l'amministrazione del personale delle aziende industriali 1994*, Jandi Sapi Editori, Rome, 1993.

9

Netherlands

Basic rights and labour jurisdiction

Compared with other EU member states labour affairs in the Netherlands are both strongly institutionalised and relatively centralised. However, a trend towards decentralisation has become increasingly apparent over the past few years.

Consultation and official authorisation are important, with a statutory obligation on government to consult the tripartite Social and Economic Council (Sociaal-Economische Raad, SER) on all major socio-economic issues. Terms and conditions of employment are governed by the law, by collective agreements, which may be declared generally binding on a whole sector, by company regulations and by individual contracts of employment.

Hierarchy of legal provision

The Civil Code lays down a hierarchy of statutory provisions governing the scope of what may be included in the individual contract of employment:

- Binding legislation (*dwingend recht*) which may not be relaxed under any circumstances (such as protection against dismissal due to marital status).
- Largely binding regulations (*driekwart dringend recht*) which can be altered to the detriment of the employee only by collective agreement (such as paid holidays).
- Partly binding regulations (*semi-dwingend recht*) which can be altered to the detriment of the employee only by a written agreement (such as a restrictive covenant).
- Supplementary regulations (*aanvulend/regelend recht*), which are deemed to apply where no written or verbal agreement provides otherwise.

Collectively agreed provisions take precedence over statute law if they are more favourable to the employee. 'Minimum conditions' laid down by collective agreement (*collectieve arbeidsovereenkomst*, CAO) can only be improved upon, not worsened, in an individual contract of employment. This would include, for example, pay levels, holiday entitlement and bonuses. 'Standard conditions' may not be altered at all in an individual contract and include, for example, the 'peace' clause, prohibiting industrial action during the life of an agreement. However, such conditions apply only to members of signatory organisations and cannot be generally extended to all companies in a given sector, unlike the minimum conditions, which may be extended by ministerial decree (*algemeen verbindend verklaren*).

Labour jurisdiction

The Netherlands does not have a separate system of labour courts or tribunals. However, the ordinary civil courts may hear employment cases using procedures intended to offer greater informality and speed, with more discretion given to presiding judges on rules of evidence and balancing the interests of the parties. The most common first instance for individual employment disputes is to go before a district judge (*kantonrechter*), with appeals through the civil court system ultimately to the High Court (*Hoge Raad*). Alternatively, complaints may also be lodged with the full district court (*kort geding*), also using employment law procedures. In addition to these procedures, there is a further option of an accelerated procedure (*spoedprocedure*), in which an interim ruling may be given pending a full hearing. Using such procedures, a court may for example order an employer to reinstate a dismissed employee until a formal court hearing is possible.

Collective agreements may lay down arbitration procedures using named arbitrators. However, using formal arbitration machinery can prove more expensive than the informal options allowed under law.

Contracts of employment

There is no legal distinction between blue- and white-collar workers, and therefore no legal differentiation in the terms of an employment contract based solely on type of employee. (Although a number of industries have weekly pay scales, most blue-collar employees are actually paid each month.) Legislation on, for example, probationary periods draws no distinction between blue- and white-collar workers. However, managers may be covered by their own collective agreement within a company or, more frequently, by individual contract only, and there may be a number of legal requirements relating to contracts for some directors or board members; however, this is regulated under a separate statute in the Civil Code rather than directly through employment law.

Company directors are not bound by the terms of collective agreements, and rarely by company regulations. Most of the terms normally laid down in contracts of employment are not covered in directors' contracts (such as job classification, pay scales etc). The most common terms are probationary and notice periods, travel costs and expenses allowances which are widespread.

Pay for company directors is normally set by the board and laid down in the individual contract, as is the frequency of payment. They are covered by the minimum wage act, and therefore entitled to holiday bonus of at least 8 per cent of salary. In addition, most directors are entitled to some profit pay-outs (*tantième*) and this must be provided for in the company statutes and referred to in the contract.

A contract of employment is defined in the Civil Code (article 1637a) as an agreement by which an employee undertakes to do certain work in exchange for wages for a certain length of time. The Civil Code lays down the rights and obligations associated with the employment relationship. All these rights and obligations, together with those specified in a variety of other laws on the employment relationship, apply as soon as a contract of employment (*arbeids-overeenkomst*) has been concluded. There is no statutory requirement for any contract of employment to be in writing. This applies to full-time, permanent contracts as much as to fixed-term or temporary contracts. On 1 January 1994 however the Netherlands implemented the EU directive on proof of an employment contract. This requires employers to provide every employee with the basic terms and conditions of their employment, in writing, no later than one month after the employment begins. It must include details of the work to be carried out, pay, holiday entitlement, place of work, periods of notice, hours of work, and the relevant collective agreement. Where this information is already set out in a written contract of employment, on a pay slip or in a collective agreement, there is no requirement to restate them separately.

No contract of employment can be concluded with anyone aged under 18 unless the consent, express or tacit, of their guardian has been given within four weeks of the contract being drawn up.

Most contracts of employment are written contracts, and usually contain at least the following information:

- Periods of notice.
- Disciplinary procedures.
- Restrictive covenants (see below).
- Pay.
- Holiday entitlement and pay.
- Hours of work.

There is no obligation to consult employee representatives on the terms of a new contract. However, works councils have a statutory right to be consulted on the terms of reference of any outside expert or consultancy brought into the company.

Types of contract

Contracts of employment can be permanent (*voor onbepaalde tijd*) or fixed-term (*voor bepaalde tijd*).

Fixed-term contracts   These can be concluded for a specific length of time or for the purpose of carrying out a specific task, including the temporary replacement of a particular employee. Fixed-term contracts may be renewed once, after which they will be deemed to be open-ended, and there is no statutory minimum or maximum period for which they must run, although there are limits on renewals. Current legislation stipulates that any extension of a fixed-term contract will be presumed to be for the same length of time – but with a maximum of one year – as the original contract, with the same terms and conditions, unless stipulated otherwise. All employment rights conferred by virtue of the existence of an employment contract apply also to fixed-term contracts, with the exception of dismissal procedures (periods of notice, authorisation, etc.; see below). However, once a fixed-term contract has been renewed, or continued without notice that it is to be discontinued, the full dismissal procedure automatically applies, unless a period of more than thirty-one days elapses between the two fixed-term contracts. (Note, however, that by law, if an employer uses the same worker during the period between fixed-term contracts, via an agency, all dismissal procedures also apply to the second fixed-term contracts.) Moreover, where an employee formerly on a permanent contract is put on to a fixed-term contract, the dismissal provisions will also apply. As of mid-1994 a number of amendments are being proposed to legislation governing fixed-term contracts affecting periods of notice, probationary periods and extension procedures.

Part-time employment   There is no statutory minimum or maximum number of hours that an employee must work to be considered a part-time employee. Part-timers are usually defined in collective agreements as those working less than the norm within a particular industry. The Central Bureau of Statistics deems part-timers to be all those working less than the norm in an industry but who are nonetheless regular, permanent employees.

Temporary workers   Temporary workers supplied through agencies are strictly regulated by a number of laws, which also forbid their use in certain circumstances. Authorisation from the Ministry of Social Affairs and Employment is required before temporary workers can be taken on. The maximum period for which an agency worker may be taken on is three months, although it may be extended by a further three if necessary. A company that has recently employed a temporary worker may not take on another in the same role until half the period of time has elapsed for which the first was employed, and in any case must wait at least one month. Temporary workers have their own collective agreement governing terms and conditions, and their own pay scales.

Flexible contracts   These include on-call contracts, zero-hours contracts and 'delayed work' contracts. Under Dutch law they may often not be regarded as true contracts of employment, and most are exempt from the dismissal authorisation procedures. For on-call work a minimum of three hours' work per call-up period is required.

Probationary periods

Probationary periods are laid down in the contract of employment and must, by law, be the same for employer and employee, with a maximum of two months. No minimum is stipulated, and a probationary period may not be renewed unless it is in relation to an employee taking up training for a new post. Temporary workers who are subsequently given permanent contracts cannot be put on a probationary period.

Restrictive covenants and confidentiality

Any restrictions relating to an employee's activities after termination of the employment contract must be set down in writing, either in the individual contract of employment or in the company's staff regulations. They should state the scope and duration of the restrictive covenant, which must not exceed what is genuinely required to protect the employer's business interests. In some circumstances employees may be compensated, but this is not a statutory requirement. Breaches of a restrictive covenant may make the employee liable for compensation payments set by the courts.

Confidentiality is an implicit duty of the employee, which may be reinforced under the terms of a collective agreement. Breaches of confidentiality may lead to disciplinary action or summary dismissal (Civil Code, article 1639p).

Copyright on an invention normally belongs to its creator. However, where the work is carried out as part of the work assigned by an employer within the terms of an employment contract, copyright falls to the employer, unless specifically agreed otherwise in writing. In cases where copyright belongs to the employee, employers may still have a right to limit the distribution or publication of the invention/research to protect their business interests.

Workplace discipline

A number of implied conditions of reasonable behaviour applying to employer and employee are detailed in the Civil Code. They include (for the employee) carrying out the work to the best of one's ability without harm or danger to others, turning up on time, and returning any tools or equipment in good condition. The employer has a duty to provide work under the agreed terms and conditions, provide the necessary tools or equipment, ensure that adequate health and safety procedures are followed, and complete any documentation required.

Discipline is laid down in three ways:

- General law and implied terms of behaviour within an employment relationship.
- The employer's instructions (*voorschrift*), as provided for by law, which are much wider than simply discipline.

- In detailed company regulations (*reglement*).

The important difference between the latter two is that the *voorschrift* is drawn up by the employer alone, whereas the *reglement* requires the agreement of the works council. (Works councils are required by statute in companies with over thirty-five staff, and are frequently set up on a voluntary basis in smaller companies.) All employees must be given and must sign a copy of the company regulations; a copy must be registered with the district judge and another copy displayed on the company's premises. The importance of company regulations has diminished as collective agreements have encompassed more and more of the terms they used to contain. Frequently company regulations do not meet the criteria laid down in statute law but are nonetheless often deemed legally binding by the courts in cases where a dispute has arisen.

Most disciplinary procedures include at least:

- Warnings, verbal and written.
- Suspension, with or without loss of pay.
- Loss of perquisites (provided these are not contractually agreed).
- Transfer or demotion.

By statute, curtailment of pay or holiday entitlement and fines can be imposed only if expressly provided for as a disciplinary measure in a collective agreement or in company regulations; in any event, statutory minima must not be exceeded. Fines may be imposed only if the amount and the use to which the money is put are stipulated by collective agreement or company regulation. There is a legal maximum of half a day's pay in any one week. The suspension or transfer of an employee may also be limited by collective agreement or company regulation. Such measures are frequently deployed as a prelude to a dismissal (see below).

Grievance procedures are often laid down by collective agreement, and may provide for trade union and/or works council involvement.

Workplace rights

In most instances rights to information are asserted through employee representatives, most frequently the works council, which has extensive statutory rights of information and consultation. A copy of the company regulations must be given to each new employee (see above), together with details of the job they are to do and any associated risks. In addition, since 1991 companies in certain sectors, and all those with more than 100 staff, must draw up an annual report on health and safety risks and policies which must be made available to all staff. This report is drawn up in consultation with employee representatives and, where necessary, individual employees.

Employment terms

Hours of work

The Labour Act (*Arbeidswet*) lays down the statutory maximum hours of work: eight and a half hours per day or forty-eight hours per week in factories and offices, based on a six-day week; nine hours per day or forty-eight hours per week in shops, based on a six-day week. In addition, the Civil Code generally prohibits Sunday working, with statutory exemptions for work in connection with public services, emergency services, repair and maintenance, health care and so on. However, employers and employees retain a considerable degree of freedom to set hours of work within the statutory maxima. Employers must apply to the labour inspectorate for authorisation if they want to exceed the statutory limits, and must have 'good reason' for wanting to do so. The authorisation may stipulate constraints such as hours outside which no work may be done, or a maximum number of hours which may be worked over a given reference period (usually four weeks or three months). Proposed amendments of the Labour Act, including the rules on hours of work, are still under debate.

Hours of work are now usually set by collective agreement. The average working week laid down by collective agreement is about 37 hours. Actual weekly working hours may be longer than the agreed average, however, especially for shift workers, with extra hours translated into additional free days (*roostervrije dagen*) to be taken throughout the year. In the textile industry agreement, hours for shift workers are specified for a variety of reference periods: eighty-five hours' maximum for two-shift workers over two weeks; 128 hours over three weeks for three-shift workers.

The agreement of works councils is required if companies wish to change their hours of work, including shift work, flexible working hours, and short-time working, unless there is specific provision otherwise by collective agreement.

Young workers

Young workers (defined as those under 18 or those following part-time education in tandem with their employment) are not allowed, by statute, to work more than eight hours per day. They must be allowed time off to attend any compulsory schooling/training. They are generally prohibited from doing night work between 19.00 and 07.00, although there are a number of exceptions such as paper rounds. They must have at least half an hour's break after four and a half hours' work, and are entitled to twelve hours' rest between working periods and to sixty consecutive hours' rest (or two periods of thirty-six hours) in any seven-day period.

Annual leave

The Civil Code (article 1638bb) provides for annual paid leave of at least four times the number of days regularly worked per week: employees working a five-day week are therefore entitled to twenty days' annual leave. The same provisions apply *pro rata* to part-timers working less than five days per week. The law also entitles employees to take two consecutive weeks' holiday or twice one full week per year. In collective agreements employers often stipulate a period during which at least ten consecutive days' holiday must be taken, usually between April and September. The remaining days are called floating days (*snipperdagen*). Companies may fix a number of these, for example to cover a shutdown between Christmas and New Year, or to bridge the gap between a weekend and a public holiday. Length of service and/or age often entitles an employee to additional days' holiday. In the textile industry, for example, the standard leave of twenty-five days increases to twenty-six for those aged over forty, to twenty-eight for those aged fifty to fifty-four and up to thirty days for those over sixty. Some collective agreements grant extra days' leave to younger workers.

Public holidays

Eight public holidays are laid down by statute: New Year's Day, Good Friday, Easter Monday, Liberation Day, Ascension Thursday, Whit Monday, Christmas Day and Boxing Day. Pay for these days is governed by collective agreements, which usually grant paid time off for the statutory holidays as well as national festivals (such as the Queen's birthday) and local festivals (such as Carnival in the southern provinces). Most collective agreements provide for ten or eleven public holidays. When a national holiday falls on a weekend it is not usual to have another day off, although this may be specified by collective agreement.

Parental leave provisions

Female employees are entitled by statute to sixteen weeks' maternity leave, four of which must be taken before the expected date of confinement, and to a minimum of eight after the birth. Most collective agreements increase this by two to four weeks. Women may also take a further two months' maternity leave on half pay (see below), provided it is within one year of the child's birth (but not necessarily immediately after the birth). A number of company collective agreements provide for additional, largely unpaid, leave. For example, the chemical concern Akzo offers up to two years' unpaid leave with a right of return to previous employment or to an equivalent post.

Parental leave on an unpaid, part-time basis is available by law to men and women who have children under 4 years of age either born to them or adopted. They must have at least one year's service and be willing to work a minimum of twenty hours per week. Pay is *pro rata* to the hours worked, and the maximum is six months' leave per child.

Time off

Employees are entitled to thirty-six consecutive hours' rest each week, and at least one Sunday in two. The minimum daily rest period is eleven hours. Daily rest breaks are set by collective agreement or by the individual contract.

Leave of absence (*georloofde verzuim*) is detailed in the Civil Code (article 1638c), which specifies an employee's entitlement to paid time off over and above paid holiday. This includes two days for the birth of a child or up to four days for the death of a close relative. Collective agreements generally extend the list of acceptable reasons and may include wedding anniversaries, weddings and the ordination of a relative. In addition, paid time off is allowed for dental and medical appointments, job-hunting (for those made redundant) and examinations. The right to unpaid leave for such things as military service, training, public office and works council or trade union activities is laid down by statute.

Individual pay and benefits

Minimum wage

The national minimum wage (*minimumloon*) was introduced in 1968 and applies to all adults over 23. It is normally revised by the government twice a year, in January and July, after consultation with the Social and Economic Council, with an adjustment to reflect the average wage increase. In the past there was an automatic link with the average increase in earnings: however, this link was severed in 1992 and since then there has been no increase in the level of the minimum wage, which remains at Fl 2,163.20 (£792.40) per month. Most collectively agreed minima are linked to the national minimum, and tend to be at least 10–15 per cent higher. The government's intention in freezing the national minimum is to encourage employers to take on more staff, as well as to try to bring down industry minimum pay rates.

Minimum rates for young people are expressed as a percentage of the adult rate, ranging from 30 per cent for 15 year olds to 85 per cent for 22 year olds. The implementation of the national minimum is monitored by the government's Loontechnische Dienst. Nonetheless, there is no penalty for infringement.

Pay indexation used to be commonly applied in collective agreements to offset increases in the cost of living. In 1982 the social partners (government, employers and unions) concluded an agreement to allocate the money intended for indexation payments to cutting working hours. Since then pay indexation has become a significantly less important bargaining issue, and no longer figures in the vast majority of agreements. It can still be found in construction and agriculture, and in a number of agreements at the port of Rotterdam. Some agreements – for example, textiles – specifically state that they will not be indexed.

The law on pay

The main piece of legislation on pay is the 1970 law on the payment of wages (*Wet op de loonvorming*), which essentially gives employers and employees the freedom to negotiate terms and conditions of employment, including the setting of pay, within the statutory framework. The semi-public sector (*gepremieerde en gesubsidieerde sektor*, G&G) is regulated by its own law, which reflects many of the provisions for the private sector.

The 1970 law requires all collective agreements to be registered with the Ministry of Labour; indeed, agreements only come into force when they have been received by the registration department – the Dienst Collectieve Arbeidsvoorwaarden. It also authorises the Minister of Labour to lay down certain binding conditions at the specific request of a trade union or employers' association, as well as to draw up overall pay policies.

Remuneration need not be exclusively monetary and can be made up of bonuses, paid partly in kind, such as the use of gas, electricity or water, clothing and food, as well as through the provision of training facilities. Wages and salaries however, must be paid in money. There are no statutory rules on the frequency of pay. It is laid down by collective agreement or in the individual contract of employment. The vast majority of employees, blue-collar and white-collar, are paid monthly or every four weeks. Annual salaries are therefore divided by twelve or thirteen as appropriate – this is not to be confused with a thirteenth-month bonus payment (see below). A considerable number of collective agreements have parallel salary scales, giving the rates for monthly and for four-weekly payment side by side. Weekly payments are now seldom encountered, even in the construction industry, where they used to be widespread. In agriculture, weekly salaries are still widely quoted in collective agreements on temporary and casual labour. Overtime and night work pay may be expressed as a percentage of the nominal hourly rate or as a percentage of the basic monthly pay (see below).

Most pay is paid net of taxation and social security contributions, which are deducted at source on a PAYE basis (*loonheffing*). The social security system consists of two parts: the national insurance schemes (*volksvezekering*), which cover all citizens, and the social security schemes (*sociale vezekering*), which cover employed persons. Contributions are payable on total earnings up to a set ceiling. Both employers and employees used to contribute to both schemes, but since 1990 only employees pay into the national schemes (covering old-age pension, widow's pension, medical expenses and basic disability benefit). To compensate for this, employees are entitled to an additional payment from their employer, the *overhevelingstoeslag*, which is set at 11.40 per cent of the total gross pay on which contributions are levied. The 1990 reforms also combined national insurance contributions with income tax for the lowest income tax bracket. The levy is deducted together but allocated separately to the various funds (for current rates see the appendix). Other contributions, e.g. to a pension or industry/company social fund, may be deducted at source if a collective agreement so provides. Union dues are charged direct to the individual employee by the union.

There are no statutory requirements governing the form of a pay slip (*loonstrookje*), other than the requirement for some form of written proof of payment. Most pay slips are fairly standard, however, containing information on the level and frequency of pay, deductions made, and so on.

In cases of insolvency, employers are required to give the statutory or agreed notice to employees, but with a maximum of six weeks. Employers can appeal to the industry boards (*bedrijfsvereniging*) for pay due for the notice period, as well as up to thirteen weeks' pay per employee, and one year's holiday pay.

Levels of pay determination

Over the past twenty years the collective bargaining system has become increasingly decentralised, with a rising number of industry and company-level agreements. The last time a central pay agreement was signed at national level was in 1982, although since then a number of central agreements have been signed on specific issues such as youth unemployment (1984) and training (1986). As economic conditions worsened throughout 1992 the government pressed strongly for a wage freeze, and in response the social partners agreed to a bargaining pause in January and February 1993, although pay rises agreed in March could be backdated to the beginning of the year. This apparently had little effect, and as the situation continued to deteriorate in 1993 the government threatened to impose a pay freeze in 1994 and beyond unless the social partners negotiated some form of framework accord. In November 1993, therefore, a social accord was signed, setting guidelines for the 1994 bargaining round. It did not, however, specify pay targets or guarantee a wage freeze; it merely emphasised that there was 'little, if any, room for manoeuvre on pay'. On a number of issues industry and company-level negotiators had shown themselves unwilling to follow nationally set guidelines and there was some scepticism about how effective the social accord would be in restraining pay rises. However, a number of important agreements signed in early 1994 settled on 0 per cent increases, in some cases over two years.

Most minimum levels of pay are laid down in industry collective agreements which cover approximately 75 per cent of private-sector employees, either directly or by extension. (In the public sector and the semi-public G&G sector the coverage is 100 per cent, although, technically speaking, these are not collective agreements as defined in the law on collective agreements – *Wet op de collectieve arbeidsovereenkomst* (CAO) – and therefore are not subject to the same legal requirements.) Figures for coverage vary considerably between industries, with 94 per cent of the work force covered in construction but only 40 per cent in some service sectors.

The number of company agreements has risen steadily over the past ten years, and they now affect some 15 per cent of the private-sector work force. They are most common in sectors not covered by an industry agreement, most notably the chemical industry, which has important company-level agreements at companies such as Akzo and Unilever. A number of large firms straddling more than one sector have opted out of the industry agreement and prefer to draw up their own collective agreements. Among them are Philips and the steel concern Hoogovens. Company agreements set out terms and conditions in line with what is laid down in industry agreements, and may only improve on those conditions. Smaller firms may have an agreement stipulating only a limited number of terms, such as pay and benefits specific to the company. Generally speaking, companies pay 10–15 per cent above industry minima, and in a number of instances the ceiling may be set by a maximum laid down in an industry-level agreement: in engineering, for example, companies can only pay up to 10 per cent above the industry minimum in basic pay. Most collective agreements specify that pay rises must apply to actual pay in order to prevent companies offsetting their pay levels against the industry-agreed minimum. However, company-level bonuses and other payments can be frozen or reduced to limit the overall increase. This has increasingly been the practice of smaller companies in hard times to minimise the impact of agreed pay rises.

Employees outside collective bargaining tend to be either the very low-paid – often, for example, in retail or other service sectors – or managerial and executive staff. A survey by the Ministry of Labour in 1990 showed that, of all non-CAO employees, 26 per cent fell into the earnings category of less than Fl 26,500 (£9,707) while some 17 per cent were earning over Fl 84,000 (£30,770) and a further 36 per cent earned between Fl 42,000 and Fl 84,000 (£15,385–£30,770). In a few companies – for example, the chemical firm Akzo – managers up to a certain income are covered by a separate collective agreement, but most have their terms and conditions of employment set individually (see below).

In recent years, works councils have begun to get involved in the setting of limited terms and conditions in some companies outside the collective bargaining process. The legal implications of this are unclear, as works councils are specifically prohibited from collective bargaining. In consequence, any accord they may sign does not qualify as a collective agreement in the legal sense. However, where there is a very limited, or no, trade union presence, employee input via the works councils is beginning to be recognised as legitimate by the unions. This whole issue of the demarcation of powers between unions and works councils is due to be examined in the light of these developments (see the volume in this series on *Employee Relations and Collective Bargaining*).

Main payment systems

Payments by results and piece rates are now very rare in the Netherlands. They may still be used for homeworking in some small companies. Most employees are on time rates or a monthly salary, although hourly rates may be used as a basis for calculating overtime.

The discussion over performance-related pay resurfaced in 1994, with employees looking to bypass pay freezes imposed during the recession. Performance-related pay is, however, little used, other than for managerial employees (see below).

Job evaluation and grading

Over 80 per cent of employees are affected by job evaluation systems (*functiewaardering*), although in some sectors, notably construction and printing, such systems are not commonly used (see below). Most systems are agreed between the employers and the unions at industry level, with details filled in at company level. They typically cover both blue- and white-collar workers and rely on a points rating system. The majority of systems have reference jobs (*normfunctie*) against which others are measured, and these are also frequently agreed with the unions. Each employee must be assigned to a given job category. Works councils have the statutory right to be consulted on any amendment of a job evaluation system where there is no such provision in a collective agreement.

Pay scales (*loonschalen/salarisschalen*) are laid down in collective agreements and typically consist of seven to ten job categories and a scale of increments for each of the categories, usually based on length of service. The scales are integrated – in other words, they cover blue- and white-collar staff. Separate scales are drawn up for adults and for those under 23 years of age. They are in monthly or four-weekly intervals.

Attempts by employers to introduce performance-related pay for non-management staff have met with little enthusiasm from the unions. Most collectively-agreed systems leave little room for individual appraisal, although it does exist within some company agreements.

In the construction industry the job classification system is very different. The industry agreement lays down five broad bands covering around 100 job functions. For each band a minimum level of pay is stipulated (*garantieloon*), and companies negotiate with individual employees or groups of employees the percentage they are willing to pay over and above this minimum. It can vary from 5 per cent to 25 per cent, and is nominally performance-related. In reality, however, it reflects market conditions in the sector.

Basic pay package

Agreed basic pay at industry level is usually improved on by 10 to 15 per cent at company level, depending largely on the size and profitability of the individual firm. Increments are normally paid according to age (especially for those under 23) and/or length of service. The number of increments varies with the level of the job. In the textile industry, for example, semi-skilled workers will have one or two increments, while skilled staff and technicians have five or six and those at the top of the scale have eight or nine increments. Some companies, such as

Hoechst, stipulate that increments for certain categories will be triggered only until the employee reaches a certain age, after which the increment will be based on years of service. Most agreements provide for a thirteenth month's pay, which may be conditional on a minimum length of service. In the banking sector, for example, all those with at least one year's service are entitled to it.

Regional differences

Despite its small size, the Netherlands shows considerable differences in pay levels from region to region, although not in every sector. The Randstad area (stretching from Amsterdam down to Rotterdam and across to Utrecht) generally pays higher wages than the rest of the country, especially for secretarial and some administrative functions. However, in the northern and eastern provinces the difficulty of finding highly qualified staff can push pay up. The difference has been evened out somewhat in the economic downturn of the past few years, but there is still a noticeable difference.

Pay increases

For employees on agreed pay scales, increases come mainly in the form of increments set by the relevant pay scales or by collectively agreed rises which apply to basic pay. Companies are free to improve on industry agreed minimum rises, and may also increase variable company add-ons. A number of agreements provide for additional, long-service increments for staff who have reached the top of their pay scale. The collective agreement in the printing industry, for example, says that, five years after reaching the top of their scale, employees in the lower pay categories are entitled to additional increments equal to the increments already payable at the top end of their scale. Staff at the top end of the pay scale are entitled to extra increments after eight years at the top of their grade. Managerial staff, especially lower and middle managers outside any collective bargaining process, will frequently have their pay increased in line with the rise agreed for lower-level employees.

There are no statutory provisions regarding payment for shift work, overtime or other work outside normal hours. These are all governed by collective agreements.

Overtime

Overtime is defined as work carried out over and above that stipulated by law or by collective agreement. Pay rates for overtime are governed entirely by collective agreement subject to a fallback rate set out in law, and is usually paid only after the first half-hour. Where no provision is made in a collective agreement or individual contract, the employer has to pay the standard, basic hourly rate for overtime work. Most agreements calculate overtime pay as a given percentage of the monthly rate: for example, the collective agreement for light engineering stipulates between 0.78 per cent and 1.12 per cent of monthly pay in addition to the basic rate, depending on when the overtime is worked. Some agreements specify different overtime rates for shift workers and other workers. The textile industry agreement provides for overtime premiums to shift workers at 0.76 per cent of monthly pay for each hour of overtime worked on a weekday; 1.06 per cent on a Saturday after 14.00 and 1.21 per cent for a Sunday or public holiday. Non-shift workers are entitled to overtime pay of 0.76 per cent of monthly pay per hour between 06.00 and 20.00 Monday to Friday; 0.91 per cent for weekdays between 20.00 and 06.00 and for Saturdays before 14.00; and 1.21 per cent for overtime worked on a Saturday after 14.00, on a Sunday or on a public holiday. Employees may also take time off in lieu, but will then receive only the overtime premiums, not the basic pay as well.

Shift work

Most collective agreements award some form of additional pay for shift work (*ploegendienst*), although in a number of instances it is incorporated into basic pay, for example in the textile industry. Where this is not the case, a premium of 12.5 per cent of monthly pay is paid for double-shift working; 18.3 per cent for three-shift work; and 22.5 per cent for four-shift work.

Other premiums

Night work is paid at the rates stipulated for overtime (see above). Additional premiums may include pay for dirty or dangerous work. A number of companies have incorporated such premiums into their basic pay; others still have separate rates. In the confectionery CAO, for example, a points system is used to calculate supplements for unpleasant work, ranging from Fl 4.9 (£1.79) to Fl 22 (£8.06) a month.

Bonuses

Holidays with pay   Employees have a statutory right to paid holidays and an additional holiday bonus (*vakantiebijslag*). The latter is set at 7.5 per cent of annual basic pay. However, most collective agreements improve on this and pay around 8 per cent of total earnings (exclusive of overtime). Most agreements provide for this bonus to be paid in May or June. In addition, some collective agreements stipulate a minimum cash payment to heads of households and employees with children. The 1993 textile industry agreement, for example, guarantees a minimum holiday bonus of Fl 2,569 (£941) for those with children. Up to 25 per cent of the holiday bonus is distributed at Christmas.

In the construction industry the system is somewhat different, to reflect the special circumstances under which it operates. As most employees are taken on temporarily, or on short-term contracts, employers with projects running over traditional holiday periods (June–August, Christmas) would find themselves liable for the vast majority of holiday pay. In addition, the industry is characterised by above-average chances of bankruptcy. The construction industry scheme therefore has the holiday bonus paid out via a special fund. Employers contribute for all their employees, even where they do no more than half a day's work. The money is then distributed to cover holiday pay, holiday bonuses and pay for public holidays. In the agricultural sector there is a similar scheme for temporary and casual workers. They are given holiday tokens by their employer which can be cashed through the sectoral holiday fund. All employers pay into the fund.

Thirteenth-month pay   Most collective agreements award an additional month's pay (*jaarlijkse extra uitkering*), commonly known as the thirteenth-month payment. Often a service requirement is attached to this bonus: in the insurance industry agreement only staff with a year's service are entitled to the thirteenth month; at Philips a bonus of 8.33 per cent of annual salary is paid out in December to employees who were in service for the entire calendar year. As a result, most salaries in the Netherlands are paid for twelve months plus the holiday bonus plus the thirteenth month. Staff on four-weekly pay scales will, of course, receive the thirteenth month as a fourteenth payment.

Other bonuses   Employees with some supervisory responsibility may be awarded additional payments by collective agreement. In the 1993/94 printing industry agreement supervisors in certain departments are entitled to between Fl 1.12 (£0.41) and Fl 2.66 (£0.97) per hour extra pay, depending on the number of staff for whom they are responsible.

Employees who temporarily take on additional responsibilities normally handled by someone in a higher grade are usually entitled by collective agreement to a corresponding pay increase equivalent to a percentage of the difference between their normal basic pay and that of the higher grade.

Allowances

A number of allowances may also be allocated by collective agreement. The horticultural industry, for example, provides an allowance for clothing and tools which varies between Fl 3.75 (£1.37) per day to a maximum of Fl 18.75 (£6.87) per week. Child care allowances are still rare, although a number of industry agreements refer to the need to make child care provision. The construction industry stipulates employer contributions at a maximum of Fl 8,400 (£3,077) per year for female employees with children under the age of 4.

Performance pay

The nature of the job evaluation system and the pay structure in most collective agreements leaves little room for merit awards. A number of industry-level agreements do specifically make provision for performance-related pay at company level, which has to be agreed with work-force representatives – usually trade unions, in the form of a collective agreement, or works councils. The collective agreement for the chemical company DSM Limburg provides a system of internal merit assessment, partly dependent on performance and/or output, with bonuses equal to 4–12 per cent of monthly pay for the top grade of the salary scale to which the employee is allocated. However, most systems are only nominally performance-related, and are often linked with the carrying out of additional tasks.

At Philips the company agreement details the procedures to be followed for appraisals which can lead to performance-related bonuses. Appraisals are carried out at least once a year and must include an assessment of employees' overall productivity, their participation within the department and their level of responsibility. Depending on the outcome of the appraisal, a consolidated pay increase of 2, 3 or 4 per cent may be awarded. The appraisals are carried out by the employee's immediate manager.

Managerial pay

Managerial and specialists' pay may be set by collective agreement or, more usually, by separate salary scales determined by the employer or by individual contracts. A number of companies have separate collective agreements to cover different management levels. For example, in the Akzo managerial and technical specialists' agreement (*CAO voor hoger personeel*), annual basic salary scales range from Fl 50,000 to Fl 185,000 (£18,315–£67,766), compared with a range of Fl 32,000 to Fl 64,000 (£11,722–£23,444) in the company's general collective agreement. In some sectors separate clauses within the terms of the general agreement stipulate certain terms including pay for higher functions: in banking, for example, the pay scale in the single-status agreement ranges from Fl 11,000 to Fl 155,000 (£4,029–£56,777).

Separate, non-negotiated salary scales are most common in larger firms, while individually determined pay is the norm for managers in smaller firms. In most cases, negotiated pay scales are merely extended upwards with the creation of additional grades for management functions. Employers may also establish a reference wage to which variable elements are added.

Over recent years a more individualised pay structure has been developing, with greater emphasis on bonuses and merit assessments. According to the Monks Partnership survey *Incentives and Benefits in Europe*, cash bonuses were paid to over 90 per cent of top and senior management, and 80 per cent of upper middle management. However, only around a quarter of top managers had more than 25 per cent of their pay at risk. At middle management level, nearly two-thirds of managers received cash bonuses of less than 15 per cent of their annual base salary.

Share option schemes are not as prevalent as elsewhere in Western Europe, reflecting the lack of a supportive tax environment (see below). Some 55 per cent of top managers were granted access to share options. In addition to cars, granted to over 95 per cent of top and senior managers, and in nearly 80 per cent of cases with fuel, the most common managerial benefits are long-term ill-health and dependants' insurance, and life assurance. Cars are taxed at 20 per cent of the list price per year where the journey between home and work is less than thirty kilometres and 24 per cent for journeys over thirty kilometres.

Financial participation

There are few tax advantages or incentives to the use of profit-share or employee-share ownership schemes. Employers and unions have called for changes in the law, and a favourable report was published by the bipartite Labour Foundation in 1991.

Nonetheless a large number of collective agreements include a clause on profit-share schemes (*winstuitkering*), especially in larger companies. When examined, however, the bonuses rarely turn out to be genuine profit-linked bonuses. Most schemes are open to all staff, only a few being restricted to management. There is some variety in the calculation methods used to allocate the bonus. At chemical company Hoechst, for example, the profit-share scheme consists of a fixed element and a variable percentage. A fixed 1 per cent of twelve times the December salary is paid out every year that Hoechst achieves a pre-tax profit through its normal business operations. The variable element is paid if the pre-tax profit is at least Fl 50 million to 100 million (£18.3–36.6 million) and ranges from 0 per cent to 4 per cent of twelve times December pay. In addition the payment is increased by 25 per cent for all employees with more than ten years' service.

Sick pay and disability benefit

Sickness benefit is provided under the state sickness insurance scheme (*Ziekenfonds*) for employed persons. Contributions are paid into the scheme by both employer and employee and are levied on all earnings up to a ceiling which is revised every year. For 1994 it was set at Fl 286 (£105) per day. Under the scheme benefit is payable at 70 per cent of earnings. However, most collective agreements make this up to at least 85 per cent, often 100 per cent, of earnings. Benefit used to be paid out after two waiting days for up to one year. However, significant changes in the sickness law took effect on 1 January 1994. They require employers to foot the bill for the first six weeks of sick pay – or the first two weeks in companies with fewer than fifteen employees. Under the new regulations, employers are required to monitor sickness absence and draw up health and safety policies. The new law also introduced a differentiation in employer sickness contribution rates, depending on whether a company's sick leave rates deviate from the average across the sector.

After one year on sick pay, employees may be transferred to the controversial state-funded long-term disability scheme (*Wet Arbeidsongeschiktheid*, WAO). This provides for benefit at a given percentage of previous earnings, depending on the extent of the disability (which can be assessed at between 15 per cent and 100 per cent). WAO recipients remain as employees of their company for one year, after which their fitness for work is reassessed. The regulations governing this scheme were revised in 1993, in an attempt to limit the escalating costs of a system that saw 14 per cent of the work force in receipt of some form of WAO benefit. Employers are now liable to pay a levy for any employee who ends up on WAO, although they are also entitled to a subsidy for taking on a WAO benefit recipient. In addition the benefits have been severely reduced for new claimants.

Maternity pay

Female employees are entitled to sixteen weeks' paid maternity leave (see above). This is paid at 100 per cent of previous earnings up to the daily contribution ceiling of Fl 286 (£105), and is administered by the joint industry boards (*bedrijfsvereniging*) from the state sickness insurance scheme. Most collective agreements give an extra two to four weeks' paid leave entitlement. In January 1991 part-time unpaid parental leave was made available to those with children under 4. At least twenty hours must be worked per week, and only hours actually worked are paid. Civil servants have the right to six months' paid parental leave at 75 per cent of their former earnings.

Equal pay and equal opportunities

The right to equal treatment and equal pay is laid down in the 1989 Act on the equal treatment of men and women (*Wet gelijke behandeling van mannen en vrouwen*), which consolidates all previous legislation on the issue.

The Act stipulates that employers must not draw any distinction between men and women as regards recruitment, terms and conditions of employment, training opportunities, promotion prospects or the termination of a contract of employment. It adds that all elements of pay must be calculated on the basis of equal criteria, provided the work is of equal value. In an employment contract there should be no differentiation between men and women arising from marital status or family situation. The only exceptions to these rules are for the specific protection of maternity rights and for positive discrimination. The Act also tackles the issue of indirect discrimination, and cites in particular the treatment of part-timers, the majority of whom are female.

Following the Act, a new Equal Treatment Commission was established. The commission has an investigative and an advisory role in the examination of alleged cases of discrimination on the grounds of sex. Any employees who feel they have been discriminated against may apply to the commission, which can launch a formal investigation and pronounce its verdict. The commission is not, however, empowered to impose sanctions, fines or compensation payments – these have to be settled in court. The 1989 Act gives unions and works councils the right to present a complaint on behalf of an employee, or group of employees, and if necessary start legal proceedings.

The trade unions and women's movement have called for legislation requiring companies to set up formal policies on dealing with sexual harassment.

Retirement

The state retirement age is set at 65 for men and women alike. The state old-age pension (*ouderdomspensioen*) is 70 per cent of the national minimum wage for unmarried pensioners or 50 per cent each for married pensioners whose partner is also over 65. Pensioners are entitled to an annual holiday bonus. The state scheme is funded by employees only, who pay contributions of 14.25 per cent for the basic pension and a further 1.85 per cent for the widows' pension fund (1994 figures). Full entitlement is gained after fifty years in the scheme, with 2 per cent deducted for each missing year. Total monthly state pension for an individual in 1994 would be Fl 1,428.40 (£523.22) plus Fl 84.75 (£31.04) holiday bonus.

In addition to the state scheme, many collective agreements at industry and company level provide for occupational pensions. These cover around 80 per cent of the work force, and the majority operate final salary schemes (*eindloonregeling*). Companies may be exempt from mandatory industry schemes if their own pension scheme provides at least equivalent benefits. Most occupational pension schemes aim to top up the state pension, bringing the total to 70 per cent of previous earnings after some forty years of service.

In general, two-thirds of pension contributions are made by the employer and one-third by the employee. Average contribution rates are around 4 per cent of earnings for the employer and 2–4 per cent for the employee. Contributions are tax-deductible. Pensionable earnings may be up to 40 per cent less than actual earnings, as a deduction is made (*franchise*) to allow for contributions to the state scheme.

Legislation on pensions and pension investments is very restrictive in the Netherlands, and until recently few people, except at executive level, had their own private schemes. The law has recently been loosened a little, and the number of private schemes is growing.

Early retirement schemes (*vervroegde uittreden*, VUT) were introduced in the early 1980s as part of a package to combat unemployment, especially among young people, and are now regarded almost as a right by unions and employees. VUT schemes are set up by collective agreement and can begin as early as age

56–7, although most run from the age of 60, 61 or 62. Typical benefits from a VUT scheme are around 70–80 per cent of final salary until retirement age, irrespective of length of service (although a minimum is required). It is normal for pension accrual to be continued between VUT age and normal retirement age. The cost of VUT schemes has risen considerably, and a number of industries and companies are looking to curtail the benefits and raise the qualifying age. At the chemicals firm Akzo agreement has been reached with the unions to phase the VUT scheme out completely over the coming ten years.

Individual termination of contract

Many foreign employers with operations in the Netherlands approach Dutch termination procedures with extreme misgivings. This view stems largely from the fact that no dismissal can take place without prior authorisation from the regional labour office (except in cases of summary dismissal). However, if an accurately prepared request is correctly presented to the director of the regional employment offices (*Arbeidsvoorzieningsbureau* – these replaced the old labour offices or *gewestelijke arbeidsbureaus*) permission is normally granted. In 1992, for example, only 5–6 per cent of applications were refused. According to official figures, around 85 per cent of dismissal authorisations are completed within eight weeks. The only alternative to the authorisation procedure is legal action. Recent government proposals to overhaul the procedures for termination of contract include the abolition of the prior authorisation requirement. Some of the greatest resistance to the proposed changes has come from small and medium-sized employers, who fear that the abolition of authorisation could lead to a greater number of lengthy and costly court cases.

Resignation and mutual agreement

In certain circumstances an employment contract can be terminated without authorisation procedures. During the probationary period either party can terminate the contract without giving notice. A contract of employment can also be terminated by mutual agreement between the employer and the employee (*wederzijds goedvinden*). Again, this requires no prior authorisation, although some sort of formal registration of the termination is often useful to prove compliance with minimum stipulations laid down by law or collective agreement. These include periods of notice, payment of outstanding wages or compensation, etc.

The expiry of a fixed-term contract also implies by its very nature the end of the employment relationship. A period of notice may be stipulated in the contract itself. Where a fixed-term contract is continued without notice that it is to terminate, any termination relating to the second contract will mean the authorisation procedures have to be followed.

Grounds for termination

An indefinite contract (*voor onbepaalde tijd*) can be terminated by the employer either summarily or by giving the requisite notice, depending on the grounds of termination. Individual dismissal can be either for economic reasons (*bedrijfs-economische redenen*), ie redundancy, or for reasons relating to the person or conduct of the employee (see below for details).

Dismissal authorisation procedures

In most cases where termination of contract includes a period of notice, official authorisation (*ontslagvergunning*) is also required. The application for authorisation must be made to the regional director of the employment bureau (RDA) covering the location where the work is normally carried out, or where the employee concerned is employed. The application must be made in writing before notice to terminate is given, and must provide details of the employee to be dismissed, the reason for the dismissal and any action taken prior to moving to termination such as warnings, offers of relocation, etc. In the case of dismissal on economic grounds adequate financial information and the reasoning behind the choice of employee must also be submitted. The regional director is required to consult a dismissal committee made up of at least one representative of a union and one from an employers' organisation. Any information provided by one party is made available to the other, including documents that may be classed as confidential by the employer. The majority (85 per cent) of authorisation procedures are concluded within eight weeks, although the law aims for a period of four to six weeks. Once the RDA has granted a dismissal licence the employer can give notice within the following two months (subject to review in 1995, which will shorten the overall waiting period). Should the employer be unable to give notice within those two months – for example, because the employee is ill – a fresh application has to be made. In cases of dismissal on economic grounds the authorisation may stipulate that for up to six months the dismissed employee must be given first refusal of any similar job that arises in the company.

Economic dismissal

Termination of contract on economic grounds (*bedrijfseconomische redenen*), ie redundancy, requires the employer to provide adequate information to the RDA, including:

- Data on the financial state of the company.
- Proof that alternatives such as reductions in working hours or relocation have been considered.
- The reasons for selecting the employee(s) in question.

In most cases dismissal is on a 'last in, first out' basis (see also 'Collective dismissal' below). Up to nineteen people can be dismissed over a three-month period without triggering the consultative procedures laid down in the law on collective dismissal (see below).

Dismissal due to employee conduct

A dismissal linked with the character or conduct of the employee (*redenen in de persoon van de werknemer gelegen*) usually falls into one of four categories:

- Unsuitability for the work (*disfunctioneren*).
- Conduct of the employee (*verwijtbaar gedrag*).
- Breakdown of employment relations (*verstoorde arbeidsverhouding*).
- Long-term illness.

Such cases will be authorised only if a well documented case is presented, backed up with personal files, proof that alternatives such as transfer or retraining have been considered, and evidence of the improbability of any improvement in the employee's performance. Where an employee's conduct is in question the employer will need to submit evidence of prior disciplinary action, including written warnings. The emphasis is usually on serious and persistent misconduct (*ernstig en duurzaam*). Dismissal in connection with the ill health of an employee is strictly regulated, and is permissible only after two years' continuous or repeated and frequent sickness. In either case the detrimental effect on the company of the employee's absence has to be shown.

Dismissal through the courts

Where an application for dismissal is refused, the employer can initiate legal proceedings in order to terminate the contract. Technically an employer can go direct to the courts without having to apply to the RDA for authorisation. However, judges are reluctant to deal with cases that have not previously been heard by the RDA unless there is good reason, such as where the dismissal is urgently necessary for economic reasons but the employer is reluctant to move to summary dismissal.

A written petition (*ontbindingsverzoek*) has to be submitted, with details of the employee and the reasons for termination. By law the court hearing has to begin within four weeks of the petition being submitted, although in practice this is not always the case, and some judges merely set a date for the hearing within the month's limit.

Only compensation payments can be awarded by the courts (see below). A judge may also rule for reinstatement of the employee. In practice, however, under the present legislation, the employer has a right to opt for a form of payment in compensation (*afkoopsom*) instead, the level of which is set by the judge.

Summary dismissal

Dismissal without notice (*ontslag op staande voet*) is permitted for very serious reasons, where it would clearly be unreasonable to expect the employer to allow an employee to continue to work out the period of notice. A list of urgent reasons, by no means comprehensive, is given in article 1639p of the Civil Code, including:

- Deliberate deception of the part of the employee when being hired.
- Persistent refusal to comply with employer's instructions.
- Negligence or incompetence.
- Persistent absence or lateness.
- Theft, deception, drunkenness, violence, threats.

An employee may be suspended prior to dismissal without notice in order to enable the employer to carry out investigations into the alleged misconduct, etc. An employee must be informed immediately of the reasons for the summary dismissal.

Periods of notice

Statutory periods of notice (*opzegtermijn*) are determined by the frequency of pay (weekly, every four weeks or monthly) and the employee's length of service. In general, the minimum period of notice must be at least equal to the interval between wage/salary payments, although this may be altered by collective agreement. There is however a maximum of six months for basic notice. Additional weeks are customarily added on by collective agreement for each year of service (over the age of 18), up to a maximum of thirteen weeks. Employees over 45 years of age are entitled to a further week's notice for each year over 45, again up to a maximum of thirteen. This results in an absolute statutory maximum notice period for an employee aged 58 or older with at least thirteen years' service of twenty-six weeks. Any employee aged between 50 and 65 with one year's service is entitled to at least three weeks' notice.

The minimum period of notice required of an employee is the same as that required of the employer. However, for every two years of service, one additional week is added, up to a maximum of six weeks. So the maximum statutory period of notice required from an employee aged 34 or over with twelve years' service is six weeks. Under certain conditions collective agreements may lengthen the period of notice, provided the employee notice period is no more than six months. Although it is not compulsory, notice should be given in writing. Collective agreements frequently stipulate this in any case. Failure by the employer to give the prescribed notice will mean payment for at least the period of notice that should have been given.

Protected employees

Dismissal is restricted by statute under certain circumstances and for several types of employee. For example, an employee's contract may not be terminated, except for very serious reasons warranting dismissal without notice:

- During pregnancy and maternity leave, or for six weeks following the maternity leave.
- In the absence of the employee owing to sickness, for a period of up to two years.
- During an employee's military service.
- If legal proceedings have been initiated following an employee's claim of discrimination.
- While an employee is a member of the works council or associated committees.

Dismissal of executives

Executives are covered by the same basic periods of notice and dismissal procedures as other employees. However, longer periods of notice and some kind of severance pay stipulations are often written into collective agreements (either where these cover executives or where there is a collective agreement specially for executives, as, for example, at Akzo) or individual contracts. The norm for executive severance pay is approximately one to two years' salary, depending on age and length of service. In most instances executives will not work out their notice. At executive level an employee will frequently be offered out-placement services in the event of dismissal on economic grounds. These can be provided for up to a year or a year and a half, and are usually at the ex-employer's expense.

Unfair dismissal and appeal

The termination of a contract before dismissal authorisation has been granted (as in summary dismissal) can be sanctioned in retrospect by the authorities. In cases where authorisation was not granted but the contract was terminated anyway, or where the employee feels that the dismissal was unfair, the employee or employee representatives may appeal within six months of the dismissal.

Statute law (Civil Code, article 1639s) defines four main categories into which unfair dismissal (*kennelijk onredelijk ontlag*) can fall, although they are not exclusive and the judge has considerable freedom to determine what does or does not qualify as unfair:

- Dismissal was based on false or distorted evidence.
- The effect on the employee is out of all proportion to the employer's reasons

for dismissal. This may apply particularly in the case of older workers whose chances of re-employment are slim.
- Dismissal involved protected employees or circumstances.
- No account was taken of the 'last in, first out' principle in selecting employees for dismissal on economic grounds.

The criteria emphasise the effect of the dismissal on the employee, and in practice mean that employers have to take this aspect into consideration. Often it results in the employer offering compensatory payments in addition to the statutory period of notice (see below).

The burden of proof in cases of unfair dismissal lies with the party lodging the appeal. Where the courts find that the dismissal was indeed unfair, compensation payments (*schadevergoeding*) are imposed by the judge or a reinstatement order is made. However, by law, employers have the right to insist on reinstatement being replaced by a payment (*afkoopsom*). The level of the payment depends on the decision of the judge, who will take into account, as with severance payments, the costs already incurred, the length of statutory notice and the vulnerability of the employee. In practice, very few employees are actually reinstated.

Severance pay

There is no statutory requirement governing severance pay, other than the requirement to a paid notice. Some collective agreements may stipulate that additional payments must be made in certain circumstances. In particular in cases of collective dismissal severance payments may be included in a social plan (see below). Any additional severance pay (*afvloeiingsregeling*) must be awarded through the courts, and is entirely at the judge's discretion. This can occur via an application from an individual employee once a dismissal authorisation has been issued and notice served. The judge will take into account the costs already incurred, the length of the required notice period and the effect of the dismissal on the employee's financial situation and chances of re-employment. There are a number of commonly used formulas which link severance pay with length of service, age, job criteria, etc. A general rule of thumb is one month's pay per year of service for those aged under 39; one and a half months' pay for those between 40 and 50, and two months for those over 50. Nonetheless, case law shows that the amounts awarded can and do vary enormously.

Employers frequently offer a dismissed employee some form of additional payment, particularly where the dismissal was by authorisation procedure, partly in order to avoid the threat of a legal appeal.

Severance payments can take a variety of forms, including:

- As a lump sum.
- As a topping-up of benefit.

- Allowing the employee to keep a company car.
- Paying for out-placement or other services.

Collective dismissal

Collective dismissal is regulated by the 1976 law on collective dismissal (*Wet melding collectieve ontslag*) and by various articles in the Civil Code. Collective dismissal is defined as the dismissal of at least twenty employees over a three-month period in the catchment area of a single regional employment bureau. Some collective agreements may narrow the definition, for example the textile CAO categorises the dismissal of 10 per cent of the work force, or twenty-five employees regardless of company size, as collective dismissal.

According to the 1976 law, employers must notify the RDA and the relevant trade union, in writing, of the intention to impose collective dismissal. One month's waiting period must then elapse before the RDA will begin its authorisation procedures. The works council must be informed of proposed collective dismissals and allowed to give its advice before the dismissals finally go ahead. No specific deadline for this is specified by statute. The RDA will, however, delay authorisation if it feels that there has been insufficient consultation with the works council.

A number of collective agreements stipulate that a social plan must be drawn up between unions and employer in cases of collective dismissal. The plan may specify severance payments due, retraining and out-placement options to be offered. Some industries or companies detail the level of severance pay in the event of collective dismissal directly in the terms of a collective agreement. For example, the printing industry agreement says that benefit will be topped up to 95 per cent of previous earnings, provided it amounts to no more than 20 per cent of net pay. Depending on the age of the employee, this top-up is paid for thirteen to fifty-eight weeks. Employees aged over 57 years are entitled to have their benefits made up to 100 per cent of earnings for eighteen months, and then at gradually reduced amounts until retirement age. Most agreed severance payments are as a one-off payment, and are usually linked to the age of the employee.

Appendix

Social security contributions

Since January 1990 social insurance contributions (covering old age and survivor's pension, medical expenses and basic disability benefit), which used to be paid by the employer, are paid by employees only. Most employed persons' social contributions are paid by employee and employer. Contributions are paid on total earnings up to a daily ceiling, and are deducted at source. They total 16.06 per cent for employees and 11.11 per cent for employers. However, to compensate employees for the increase in contributions, employers have to pay an extra allowance of 11.40 per cent of total gross pay on which contributions are levied (to a maximum of Fl 76,350 (£27,967) p.a.).

Income tax

Income tax is levied on total gross income less a personal allowance, mortgage interest and a variety of fixed expenses deductions. There are three tax brackets, the first being levied inclusive of national insurance contributions. The rates are 38.25 per cent on the first Fl 43,267 (£15,849) of taxable income; 50 per cent on the next Fl 43,267 and 60 per cent on earnings over Fl 86,534 (£31,698).

Organisations

Ministry of Social Affairs and Employment (*Ministerie van Sociale Zaken en Werkgelegenheid*)
Postbus 90808, 2509 LV The Hague
Tel. + 31 70 333 4444

One of the Ministry's major functions is to monitor and register the content of collective agreements. This is done by the Information and Inspection Service, known as Dienst I-SZW, located at the same address as the Ministry.

Economic and Social Council (*Sociaal-Economische Raad*, SER)
Bezuidenhoutseweg 60,
2594 AW The Hague
Tel. + 31 70 349 9499

The SER is a tripartite discussion forum and advisory body, made up of equal numbers of employers' and union representatives and independent experts. The government is under a statutory obligation to seek its advice on all prospective major social and economic legislation. The SER's role is purely advisory and it is not required to give a unanimous opinion. However, its influence on policy is considerable.

Federation of Netherlands Industry (*Verbond van Nederlandse Onderneming*, VNO)
5 Prinses Beatrixlaan, Postbus 93093,
2509 AB The Hague
Tel. + 31 70 349 7373;
fax + 31 70 381 9508

The VNO is the largest employer's organisation. Some 10,000 companies with more than ten employees belong to its 100 or so member federations, as well as a number of individual large companies. In addition to representing its members' interests on a variety of issues, it also carries out social and economic research.

Dutch Association of Personnel Managers (*Nederlands Vereniging van Personeelsbeleid*, NVP)
Catharijnensingel 53, Postbus 19124,
3501 DC Utrecht
Tel. + 31 30 367137;
fax + 31 30 343991

The NVP is the main professional body for personnel practitioners in the Netherlands, and is a member of the EAPM. It offers individual membership and provides training courses.

Netherlands Trade Union Confederation
(*Federatie Nederlandse Vakbeweging*,
FNV)
Naritaweg 10, Postbus 8456,
1005 AL Amsterdam
Tel. + 31 20 581 6300;
fax + 31 20 684 4541

The FNV is the largest trade union
confederation, with a membership of some
1,092,000 – nearly 80 per cent of the
unionised work force. Its member unions
represent blue- and white-collar workers in
industry or sector groupings, as well as
civil servants.

Main references

Zakboek Arbeidsrecht, looseleaf edition published by Kluwer.
Arbeidsovereenkomst en ontslag, in the Memo Plus series, published annually by
    Kluwer.
CAOs in Nederland, Ministry of Labour.
Assorted collective agreements.
Maatwerk, Verbond van Nederlandse Onderneming.

10

Portugal

Basic rights and labour jurisdiction

Although the parties are in principle free to negotiate the terms of an individual employment contract, it must respect the fundamental rights enshrined in the Portuguese constitution, as well as statutory minimum rights embodied in a wide range of labour laws. It has been held that the comprehensive legal framework leaves limited scope for elaboration of terms and conditions by collective negotiation. Employers' organisations have for some time been seeking changes in labour legislation to allow them more flexibility but their proposals have been resisted by unions concerned not to exacerbate rising unemployment at a time of recession.

Sources of employment law

The hierarchy of legal provisions is as follows:

- The constitution of the Portuguese Republic: this guarantees sex equality, the right to work, trade union rights to organise and to bargain, the right to strike, workplace representation, individual employment rights, protection of maternity and parternity, and of young people.
- European Union and international labour law (including ILO conventions).
- Legislation approved by the Assembly of the Republic (unicameral), orders-in-council issued by the government and legislative orders issued by regional assemblies.
- *Assentos* of the Supreme Court of Justice, which have the force of law. These rulings are intended either to clarify a point of law where the court had previously issued two conflicting judgements on the same point or to interpret the terms of a collective agreement. In this latter case, rulings are published in the Employment Gazette (*Boletim do Trabalho*).
- General government regulations.
- Collective agreements, decisions of joint committees responsible for interpreting individual agreements, arbitration rulings.
- Orders which extend the coverage of collective agreements, and orders which regulate conditions in unorganised sectors.
- Custom and practice.
- Internal works rules.

286

System of labour jurisdiction

Labour tribunals, which are magistrates' courts with specialised functions, operate as courts of first instance. They handle civil law relating to the legality of regulatory instruments, working conditions, industrial accidents and occupational diseases, social safeguards, apprenticeships, trade union legislation and strike law. In addition, they deal with criminal law matters which arise from infringements of employment law concerning factory closures, health and safety regulations and strikes.

Appeal is usually to the Court of Appeal (*Tribunal de Relação*), except where the value of the claim exceeds a certain ceiling, in which case the matter is referred direct to the Supreme Court of Justice.

The Constitutional Court, the highest Portuguese court, can be called upon to verify a law's conformity with the constitution before its promulgation, at the instigation of the President or government Ministers. President Soares has on occasion sought the court's advice on labour legislation in this matter. The court also monitors government regulations which do not require parliamentary scrutiny, and can intervene when requested by designated officials. Moreover, lower courts may also seek clarification on whether or not established legal principles conform with the constitution.

Contracts of employment

The statutory framework regulating individual contracts of employment is set out by decree law 49 408 of 24 November 1969 (*Lei do Contrato de Trabalho*). This covers the different types of contract, the rights and obligations of the contracting parties, disciplinary procedures, hours of work, holidays, pay, the employment of women, the employment of minors and the disabled, and penalties for infringing legal provisions. The basic law has been subject to amendment since 1969 and separate pieces of legislation make additional provision in a number of areas.

Types of employee

Under an individual contract of employment (*contrato de trabalho*) an individual is committed to work under the direction of the employer. The work can be permanent, seasonal or casual. A number of rights and obligations attach to each party; broadly, the employer must provide appropriate pay and working conditions – in return the employee must work with loyalty, zeal and diligence.

Under a contract for services (*prestação de serviço*) the individual agrees to furnish specified services in return for a fee, and is paid directly for the results of their labour. This form of contract is becoming more widespread as a transitional phase where an employment contract has been terminated by mutual consent, or through retirement or early retirement.

Individuals may also work under a contract for the rendering of a service (*regime de trabalho em comissâo de serviço*) in certain circumstances. This type of agreement covers some assignments of a temporary nature in a senior management capacity, or in administrative positions where a high degree of trust and confidentiality is necessary (e.g. personal secretary). Such contracts can be terminated by either party at any time without the need to give a reason.

Form of contract

Under decree law 5/94, which incorporates EU Directive 91/533/EEC on proof of the employment relationship, once a contract is signed employers are obliged to inform employees in writing of the terms and conditions of their employment. The only exceptions are where the weekly hours are less than eight, or where the contract lasts for less than one month.

As far as contract itself is concerned, if it is for an indefinite term it can be oral or written, though either party may insist that it must be in writing. On the other hand, fixed-term contracts have to be in writing.

Workplace workers' committees (*comissôes de trabalhadores*) must be informed about the company's employment policies in general and on specific issues, such as the introduction of part-time work or the recruitment of temporary agency staff.

Content of the contract

There are no specific rules on what terms the contract should include, although the written details which must comply with proof of contract law (decree law 5/94) are as follows:

- Identity of the parties.
- Place of work.
- Starting date and expected duration of the contract (i.e. for employment for a fixed-term).
- Notice periods.
- Job category and duties.
- Rate of pay and frequency of payment.
- Hours of work/operating schedules.
- Leave entitlement.
- Reference to collective instruments governing the employment, and internal works rules.

The parties are free in principle to set the terms of a contract, provided that the terms are at least as favourable as legal or applicable agreed provisions. A higher source of law takes precedence over a lower one, except where the latter gives more favourable treatment to the worker in accordance with the *favor laboratoris* principle. Thus neither collective agreements nor individual contracts can make provisions less favourable than the law.

In addition to express contractual terms, an employer must not discriminate between employees in setting terms and conditions, nor discriminate on the grounds of sex, religion, political or trade union affiliation.

The general rights and duties of the contracting parties are outlined in law, including principally the right to payment in return for the employee's labour. An employer must not apply pressure which could deny the exercise of individual employment rights or worsen working conditions. Specifically, employers must not reduce pay or transfer anyone to a lower job category or to another workplace, except within narrow limits defined by law. Any change in the contractual terms must be mutually agreed. Changes involving reduced pay must be submitted to the Ministry of Employment for approval. Most collective agreements reiterate the respective rights and obligations set out in law.

Types of contract

The basic type of contract is either for an indefinite term or for a fixed term or task. Part-time work – which is not defined in law – is much less widespread than in the UK, although employees with children under 12 have a right to work part-time or flexible hours over a period of three years, with full reinstatement to full-time status thereafter. Job-sharing and 'zero hours' contracts are virtually unknown.

Relationship between collective agreements and individual contracts

As noted above, an individual contract of employment may not contain any provision which is less favourable than that embodied in statute law or a collective agreement, which also has the force of law. The contract of employment should make reference to the relevant collective regulatory instruments or agreements.

Probationary periods

By law the probationary period for most employees is sixty calendar days (or ninety in firms with fewer than twenty workers), rising to 180 for tasks which are technically complex or which require a high level of responsibility or trust. In the case of directors and senior management the probationary period lasts 240 days. A collective or individual contract can reduce or lengthen the probationary period. A contract can be terminated within the probationary period without notice and without compensation becoming payable.

Restrictive covenants and confidentiality

Restrictive covenants are rare in Portugal, partly because of the impracticability of enforcing them in a small labour market. By law any limitation on future employment has to be directly related to the harm which would be suffered by the former employer's business. The restraint cannot last more than three years, during which period the individual must be paid. An employee might be obliged to repay training costs as a penalty for breaching a restrictive covenant.

Workplace discipline

The law broadly outlines the employer's disciplinary authority over the employee, which can be exercised by the employer directly or by a designated person within the corporate hierarchy. A collective agreement may supplement these provisions. Within the context of a written disciplinary procedure an employer may impose a range of penalties on an employee who has committed an offence, including verbal and written warnings, fines of up to ten working days' pay a year (rarely imposed), suspension without pay (twelve days for each offence, with a limit of thirty in any one year) and summary dismissal without compensation. However, the sanction must not be disproportionate to the severity of the offence and the degree of blame attributable to the individual. During proceedings the individual may be suspended without loss of pay.

Disciplinary proceedings must commence within a year of the alleged offence having been committed, and must be implemented within sixty calendar days of an offence becoming known to a superior. Failure to let an employee put their case will render the proceedings null and void.

The first step is for the employer to identify the employee, outline the alleged misconduct and indicate whether dismissal is intended. The burden of proof lies with the employer. A copy of the charge is sent to the employee, to the enterprise workers' committee and to the employee's trade union.

Within five working days the employee must answer the charge (a copy of the answer should be sent to the workers' committee). The workers' committee may issue a non-binding opinion on the proceedings. Within thirty days of completing the disciplinary procedure the employer must reach a decision and communicate it in writing, giving reasons, to the employee. (See also 'Dismissal' below.)

The law provides for compensation where the employer has unlawfully imposed a penalty on an employee.

Individual workplace rights

Individual employees are entitled not to have their pay reduced or to be transferred to a lower job category or another place of work, other than in the exceptional circumstances noted above. They can belong – or not belong – to a trade union of their choice, and may be assisted by a union representative in disciplinary proceedings or in pursuing other grievances.

Where a grievance relates to the interpretation of the terms of a collective agreement (for example, on job classification or promotion) the appropriate bipartite 'interpretation committee' may be asked for a view, which if expressed unanimously has the force of law.

Workplace issues

Issues specific to a given workplace would normally be covered in the establishment's internal works rules, and in appropriate cases would be stated in the disciplinary procedure. Workers' committees have a right to be consulted on any changes in such rules.

Employment terms and conditions

Hours of work

The length and organisation of working hours are governed by decree law 409/71, and on overtime by decree law 421/83. These laws were amended by decree law 398/91.

Normal working hours may not exceed eight per day or forty-four per week. For office employment, however, the maximum is a seven-hour day and forty-two hours a week. Under the 1990 tripartite Economic and Social Agreement the social partners made a commitment to negotiate a progressive reduction in working hours by one hour per year down to forty by 1995. In 1994 normal weekly hours by collective agreement ranged from thirty-four to forty in services, and from forty-two to forty-four in industry.

Where working hours are defined by using a weekly average figure, hours may not exceed the eight-hour daily limit (seven hours in offices) by more than two hours, nor exceed fifty hours on a weekly basis. The reference period for calculating the average is three months by law, although an alternative period can be specified by agreement.

Employees performing management and supervisory functions, acting in positions of trust, carrying out preparatory work or working outside the company may, by law, be exempt from the upper limits on normal working hours, although minimum levels of compensation are set for work done outside normal hours in such cases. Minimum rest day provisions (at least one – either Saturday or Sunday) and annual leave, however, apply to these staff.

Flexible hours

Hours of work which depart from normal hours are usually defined by collective agreement, with any changes subject to negotiation. Limits on the maximum working day and week are stated above; the latter can be exceeded if the hours are expressed as an average.

Overtime

This is defined as work done outside the normal work schedule. Some designated employees, usually those in management who are exempt from normal working hours limits, are not covered (see above). Overtime is permitted in order to meet an unexpected increase in demand which does not justify recruiting extra staff, or in the event of *force majeure*. Total overtime must not exceed 200 hours per annum by law (i.e. two hours per day per worker). Employees who work overtime on a normal weekly rest day are entitled to an extra paid day off within the following three days.

Night work

Night work is defined as work done between 20.00 and 07.00. In industry employees who regularly work nights must be medically examined at least once a year. As the law stands, women's night work is subject to special authorisation, with some exceptions. Following a European Court ruling on women's night work in 1991, five member states, including Portugal, were required to bring national law into line with the 1976 Equal Treatment Directive. In spring 1994 the European Commission instituted court proceedings for continued non-compliance.

Public holidays and annual leave

There are twelve national public holidays, which are normally paid. When a holiday falls on a day not normally worked no extra day's leave is granted. The holidays are New Year's Day, Good Friday (although this may be moved to another day over Easter), 25 April (Liberation Day), 1 May, Corpus Christi, 10 June (Portugal Day), 15 August (Assumption), 5 October (Republic Day), 1 November (All Saints' Day), 1 December (Restoration of Independence), 8 December (Immaculate Conception), 25 December.

The granting of one additional local holiday and Mardi Gras is optional. The local holiday for Lisbon falls on 13 June and that for Oporto on 24 June.

Minimum statutory paid annual leave entitlement is twenty-two working days (no longer than thirty consecutive calendar days) per annum. This can be improved upon by agreement. Holiday must normally be taken in the calendar year in which entitlement falls and cannot normally be cashed in. However, under certain circumstances, leave in excess of fifteen days may be cashed in. Days off sick do not count against leave entitlement, provided the employer is informed of the fact.

Maternity and paternity leave

Pregnant employees are entitled to 98 days' leave, sixty of which must be taken after confinement. Expectant mothers may take paid time off to attend antenatal medicals. Nursing mothers have the right to two one-hour breaks off per day until the child is one year old. If a mother dies during maternity leave, any outstanding leave is transferred to the father. Paternity leave is provided for by collective agreement, although other rights to parental leave, and time off to care for sick children, apply to either parent (see below) and are statutory.

Other time off

There are a range of statutory provisions on time off. Broadly, the law protects the employee against loss of pay when the absence is due to reasons beyond their control – sickness, medical treatment, family reasons, jury service or court hearings, specified study periods and examinations. They are also entitled to fulfil duties as an employee or trade union representative up to a specified time limit without loss of pay.

By law an employee has a right to the following time off for family reasons:

- Death of a spouse or close relative: five consecutive days.
- Death of a direct relation or cohabiter: two days.
- Marriage: eleven consecutive days.

Thirty days' carer's leave is available to attend a dependent sick child under 10 (or to cover a period of full hospitalisation) during which time state sickness benefit is payable. Carer's leave of fifteen days is available to attend a sick spouse, parent or child over 10 but without state benefit entitlement.

Members of workers' committees are entitled to between eight and fifty hours off per month, depending on the enterprise level for which the committee is responsible (sub-committee, main enterprise committee or co-ordinating committee in a group of companies).

Trade union representatives are also entitled to time off to attend to union duties, which cannot be less than five hours a month. Collective agreements include supplementary provisions.

Employees continuing their education are entitled to two paid days off to take examinations, the day before and the actual day of the exam. Extra paid time off up to six hours a week may be granted where attending classes clashes with working hours.

The period of military service was cut in 1993 from eighteen to four months. Often fixed-term contracts are used to fill posts temporarily vacated by men who are called up.

Promotion and transfer

As noted above, employees are protected by law against demotion or transfer to another workplace, except within closely defined limits. There is also a large body of case law on this issue. Collective agreements, concluded both at sector and at company level, often play a major role in the areas of recruitment, promotion and transfer.

Agreements may set minimum requirements on age and qualifications for hiring new recruits. In a situation where applicants are otherwise equal, preference may be given to those who have previously worked for the company on a temporary or part-time basis, or even to dependants of present workers who are disabled. Company agreements usually outline detailed procedures for progression within and between grades, including compulsory promotions which depend on time served in grade and those which are subject to merit.

Pay and benefits

Statutory minimum wage

By law (decree law 69-A/87) a gross guaranteed monthly minimum wage (*remuneraçâo mínima mensal garantida*, RMMG) is payable to all employees over 18. Younger workers receive 75 per cent of the adult rate, and apprentices and trainees aged under 25 have a right to at least 80 per cent of the adult rate for a period of up to two years. A reduction of up to half may apply to a worker with a disability which affects the capacity to work.

The law on pay

By law wages must be paid weekly, fortnightly or monthly; an agreement may specify an alternative arrangement. Monthly payment has become the norm, except for some manual workers and in sectors such as construction. Most employees receive fourteen monthly payments a year (two in the form of bonuses). Wages are normally paid by cheque or credit transfer.

By law, employees must be issued with a written itemised pay statement detailing all elements of pay and deductions. Deductions at source include social security contributions, income tax, loan repayments or fines for a disciplinary offence. Union subscriptions may be deducted if a collective agreement so provides.

The state undertakes to pay an employee's wages in the event of an employer's insolvency, bankruptcy or closure, in line with the 1980 European Insolvency Directive. Compensation is limited to pay for up to four of the last six months prior to the insolvency, bankruptcy or closure, with a ceiling of three times the statutory monthly minimum wage.

There is separate legislation guaranteeing wages when payment falls into arrears – a situation which crops up in sectors such as textiles which are undergoing restructuring and contain many small firms. If wages are not paid within thirty days of the due date an employee can cease working without loss of rights and claim unemployment benefit until the situation is rectified. Alternatively, employees may terminate their employment contract and claim compensation according to length of service (one month's pay per year served) plus a minimum three months' pay.

Levels of pay determination

The scope of statutory minimum wage legislation is national. Around 60 per cent of the employed work force is, however, covered by some form of collective agreement at sectoral, regional or company level which sets binding pay minima.

There is no formal hierarchy of collective agreements. For example, companies with their own agreements are not bound by agreements covering their industry, although in practice they usually offer better terms. Company agreements are usually found in public companies or foreign-owned multinationals. Owing to the fact that 90 per cent of Portugal's firms employ fewer than ten people, the terms set by sectoral agreements play an important role.

Collective agreements can be concluded on a number of levels. The following provides an overview of the various types of agreement. (A detailed presentation of bargaining arrangements and the law on collective agreements is to be found in another volume in this series, *Employee Relations and Collective Bargaining*.) A collective agreement (*contrato colectivo de trabalho*, CCT) is concluded between an employers' association/s and a trade union/s and covers most major sectors or industries either on a national or on a regional basis. Around four-fifths of organised employees are encompassed by such agreements, which are important in the Portuguese economy, where there are many small firms without their own agreement. Collective accords (*acordo colectivo de trabalho*, ACT) bind a trade union and several companies operating either in the same area or in the same sector. Only 4 per cent are covered by such deals. Company agreements (*acordo de empresa*, AE) are between a union/s and a single employer and are most prevalent in large publicly owned companies (7 per cent of organised employees). Employers and trade unions may jointly apply to join an existing agreement by means of an adherence agreement (*acordo de adesâo*).

Official intervention can extend agreed terms to employers not covered by the original agreements. Some sectoral agreements have been extended by request of the signatory parties through an extension order (*portaria de extensâo*, PE) to firms in the same sector, not affiliated to signatory organisations, or to workers in similar occupations. Some basic terms may be regulated in non-unionised sectors through a regulation of work order (*portaria de regulamentaçâo de trabalho*, PRT).

Senior management is unlikely to be covered by collective agreement, even where other senior white-collar staff are included, except in public companies.

Main payment systems

The vast majority of employees receive their salary, usually based on time rates, on a monthly basis paid fourteen times a year. Remuneration is largely comprised of fixed elements, since incentive payment systems are as yet little developed. Overtime (including exemption from hours of work allowances) constitutes the most important variable component.

Job grading and evaluation

Pay is determined with reference to an individual's position in an agreed grading structure. Collective agreements usually include broad job descriptions (*definiçâo de categoria*) for each function, which are then structured into a hierarchy according to level and group. At each level equivalent jobs across all functions are grouped and graded, the minimum point in the pay scale being set for each level.

Make-up of the pay packet

Basic pay is determined by statutory minimum wage legislation, binding agreed minima (through sectoral, regional or company agreements) or – for most senior managers – by individual agreement. Public holidays are normally with pay. Monthly pay includes all regularly paid elements of salary. By law it must be paid thirteen times a year (this includes a holiday bonus) and most employees enjoy a fourteenth month, by agreement, payable at Christmas.

Length of service payments (*premio de antiguidade/diuturnidade*) are not governed by law but they do feature in agreements, particularly in the public sector. They may be paid according to seniority with the company, or seniority in a given job, especially where a job holder is not promoted to the next grade.

Other bonuses are related to the nature of the business and the particular job being done, including punctuality, attendance and loyalty bonuses and, for production line workers, those linked with output and productivity.

Employees responsible for handling money are often paid a special responsibility allowance (*abono para falhas*). (Any enhancement exceeding 5 per cent of base pay is subject to tax.)

Pay increases. The vast majority of the approximately 400 collective agreements in force relate to pay. By law, an agreement may not be revoked within ten months of its being registered with the Ministry of Employment. In practice, deals are valid for a year. Thus pay reviews are usually conducted once a year – with possibly an additional review where pay is related to performance targets.

Overtime, night work and shift pay

There are a whole range of premium rates payable for specific working hours arrangements, some regulated by law (and supplemented by agreement), others determined by agreement only.

Premium rates, paid for work performed outside normal working hours, including at night, are regulated by law, with collective agreements often improving on minima. There is a legally prescribed formula for calculating the normal hourly pay as the basis of supplementary rates: $(Rm \times 12)/(52 \times n)$, where Rm is monthly base pay and n is normal weekly hours.

Overtime is defined as work performed outside the normal work schedule; this also applies to part-timers (i.e. outside the hours they normally work). Overtime pay (*remuneraçâo do trabalho suplementar*) is the most important variable element of pay for non-managerial staff. For the first hour of overtime each day a 50 per cent supplement on basic rates is payable, with 75 per cent thereafter, except extra hours worked at weekends and on public holidays, where 100 per cent is due. Some agreements give a 200 per cent supplement for overtime working on public holidays.

Night work, defined as work performed between 20.00 and 07.00, attracts a 25 per cent premium (*subsídio por trabalho nocturno*). Overtime worked at night attracts a 75 per cent premium, rising to 100 per cent thereafter, with 125 per cent at weekends or public holidays. The amount of overtime and night work worked is regulated by law.

By contrast premiums paid for operating different hours of work schedules are governed by agreement. Shift premiums (*subsídio por turnos*) vary according to schedule, with progressively higher rates for two-shift, three-shift and continuous working schedules (12.5 per cent, 18.75 per cent and 20.4 per cent, for example, respectively in the ceramic, cement and glass sectors). Companies may also pay a general supplement for working irregular hours; this amounts to 20 per cent in the insurance industry, for example.

As a separate item the law provides for an 'exemption from working hours' allowance (*subsídio por isençâo de horário de trabalho*) which can be paid to staff in certain positions of responsibility, such as accountants, who are not bound by their employer's normal working hours. Although agreements normally cover such situations, the law stipulates that the allowance must equal at least one hour's overtime daily. A 25 per cent enhancement is quite common. In practice the allowance is paid to a wider group of staff who may even receive overtime payments in addition.

Thirteenth- and fourteenth-month payments

By law employers must pay a holiday bonus (*subsídio de ferias*) equivalent to statutory leave entitlement, that is one additional month's salary. It is payable in June or July. Under agreement, or by custom and practice, most employees are entitled to a fourteenth-month's payment at Christmas (*subsídio de Natal*).

Merit pay

Merit pay plays an important role among senior staff – whose increases do not usually derive from collective agreements. A major part of any increase would be attributable to performance.

Financial participation

Most companies in Portugal are small. Many are family-owned, and therefore resistant to the idea of shared ownership or financial participation. In larger publicly owned enterprises, some of which are preparing for privatisation, existing schemes are as yet unco-ordinated. These structural factors may explain why the social partners have shown little interest.

By contrast, the subsidiaries of international companies often include their most senior managers in share option schemes, typically using parent company stock, but share schemes are seldom extended below managing director level.

Profit-sharing

Profit-sharing is more prevalent in publicly owned firms but on an *ad hoc* basis. However, as a system it is tax efficient as companies can write payouts from schemes off as business expenses, and employees are not liable for income tax.

Sick pay

Employees have a right to statutory sick pay after three waiting days, provided they have six months' social security contributions to their credit. This amounts to 65 per cent of average earnings over the six months prior to the two months before illness, payable for a period of one year and at 70 per cent for up to 1,095 days. Under some collective agreements employers may have to make payment for the three waiting days and top up statutory payments to full pay. However, employers often use the first three days as a mechanism to discourage absenteeism.

Maternity pay

Statutory maternity pay, made over by social security is paid for the 98 days of maternity leave. It is based on average earnings over the six months preceding the two months before maternity leave commences.

Cars, insurance, health care

The award of a company car for business and personal use is a highly tax-efficient benefit for executives and can be worth around a quarter of base pay.

Vehicles are most likely to be supplied – including insurance, maintenance and fuel – to senior and middle management and to others on a needs-only basis.

Medical insurance providing benefits for employees and their family outside the state health system is a common perk for executives. Schemes may cover all employees in larger companies. Personal accident insurance and life insurance are also a very common benefit at managerial level.

Retirement

Pension age

Whilst there is no mandatory retirement age, as from 1 January 1994 the age at which women can claim a state pension is to be progressively raised from 62 to 65 (the age for men). The reform will be phased over six years, retirement age being raised by six months each year. Most companies already have a common retirement age.

The harmonisation of pension ages is part of a total reform of the state pension system, approved in 1993. This was prompted by increased demands on the social security system, following industrial restructuring and recession, which had plunged the fund into the red.

As from 1 January 1994 state pensions are calculated on the basis of the best ten years' earnings over the previous fifteen contribution years – the minimum contribution period. Monthly reference earnings are multiplied by 2 per cent for each contribution year – any year when earnings were received for 120 days at least. Under the reforms an employee will qualify for a maximum pension after forty years' contributions, compared with thirty-six before. There is a guarantee of a minimum 30 per cent and a maximum of 80 per cent of reference earnings; additions to pensions arise where there is a dependent spouse. Like wages, pensions are paid fourteen times a year.

Contributions into the state scheme, which also pays out benefits other than pensions, are 24.5 per cent for employers and 11 per cent for employees. The employers' contribution is expected to fall to 23.75 per cent in 1995.

Supplementary pensions

Company pensions are regulated by 1986 legislation, which provides a framework for the financing of schemes which supplement the state scheme.

In the past, state pensions were regarded as fairly generous. However, the reform of the state system is likely to boost the spread of private schemes, many of which offer a pension based on final earnings, instead of the average reference earnings used in the state scheme. Most schemes are non-contributory and are able to offer incentives to voluntary retirement, given that retirement cannot be enforced at state pension age.

Right to continue at work

Retirement is voluntary. If an employee is at work thirty days after the date which both parties have accepted as the individual's retirement date, then the employment contract becomes a fixed-term one for six months, renewable, and terminable at sixty days' notice by the employer or at fifteen days' by the employee. If the employee is still in service at the age of 70 the employment contract automatically becomes a fixed-term one. The dismissal of an employee who has been forced to retire will constitute unfair dismissal.

Early retirement and pre-retirement

Employees may retire early at the age of 60 under the state scheme. In 1991 legislation introduced the option of pre-retirement from the age of 55, under which employees have the choice of either suspending their employment contract or working reduced hours in return for a monthly payment from the company until retirement age. At a time of recession and restructuring this option offers an alternative to dismissal on the grounds of unsuitability (that is, where an older worker finds it difficult to adapt to new working conditions following restructuring).

Pre-retirement arrangements must be the subject of a written agreement approved by the local social security office. The agreement should state when the scheme started, the amount of payment and the number of hours to be worked should the employee continue working reduced hours. The amount of payment cannot be less than 25 per cent of previous pay, adjusted either by the rate of pay increases the employee would have received had they remained in post on normal terms or, if that is impracticable, by the amount of inflation.

The reduced hours option is more advantageous to employees because it retains the individual's entitlement to *pro rata* sickness and unemployment benefit. But in either case, under certain conditions, the employee may take up other paid work. During pre-retirement both parties continue to pay social security contributions (3 per cent for the employee and 7 per cent for the employer) where the employee has thirty-seven years' contributions or 7 per cent and 14.6 per cent respectively for fewer contribution years. No contributions are payable where forty years' contributions have already been made.

Equal pay and equal opportunities

Legal framework

Equality of opportunity is enshrined in the Portuguese constitution. Article 13 forbids discrimination on the grounds of sex, race, language, country of origin, political or religious belief, education, economic or social position.

Equality of opportunity and treatment between men and women in employment is covered by 1979 legislation (decree 392/79) for the private sector and by decree 426 in public administration. Employers are forbidden to obstruct access to employment by discrimination based on sex, whether directly or indirectly, or by reference to marital status and family circumstances. Any laws, agreements or regulations which contravene this principle are null and void.

During the recruitment process the law prohibits gender-biased job advertisements, or mention of physical requirements unrelated to the vacancy, with certain exceptions, such as fashion and the performing arts. It also forbids women to do work which could pose an actual or potential risk to procreation, a restriction under review in the light of scientific progress.

The law requires equal pay for work of equal value in the workplace. Job evaluation systems must be based on objective criteria. An employee alleging discrimination must indicate a comparator of the opposite sex; the employer then has to establish that any differences in pay are based on factors other than sex.

Employers must ensure equality of access to training and promotion. In the latter case a complainant is protected from dismissal for a period of a year after raising a grievance.

The 1979 legislation also established a Commission on Equality in Work and Employment charged with promoting equality. It is empowered to:

- Recommend measures to the Ministry of Employment (of which the commission is part) for making the equality decrees more effective.
- Promote public awareness, not least by publicising cases involving manifest discrimination.
- Issue opinions on complaints of discrimination at the request of the labour inspectorate, the courts, employers or trade unions.

The issue of sex equality has not commanded a high priority in Portugal, and company Equal Opportunity policies are rare. Despite formal legal guarantees, women suffer a higher unemployment rate, they are more likely than men to be employed on a temporary contract and a large differential persists between male and female earnings. The network of child care facilities is poorly developed and flexible working hours are not widespread, although in principle working parents of young children have the right to work part-time or flexible hours. Only 4 per cent of the work force are employed part-time.

Sexual harassment

Complaints of sexual harassment – which is not precisely defined in law – can be brought under the Civil and Penal Codes and under the respective decrees concerning individual contracts of employment and equality of opportunity.

If an employee can establish that sexual harassment has occurred in the context of discrimination on grounds of sex, then the matter can be dealt with under decree 392; employers may be held liable for discriminatory acts by a member of their staff. Equally, any worker whose conduct corrupts or endangers the morals of fellow employees, or who is guilty of physical and verbal assault, is subject to disciplinary action by the employer under a company's code. Sanctions could range from a warning, through a written warning, fine, suspension from work with loss of pay to summary dismissal without compensation. Employees are entitled to compensation if the harassment led to their dismissal, to a disciplinary measure or to any other steps being taken against them.

There are no special procedures for dealing with sexual harassment, although if there are doubts about whether the behaviour complained of constitutes harassment the employer can refer to the Commission for Equality in Work and Employment before taking disciplinary action.

Individual termination of contract

The constitution guarantees the right to work and the right to security of employment. Until 1989, when the possibility of dismissal on economic grounds was introduced through decree law 64A/89, the grounds for lawful dismissal were limited to those connected with disciplinary offences. A further law of 1991 permitted dismissal on grounds of unsuitability for a job, under certain restricted circumstances. Nevertheless, the dismissal laws remain restrictive and, by law, other avenues short of dismissal must be explored first.

Termination by mutual consent and resignation

Either party can terminate a contract during the probationary period without notice being due or compensation payable. Employees resigning their post without 'just cause' (that is, on the basis of a breach by the employer) must give thirty days' notice if their length of service is less than two years, or sixty days' if it is longer.

Termination of the contract by mutual consent must be recorded in writing, giving the date and reasons for termination.

Expiry

A contract can come to an end on the expiry of its term, for example at the end of a fixed-term contract (with eight days' notice from the employer if it is not to be renewed) or in the case of *force majeure* (accident, death, company closure). The fact that an employee has reached the state retirement age does not allow the employer to terminate a contract; in the private sector, the employee can opt to stay on until the age of 70, after which the contract is converted into a renewable fixed-term one. However, there is an increasing tendency to offer incentives to encourage older employees to retire, either through pension schemes or through early retirement arrangements.

Constructive dismissal

As part and parcel of the rights and obligations attached to the employment relationship an employer may not prevent employees from exercising their individual rights, and may not exert pressure which impinges negatively on working conditions, or reduce their pay, or transfer them to a lower job category, except within narrow limits defined in law.

Consequently, an employee may terminate the contract, with just cause, on the grounds that its terms have been seriously breached. The reasons could include non-payment of wages (see also under 'The law on pay' above) substantially changed working conditions, infringement of individual rights and inadequate health and safety protection. In such instances the aggrieved employee has a right to claim compensation equivalent to one month's pay for each year of service. If a tribunal finds in favour of the employer the employee must reimburse the company to an amount equal to that for the period of notice which would have applied had the contract been terminated voluntarily by the employee, that is, thirty or sixty days.

Disciplinary dismissal (see also 'Workplace discipline' above)

By law, any disciplinary procedures must be initiated within one year of the alleged offence having been committed. Furthermore, once an offence has been brought to the attention of a superior, proceedings must be implemented within sixty calendar days. Although the employee may be suspended from work without loss of pay during the course of proceedings, the employer may not impose any sanction until the employee has had the chance to give evidence; denial of a fair hearing could nullify the whole proceedings.

At the first stage of the disciplinary procedure employers must identify the accused employee, outline the alleged misconduct and indicate whether they intend to dismiss. A copy of the allegations must be sent to the employee and, where appropriate, to the workers' committee as well as the individual's trade union representative. At the second stage the employee must respond to the charges within five (working) days and inform the workers' committee, which has a right to give a non-binding opinion on the proceedings. The burden of proof is upon the employer, who has a further thirty days to hear witnesses, complete procedures and reach a decision. This must be communicated to the employee in writing, stating the reasons, and copied to the workers' committee, and/or trade union as appropriate.

Disciplinary dismissal with 'just cause'   Dismissal with 'just cause' arises in situations where the employee's action is such as to render the continuation of the employment relationship impossible. Such behaviour would include unwarranted refusal to carry out reasonable instructions, failure to observe health and safety regulations, violence at work, an abnormal fall in productivity and making false statements to justify work errors. Such dismissals are still subject to formal disciplinary procedures, although employees may be suspended while the case is being dealt with.

Dismissal on grounds of unsuitability   As from 1991 employers may dismiss on the grounds of the employee's unsuitability for the job. This might include repeated reductions in productivity, damage to equipment, presenting a health or safety risk to other workers or third parties, or failure to achieve individual work targets which involve managerial or technically complex tasks.

In order lawfully to dismiss an employee who has failed to adapt to a job, the employer has to establish that no changes involving new technology have been made to the job within the previous three months, that adequate training has been given and that a period of adaptation has elapsed since the training, or that the employee has refused an alternative job offer compatible with their qualifications. The employer must also ensure that the unsuitability cannot be attributed to poor health and safety standards in the workplace. Workers dismissed in these situations have to be paid compensation of one month's pay for each year of service.

Employers may not use this reason for dismissal simply to shed labour. If an employee is dismissed on these grounds, a replacement must be hired or an employee on a fixed-term contract offered a permanent one. In practice, problems have been encountered in training older workers in new technology – given Portugal's lower education base – and therefore older individuals dismissed for this reason may also be offered early retirement.

Individual dismissal on economic grounds

Under legislation introduced in 1989 individuals may be dismissed because their posts have ceased to exist owing to economic, market, technical or structural reasons. Where jobs cease to exist, preference for continued employment must be given to workers with the longest service, and in the highest grades.

Employers must establish that dismissal on economic grounds is not in any way attributable to factors personal to the employer or employee, and that the situation is not covered by the provisions of a collective agreement. They must also establish that no other appropriate job exists, subject to training, and that the job vacated is not being done by a worker on a fixed-term contract.

Individuals and the workers' committee must be informed of any intention to dismiss on economic grounds. The employee(s) affected and/or the workers' committee have fifteen days in which to pronounce an opinion on the reasons stated for the decision, or they may request the labour inspectorate to review the grounds. After a further five days the employer may notify individuals that their contracts are being terminated, stating the grounds, the date of dismissal (with at least sixty days' notice), the amount of compensation due and the evidence that preference in continuing employment has been given to long-serving employees.

Compensation payable is the same as for 'lawful dismissal', that is, one month's pay per year of service.

Unlawful dismissal

If a dismissal is found unlawful the employer must pay compensation for remuneration between the date on which the dismissal took place and the date of a court decision. If the court orders reinstatement, and the employee accepts it, then the employer must reinstate on the previous terms and conditions and pay wages from the date of dismissal to the date of the court judgement. An employee who does not wish to accept reinstatement is entitled to compensation of one month's basic pay for each year (or part of a year) of employment, with a minimum of three months' pay.

Collective dismissal on economic grounds

The procedure to be followed in the case of collective dismissal on economic grounds is similar although not identical to that applied in the cases of individual dismissal. Under Portuguese law a collective dismissal is defined as one affecting at least two employees in establishments with up to fifty staff, or five employees in firms with more than fifty staff, over a three-month period.

Statutory consultation requirements

The employer must notify the workers' committee or, in the absence of one, the trade union committee or the workers themselves – who may form their own committee for representation purposes – of the intention of effecting economic dismissals. The reasons must be given, as must details of the groups of staff and departments affected, the criteria for selection (laid down by law), the actual number of workers concerned and their skill category. The Ministry of Employment must be informed and is responsible for making sure the correct procedure is followed: where necessary, it may seek to conciliate the parties. Within a fortnight the management and the workers' committee must negotiate over measures to reduce the impact of the dismissals, specifically examining the scope for short-time working, reductions in working hours, temporary lay-offs, skills conversions and pre- or early retirement.

Compensation terms

Within thirty days of the original dismissal notification, the employer must inform individuals of their dismissal, giving reasons and the date on which it will take effect; this cannot be less than sixty days from the date of notification. During this period individuals may resign at three days' notice without prejudice to their severance payments. Severance compensation is equal to one month's pay for each year of service, with a minimum of three months' pay.

Transfer of undertakings

Transfer of undertakings is covered by article 37 of the law on contracts of employment. Contracts of employment are automatically transferred to the new owner, who is responsible for any obligations entered into by the former owner during the six months preceding the transfer.

Appendix

Social security contributions and income tax

Total statutory employer social insurance contributions are 24.5 per cent for the employer and 11 per cent for the employee paid a monthly salary (i.e. fourteen times a year).

Income tax is payable on taxable income, which is equivalent to gross income less statutory social insurance contributions, additional health and life insurance contributions, educational expenses and personal and child allowances. There are four rates: 15, 25, 35 and 40 per cent.

Organisations

Ministry of Employment and Social Security (*Ministério do Emprego e da Segurança Social*)
Praça de Londres 2, 1000 Lisbon
Tel. + 351 1 80 44 60

Institute of Employment and Vocational Training (*Instituto do Emprego e Formação Profissional,* IEFP)
11 Avenida José Malhoa 11, 1100 Lisbon
Tel. + 351 1 726 25 36

Office of Technological, Artistic and Vocational Education (*Gabinete de Educação Tecnológica Artistica e Profissional,* GETAP)
Avenida 24 Julho 140, 1300 Lisbon
Tel. + 351 1 395 34 07
A section of the Ministry of Education.

Directorate General of Occupational Safety and Health (Direcção Geral de Higiene e Segurança do Trabalho)
Avenida da República 84, 5°, 1600 Lisbon
Tel. + 351 1 77 28 22

Association of Portuguese Human Resource Managers (*Associação Portuguesa de Gestores e Técnicos de Recursos Humanos*, APG)
Avenida do Brasil 194, 7°, 1700 Lisbon
Tel. + 351 1 89 97 66;
fax + 351 1 80 93 40

In Oporto: Rua Formosa 49, 1°
tel. + 351 2 32 32 34;
fax + 351 2 200 07 64

The APG is the professional organisation of personnel practitioners with some 2,000 individual members; companies may also affiliate. APG is a member of the European Association of Personnel Management and of the World Federation of Personnel Management Associations.

Confederation of Portuguese Industry (*Confederaçâo da Indústria Portuguesa,* CIP)
Avenida 5 de Outubro, 35, 1º
1000 Lisbon
Tel. + 351 1 54 74 54

The central employers' organisation for industry.

Confederation of Portuguese Commerce (*Confederaçâo do Comércio Português,* CCP)
Rua Saraiva de Carvalho, 1000 Lisbon
Tel. + 351 1 66 85 39

The central employers' organisation in trade and commerce.

Confederaçâo Geral dos Trabalhadores Portugueses–Intersindical Nacional (CGTP-IN)
Rua Vitòr Cordon 1, 3º, 1200 Lisbon
Tel. + 351 1 34 72 181/8

Uniâo Geral de Trabalhadores (UGT)
Rua Buenos Aires 11, 1200 Lisbon
Tel. + 351 1 67 65 03/5

Portuguese–British Chamber of Commerce (*Câmara do Comércio Luso-Britânica*)
Rua da Estrela 8, 1200 Lisbon
Tel. + 351 1 396 14 86;
fax + 351 1 60 15 13

APETT (Association of Temporary Employment Agencies)
c/o Marcelina Pena Costa, Rua Quirino da Fonseca 15, 1000 Lisbon
Tel. + 351 1 57 04 15

APPC (*Associaçâo Portuguesa de Projectistas e Consultores*, management consultants' organisation)
Avenida Antonio Augusto Aguiar 126, 7º, 1000 Lisbon
Tel. + 351 1 52 04 76

Main sources

A. Neto, *Contrato de Trabalho: Notas Práticas*, 12ª Edição, 1993.

Associaçâo Portuguesa de Gestores e Técnicos de Recursos Humanos, APG, *Pessoal* (bimonthly journal), Lisbon.

Instituto do Emprego e Formaçâo Profissional, IEFP, *Emprego e Formaçâo* (quarterly journal), Lisbon.

Ministério do Emprego e da Segurança Social, MESS, *Quadros de Pessoal*, Lisbon.

11

Spain

Basic rights and labour jurisdiction

Legal framework

Legislation governing employment contracts stems from the provisions of the 1978 constitution, the 1980 Workers' Statute, the 1980 Basic Employment Law and the 1994 reform of the Workers' Statute. Under legislation governing the regional governments of Spain (the *autonomías*), the Ministry of Labour and Social Security is gradually transferring powers relating to several employment precedures to the regional governments. By 1994 Andalusia, the Canary Islands, Catalonia, Galicia, Navarre, the Basque country and Valencia had assumed these powers, leaving the other ten regions directly dependent on the Ministry of Labour.

The important and controversial reforms of the Workers' Statute in May 1994 imply a major overhaul of the whole structure of labour relations, forms of contract, and individual and collective bargaining by introducing deregulation of a formerly highly centralised and regulated system. Prior to the reforms, one central underlying feature of the Spanish system of employment relations was that the structuring of many company work forces continued to reflect the employment philosophy of the corporatist and paternalistic state under Franco, with functions, procedures, staffing, pay, promotion and many other features still shaped by the labour ordinances (*ordenanzas*) through which employment conditions were regulated under the dictatorship. Although collective bargaining has been free to evolve since 1977, only a very few ordinances were formally abrogated and many of the assumptions and concepts they contained were incorporated into collective agreements. One important element of the 1994 reform of the Workers' Statute was the Spanish government's decree that ordinances should be replaced by collectively agreed provisions by the end of 1995. The implications for both individual and collective contractual arrangements may be considerable, although at the time of writing it is still too early to venture a detailed forecast.

Labour jurisdiction

Employment cases are brought in the first instance before a Social Court (*Juzgado de lo Social*) generally located in provincial capitals. Cases which are deemed to entail issues whose significance transcends the local level or appeals are heard by the Social Chambers (*Sala de lo Social*) of the Higher Court of Justice (*Tribunal Superior de Justicia*) which serve each Autonomous Community and are located in their respective capitals. Cases of national significance and appeals are heard in the Social Chamber of the national High Court in Madrid. Appeal can be had from here to the Supreme Court (Tribunal Supremo). Constitutional matters are ruled on by the Constitutional Court (Tribunal Constitucional).

In cases of contested dismissal the employee has a statutory right to have initial recourse to the national conciliation, mediation and arbitration service, the Servicio de Mediacion, Arbitraje y Conciliacion (SMAC). This is located either in the employment departments of those Autonomous Communities which have had powers transferred to them, or in the provincial offices of the Ministry of Labour and Social Security (see below, 'Dismissal').

Contracts of employment

Types of employee

Employment regulations do not distinguish between blue-collar and white-collar employees, but employees are divided into categories for the purpose of levying social security contributions (see the appendix). Special provisions regulate the employment conditions of a range of different occupations, including sportsmen, the disabled, domestic servants, artists, commercial agents, merchant seamen and dockworkers. Executives' employment conditions and dismissal procedures are also covered by separate legislation (laws 8/80 and 2/91) which requires that they must be set out in writing where employees are promoted to executive positions. Unless it is specifically agreed otherwise, normal employment legislation does not apply to executives.

Employee grading

The employer is required to assign an employee to a job grade (*categoría profesional*) and agree a job description. Formerly this was either as defined in the appropriate collective agreement or in a category set out in legislation or a labour ordinance. The employee's grade defines contractual duties as well as pay, and possibly hours of work, holiday entitlement and other terms and conditions. Under the 1994 reforms, collective bargaining has been entrusted with responsibility for agreeing job descriptions and the grading system on the basis of the employee's qualifications, professional role and job content.

Form of contract

Contracts may be verbal or written, and freely agreed between an employer and a person aged at least 18 (or a 16–18 year old who lives independently or has parental permission). Contracts for a fixed term of more than four weeks, or for a specific job, must be in writing. In the case of a contract lasting for more than four weeks the employer must write to the employee to identify any aspects of the employment not expressly detailed in the contract. In any event, either party may require the contract to be in writing. Contracts are no longer presumed to be permanent unless otherwise stated (as was the case until 1994); collective bargaining may determine which contracts are to be fixed-term. Failure to issue a written contract where statute law requires one (for part-time employment, Spanish personnel working abroad for their company, dockworkers, sportsmen, artists, commercial travellers, the disabled, and a variety of atypical contracts) is regarded as a serious offence, punishable by a fine of Pta 50,000 to Pta 500,000 (£250–£2,500).

Since 1991 the government has required employers to issue a copy of all employment contracts issued, except those for executives, to employee representatives within ten days, a step designed to combat social security fraud. (Details of the mechanisms of employee representation are to be found in the volume in this series on employee relations and collective bargaining.)

Statute law requires written contracts to indicate the type of employment, hours of work and rest, pay, social security arrangements and information on training provision.

Types of contract

In addition to normal open-ended contracts of employment there are a plethora of atypical contracts governed by statute law and introduced mostly since the 1980s to create employment and training opportunities for selected groups of employees. In addition, there are incentives to conclude open-ended contracts with people aged over 45 who have been unemployed for at least a year.

The labour market is characterised by a high proportion of employment on fixed-term contracts, following a number of legislative changes since the mid-1980s intended to create new employment opportunities. Around one-third of all contracts of employment are currently fixed-term, and in 1993 as many as 48 per cent of all new hirings were accounted for by fixed-term contracts.

Part-time contracts   Part-time contracts have been widely permitted only from 1984 onwards, but they have become a major source of new employment opportunities. They must be written, in the approved format, and must indicate whether the contract is temporary or permanent, and the number of hours per day, week, month or year involved. Employees working for less than twelve hours weekly, or forty-eight hours monthly, are not entitled to unemployment benefit. Under special provisions, employees aged at least 62 may move to half-time working until retirement and be replaced by an unemployed part-time worker.

Temporary job creation contracts These may be concluded by small firms for employing certain groups of the registered unemployed. They may be from twelve months up to three years, and on termination the employee is entitled to compensation of twelve days' pay per year's service. Currently these contracts are permitted for over 45 year olds and the disabled (or the under-45s in firms of fewer than twenty-five employees). They entitle the employer to a reduction in social security contributions of 75 per cent (or 50 per cent for the under-45s, where relevant). The benefit rises to 100 per cent and 75 per cent respectively if a self-employed person recruits another employee in these conditions.

Apprenticeship contracts Since 1994 these have become available for those aged 16–25 and lacking formal qualifications. There is a limit to the number allowed in an undertaking, ranging from one employee in a work force of five to 4 per cent of the work force in a company with more than 500 staff. Contracts may last from six months to three years and must allocate at least 15 per cent of working hours to training. Pay must be at least 70 per cent of the legal minimum wage in the first year, rising to 80 per cent and 90 per cent in the second and third years. The employer pays reduced social security contributions, and the employee is not entitled to unemployment benefit on termination. An employee may be recruited on an apprenticeship contract only once.

Work experience contracts Work experience contracts may be concluded with qualified graduates or diploma holders within four years after they have qualified. The contract may last from six months to two years. Pay must be at least 60 per cent of an appropriate regular employee's wage in the first year, rising to 75 per cent in the second year.

Contracts for a specific job or service, and casual contracts Task-related contracts may be concluded for a specific job or service of limited or uncertain duration, as in the construction industry. Should the job last for more than a year the employer must give fifteen days' notice of termination. Casual contracts to meet seasonal or market fluctuations in demand or a backlog of orders may be concluded for a period of up to six months in any twelve-month period. Temporary replacement contracts allow the replacement of employees on temporary leave of absence.

Contract for starting up a new activity Newly established companies or existing firms that want to initiate a new area of production, open a new workplace or launch a new product may conclude fixed-term contracts of between six months and three years. Short-duration contracts may be agreed and renewed, provided the overall period does not exceed three years.

Probationary periods

Collective agreements may establish probationary periods. In the absence of any agreed period, the maximum probationary periods are six months for qualified technical staff and two months for other staff. They may be extended to three months for other staff in companies with fewer than twenty-five employees. Probationary employees enjoy the same employment rights as other employees.

Restrictive covenants and confidentiality

Statute law forbids simultaneous employment with more than one employer if the work in question constitutes unfair competition, or should one employer specifically wish to forbid it in the employment contract. The employer may extend the prohibition for a period of up to two years after termination of the contract for technical staff and up to six months for unskilled staff, provided that there is genuine competition from another employer, and provided that the employee is adequately compensated. Where the employee is remunerated specifically for abiding by such an agreement, he may withdraw from it upon thirty days' notice, in writing, to the employer. There is no statutory definition of what is a competing activity, but the courts have ruled that unfair competition includes competing in the same commercial sector, producing concurrent competing products, and poaching customers and fellow employees. Any restriction also applies during vacation periods, sick leave or the suspension of the contract for disciplinary reasons.

When an employee receives special technical training at the employer's expense there may be a written agreement between them that the employee will remain in employment with the employer for a certain period of time – which may not exceed two years. If the employee breaks this agreement by leaving within the agreed term, the employer is entitled to seek compensation and damages.

Infringing confidentiality is customarily viewed as a very serious breach of contract and some collective agreements define it as 'an activity contrary to the interests of the company'. Sanctions render the employee liable to suspension and fines of between twenty and ninety days' pay, and some agreements make it a dismissable offence. Confidential information, e.g. about company inventions or manufacturing systems, economic and social reports on the company's progress, markets, client lists, and raw material use, must not be divulged. The obligation lasts for the lifetime of the contract and beyond. Infringement renders the employee liable to dismissal, payment of damages and fines of up to Pta 1 million (£5,000).

Employee inventions and copyright

Legislation dating from 1944 rules that inventions by the employee working under the terms of an employment contract belong to the employer. Employees are not entitled to any extra payment for them, except when their own contribution to the discovery is so exceptional, or the discovery is so important, that such factors exceed the normal suppositions of the employment contract. Inventions by the employee in other circumstances remain the employee's own property, except where the invention is due primarily to knowledge acquired through working for the employer, in which case the employer has rights of ownership in the invention, or preferential use. In such cases, when the employer claims ownership of the invention, the employee is entitled to compensation appropriate to the commercial value of the invention. Any employee claim to benefit from an invention must be registered within three months. The employee is obliged to inform the employer in writing, within three months, of inventions he has discovered while working under contract. Inventions submitted for patent within one year of termination of a contract of employment may also be claimed by the employer.

Collective agreements and contracts of employment

Contracts of employment must by law respect any collectively agreed terms and conditions that apply. Collective agreements at undertaking level must in turn conform with the minimum conditions agreed at a higher level, such as provincial or national industry level. Under the 1994 reform of the Workers' Statute collective bargaining may designate which company functions are appropriate to fixed-term contracts. National industry-level bargaining is charged with identifying which seasonal activities may justify fixed-term contracts lasting longer than the six months' maximum normally permitted.

In contrast to the situation which prevailed before 1994, the terms of collective agreements no longer continue to be binding once the contract has expired. Companies in financial difficulties may negotiate exemption from pay clauses in sectoral or provincial agreements. Collective agreements may now include procedures for resolving disputes. They may also be endorsed by a simple majority of each of the negotiating parties, rather than by the 60 per cent approval previously needed on both sides. (Details of bargaining arrangements and procedures are dealt with in another volume in this series, on employee relations and collective bargaining.)

Workplace discipline

Article 5 of the Workers' Statute requires the employee to carry out the employer's instructions and to 'contribute to improvements in productivity'. There are statutory procedures for disciplinary action against individual employees, under which the employer may impose sanctions on employees for breaches of discipline. Statute law outlines those breaches of conduct which may warrant dismissal; they include:

- Repeated unjustified absence or unpunctuality.
- Indiscipline or disobedience.

- Verbal or physical abuse of employers, colleagues or their families.
- Breach of faith or confidence.
- Poor working habits.
- Repeated drug or alcohol abuse.

(See also 'Dismissal', below.)

Collective agreements (or surviving 'labour ordinances') also detail infringements of workplace discipline and permissible sanctions. In the chemical industry, for example, the national collective agreement establishes three levels of indiscipline (light, serious and gross). A light breach, for example, would be failure to register when absent through sickness, a serious breach would be two days' unjustified absence each month, and a gross breach would include verbal abuse of management. Sanctions in the three categories range from two days' unpaid suspension, three to fifteen days' unpaid suspension, and sixteen days' unpaid suspension up to dismissal in the most serious cases.

Individual workplace rights

There is no specific legislation protecting the privacy of employees, and a data protection law is still awaited. However, legislation introduced in 1982 on rights to respect, privacy and dignity (*Ley Orgánica sobre el derecho al honor, a la intimidad y a la propia imagen*) does contain general safeguards against undue interference or investigation by the employer. The Workers' Statute (article 4) states that employees are entitled to 'actual occupation, promotion and training . . . respect for personal privacy and dignity, including protection from verbal, physical and sexual abuse and the right to receive punctual salary payments'. There are fines for infringement ranging from Pta 30,000 to Pta 300,000 (£150–£1,500). Statute law requires the employer to treat the employee 'in a dignified fashion'.

Variation of terms

An employer who wishes to modify an employee's working conditions as regards pay, hours of work, shift work or grade of work, must give thirty days' notice of the intention. If the employee would be seriously affected by a proposed change in hours of work, the timetable or shift-work arrangements, they have the right to ask for the contract to be terminated, with twenty days' compensation per year of service, up to a maximum of nine months' pay. Where the employer wishes to transfer the employee to work of a grade other than that originally contracted for, employees must accept the move if their qualifications are appropriate to the new job. If, however, the employer wishes to effect a transfer to lower-grade work the decision must be agreed with employee representatives, and the employee must suffer no loss of pay or entitlement to training and promotion, and must be retained on the lower-grade work for only the minimum time necessary. If any proposed changes affect more than 10 per cent of the work force, the employer must negotiate with employee representatives during a two-week period of consultation.

Any proposal to relocate the employee on reasonable commercial grounds requires a two-week consultation period with employee representatives and notification of the labour authorities. The employee may opt for termination of contract, with twenty days' pay per year of service in compensation, up to a maximum twelve months' pay, or may appeal to the labour courts for retention of the original post. The courts may order a freeze on the transfer order of up to one year. Such procedures apply to all proposed transfers which entail a total of twelve months' relocation in a three-year period. Elected employee representatives take priority in retaining their posts in cases of proposed transfer.

Employment terms and conditions

Hours of work

By statute, the maximum working week is forty hours, which may be averaged over the working year. In 1993 the national average agreed working year was 1,765 hours, with the average figure in company agreements somewhat lower, at 1,727 hours. The maximum working day is normally nine hours, unless collective agreements provide otherwise. Under-18s may not do more than eight hours' effective daily work, including training. There must be a minimum fifteen minutes' break in a six-hour shift, with thirty minutes for under-18s.

One feature which still distinguishes hours of work in Spain is the persistence of the siesta. Many companies, especially in the commercial and office sectors, have a working day of 08.00 to 14.00, and some return to work from 17.00 to 20.00. This provides an alternative to the 09.00–17.00 day, especially in the summer months. There is a statutory minimum one and a half days' rest per week (two days for under-18s), which may be calculated over a two-week reference period. Collective agreements occasionally allow some element of flexible hours, with a thirty-minute 'envelope' of variable arrival and departure times. More typically, seasonal fluctuations allow flexible choice according to season. 3M, for example, works a six hours thirty minutes day in summer and an eight hours fifteen minutes day in winter. Many companies work a shorter continuous day in the period May to September, and a longer split day from October to April.

A number of occupations have separate statutory regulations on the maximum length of the working day; among them are road haulage, farming and maritime transport. Some occupations distinguish between attendance hours and actual working hours, such as rail and local public transport, which allow up to twenty hours' extra 'attendance time' weekly.

Overtime

Statute law limits maximum regular annual overtime to eighty hours per year for an employee. Overtime is prohibited for under-18s and on night-shift work. Employers have a statutory right to use overtime to recoup working hours lost due to *force majeure* at a maximum rate of one hour daily. There is no longer any statutory minimum supplement for overtime work. Instead, such supplements must be collectively, or individually, agreed and may be compensated by time off in lieu.

Night work

Night work is forbidden by statute for under-18s, and no employee may be obliged to work more than two consecutive weeks of night shifts. Most collective agreements provide that an employee working the last shift one week should not have to work the first shift the following week. Night shifts are commonly an hour shorter than the day shift. Since the 1994 reform of the Workers' Statute there is no longer any statutory pay supplement for night work.

Annual leave and public holidays

There is a statutory minimum period of thirty calendar days' paid annual leave, equivalent to twenty-two working days. Specific arrangements are left to collective bargaining or, in its absence, to individual agreement. Traditionally, most employees take their annual leave in August, and many companies close down in that month. However, there is a small but growing trend towards taking annual leave at other times, especially at Christmas. Disagreements over holiday arrangements may be resolved by the labour authorities. The employer is required to arrange vacation entitlement with at least two months' advance notice to the employee. Collective agreements often improve on the statutory minimum, and often grant more days' annual leave to employees with longer service.

All employees are entitled to a maximum of fourteen days' public holiday with pay per year in addition to paid annual leave. Each December the government fixes the calendar of public holidays for the following year, announcing twelve dates which apply to the whole country, and allowing local authorities (at the Autonomous Community level) to allocate another two days for local celebrations (*fiestas*). Of the twelve dates announced by the national government, three may be substituted for others of local importance by the governments of the Autonomous Communities. The twelve days normally established by central government are New Year (1 January), Epiphany (6 January), St Joseph (19 March), Good Friday, May Day (1 May), St James (25 July), Assumption (15 August), Virgen del Pilar (12 October), All Saints (1 November), Constitution Day (1 December), the Immaculate Conception (8 December) and Christmas Day (25 December). Most of the Autonomous Communities have a particular date to celebrate their inauguration, which they take as a local holiday: Andalusia, 1 March; Aragón, 23 April; Castilla la Mancha, 31 May; Catalonia, 11 September; Valencia, 9 October; Extremadura, 8 September; Galicia, 17 May; Murcia, 9 June; La Rioja, 9 June. The government has statutory powers to move a public holiday to a Monday if it considers it in the best interest of the working week. When a public holiday occurs during annual leave or during a weekend no extra day has to be allowed in compensation.

Maternity and paternity leave

There is a statutory right to sixteen weeks' maternity leave, increased to eighteen weeks in the event of multiple birth. At least six weeks of the leave must be post-natal. In the event of the mother becoming seriously ill or dying because of the delivery, the father is entitled to the six weeks' postnatal leave. When both parents work, the father may take four out of the ten weeks' antenatal leave, provided they are not taken as leave by the mother. The father is also entitled to two days' paid leave for the birth. There is also entitlement to eight weeks' leave upon the adoption of a child under nine months, and six months for 5–9 year olds.

Either the father or the mother has a statutory right to up to three years' unpaid leave to care for a child, or to reduce hours of work by between 33 per cent and 50 per cent, to care for a child under 6. Mothers also have a statutory right to one hour's absence from work daily to feed a child under nine months. The hour may be divided, or the mother may shorten her working day by half an hour.

Other time off

Elected works council members or workers' delegates have a statutory right to paid leave to carry out their duties. The amount of leave is based on the size of the company, and ranges from fifteen hours monthly per representative in a company of fewer than 100 employees to forty hours monthly in companies of 751 or more employees. By collective agreement the hours may be consolidated to allow representatives to act as such full-time without loss of pay or entitlement.

Military service (of nine months) carries a statutory obligation on the employer to reserve the job for the employee for up to thirty days after completion of the service.

Statutory paid leave is available in a variety of personal circumstances. It includes fifteen calendar days for marriage, two to four calendar days for the birth, serious illness or death of a close relative, one day for moving house, and any time necessary to perform public duties.

Unpaid leave

There is a statutory right to unpaid leave of between two and five years when an

employee has had at least one year's service and has not had other unpaid leave
within the previous four years.

Promotion and transfer (see also 'Variation of terms' above)

Statute law requires collective bargaining, or some other form of agreement
between the employer and employee representatives, to define the criteria and
procedures for promotion, which must expressly apply equally to both sexes. An
employee who is required to accept the responsibilities of a higher grade is entitled after six months to apply to be allocated to a post in the higher grade.
Collective agreements often include detailed provisions on promotion, specifying
the composition of promotion panels, the types of competitive examination or
test to be applied, relative preferences for internal or external candidates, the
weightings to be given to different factors such as qualifications, experience and
aptitude.

Under the amended Workers' Statute an employer has much more freedom to
transfer employees between jobs and locations than before. Provided an
employee has suitable qualifications, the employer may effect a transfer to work
of a similar grade, and may also, where management or technical reasons require
it, transfer to lower-grade work, for the minimum time necessary, while protecting the employee's previous pay level. When an employer wishes to relocate the
employee to another workplace which would mean the employee having to move
house, the employee has the right to request that the contract should be terminated, with severance compensation of twenty days' pay per year of service, up to
a maximum of one year's pay, or to appeal to the labour authorities against the
compulsory relocation.

Where 10 per cent or more of a work force is affected by a relocation order the
employer must inform the employee representatives, consult them at least fifteen
days ahead of implementation, and notify the labour authorities. The labour
authorities have the power to delay implementation for a period of up to one
year. An employer also has the right to relocate employees temporarily, provided
they are given at least five days' notice of a relocation lasting three months and
granted at least four days' paid leave each three months. All expenses must be
reimbursed. Employees may appeal against the decision.

Relocation packages tend to be generous, to overcome the reluctance of
Spanish employees to uproot themselves. In banking, for example, an employee
accepting voluntary relocation receives a resettlement accommodation allowance
of between Pta 50,000 and Pta 120,000 monthly (£250–£600) for between three
and five years, plus nine months' advance rent payments, a low-interest mortgage of four times annual salary, and promotion. A motor vehicle component
company (Valeo), transferring staff from Barcelona to Andalusia, offered
employees Pta 3 million (£15,000) disturbance allowance plus removal costs.

Pay and benefits

Statutory pay determination

A statutory minimum wage (*salario mínimo interprofesional*, SMI) is imposed by decree. The level is usually set in December for the following year, after consultation with unions and employers' organisations. The minimum wage is designed to be a subsistence wage, and it establishes minimum pay levels for over-18s, day labourers and domestic servants. It is important not only as an absolute minimum pay requirement but also because it is used as the basis for calculating statutory compensation payments for severance, for pensions and for sick pay. In 1994 the SMI was Pta 60,570 monthly (Pta 2,019 daily) for over-18s (£303 and £10.10), and Pta 40,020 monthly (Pta 1,334 daily) for under-18s (£200 and £6.70).

The law on pay

Form of payment   For tax and legal purposes, pay is defined as all remuneration except 'justifiable expenses', social security benefits and compensation paid in the event of transfer, redundancy or temporary lay-off. No more than 30 per cent of pay may be in the form of pay in kind (except for domestic servants, for whom it may be up to 45 per cent). Pay must be accompanied by a pay slip in the officially approved format, which has to be signed by the employee and a copy held by the employer for five years. An employer may pay by cheque or other form of non-cash payment, provided the works council or employee delegates are informed in advance. Employees have the right to 10 per cent interest on delayed payment. Payments must not be more than one month apart. Pay must be distributed at the place of work, and expressly may not be distributed in recreation centres, bars, canteens or shops – except in the case of employees of such establishments. When employees are paid more frequently than monthly, such pay is considered as an advance on monthly earnings, and pay statements must still be set out in monthly terms as well.

Deductions   The employer is required to deduct social security contributions from pay. Legislation allows employers and unions to agree on procedures for union dues to be deducted at source. Collective agreements sometimes include this provision, and employees must give their written consent for it to proceed. Salaries are liable to a court order for attachment of earnings if a creditor is seeking redress from an individual. Legislation specifies the limits which apply in such cases: an employee must retain at least the amount of the statutory minimum wage, and thereafter deductions are permitted on a sliding scale.

Grading and job evaluation   Statute law requires that employees are guaranteed the level of pay appropriate to the job classification they are assigned on recruitment. An employee's basic pay is fundamentally determined by allocation to a job grade which carries with it a monthly or annual rate. In many cases such a pay structure reflects long-standing definitions which stem from the ordinances. There is great government pressure for these to be replaced by collectively agreed arrangements, a procedure which has occurred at national sectoral level in a few industries, notably chemicals and banking. The reform of the Workers' Statute in 1994 considerably strengthened the role of collective bargaining in determining the structures which define an individual employee's pay. Collective bargaining is expected to determine basic pay and supplements by taking into account the employee's individual functions and circumstances, as well as the financial situation of the company.

Job evaluation procedures are often formally established by collective agreement and monitored jointly in the workplace. Model schemes, such as that specified in the chemical industry agreement, require management to inform employee representatives of any proposed introduction of evaluation systems, with recourse to external arbitrators if agreement cannot be reached.

Make-up of pay

Individual remuneration customarily consists of a large number of elements which can, in some cases, virtually double the agreed minima. The main components, some of which are detailed below, include the *plus de convenio*, a collective agreement ratification supplement, seniority payments, bonuses, incentive payments, a variety of allowances, profit-sharing payments and any payments for overtime, shift work or night work. For the employer, these basic employment costs can also be supplemented by loans to employees, canteen and housing subsidies, and other social benefits.

Extra payments

Traditionally pay in Spain is composed of several extra payments on top of basic pay.

Agreement ratification allowance   This allowance, the *plus de convenio*, was formerly given as a 'sweetener' for signing a collective agreement. Many agreements retain the concept, though there have been moves to consolidate it into basic pay, as has happened in some national sectoral agreements. Where it persists, however, the payment can be large in comparison with basic pay, at times amounting to some 60 per cent of an employee's gross pay.

Seniority supplement   These payments are not statutory, although until 1994 statute law restricted them to no more than 60 per cent of basic pay after twenty-five years' service; now there are no statutory restrictions. Collective agreements typically provide for increments such as 2.5 per cent every two years, 6 per cent every four years, 5 per cent every three years, 5 per cent every five years – or a variety of fixed cash amounts.

Punctuality and attendance bonus   This is still a fairly common supplement, though it is being absorbed in some newer agreements. Examples range from Pta 120–282 daily (£0.60–£1.40) to Pta 1,758 monthly (£8.80) for regular punctual attendance.

Dangerous, noxious or arduous conditions supplement   These are all common payments where such conditions apply, and are negotiated according to the specific job. Examples range from 10 per cent extra on basic pay for working with toxic substances to 25 per cent extra on basic, to 20 per cent if one of the factors applies, 25 per cent if two apply and 30 per cent if three apply. This supplement may also be called a 'special job premium'.

Responsibility supplements   Agreements often allow for extra payments to staff with particular responsibilities. Section heads, for example, may be paid from 4 per cent to 20 per cent extra on basic pay. Team leaders in one agreement receive two extra monthly payments in July and December of approximately Pta 57,000 (£285).

Overtime, night work and shift pay

As from 1994 statute law no longer guarantees higher pay for overtime. There is still a statutory restriction of eighty hours' annually permitted overtime per employee – a 'job creation' practice which has been in force since 1981. However, the rates for overtime work are now to be agreed either individually or collectively. Time off in lieu is permitted, provided it is taken within four months. Pay for overtime working must be at least the rate of normal working; agreements typically provide 175 per cent of normal rates for weekday overtime and up to 225 per cent of normal rates for Sunday and public holiday overtime. There is no statutory rate for night work (22.00–06.00), but agreements typically provide for between 30 per cent and 40 per cent extra on basic rates.

Agreed provisions on shift work range widely. Current examples range from Pta 28,360 monthly (£142) for working a full three-shift rota to a 10 per cent supplement on basic pay for working alternate shifts, or daily and hourly based supplements. It is fairly common for employees liable to be called out at unsocial hours to receive an extra supplement. Agreements currently provide amounts ranging from Pta 1,271 (£6.35) for being on call over a weekend to 10 per cent on basic pay for being on call for two weeks per month, and up to 20 per cent for being on call for three weeks per month. Being permanently on call can attract supplements of up to 30 per cent on top of basic pay.

Bonuses

Employees have a statutory right to receive two extra payments per year, one at Christmas and the other to be determined by collective agreement, normally paid in July. Annual salary is therefore divided into fourteen payments. Employees may opt by collective agreement for these payments to be consolidated into twelve monthly payments. Collective agreements often vary or add to this pattern; a fifteenth payment is not unusual, and a fifteenth payment of 50 per cent of monthly pay is sometimes agreed; some agreements even include a sixteenth payment.

Long-service awards   It is quite common for company agreements to establish cash awards for employees with long service. Current sample practices range from two months' pay after twenty-five years to one month's pay after fifteen years. These are often in addition to extra holidays and other awards.

Profit-sharing   This is a long-established component of many agreements, and in several cases it is paid whether or not the company is in profit. The term is often used merely to describe a fifteenth monthly payment. One example of a genuine profit-sharing agreement is at the power company Fenosa, where employees receive a bonus of 16 per cent of their May salary × 12 in June if the company makes profits of 5 per cent or less on turnover, 20 per cent if profit is 5–7 per cent on turnover, and 24 per cent if it is over 7 per cent.

Pay for performance

Productivity-based reward schemes are not generally well developed in Spain. Variable pay is thought to represent some 14 per cent of all pay in large companies. In recent years, however, there has been a small but significant growth in the number of employees in larger companies whose pay and conditions are agreed outside collective agreements, and who often have an element of performance pay in their salary. The numbers 'exempted' in this fashion are estimated at some 1.9 million (having risen from 1.2 million in 1985), and are thought to total some 4 per cent of the non-executive work force, especially in marketing and commercial activities, earning some 14 per cent more, on average, than other employees.

Managerial pay

The rapid growth of the economy in the late 1980s exposed the country's shortage of qualified managers, and boosted the real net pay of executives to some of the highest levels in Europe, trailing only Switzerland, Germany and France. The recession of the early 1990s eased the pressure somewhat, although managerial salaries continued to rise in real terms – if with a smaller margin over inflation –

despite a period of economic slackness. For the first time for several years, executive pay rises in 1993 were broadly in line with those of other groups of employees.

The predominant influences on salary levels are turnover and the size of the work force. Pay is higher on a regional basis in the Barcelona and Madrid areas, but the differential is not enormous, with executive pay in Madrid some 5 per cent above the national average. Geographical mobility can present problems, and young managers may be reluctant to leave established centres. Some industries, such as petrochemicals and electronics, have built up higher pay levels than more traditional sectors.

There is a small but growing trend towards greater pay flexibility for middle management, although the element at risk is likely to be tied to corporate rather than individual performance. According to the Monks Partnership survey *Incentives and Benefits in Europe 1993–4*, 93 per cent of top managers and 82 per cent of senior managers were eligible for cash bonuses – in both cases an increase on the previous year. For top management the amount at risk was substantially higher: for 37 per cent of top managers the value of the bonus was more than a quarter of annual salary, but it was less than 15 per cent of salary for nearly half of all senior managers. Share options are a rarity and mainly confined to international companies.

By function, the Monks Partnership survey *Management Remuneration in Europe 1993–4* found that, compared with differentials elsewhere in Europe, administration was comparatively highly remunerated and finance less well rewarded than the average. Among the Spanish companies surveyed, the head of a major sub-function in a company with a turnover of Pta 5.8 billion (£29 million) earned some 60 per cent of the managing director's total earnings, with finance slightly ahead at 62 per cent and administration and personnel the lowest paid head of function, with 50 per cent.

Sick pay and maternity pay

The state social security scheme provides sickness benefit for temporary incapacity for work. To qualify, the employee must have a record of 180 days' contributions in the preceding five years. The amount of benefit is 60 per cent of the social security calculation base from the fourth to the twentieth day of sickness, and 75 per cent thereafter, payable for up to twelve months, and renewable for a further six months. For the first fifteen days, benefit is paid directly by the employer. A variety of provisions govern permanent disability benefits. Collective agreements usually improve on the state arrangements for sickness benefit by requiring the employer to top up payments to 100 per cent of normal earnings.

To qualify for maternity benefit, the mother requires 180 days' contributions in the year before the birth, and to have been registered with the social security scheme for at least nine months before that. Maternity benefit amounts to 75 per cent of basic pay (and another 75 per cent for each extra child) for the statutory sixteen-week leave period. Collective agreements often provide extra payments, in some cases topping up benefit to normal earnings. Collective agreements often also provide for a one-off maternity allowance; examples range from Pta 5,000 to Pta 19,868 (£25–£99).

Main benefits

Cars are virtually a standard part of the package for top management, and are provided to the vast bulk of function heads. However, according to the 1993 Monks Partnership *European Company Car Survey*, the incidence of cars as a benefit falls off rapidly for posts below director level. For example, only 20 per cent of senior managers in finance, reporting to a finance director, have cars, compared with 96 per cent of those in a comparable position in the UK. However, Spanish companies are more inclined than others to provide housing assistance to executives.

As noted elsewhere, company pensions remain relatively undeveloped, despite legislation intended to promote them having been on the statute book since 1987. Between 50 and 60 per cent of managerial posts were eligible for company pensions in 1993/94, a slight increase on the previous year, but still substantially below provision elsewhere in Europe.

Equal pay and equal opportunities

Discrimination against women

The constitution affirms equality between the sexes, and the Workers' Statute requires employers to pay equally for equal work. Spain has ratified EU and ILO directives on equality and non-discrimination. The Instituto de la Mujer, part of the Ministry of Social Affairs, is charged with monitoring conditions for women and proposing measures to promote equality. Nevertheless, studies show that on average women earn some 20 per cent less than men. Although the female participation rate is very low, the number of women in the work force has risen rapidly in recent years, from 3.7 million in 1981 to 5.5 million in 1993. One measure the government has adopted is the creation of a special contract to boost the employment of women. An employer can earn a subsidy of Pta 500,000 (£2,500) towards the creation of a new post by hiring a long-term unemployed female or a woman over 25 wishing to return to employment, on a permanent full-time contract. Collective agreements occasionally include provisions to promote greater female equality of access to employment.

One persistent problem in this respect has been the labour ordinances, which in many cases included job classifications which distinguished between male and female employees. Court cases in 1993 and 1994 have declared them to be unconstitutional, and the government is committed to revoking the remaining ordinances by 1995.

Sexual harassment   Physical or psychological harm suffered as a consequence of sexual harassment at work is treated as an occupational accident. The female employee affected has the right to ask for termination of contract, with full compensation rights. Sexual harassment at work is punishable by fines on the employer of Pta 500,000 to Pta 15 million (£2,500–£75,000).

Retirement

The past three decades have seen a substantial increase in the number of pensioners. Those drawing state retirement and disability pensions had risen from 3.8 million in 1971 to 6.5 million by 1993. The maximum permissible age for employment is 69, but the retirement age for a state pension is 65. Employees in dangerous, arduous or unhealthy occupations, such as railway workers, aircrew, artistes and bullfighters, may retire earlier.

State pensions are earnings-related and yield a minimum of 60 per cent of covered earnings after fifteen years, rising to 100 per cent after thirty-five years. Maximum possible covered earnings are Pta 3.3 million (£16,500). In 1994 the minimum retirement pension for a married pensioner was Pta 57,680 monthly (£288) and for a single pensioner Pta 49,020 (£245). The average pension was approximately Pta 86,000 monthly (£430).

Where the employer is operating a job creation scheme, early retirement on full pension is permitted at 64, provided the employer recruits a replacement employee from among the registered unemployed. Under a different job creation measure, the 'relief contract', employees may take partial retirement from the age of 62, with full *pro rata* pension entitlement, provided the employer recruits a replacement employee from among the registered unemployed on a part-time contract. In addition there are a number of provisions for early retirement on a full pension at 60 for employees in various industrial sectors covered by the government's industrial restructuring legislation.

Company schemes detailed in collective agreements often improve on statutory measures, and frequently include a one-off retirement bonus. Examples range from two months' pay at age 65 to two months' pay per year of service, up to a maximum of nine months. Early retirement premiums may also be payable: for example, they may start at sixteen months' pay at 60, falling to four months' at 64.

Legislation to regulate private pension schemes dates from 1987. Despite considerable government promotion of the benefits, private pensions have been slow to develop. Three types of pension plan are granted favourable tax treatment:

- Company schemes run for the benefit of employees, financed by employer and employee contributions.
- Associated schemes for such groups as unions and professional associations, financed by members' contributions.

- Individual schemes run by financial institutions such as banks or insurance companies.

Group schemes are of two types: defined contributions or defined benefits. The current limit for tax exemption for the employer is Pta 750,000 per employee (£3,750). Individuals may also set off against taxable income in each tax year either Pta 750,000 (under new proposals Pta 1.5 million (£7,500) when a joint tax declaration is made) or 15 per cent of earned income, whichever is the lower.

Individual termination of contract

Resignation

Employees are required to give whatever period of notice appears in collective agreements, is in line with local custom or is set down in the individual contract of employment. It is typically two weeks for most employees, though in some cases technical staff are required to give four weeks' notice, and manual workers may on occasion be required to give only one week's. Employees who terminate a contract at their own request forfeit the right to unemployment benefit.

Employees are entitled to ask for the contract to be terminated if the employer substantially modifies their working conditions or terms of employment in a way which is detrimental to their professional development or their human 'dignity', or if the employer habitually delays paying their wages. Where employees can establish such a breach of the original contract they may be entitled to compensation of forty-five days' pay per year of service, up to a maximum of forty-two months' pay.

Termination by mutual agreement

When both sides agree upon termination, a document known as the *finiquito* is signed, recording the employee's pay, and the contract terminates, with no entitlement to compensation. There may also be situations in which each party wishes to agree upon harmonious departure, and voluntary severance terms in line with the statutory provisions may be included in a settlement.

Both sides can also agree provision for termination in the contract of employment, provided the employee's statutory rights are not infringed.

Retirement of the employee

The contract may be terminated when the employee reaches the state retirement pension age of 65. Compulsory retirement is unlawful, but collective agreements may decide on an enforceable retirement age other than the statutory upper limit of 69.

Grounds for dismissal

Individual dismissal is taken to be dismissal involving fewer than 10 per cent of the work force (see below, 'Collective dismissal'). There are a variety of grounds for dismissal. In the case of fixed-term contracts for less than a year, termination is automatic when the expiry date is reached. When fixed-term contracts last for more than one year, the employer is obliged to give fifteen days' notice, otherwise the contract is considered to have been extended indefinitely, except in cases where the temporary nature of the job is self-evident.

Should the employee be declared permanently disabled as far as normal duties are concerned, the employer is entitled to terminate the contract or offer an appropriate job.

If the business ceases to function, owing to the death, retirement or legal incapacity of the employer, the employee is entitled to statutory compensation.

The Workers' Statute envisages two main grounds for individual dismissal: dismissal for 'objective reasons' and dismissal on disciplinary grounds. 'Objective reasons' justifying dismissal include such factors as:

- An employee's proven incapacity for the job they were employed to do.
- Unjustified absence amounting to 20 per cent of working hours in two consecutive months, or 25 per cent of working hours in any four months of a year, provided that the company's overall absenteeism rate exceeds 5 per cent in those periods.
- An employee's inability to adapt to changed working practices, such as new technology, after a familiarisation period of up to two months, and up to three months' retraining.
- The company's need to reduce posts for economic, technical, organisational or production reasons (when less than 10 per cent of the work force are affected).

Dismissal for disciplinary reasons is recognised in statute law as justified for habitual absenteeism or unpunctuality, indiscipline or disobedience, verbal or physical aggression towards the employer, colleagues or their families, abuse of contractual good faith or breach of confidence, 'consistent and deliberate reduction of normal or agreed output', or habitual drug or alcohol abuse which adversely affects performance at work. Collective agreements may specify termination on disciplinary grounds as the final stage of a graduated series of penalties for offences of progressively increasing gravity. Such agreements may define a 'very serious' offence meriting dismissal as, for example, unjustified absence of two days in one month, repeated within six months, or more than ten arrivals five minutes or more late in a period of six months.

Notice must be served in all cases of disciplinary dismissal.

Dismissal procedure

Disciplinary dismissal notice must be given in writing, stating the reasons for dismissal, and must follow within sixty days of the employer becoming aware of the offence and within six months of the offence itself. The employer must allow a hearing from representatives of the employee's trade union and, in the event of the employee being a union official, from other union officials. An employer who fails to meet these requirements may reissue the notice of dismissal within twenty days of the first dismissal.

The procedure for dismissal on objective grounds requires written notice of at least thirty days, with details of the alleged reasons for dismissal (see also 'Periods of notice' below). The employee is entitled to six hours' leave per week in this period in order to look for other employment.

Terminating executives' employment

Employees classified as executives must, by law, give three months' notice of termination of their contract. In certain circumstances, such as substantial changes in working conditions, delay in receiving pay, failure by the employer to meet contractual obligations or a change in the ownership of the company which has substantial repercussions on personnel or business activity, an executive may terminate the contract with a right to compensation in certain circumstances. Compensation can be seven days' pay per year of service, up to six months' pay. Employers who dismiss an executive for failing to fulfil contractual obligations may be liable to pay compensation of twenty days' pay per year of service, up to twelve months' pay, should the dismissal be held to have been unlawful.

Periods of notice

In cases of dismissal on objective grounds the employer must give written notice of at least thirty days, and a copy of the dismissal notice must be given to workers' representatives at the same time. Notice increases with service, to two months for employees with one to two years' service, and to three months for two or more years' service. An executive must receive at least three months' written notice.

Severance payments

In cases of objective dismissal the employee is entitled to compensation of twenty days' pay per year of service, up to a maximum of twelve months' pay. Dismissed executives are entitled to whatever compensation was agreed in their contract, or a statutory seven days' pay per year of service, up to a maximum six months' pay. Studies suggest, however, that many dismissals have been receiving compensation substantially above the legal minimum. In late 1993 it was estimated that the average redundancy compensation in large companies was Pta 6.5 million (£32,500). In many cases, instead of twenty days' pay per year of service, redundant employees received nearly three times that amount.

Unfair dismissal

The first stage in the appeal procedure should an employee contest objective or disciplinary dismissal is the conciliation procedure at the local office of the official mediation, conciliation and arbitration agency, the Servicio de Mediacion, Arbitraje y Concilicacion (SMAC). SMAC branches are attached to the offices of the Autonomous Regional governments. The agency handled 61 per cent of the 3 million redundancies in the decade before 1994, and is often used by employers to speed the redundancy process and avoid the labour courts. Employees may submit a request for conciliation to the local offices of SMAC or the appropriate office of the Autonomous Regional government in the seven Autonomous Regions which have had these powers transferred to them. The appeal must be lodged within twenty working days of receiving notice. The authorities will call on both sides to reach one of three resolutions:

- Agreement, involving either reinstatement or the payment of compensation due.
- Non-agreement – in which case the employee may take the appeal to a Social Court (*Juzgado de lo Social*).
- Non-appearance of either side – in which case, if the judge rules against the absent party, they may impose a fine of up to Pta 100,000 (£500) and award costs.

In SMAC proceedings it has been the convention since the 1984 law governing the unemployment benefit system (law 31/84) for dismissed employees to claim at least thirty-five days' compensation following 'objective' dismissal and for SMAC to rule in their favour. This is partly to give employees an official guarantee that their application for unemployment benefit will be accepted, by showing that the individual is not voluntarily unemployed. It is also partly to avoid the employer's having to pay forty-five days per year of service if the appeal to the court is rejected and the dismissal declared unlawful. Some 80 per cent of dismissal cases handled by SMAC involve employees in companies with fewer than fifty employees, and 68 per cent of cases result in agreed compensation.

Should the parties appeal, the court will proceed as follows. After taking evidence in the case, the court will rule, also in one of three ways:

- Dismissal annulled (*despido nulo*). For a variety of reasons the court may judge that the employer has no good grounds for dismissal, or has not followed the dismissal procedure properly. In that case the court will order the employee to be reinstated and any pending wages paid.

- Unlawful dismissal (*despido improcedente*). In this case the court does not uphold the employer's claim. The employer must decide within five days whether to reinstate the employee or to pay compensation of forty-five days' pay per year of service, up to a maximum of forty-two months' pay, together with any pay owing from the time of dismissal to the time of the ruling. Employers who opt for compensation are liable for pay due only up to the time of a previous conciliation hearing if in that hearing they acknowledged that the dismissal was unlawful. If the employee in question was an employee representative or trade union official, the employee has the right to choose between reinstatement and compensation.
- Lawful dismissal (*despido procedente*). If the court rules in favour of the employer, the employee has a right to compensation only where dismissal was on objective grounds (twenty days' pay per year of service, payable at the time of dismissal).

Both the employer and the employee may appeal against a labour court ruling to the Social Chamber of the High Court (Sala de lo Social del Tribunal Superior de Justicia). The Supreme Court (Tribunal Supremo) may also handle appeals at a higher level. A ruling at a higher level in favour of the employee renders the employer liable for payment of wages due the employee; if the ruling goes the other way the employer is entitled to compensation by the authorities for any wages paid after the earlier ruling and for costs. When an employer appeals against a ruling of *despido nulo* or *despido improcedente* the employee must be provisionally re-employed during the hearing.

Of the 14 per cent of dismissal cases which reach the labour courts, the average compensation paid in 1993 was Pta 897,400 (£4,487). Authorised dismissals in small companies resulted in average compensation of Pta 662,000 (£3,310).

Collective dismissal

Collective dismissal provisions apply when economic dismissals on the following scale are envisaged:

- Ten employees in a work force of 100.
- Ten per cent of employees in a work force of between 100 and 300.
- Thirty employees in a work force of 300 or more, in any period of ninety days.

Whatever the size of the company, if the whole work force is to be dismissed, then collective dismissal procedure will also apply when the company ceases to operate for economic, technical, organisational or production reasons.

Collective redundancies are tightly controlled by the provisions of the Workers' Statute. Any employer who wishes to declare collective redundancies requires official permission, known as a *regulación de empleo* and obtained from the employment authorities. While requesting permission from the authorities the employer must at the same time begin consultations with employee representatives. These are elected staff representatives in small companies and works committees or trade union representatives in larger firms. (See the volume on employee relations and collective bargaining in this series.) Documented evidence of the need for redundancies has to be made available to both parties. The labour inspectorate is responsible for investigating the basis of the employer's claim. Consultations with employee representatives may last for a thirty-day maximum period, reduced to fifteen days in companies with under fifty employees. Both sides are charged to negotiate in good faith to investigate possible alternatives to dismissal. If agreement between the sides is reached, the labour authorities will endorse the agreement; failing agreement, the authorities will rule on the request within fifteen days, and will support the employer's request where the documentation clearly establishes the justification for the dismissals.

Employee representatives have preferential rights to retain their jobs when dismissals are authorised. Employees dismissed as part of collective redundancy have the right to compensation of twenty days' pay per year of service, up to twelve months' pay.

Transfer of undertakings

Under the Workers' Statute a transfer of the ownership of a company, workplace or unit of production does not terminate an employment relationship. The new owner inherits the employment rights and obligations of the former owner. The existing owner must notify employee representatives of any change of ownership, and both transferor and transferee are jointly liable for a further three years for any undischarged obligations arising out of the employment relationship prior to the transfer.

Appendix

Non-wage labour costs

Social security contributions are levied on gross earnings, with upper and lower limits established for each of eleven occupational categories. Employer contributions are approximately 32 per cent of eligible earnings and employee contributions 6 per cent. There are supplementary employer contributions on some forms of overtime, and employer social insurance contribution reductions for workers hired on any of the special job creation contracts available for targeted groups such as the long-term unemployed, the young and people with disabilities.

Organisations

Ministerio de Trabajo y Seguridad Social
(Ministry of Labour and Social Security)
Agustín de Bethencourt 4, Madrid
Tel. 010 341 553 6278;
fax 010 341 533 2996

The Ministry of Labour and Social
Security deals with all aspects of labour
legislation, employment, the labour
inspectorate, health and safety and social
security.

Instituto Nacional de Empleo (INEM)
Condesa de Venadito 9, Madrid
Tel. 010 341 585 9888;
fax 010 341 268 3981

INEM is attached to the Ministry of
Labour and Social Security, and is
responsible for the management of the
employment offices. It also processes
unemployment statistics and manages the
government training schemes. It has an
office in each provincial capital, entitled
*Dirección Provincial del Instituto
Nacional de Empleo*, which handles
recruitment and registers the unemployed.

Instituto Nacional de Seguridad Social
(INSS)
Padre Damian 4, Madrid
Tel. 010 341 564 9023;
fax 010 341 564 7822

INSS is a department of the Ministry of
Labour and Social Security. It manages
employers' and employees' contributions,
and processes pensions, sick pay and other
social security benefits.

*Instituto Nacional de Seguridad e Higiene
en el Trabajo* (National Health and Safety
at Work Institute)
Torrelaguna 73, Madrid
Tel. 010 341 403 7000;
fax 010 431 403 0050

*Diracción General de Inspección de
Trabajo y Seguridad* (the labour
inspectorate)
Agustín de Bethencourt 4, Madrid
Tel. 010 341 553 6000

Also a department of the Ministry of
Labour and Social Security, the labour
inspectorate is empowered to investigate
working conditions, hours and
remuneration.

Union General de Trabajadores (UGT)
Hortaleza 88, Madrid
Tel. 010 341 308 3333

The UGT, with some 720,000 affiliates,
has for the past century been the trade
union base of the Spanish Socialist Party,
the PSOE. It is the largest trade union
confederation, and in the trade union
elections of 1990 its representatives
constituted 44 per cent of those elected.
Despite its links with the governing PSOE,
relations have been strained since the
mid-1980s, and in December 1988 and
January 1994 the UGT led one-day general
strikes in protest against PSOE policies.
General secretary: Candido Mendez.

Comisiones Obreras (CC.OO)
Fernández de la Hoz 6, 28010 Madrid
Tel. 010 341 419 5454

The CC.OO union confederation, which
has some 700,000 members, was formed in
the mid-1960s and operated underground
during the first decade of its existence
under Franco. Although it initially
attracted a broad alliance of anti-Franco
members, its main influence was the
Spanish Communist Party. In the 1990
trade union elections the CC.OO had some
36 per cent of the elected representatives.
It led the two one-day national stoppages
in December 1988 and January 1994
jointly with the UGT. General secretary:
Antonio Gutierrez.

Union Sindical Obrera (USO)
Príncipe de Vergara 13, 7º, 28001 Madrid
Tel. 010 341 262 4040

With some 80,000 members, the USO is
the third largest trade union. However, in
the 1990 trade union elections its
representatives were less than 10 per cent
of the total elected, and it therefore failed
to reach the status of 'most representative
union', which would have allowed it to
share in national-level bargaining and
representation in national institutions.
General secretary: Manuel Zaguirre.

Confederación General de Trabajo (CGT)
Sagunto 15, 28010 Madrid
Tel. 010 341 447 5769

The CGT union's roots lie in the anarchist
movements which had a significant base in
the late nineteenth and early twentieth
centuries. In the 1930s the CNT (its former
title) was Spain's largest trade union, with
well over a million members, especially in
Catalonia. However, it never recovered
from its defeat by Franco, and now has
some 40,000 members. General secretary:
Emilio Lindosa.

*Confederación Sindical Euzko Laguillen
Alkatasuna–Solidaridad de Trabajadores
Vascos* (ELA–STV)
Euskalduna 11, 1º, 48008 Bilbao
Tel. 010 344 4442504

ELA–STV is the largest union in the
Basque country. It won 7,325 places in the
1990 trade union elections (ahead of the
UGT with its 5,203 and the CC.OO with
its 6,209). It has historically co-operated
with the *Partido Nacionalista Vasco*
(PNV) and has had a constructive relationship with the Basque employers' federation. It is essentially a local trade union,
but a recent amendment to the Workers'
Statute which allows a 'most representative union' at regional level to negotiate at
regional level collective agreements not
bound by higher national-level agreements
should allow ELA–STV to develop much
more local influence in the Basque coun-

try, which has traditionally had a more
progressive framework of labour relations
than many other parts of Spain. General
secretary: Jose Elorrieta.

INTG
Couto de San Honorato 92, Vigo
Tel. 010 3486 425544

INTG represents workers in Galicia, and
claims some 25,000 affiliates. It won 3,519
places in the 1990 trade union elections. It
merged with the small Galician nationalist
trade union CXTG in March 1994. General
secretary: Manuel Mera Sanchez.

*Confederación Española de
Organizaciones Empresariales*, CEOE
(Confederation of Spanish Employers)
Diego de León 50, 28006 Madrid
Tel. 010 341 563 9641;
fax 010 341 262 8023

The CEOE was founded in 1977 and
represents the vast majority of Spanish
companies. It negotiates with unions and
government at national level, and has an
important influence in establishing
employers' guidelines for collective
bargaining each spring. General secretary:
Jose Maria Cuevas.

*Confederación Española de Pequeñas y
Medianas Empresas* (CEPYME)
Diego de León 50, 28006 Madrid
Tel. 010 341 261 6757

An associate organisation of the CEOE,
the CEPYME represents the interests of
small and medium-sized companies.

*Asociación Española de Directores de
Personal* (AEDIPE)
Moreto 10, Madrid
Tel. 010 341 468 2217

AEDIPE is Spain's largest personnel
management association and is a member
of the European Association of Personnel
Management. President: Pedro Blasquez.

Main sources

Ministerio de Trabajo y Seguridad Social, *Boletín de Estadísticas Laborales*, various issues.

Ministerio de Trabajo y Seguridad Social, *Guía Laboral*, various issues (annual review of labour legislation).

Edersa-Francis Lefebvre, *Memento práctico, Social*, Lefebvre, Madrid, 1992.

Ministerio de Economía y Hacienda, *La negociación colectiva en las grandes empresas*, various years (annual survey of collective bargaining in large companies).

J. Vidal Soria, *Código de las Leyes Laborales*, BOE, Madrid, 1991.

Industry collective agreements, published in *Boletín Oficial del Estado* (Official Gazette).

12
Sweden

Basic rights and labour jurisdiction

Legal framework

The terms of the employment relationship in Sweden have traditionally been a matter for collective agreement between employers and unions. However, the 1970s saw the adoption of a range of laws covering nearly all aspects of industrial and employment relations – the exception being pay, which is unregulated by law.

The core of Swedish labour legislation is contained in two laws:

- The Act on Co-determination at Work (*Lag om medbestämmande i arbetslivet*, MBL) imposes upon employers and unions the duty to negotiate on all matters which affect employer–employee relations, including conditions of employment, production and the management of the enterprise. The Act also guarantees employers and employees full freedom of association.
- The Act on Security of Employment (*Lag om anställningsskydd*, LAS) gives security of employment to nearly all categories of employee, defines types of employment and includes rules on termination of contract.

Other laws cover areas such as leave and holidays, including payment during time off, hours of work, the working environment, anti-discrimination measures, the protection of union representatives and employee board representation.

The Co-determination Act and the Security of Employment Act are to some extent invariable, although they do contain provisions which allow departures from the law by collective agreement.

Labour jurisdiction

Disputes over breaches of contract, collective agreements or public law may be heard either before the civil courts or before the Labour Court (Arbetsdomstolen, AD). The Labour Court is composed of seven members, three appointed by the state and two each appointed by the central employer and employee labour market organisations. For a case to be taken directly to the AD, three conditions must be met:

- the case must be brought by an employer or employee organisation.

- The case must definitely concern a labour market question.
- The case must involve parties who are bound by the terms of a collective agreement, or concern an organised workplace.

If these conditions cannot be met the case is dealt with in a civil court. However, appeals against a civil court's judgement on an employment matter will be heard by the Labour Court, which is the court of final instance in such cases.

The characteristic penalty under Swedish law is damages, which have a character closer to that of fines rather than compensation for actual losses, with the crucial difference that the sums involved are paid to the injured party. Damages against employees – for example, for participation in unlawful industrial action – are usually low.

Contracts of employment

Types of employee

Swedish labour legislation does not recognise any distinction between different types of employee, and no attempt is made to classify them formally. However, the Security of Employment Act does explicitly exclude those in a managerial or comparable position.

The traditional distinction between blue-collar workers (*arbetare*), white-collar employees (*tjänstemän*) and professional employees (*akademiker*) is still relevant in the context of collective agreements, since they have different union organisations and will usually negotiate different agreements.

Form of contracts

By law, all contracts of employment must be in writing. Employers' organisations produce standard forms for employment contracts.

There is no general legal or collectively agreed requirement to consult employee representatives on new contracts. However, the Co-determination Act obliges employers to negotiate before taking any action which will entail major changes in the workplace. Thus if any new hiring would mean an important change in, for example, the distribution of work, workplace unions would have to be consulted. The employment of new supervisory and managerial staff is also considered to fall into this category.

Types of contract

The types of employment contract which may be entered into are specified in the Security of Employment Act. There are two broad categories – permanent (*tillsvidare*) and fixed-term (*tidsbegränsad*). However, collective agreements may specify that only certain fixed-term contracts are allowable. Permanent contracts are considered to be the norm, and a contract will be considered permanent unless it is expressly agreed otherwise on recruitment.

The Security of Employment Act allows a number of types of fixed-term contract, and some 13 per cent of people in employment work under such arrangements. Contracts may be limited to a certain period of time or to the performance of a specific task. The different types are:

- Contracts for a specified time, season or task, where they are necessitated by the nature of the work.
- Contracts for a specified period spent as a temporary replacement, a trainee or as holiday employment.
- Contracts for a specified period, up to a maximum of twelve months over a period of two years, where necessitated by a temporary accumulation of work.
- Contracts for the period leading up to the commencement of compulsory military or other comparable service lasting over three months.

Employers covered by collective agreements are required to inform the relevant trade union of all temporary contracts lasting over one month.

Part-time work is permitted, with employees having the same rights *pro rata* as full-timers. Some 28 per cent of employees work part-time.

Contents of a contract

Standard contracts of employment are available both commercially and from employer organisations.

Since contracts contain details of areas which may be covered by law, collective agreements and employer–union negotiation, there are many possible variations. However, the following elements should be taken into consideration:

- Personal details (including work permit details, if applicable), job title and description.
- Hours of work and holiday entitlement.
- Starting date (and end date if the contract is a fixed-term one).
- Pay and other benefits, and frequency of payment.
- Relevant collective agreement.
- Restrictive covenants.

In addition to being signed by the employer and employee, the agreement should also bear the signature of a union representative if applicable.

Probationary periods

The Security of Employment Act also sets out rules concerning probationary periods, which may last up to twelve months. The contract may be terminated at any time during the period at fourteen days' notice on either side, unless otherwise agreed. If an employer neglects to inform the employee that he does not wish the employment to continue after the expiration of the probationary period, the contract automatically becomes permanent. However, this clause is often dispensed with in agreements for white-collar employees. Some collective agreements contain clauses which oblige employers to obtain union agreement before using probationary periods. Unions must also be informed if the probationary period is to last for more than one month.

Restrictive covenants and employee inventions

Many collective agreements contain provisions which stress employees' duty to observe discretion about the employer's affairs and forbid employees to carry out work which conflicts with an employer's interests. However, for more senior employees a restrictive covenant (*konkurrensklausul*) may be included in the contract of employment.

An agreement between the employers' federation, the SAF, and the SIF, SALF and CF – the unions for industrial white-collar workers, supervisors and civil engineers respectively – lays down rules for such covenants. (The volume in this series on employee relations and collective bargaining outlines negotiating arrangements in Sweden.) The most important provisions are that the covenant may not last for more than two years and that compensation paid by employees for breaking a covenant should not be more than six months' salary. The terms of the covenant should be included in the contract of employment.

Employers' rights to employee inventions and employee compensation are regulated in law, but much the same ground is covered by a SAF–SIF–SALF–CF collective agreement. This contains rules on entitlement to inventions and gives general guidelines on how compensation should be calculated. Both the law and the agreement apply only to patentable inventions. Non-patentable inventions are dealt with through internal suggestion procedures, and guidelines for these have been set out in an agreement between the SAF, the blue-collar union federation, the LO, and the white-collar bargaining cartel, the PTK.

Workplace discipline and rights

Internal personnel policy and disciplinary procedures are largely a company matter. However, employers' use of disciplinary measures is limited by law. The Co-determination Act states that only measures already specified in law and in collective agreements can be taken against employees. The legal sanctions tend to be limited to compensation, which can be claimed either for material injury or for breaches of contract. Collective agreements often contain general rules of conduct but no specific disciplinary procedures.

Suspension may be used only if an employee has already been given notice of dismissal, unless rules are laid down in collective agreements. Written warnings concerning employee conduct are often used, however, because of employers' need to provide extensive justification when dismissing employees.

Promotion and transfer

Many larger companies use proprietary or in-house appraisal systems to assist in promotion, and some have a two-track (i.e. technical and managerial) promotion structure. However, any systems or policy used are a matter of internal company policy.

The transfer of employees is similarly a matter for company policy. However, union representatives have special protection in this respect, since they may not be given worse conditions of employment because of their union activities. This means that, even if a shop steward is moved to a worse-paid job in order to be able to carry out union duties, they must still be granted the same pay as in their old job.

In addition, the Co-determination Act allows union representatives to demand consultation on any matter concerning the employment relationship; this would include such matters as transfer and promotion.

Employment terms and conditions

Hours of work

Working hours are subject to statutory regulation under the Hours of Work Act (*Arbetstidslagen*), which may, however, be departed from by collective agreement. The law specifies a maximum length of forty hours for the normal working week. Under some circumstances this figure may be achieved by averaging out over a maximum reference period of four weeks, subject to weekly maxima set by collective agreement.

The maximum of forty hours is generally the norm, and is complemented with maxima for shift and other forms of working. For instance, the agreement covering blue-collar workers in manufacturing industry has a normal weekly maximum of forty, with thirty-eight hours for workers on discontinuous three-shift systems, thirty-six hours for continuous rotating shifts and thirty-five hours for continuous shifts with regular work on public holidays. The white-collar agreement for the same industry has maxima of forty, thirty-eight and thirty-six hours per week.

Averaging periods may also be varied by collective agreements; for shop and office workers in retailing the period is one year, but no one week may be more than forty-five hours. Agreements usually state that different averaging periods may be used, subject to local collective negotiations.

The distribution of hours is partly regulated by the Act because of statutory provisions on rest periods. The period between 24.00 and 05.00 should normally be included in the daily rest period, although this can be changed by collective agreement. Employees also have the right to a continuous thirty-six-hour rest for each period of seven days which should be at the weekend if possible. Collective agreements' regulation of the pattern of working hours varies widely between sectors because of the requirements of different industries.

Flexitime is widely practised by white-collar employees in several variant forms, but much less commonly by blue-collar workers.

Short-time working (*permittering*) can be introduced, although it usually has to be negotiated with unions, and the County Labour Board (*Länsarbetsnämnden*) must be informed at least one month in advance.

The Act also allows the use of 'on call' work for at most forty-eight hours per four weeks or fifty hours per calendar month.

Employees are entitled to two types of break under the Act. A *rast* (a break during which the employee may leave the workplace) must be allowed after five hours' work. Employers must also give *pauser* (short breaks) as necessary. The Act does not specify the length of either of these, and their duration and timing are both subject to local agreement. *Raster* are not counted as part of working hours but *pauser* are.

Overtime

Overtime is regulated by the Hours of Work Act, supplemented by collective agreements. Overtime is defined in the Act as any time worked outside normal working hours (including on-call time, if any). The Act also defines different types of overtime. *Allmän övertid* (general overtime) may be worked for at most forty-eight hours per four-week period, or fifty hours per calendar month, up to a limit of 200 hours per year. However, employers and unions may negotiate short-term (up to one month) exceptions for extra overtime with no limit. If such agreement cannot be reached, employers have the right to apply to the Labour Welfare Board (*Arbetarskyddstyrelsen*), which may grant an extra 150 hours per year over and above ordinary overtime.

The Act also covers *nödfallsövertid* (emergency overtime), which may be worked without limit in the event of accidents and emergencies. However, if employers are covered by collective agreement they must notify the relevant union. If overtime still has to be worked more than forty-eight hours after the emergency, permission must be obtained from the Labour Welfare Board.

These provisions are usually included in blue-collar collective agreements, which also expressly state that employers have the right to require that overtime must be worked, subject to reasonable notice.

However, white-collar workers are often covered by an SAF–PTK collective agreement on working hours. It specifies a maximum 'ordinary overtime' of 150 hours per year. An extra seventy-five hours can be worked by local agreement and a further seventy-five hours by agreement between an individual employer and the PTK.

Overtime may be compensated either by payment or by time off in lieu. In the case of white-collar workers, overtime up to seventy-five hours per year which is taken as time off is not counted towards the annual maximum, which means an effective annual limit of 225 hours.

Overtime worked by part-timers is known as *mertid*. The Act specifies an annual limit of 200 hours for such work. The limit may be increased by collective agreement.

Time off

Annual leave and public holidays

Employees are guaranteed leave under the terms of the Annual Leave Act (*Semesterlagen*). Their right to pay during this period is also governed by the Act. The entitlement is twenty-five days per year, with very few exceptions (mainly those on very short employment contracts and employees joining a company later than 31 August, who have a right to no more than five days' leave). The amount of holiday due to part-time workers is on a sliding scale according to the number of days worked per week. Collective agreements may improve on the provisions of the Act. For example, the banking agreement grants up to thirty days' annual leave, depending on age and responsibility.

Pay during annual leave is accrued during the previous holiday year, which runs from 1 April to 31 March. According to the Annual Leave Act, holiday pay is 13 per cent of wages during the accrual year. However, some blue-collar collective agreements improve on this. White-collar workers are generally entitled by agreement to usual wages plus 0.8 per cent of monthly salary per day of annual year.

Employers are required to negotiate with employees in fixing annual leave dates. If agreement cannot be reached, the law states that leave dates should usually be arranged so that employees have four consecutive weeks' holiday during the period from June to August. Until recently entire companies shut down for the whole of July. This practice is gradually giving way to a more even spread of leave within the period.

Leave entitlement is transferable, and the Act therefore gives employees, on termination, the right to a written statement of how many days' leave have been taken during the current year. Holiday may be carried over at the rate of five days per year for up to five years: it is thus possible to take ten weeks' leave every fifth year.

There are eleven public holidays in Sweden: Christmas Day, Boxing Day, New Year's Day, Epiphany, Good Friday, Easter Monday, May Day, Ascension Day, Whit Monday, Midsummer Holiday and All Saints' Day. Shops and businesses usually close early on the day before.

Maternity, paternity and parental leave

Provisions on maternity, paternity and parental leave are contained in the Parental Leave Act (*Föräldraledighetslagen*).

As part of the overall parental leave system mothers have the right to take parental leave from the sixth week before the expected date of the birth to the sixth week after the birth. If the mother's work is strenuous, or there are environmental dangers, she is additionally entitled to leave from the sixtieth to the eleventh day before the birth (instead of parental leave) provided that alternative work cannot be found with unchanged pay and benefits. Fathers have the right to ten days' leave within sixty days of the birth.

Either parent has the right to full leave until the child is 3 years old, and to cut working hours by 25 per cent until the child is 8 years old. Only one parent may be on leave at any one time. Parents are also entitled to sixty days per child per year of 'temporary parental leave'. This may be taken:

- For the care of a sick child.
- For visits to clinics.
- If the parent who normally cares for the child falls ill.
- For the care of a child at home while the other parent takes a sick child to a doctor or clinic.

There is an additional entitlement of two 'contact days' per year for each child aged between 4 and 12, which may be used to visit the child's nursery or school. Any type of parental leave may be taken by either parent. Adoptive parents enjoy the same rights to leave as natural parents.

Other time off

Employees who have been with the same employer for the last six months or twelve months over the last two years have a statutory right to unpaid leave for educational purposes. Leave cannot be granted for private study or for courses related purely to hobbies. The length of the leave is unlimited (but should be agreed in advance). Length-of-service requirements do not apply to training concerned substantially with trade union matters. An employer may postpone the granting of a request for educational leave (with union agreement for organised employees).

Union representatives have a statutory right to time off for union activities. This includes central negotiations outside the workplace, attendance at trade union courses and conferences, and educational courses important to the representative's duties. There is no limit on the length of the leave, but it must be 'reasonable' in relation to workplace conditions. Representatives are entitled to pay whilst on leave only if their activities have relevance to their workplace. Union members have the right to five hours' paid leave per year for workplace-related union meetings.

Under the terms of collective agreements, employees may be granted one-day leave of absence with pay for such events as weddings, visits to the doctor or dentist or the death of a close relative. White-collar employees may also request unpaid leave of at least one day.

Other types of leave entitlement include:

- Paid time off to look for a job (for employees working out notice).
- Paid time off for employees who are elected representatives in local and national government.
- Seven hundred hours' leave for immigrant workers to learn Swedish.
- Time off in connection with compulsory military service.

Individual pay and benefits

There is no statutory minimum wage in Sweden, nor are there any laws governing how pay is determined. Neither is wage indexation practised. Pay is usually set, for organised employees, by collective bargaining at industry and company level and, for unorganised workers, by individual negotiation.

The form and frequency of wage payments are specified in collective agreements and are not covered by legislation. For instance, the manufacturing industry agreement states that wages must be paid at least monthly; the retail agreement states that wages should be paid monthly or fortnightly.

Employers are legally obliged to make certain deductions from gross pay. These are, in order of precedence:

- Income tax (PAYE).
- Maintenance payments.
- Tax arrears.
- Other debts, e.g. fines.

Other deductions may also be required. They may include: money owed to the employer, such as wage advances or loans, voluntary insurance, trade union dues, and voluntary saving schemes.

There is a wage guarantee fund, financed by employer contributions, which guarantees employees' wages (up to a ceiling of Skr 100,000 (£8,826)) in the event of an employer's insolvency.

Levels of pay determination

For around 90 per cent of employees, pay is determined by collective bargaining. This is currently carried out mainly at industry and company level, with central employer and employee organisations fulfilling a co-ordinating role. Agreements are usually concluded for a period of two years, although shorter agreements are not uncommon. (The pattern of collective bargaining is dealt with in another volume in this series, on employee relations and collective bargaining.) However, the fact that collective agreements often set only minimum rates leaves considerable scope for company-level and individual supplements.

Since there are no provisions for extending collective agreements to non-unionised employees and non-signatory firms, wage-setting for the remaining 10 per cent of employees is theoretically by individual negotiation. However, having a single member employed in a company gives a union the right to demand negotiations. In such situations, companies will usually join an employers' federation for support in bargaining, and in doing so are automatically bound by the industry collective agreement and obliged to pay the rates specified in it.

Main payment systems

There are two main methods of payment for blue-collar workers: fixed hourly rates (*tidlön*) and piece rates (*ackordlön*). Piece rates may either be comprehensive or consist of a fixed rate plus a variable element. An SAF survey from the mid-1980s found that 39 per cent of workers were on fixed rates, with 12 per cent on comprehensive piece rates and 49 per cent on other systems of payment by results.

There are also two types of pay agreement for blue-collar workers: agreements on actual pay and agreements on industry minima. Most workers covered by collective agreements have their pay set according to the former, although even these often specify that personally agreed pay supplements are allowable for especially demanding or responsible work.

The main example of an agreement specifying minima only is the manufacturing industry agreement. It specifies minimum fixed and piece rates for four types of workers, divided by job difficulty, together with minima for young workers (under 18). The agreement also has provisions specifying higher minima for workers with two and four years' seniority.

Both types of agreement contain supplements for overtime, unsocial hours and shift work.

Pay agreements for white-collar employees do not usually set anything other than minima, and much more emphasis is put on individual salary setting, although they do include a general percentage pay increase. A new departure for the Swedish labour market was the introduction, from 1993, of an industry-level agreement between Almega, the General Employers' Federation, and SALF, the supervisors' union, which devolved wage-setting totally to company level, with no recommended percentage increase.

Job evaluation

In principle, companies are free to choose to use (or not to use) any type of job evaluation system. Company, company/consultant and proprietary systems exist, as well as some which have arisen from employer–union projects. For instance, the SKF system, widely used for the evaluation of senior white-collar jobs, was developed solely by the company of the same name. The IPE system, used to evaluate similar positions, is the result of co-operation between consultants and the personnel departments of several large Swedish companies. The BVT system, for other white-collar positions, and the Manufacturing Industry Job Evaluation System, for blue-collar jobs, are the result of employer–union co-operation. These systems are all based on points awarded for such factors as skill, responsibility, effort and the working environment.

The collective agreement for manufacturing industry, which contains pay minima for four groups of employees, requires that job evaluation, if carried out, should be done by a committee with equal employer/employee representation. Where such systematic evaluation is not undertaken, the agreement contains guidelines for placing workers in the four groups.

Components of basic pay

Basic pay is made up of either a flat rate or a minimum improved upon by local bargaining, with the possibility that either may be affected by productivity schemes.

Real wage rates are considerably higher than the rates specified in agreements. For example, the highest minimum wage in the engineering agreement for 1993/94 is Skr 65.43 (£5.77); the average wage in the sector in March 1994 was around 28 per cent higher at Skr 83.60 (£7.38). Indeed, the agreement itself requires that 'capable workers with several years' service in the engineering industry shall receive a wage that is higher than the minimum hourly wage'.

Exactly which rate or minimum is applied will depend, for organised workers, on the contents of the collective agreement. Rates are set to take account of such factors as seniority, age – under-18s usually have lower pay rates – and job classification. It is usual for increments to be awarded for the achievement of specific qualifications.

Overtime

Overtime pay is generally set in collective agreements. Agreements will also include limits on overtime, provision for time off in lieu, periods of notice, etc. Current overtime supplements in the retail sector are 50 per cent for the first two hours, 70 per cent for other hours and 100 per cent for overtime on Sundays and holidays. In manufacturing, overtime compensation is expressed in cash terms, and ranges up to around double time for weekend and holiday work.

Night work, shift and other premiums

Compensation for these is specified in the relevant collective agreements. The latter will commonly include supplements for unsocial hours, night work and various types of shift work. Any other premiums will depend upon the sector. For instance, the manufacturing agreement contains rules on extra payment for work underground and payment for rejected work in foundries.

Bonuses and financial participation

There is no legal requirement to pay thirteenth-month or Christmas bonuses. However, profit-sharing schemes are fairly common. Share option plans for managers are not typical, although cash bonuses, typically tied to a measure of profit, are customary for top and senior management.

Until 1991 the main form of employee financial participation was the wage-earner funds (*löntagarfonder*), introduced by the Social Democratic government in 1984. The funds, financed by taxes on profits and by statutory employer contributions, were used to acquire collective employee stakes in companies. However, the centre-right government elected in 1991 has been progressively winding down the funds, whose assets have reached around Skr 20 billion (£1.7 billion). Most of the money so far released has been used to set up risk capital companies. It is also planned to use the fund's money to support regional development agencies and new product development.

Executives' and managers' pay

Although Sweden has a high rate of union membership and this reaches fairly high up the employment hierarchy – the SACO organisation, for instance, has member associations representing doctors, lawyers and personnel professionals – the pay of executives and senior managers is not usually the subject of collective bargaining. Executive pay is usually set by company boards, and the pay of senior managers is set on the 'grandfather principle' (*farfarsprincipen*). This means that a manager's pay is set by an immediate superior and checked in turn by that person's superior. By far the most common benefit is a company car, enjoyed by over 70 per cent of executives and managers, followed by mobile phones and company pensions.

Managerial pay levels are not especially high by international standards, particularly considering the high taxation levels and the cost of living. However, the high level of severance payments for executives dismissed for incompetence has triggered considerable public debate.

According to the 1993–94 Monks Partnership survey of incentives and benefits, share options were available to only 55 per cent of top managers and 20 per cent of senior managers. Cash bonuses, overwhelmingly tied to an objective measure of profit, were almost universal at top management level, and were paid to some three-quarters of second-tier managers. Additional company-level pensions are infrequent, owing to the pensions provided under the various national statutory and agreed schemes (see below).

Sick pay

Sick pay is regulated by law. After one waiting day, sick pay for the second and third day of illness is 65 per cent of earnings. This rises to 80 per cent until the 365th day and falls to 70 per cent thereafter. Employers are responsible for the first fourteen days of sick pay, after which the state takes over. There is no qualifying period for sick pay, although employees on very short contracts (less than one month) need to have been working for at least fourteen days before the illness occurred.

For white-collar employees, benefits are often made up to full pay for the remainder of the month in which sickness occurs and one month thereafter by collective agreement. For blue-collar workers, a collectively agreed sickness benefit scheme gives an additional 12.5 per cent of wages from the fifteenth to the ninetieth day of illness.

Parental benefit

Full parental leave is compensated by state parental benefit, which is paid for 360 days. Either parent may take leave; the decision as to which may affect the level of benefit paid. Ten months' benefit is paid at 80 per cent of previous income, with one month each reserved for the mother and father respectively at 90 per cent of income. The benefit is taxable. It is not mandatory for the mother or father to take the month reserved for them, but if it is taken by the other partner the level of benefit drops to 80 per cent of income. 'Temporary' parental leave attracts benefit of 80 per cent of income.

Equal pay and equal opportunities

The Equality Act (*Jämställdhetslagen*) prohibits discrimination on grounds of gender in connection with recruitment and dismissal, terms and conditions of employment, and the management and allocation of work. Other provisions protect employees from sexual harassment by employers and punitive action taken by employers where an employee has made a complaint under the Act.

However, the Act does not confine itself to passive measures – several active duties are also imposed on employers. They include addressing gender imbalances when recruiting, taking measures to eradicate sexual harassment and to 'facilitate, for both male and female employees, the combination of work and parenthood'. Other active measures are the requirement that workplaces should be adapted to both genders and a legal obligation upon employers with more than nine employees to draw up a yearly equality plan.

The Act is overseen by the *Jämställdhetsombudsman* (JämO), the Equality Ombudsman. The JämO may forward cases to Jämställdhetsnämnden, the Equality Board, which may order employers to change their practices and can impose fines on those who do not. The JämO may also represent workers who are not union members, or whose unions have chosen not to represent them. In that case, the JämO will initially try to reach a negotiated settlement, but can then take cases to the Industrial Court if this is not possible. Employees represented by neither the JämO nor a trade union may personally pursue cases through the civil courts, and thence to the Labour Court. In both cases, damages may be awarded against employers.

Collective agreements may be negotiated to replace the Act's active measures, but the ban on sexual discrimination is non-negotiable.

Retirement

State old-age pension

The normal retirement age for men and women is 65. Employees choosing to retire at 65 receive a full state pension, which consists of two parts: the basic pension (*folkpension*) and a supplementary pension (ATP). The basic pension is 96 per cent of the 'base amount' (*basbelopp*), a figure uprated annually in line with inflation and used for fixing benefits. For 1994 the base amount was Skr 35,200 (£3,107) per year. ATP pension benefits are calculated on a points system and paid according to the fifteen best-paid years of working life. The basic pension and ATP together represent a figure which is around 65 per cent of income during the fifteen best-paid years.

Although retiring at 65 gives full basic and ATP pensions, they can be taken out at any time between 60 and 70 years of age. For every month of retirement before the age of 65 the amounts are reduced by 0.5 per cent; for every month after 65, payments are increased by 0.7 per cent.

Collectively agreed supplementary pensions cover the vast bulk of blue- and white-collar employees, and are compulsory for member companies of SAF. Additional company-level schemes are extremely rare. STP, the blue-collar scheme, gives around 10 per cent of pay up to 7.5 times the base amount, based on average earnings between the ages of 55 and 59. ITP, the scheme for white-collar workers, gives 10 per cent of final salary up to 7.5 times the base amount, 65 per cent of salary between 7.5 times and 20 times the base amount and 32.5 per cent of salary between 20 and 30 times the base amount. Full entitlement to these pensions requires thirty years of pensionable service.

Partial early retirement

Employees aged over 61 who reduce their working week by up to ten hours but still work for at least seventeen hours per week are entitled to *delpension* (partial pension), which compensates for 55 per cent of lost income. The amount of subsequent pensions is not reduced by taking *delpension*. Introduced in 1976, this option has proved very popular. ITP (see above) may also be taken on similar terms.

Individual termination of contract

Termination of contract is governed by the provisions of the Security of Employment Act, supplemented by collective agreements.

A permanent contract of employment is valid until an employee resigns or is dismissed. A temporary contract ends when the agreed period or task is finished. However, temporary contracts of twelve months over a period of two years and seasonal work of six months in a period of two years give the employee the right of priority if any new recruitment takes place up to one year after dismissal.

Termination by employees

Employees may terminate their contracts of employment after working out a period of notice. The Security of Employment Act prescribes one month for all workers, although white-collar staff usually have longer periods of notice by collective agreement, depending upon age and service. For instance, the engineering industry white-collar agreement has notice periods of up to three months for employees over 35 with six years' service. Employees may resign without notice if an employer has seriously breached the provisions of the contract of employment, for example if wages have not been paid.

There is no legal requirement for employees to give written notice; however, the desirability of doing so may be stated in collective agreements.

Termination by employers

Termination of contract by employers must always be in writing. If required by the employee, reasons for dismissal must be given (in writing if required). In all dismissals, if the employee is a union member the local representative must also be informed. Notification must be given to both employee and union at least fourteen days before formal notice of dismissal is issued.

Probationary employment

Probationary contracts automatically become permanent unless the employer (or employee) takes steps to prevent them from doing so. To accomplish this, notice must be given no later than the expiry date of the contract. Employment may also be terminated early, unless it has been agreed otherwise in the employment contract.

Termination of permanent employment

The Security of Employment Act states that employment can be terminated only on 'objective grounds'. Such grounds are deemed not to exist if an employer can reasonably offer an employee alternative work within the company. Two main reasons for dismissal are specified – lack of work and personal circumstances.

Lack of work   As part of its requirement for 'objective grounds', the legislation demands that no alternative employment should be available within the company. Dismissal of an individual employee because of lack of work invokes the duty to negotiate embodied in the Co-determination Act.

The main steps in dismissal on economic grounds are as follows:

- Written notice to both the employee and the union that negotiations are requested.
- Negotiations take place.
- After negotiations have been carried out, notice of dismissal may be handed to the employee if the dismissal is accepted.

Employees who have been employed for twelve months before dismissal have a right of priority to comparable new jobs in the company for twelve months after dismisssal. Employees must inform employers in writing that they wish to exercise this right.

Personal circumstances   These may be a basis for dismissal (with or without notice), although the legal requirements for 'objective grounds' make it a thorny issue. Indeed, the *Employer's ABC*, produced by the employers' association SAF, recommends that no dismissal on personal grounds should be undertaken unless the employer has consulted a central employer organisation. As with dimissal for lack of work, 'objective grounds' will not be upheld if the problem can be solved by redeployment within the company.

Some common grounds for dismissal with notice (*uppsägning*) are:

- Repeated unauthorised absence.
- Documented lack of co-operation.
- Refusal to work.
- Long-standing lack of competence.
- Repeated drunkenness at work, unless the employee in question is a medically certified alcoholic.
- Continued participation in illegal industrial action.

An important provision of the law is that dismissal may not be based on events which happened longer ago than two months before notice is given. This does not prevent employers from using such events as evidence when justifying dismissal; it simply means that the last occurrence of unacceptable behaviour must have been less than two months before notice was given. Since the validity of the above grounds is based on the existence of a *long-standing* problem, it is standard practice to give at least one written warning before dismissal.

As long as 'reasonable grounds' can be proved, the following order of events is observed. The employer informs employee and union of intended action at least fourteen days before notice of dismissal is issued. The employee and union may request consultation, which must begin no later than seven days after the notification of the intention to issue notice of dismissal. If consultation is not requested, notice of dismissal may be issued, but not until fourteen days after the initial notification at the earliest. If consultation is requested, notice of dismissal may be issued after it has concluded only, and again at least fourteen days after initial notification.

Summary dismissal (*avskedande*) is reserved for very serious breaches of conduct, and is also governed by the Security of Employment Act. Examples of behaviour which can lead to summary dismissal are:

- Violence or threats of violence.
- Disloyal competition.
- Disclosure of professional secrets.
- Fraud, theft or embezzlement.

The chain of events preceding summary dismissal is the same as that for dismissal with notice, with the difference that only one week's notification need be given.

Notice periods and pay

Periods of notice to be given by employers are also governed by the Security of Employment Act, and depend upon age and length of service. Any worker employed for less than six months prior to dismissal is entitled to one month's notice. However, workers who have been employed for longer (or for at least twelve months during the previous two years) are entitled to the following periods of notice:

- Two months after 25 years of age.
- Three months after 30 years of age.
- Four months after 35 years of age.
- Five months after 40 years of age.
- Six months after 45 years of age.

There are no legally required redundancy payments, but employees are entitled to wages during the period of notice; however, this requires them to be at the employer's disposal during the period, even if the employer has no work or chooses not to offer it. Employers have the right to deduct from notice pay any income which employees have earned from other jobs during the period of notice.

This lack of statutory redundancy payments is due to the traditional generosity of the unemployment insurance system. Even after recent reforms, unemployment insurance is payable for a total of 600 days, although a period in one of the state-sponsored employment schemes is mandatory after the first 300 days. Compensation is 80 per cent of former wages, subject to (for 1994) a floor of Skr 245 (£21.62) per day and a daily ceiling of Skr 564 (£49.78).

White-collar workers over 55 with at least ten years of service are often covered by a 'Security Agreement' (*Trygghetsavtal*) concluded between the SAF and PTK, a union bargaining federation. Among other things, the fund set up under this agreement provides employees with financial help, training advice and help in setting up a business in the event of dismissal. It also provides an individually calculated severance payment (called AGE) to white-collar employees over 40 with at least five years' service. There is a similar scheme (AGB) for blue-collar workers.

Executives are not covered by the Security of Employment Act and their periods of notice are therefore freely negotiable upon recruitment. Notice periods average around two years and are sometimes even longer. It is common practice to pay remuneration during the period of notice in six-monthly tranches to avoid having to reclaim large sums of money if executives find other employment during the notice period.

Recourse to law and compensation

If a dismissal is felt to be unfair, the employee must inform the employer within two weeks of the notice of dismissal. The period is extended to four weeks if the company has not informed the employee of the appeal procedure in the dismissal notice. Negotiations (with union representation if the employee is a member) should then take place within two or four weeks respectively. If agreement cannot be reached, the matter may be taken to court either by the individual employee or by the union. If the employee is working a period of notice, he or she may not be suspended from work because of it, save in exceptional circumstances.

Employers who are found to have effected a dismissal without 'objective grounds' are liable to pay compensation to the employee on a scale set out in the Security of Employment Act, according to age and length of service. Damages are payable only if the employer refuses to reinstate the employee concerned. The amounts are (employees over 60 in parentheses):

- Sixteen (twenty-four) months' pay with less than five years' service.
- Twenty-four (thirty-six) months' pay with between five and ten years' service.
- Thirty-two (forty-eight) months' pay with ten or more years' service.

Collective dismissal

The provisions which apply to collective dismissal are broadly the same as those for individual dismissal, with some further requirements to be taken into account. Firstly, the Security of Employment Act states that, in the event of redundancies 'an employee with a longer period of service is to take priority over an employee of shorter standing'. However, an employer may exempt two employees from this rule. Other orders of priority are permissible; for example, most LO sectoral collective agreements contain a clause which allows parties to negotiate another order of priority at local level. The same is true of the SAF–PTK Security Agreement. This order of priority – *turordning* – will be worked out at the consultations which by law must precede all dismissals.

In addition, any dismissal of five or more employees must be notified to the County Labour Board, the Länsarbetsnämnd, in advance, with the period dependent on the number of proposed dismissals. The rules are:

- Five to twenty-five employees: two months in advance.
- Twenty-six to 100 employees: four months in advance.
- Over 100 employees: six months in advance.

Details must be given of the nature of and reason for the planned job cuts, the date on which they will be carried out and the number of employees involved.

Final formalities

Employers are legally required to provide a certificate of service. If employment has been for a short time, this will be a *anställningsintyg* (certificate of employment), which gives only dates of employment and job description. For longer employment a worker is entitled to a *tjänstgöringsbetyg* (certificate of performance), which in addition provides details of competence and conduct, and the reason for the termination of the contract; however, these may be omitted at the employee's request. Some collective agreements also contain provisions regarding these certificates; for example, the engineering industry white-collar agreement states that the certificate must be provided within five days of a request being made.

A separate certificate showing how many of the statutory twenty-five days' annual leave have been taken must also be provided on request.

Appendix

Non-wage labour costs and income tax rates

Employers pay approximately 31 per cent of gross pay for all employees in statutory charges, with an additional 7 per cent in collectively agreed levies for blue-collar workers and 8.5 per cent for white-collar workers.

Both local and national income tax is payable. The rate of national tax is 20 per cent. The rate of local tax varies between authorities, but is generally between 34 per cent and 27 per cent. Liability depends upon whether annual income is above or below an annually revised yearly threshold (*brytpunkt*). For 1994 this was Skr 198,700 (£17,476).

Income between Skr 8,800 (£776) and the threshold attracts local tax plus a nominal Skr 100 (£8.83) in national tax. Income above the threshold attracts full local and national taxes.

Organisations

Landsorganisation i Sverige, LO
(Swedish Confederation of Trade Unions –
blue-collar)
Barnhusgatan 18, S-105 53 Stockholm
Tel. + 46 8 796 25 00;
fax + 46 8 20 03 58

Tjänstemännens Centralorganisation,
TCO (Central Organisation of Salaried
Employees)
Linnegatan 14, S-114 94 Stockholm
Tel. + 46 8 782 91 00;
fax + 46 8 663 75 20

*Sveriges Akademikers
Centralorganisation*, SACO
(Confederation of Professional
Employees)
Lilla Nygatan 14, S-103 15 Stockholm
Tel. + 46 8 613 48 00;
fax + 46 8 24 77 01

Svenska Arbetsgivareföreningen, SAF
(Swedish Employers' Federation)
Södra Blasieholmshamnen 4A, S-103 30
Stockholm
Tel. + 46 8 762 60 00;
fax + 46 8 762 62 90

Arbetsmarknadsdepartementet (Ministry
of Labour)
Drottninggatan 21, S-103 33 Stockholm
Tel. + 46 8 763 10 00;
fax + 46 8 20 73 69

Main sources

Svenska Arbetsgivareföreningen, *Arbetsgivarens ABC*, Stockholm, 1992.
Svenska Arbetsgivareföreningen, *Företagets sociala kostnader 1994*, Stockholm, 1994.
Runhammar, Urban, and Stare, Peter, *Handbok i arbetsrätt*, Stockholm, 1991.
Sveriges Verkstadsförening and Svenska Metallindustriarbetareförbundet, *Verkstadsavtalet 1993–94*, Stockholm, 1993.
Sveriges Verkstadsförening, Svenska Industritjänstemannaförbundet, Sveriges Arbetsledarförbund and Sveriges Civilingenjörsförbund, *Tjänstemannaavtal 1993–94*, Stockholm, 1993.
Handelns och Tjänsteföretagens Arbetsgivarorganisation and Handelsanställdas-förbund, *Avtal 1993–94*, Stockholm, 1993.

13

Switzerland

Basic rights and labour jurisdiction

The regulation of employment in Switzerland is governed by general principles set out in the federal constitution, federal law, cantonal law and case law. Collective agreements, concluded under the provisions of the Code of Obligations (see below) are legally binding. Individual contracts of employment may either improve on collective agreements or may make wholly independent arrangements, provided no binding collective agreement applies. In addition, company handbooks, custom and practice and in the final analysis the employer's right to direct and control also constitute sources of regulation which may be considered by the courts in the event of a dispute over terms and conditions of employment. In what follows, German names and titles have been used. (Swiss-German is spoken by about 65 per cent of the population. French is spoken by just under 20 per cent, and Italian by 10 per cent. Approximately 1 per cent of the population speak Romansch.)

Swiss employment law offers the contracting parties considerable flexibility. On many issues statutory provisions are not mandatory but allow either deviation, so long as it is to the advantage of the employee, or derogation, by collective or individual agreement, even where this might be to the detriment of the employee.

Federal law comprises:

- The Code of Obligations (*Obligationsrecht*), which is private law setting out the legal foundations for contracts of employment, both collective and individual. There is also separate federal legislation on the extension of collective agreements. As explained below, and depending on the subject, the provisions of the Code of Obligations may be binding absolutely, may be departed from to the benefit of the employee, or may also be departed from to the disadvantage of the employee, subject to a written individual agreement to that effect.
- The Labour Code (*Arbeitsgesetz*), and its associated regulations, which are public law regulating working hours and breaks, protective legislation for young people and women, provisions on company rule books, and special provisions on hours of work in industry and other specific types of establishment.
- There is specific federal legislation covering temporary work (see below), vocational training, employee information rights (see below), sickness and accident insurance, transfer of undertakings and collective dismissal (see below). Legislative proposals in the pipeline or proposed in 1994 included a

355

law on sex equality and a number of amendments to legislation on working hours.

In the period preceding the December 1992 referendum on Swiss membership of the European Economic Area (EEA) a package of measures (known as 'Eurolex') was put forward to bring Swiss law in some areas of employment closer to that of European Union member states. Although the electorate voted against membership of the EEA, a number of the measures were retained and progressed through the legislature under the rubric 'Swisslex'. They include legislation on employee information, a law on collective dismissal, and legislation regulating the transfer of undertakings.

Cantonal law in the employment field is concerned only with procedures in the field of labour jurisdiction, and does not affect substantive matters. However, tax law – in particular taxation of incomes – is determined at cantonal level, and this can affect the design of remuneration schemes (see below).

Contracts of employment

Individual contracts of employment are governed by the Code of Obligations, by the provisions of any applicable collective agreements, and by individual agreement. Under the Code of Obligations certain provisions are absolute, and allow no form of deviation. In addition, and in common with many other jurisdictions, other provisions can be varied by collective or individual agreement, provided it is to the benefit of the employee. Variation of other terms is also permissible, even if it means the individual contract of employment makes less favourable provision than the law (*dispositives Recht*). This makes it difficult to speak of a 'statutory minimum' in many areas of employment, and also explains the great flexibility of employment regulation in Switzerland. Statute law on employee protection, embodied in the Labour Code, is also subject to a wide variety of exemptions, facilitating a high degree of flexibility provided official permission is obtained to depart from the legal minima. Where collective agreements apply – and they are estimated to cover some 40–60 per cent of the workforce – they are binding on signatory parties and may be extended to non-signatory employers (see below; another volume in this series deals with employee relations and collective bargaining).

In addition to the regulatory instrument of law and collective agreement, Swiss law also has the concept of the 'normal' or 'standard' contract of employment (*Normalarbeitsvertrag*). Under this provision, either the cantons or in some cases the federal authorities can draft employment contracts and put them into force by decree for specified employee groups, mostly in branches with weak trade union organisation. The contracts prescribe hours of work arrangements, social benefits, sickness insurance, holidays and other terms of employment. The sections of the Code of Obligations which govern this type of employment contract are amongst those which may be departed from to the disadvantage of the employee, even by oral agreement. However, where no agreement is made the statutory provisions apply. The employee groups covered are mainly in agriculture and domestic employment.

Types of employee

There is no difference in the legal status of salaried and manual employees. In the case of managers, there may be a question of the relationship between the employee and the body which represents the legal personality of the company. Managers are excluded from the provisions of the Labour Code, which regulates hours of work and provides for statutory payments for overtime (see below). Managers are also subject to a more stringent duty of fidelity, both during and after employment, and are more likely to be covered by a restrictive covenant. In general, managerial employees work on ordinary permanent contracts, although they tend to have longer periods of notice and more generous holiday provisions (see below).

Form of contract

Contracts of employment do not, in general, have to take a particular form, and may be implied from the conduct of the parties. However, written contracts are required for apprenticeship agreements, for sales representatives, for employees of temporary employment agencies, and where special provisions are involved, such as restrictive covenants and terms on employee discoveries (see below). Some collective agreements – for example, in the banking sector – may require written contracts.

In practice, most employers conclude written contracts of employment. The contract may consist of a short letter of engagement, setting out the main elements of the employment relationship, together with the company's own handbook and a standard statement of contractual terms. All the documents together are deemed to constitute the contract of employment.

Types of contract of employment

Part-time work   Around 14–15 per cent of the work force are part-timers, with a gentle but steady increase in part-time work since the early 1970s, following rapid expansion during the 1960s. Some 80 per cent of part-timers are women.

Part-time contracts are subject to the Code of Obligations, with no specification of a minimum number of hours to be worked, provided the employment is 'regular'. Moreover, there is also a basic presumption that employees must be treated equally, in the absence of a material reason which would warrant differential treatment. In theory this entitles part-time workers to sick pay, and *pro rata* pay, holidays and other benefits.

Collective agreements may make some supplementary provisions. For example, the agreement in the engineering industry excludes part-timers who work fewer than twelve hours a week from all the provisions of the agreement except for those detailing terms and conditions of employment: that is, they are not covered by provisions on employee participation and training. In the chocolate industry, the terms of the collective agreement only apply to employees who work for at least twenty hours a week.

'Work on call' is generally regarded as a sub-species of part-time work. The main area of application has been in the retail sector.

Fixed-term contracts A fixed-term contract may be concluded when both the start and the finishing point of the contract are clearly identifiable in advance. This does not necessarily mean that a finishing date has to be agreed: a contract may be agreed for a particular task, provided the time of completion can be estimated during the work in question. In contrast, a contract to deputise for a sick employee until they recover would not meet these criteria, and could be deemed to be open-ended.

Successive fixed-term contracts (known as *Kettenarbeitsverträge*), intended to restrict the statutory rights of an employee, could, if contested, be held to constitute a permanent contract. (See also 'Individual termination of contract', below.)

Employment agency workers Temporary agency work is regulated by the 1989 Federal Law on Job Placement and Agency Employment, which came into force on 1 July 1991. Temporary agency workers are employed by the agency, which is responsible for the payment of wages and compliance with other employment and social insurance legislation. The client employer enjoys a right to supervise and direct the employee on their premises. The contract of employment between agency and employee must be in writing, and the law lists those elements which must be specified. Contracts may be permanent or fixed-term. In general, there is no legal difficulty in concluding a series of fixed-term contracts where different client employers are involved: however, repeated fixed-term contracts assigning the employee to the same employer might lead to problems, and to the presumption of a permanent contract between agency and employee. As a rule, employees conclude an outline agreement (*Rahmenvertrag*) with the agency, which sets out basic terms and condition but allows the agency to call them in for particular tasks on an assignment contract (*Einsatzvertrag*). The outline agreement should allow the employee to turn assignments down. Any employment contract which seeks to prevent the employee taking on permanent employment with the client company will be null and void.

There is a trade association for temporary employment agencies (SVUTA) which has a code of conduct and whose members are covered by a collective agreement concluded with the white-collar union, the Schweizerischer Kaufmännischer Verband. This specifies minimum requirements on periods of notice, holidays and other time off, overtime and weekend/holiday work compensation, sick pay and other social benefits. Beyond this, agency employees will be covered by any other collective agreement applicable to a client company. (A fuller treatment of agency employment is to be found in another volume in this series on recruitment, training and development.)

Collective agreements and individual contracts of employment   Approximately 40–60 per cent of the labour force is covered by collective agreement. The coverage of the work force of signatory employers in particular industries may be regulated by the collective agreements themselves. For example, the agreement in the engineering industry covers 'all employees of member companies of the Swiss Engineering Employers' Federation in Switzerland . . . How the agreement is to be applied to managerial employees is to be regulated in member companies.' In some companies this local regulation may embrace a provision that no more than a set percentage of the work force may be outside the scope of the collective agreement.

Collective agreements may not breach inalienable federal or cantonal law, but may improve upon it where appropriate. Collective agreements themselves are directly binding and legally enforceable as far as signatory organisations are concerned, and may be departed from only where it benefits employees or if the agreement expressly provides for derogation. Collective agreements may also be extended to cover non-signatory employers, provided certain minimum criteria of representativeness are met. In addition, individual employers can adopt the terms of a collective agreement, with the permission of the negotiating parties, and become parties to it. Where an employer extends a collective agreement to employees who are not trade union members, provision may be made to collect 'solidarity contributions' from the employees to meet trade union concern about 'free riders'. For example, in the collective agreement for the engineering industry, non-trade union members covered by the agreement pay SFr 5 (£2.45) a month into a special fund, which may be used for social purposes. (For administrative convenience trade union members also pay into the fund.) (Collective bargaining and collective agreements are dealt with more fully in another volume in this series on employee relations and collective bargaining.)

The substantive provisions of collective agreements on terms and conditions of employment are set out in the relevant sections below. These form part of the individual contract of employment via incorporation but are directly enforceable without this provision.

Probationary periods

Probationary periods may be concluded. Under article 335 of the Code of Obligations, employment can be terminated during a probationary period upon notice of seven days. This may be extended, in some instances as long as two weeks. In general, the first month of an indefinite contract is regarded as a probationary period in the absence of any specific agreement. The period may be lengthened by written individual agreement or by collective agreement but may not exceed three months (unless sickness or the fulfilment of a statutory duty reduces the period of actual employment).

Restrictive covenants and confidentiality

During employment, employees may not engage in any other employment which would constitute a breach of their contractual duty of fidelity, especially if it entails direct competition with the current employer. Employees may not divulge technical or commercial secrets obtained in the course of employment, and are required to maintain confidentiality after employment where this is in the reasonable interest of the employer. Company handbooks may set out more specific rules, relevant to particular industries (such as regulations on financial transactions), and the penalties for infringement may be severe. For example, bank employees who breach professional secrecy may not only be dismissed but also prosecuted under the Penal Code, fined and imprisoned. Insider dealing is also punishable under article 161 of the Penal Code.

In some cases the employer's permission must be obtained before an employee takes on any form of paid work for another party, or seeks public office – although the latter may be refused only in exceptional circumstances.

Company handbooks may contain very tightly worded injunctions on employees not to disclose any material about the business, including details of employees' pay.

Restrictive covenants for the period after employment are governed by article 340 of the Code of Obligations. Some clauses are mandatory, others may be altered only to the benefit of the employee, and others are open to negotiation between the parties. Restrictive covenants must be in writing and must be specific as to region, period and scope. Unless otherwise individually agreed, such a restrictive covenant is valid only if the employee concerned has had access to the employing organisation's regular customers or to technical, commercial and business secrets, and the disclosure of such information could substantially harm the interests of the former employer.

Restrictive covenants must meet criteria of reasonableness as far as location (which may extend beyond national borders), period and scope are concerned: in general, scope and duration should be in inverse relation. The courts have intervened to shorten the duration of covenants which they regarded as too long for employees not in senior positions. In general, a restrictive covenant must not unfairly impede the professional advancement of the employee. The difficulty of enforcing covenants because of past court interpretations of this latter provision has led many companies to avoid them. They may exceed three years only under exceptional circumstances. The courts may curtail any covenant which they deem to be excessively restrictive, subject to the compensation paid to the employee.

The law provides either for the payment of damages or for some other penalty specified in the contract itself.

A restrictive covenant will lapse if the employer no longer has a justifiable interest in its maintenance or if the employer dismisses the employee without good cause (including constructive dismissal).

Workplace discipline

Under article 321(d) of the Code of Obligations, the employer may issue general regulations on the conduct of employees as well as specific instructions. Employees are required, by law, to comply with general regulations and specific instructions in good faith. The Labour Code requires industrial undertakings to draw up a company handbook (*Betriebsordnung*). Non-industrial organisations can issue regulations, and any firm can do so voluntarily. Company handbooks must be agreed in writing between management and elected employee representatives, but may also be issued unilaterally by the employer after consultation with the work force. (Employee representation is dealt with in another volume in this series, covering employee relations and collective bargaining.) Once agreed, they are binding on both parties. Company handbooks must include provisions on health, safety and accident prevention, and may also contain rules on employee conduct and set out penalties for infringement. In general, penalties for employee misconduct, which may include fines, will be lawful only if they are specified in a written handbook. Where employees are unfit for work, or their conduct is prejudicial to the operation of the business, they may be suspended (without pay). Handbooks may not violate mandatory statute law or the provisions of any collective agreement. Company handbooks must be submitted to the relevant cantonal authorities for inspection: the authorities can amend them where any contravention of law or collective agreement is found.

General disciplinary principles, for example on non-competition during employment, may also be included in collective agreements.

Individual employee rights

Employers are under a statutory injunction to respect and protect the person of the employee, and to take all appropriate and reasonable measures to safeguard employees' health and safety at work. Under this general duty of care employers may not, for example, bug employees' telephones or release information to third parties which is not on the employee's employment certificate (*Zeugnis*).

Under legislation introduced in 1993 (article 328(b) of the Code of Obligations) employers may process data on employees only where they are relevant to assessing their suitability for the position or to carry out the terms of the contract of employment. General data protection legislation, introduced in 1992, also regulates the storage and use of information on individuals. Company handbooks typically grant employees access to their files.

Individual employee rights may also be dealt with by collective agreement.

For example, in addition to clauses on equal opportunities for women (see below), the collective agreement for the engineering industry lays down a number of basic principles on the protection of the individual employee. These commit 'managers and work-force representatives to work together to create a climate of personal respect and trust which will prevent abuses, excesses and sexual harassment'. Under the agreement, employee representatives must be consulted over proposals to introduce systems of electronic monitoring of the movement of employees. Systems intended solely to control and exercise surveillance over the conduct of employees in the workplace may not be installed.

There is a general constitutional principle of equal treatment for all employees, above and beyond sex equality, which forbids arbitrary and unequal treatment. For example, an annual bonus would need to be paid to all employees unless the employer had a material reason to act selectively. However, the extensive individualisation of pay and the lack of an open culture on pay issues, combined with freedom of contract, mean that making comparability claims could be very difficult for employees.

Under a regulation implementing the Labour Code, employers are required to ensure that, subject to the limitations of their premises, non-smokers should not be inconvenienced by the smoke of others. This provision is often written into company handbooks. However, no-smoking policies are rare, and as yet there have been no court cases to determine whether an employee has an enforceable right to a smoke-free environment or whether employees can continue to claim their pay but refuse to work until it is provided. There is a No Smoking Association (Arbeitsgemeinschaft Nichtrauchen) which can offer advice.

Grievance procedures

Grievance procedures may be outlined either in company handbooks or collective agreements. They may be used to resolve both individual and collective differences. In some industries, conciliation committees and arbitration tribunals are established by collective agreement, often in the latter case in conjunction with the public arbitration authorities. These offer a final recourse when scope at the place of work has been exhausted.

Employment terms and conditions

Statutory provisions on a number of aspects of terms and conditions of employment, in particular health and safety and working hours, are set out in the Labour Code and its associated regulations. The code applies to the vast bulk of commercial and industrial businesses in the private sector. It excludes sales representatives, academics, artists and senior managers. The law is complex because of the special provisions for individual types of establishment and the large number of possible exemptions which may be applied for in the area of working hours.

Hours of work

As the statutory and agreed provisions set out below indicate, Switzerland has the longest working week and working year in Western Europe, amongst the OECD countries exceeded only by Japan and the United States. In 1992, for example, according to a study carried out by the German employers' confederation, the BDA, average agreed hours in manufacturing were 1,865 a year, compared with 1,777 in the United Kingdom, 1,667 in Germany and 1,912 in the United States.

At the time of writing, legislation was in the pipeline to amend the law governing hours of work, in particular to allow night work for women, backed up by improved health and safety procedures for all shift workers, and to introduce scope for greater flexibility in working hours.

Working week   The statutory maximum working week in industrial establishments, for office staff and in large retail establishments with more than fifty employees is forty-five hours: for all other employees it is fifty hours. This maximum can be raised by four hours with official permission in workplaces with pronounced seasonal business fluctuations, provided the annual maximum is not exceeded. Other extensions may be granted to meet peak work needs, with shorter reference periods: in retailing, for example, the reference period for achieving the average is twelve successive weeks.

The working day may not start before 05.00 in summer or 06.00 in winter, and must finish by 20.00. Both limits may be altered with the permission of the Federal Labour Office (BIGA) in the case of industrial workplaces, or of the cantonal authorities in other cases.

In practice, collectively agreed and customary hours are shorter than the statutory maximum. The agreement in the engineering industry, for example, establishes a forty-hour week, and also sets out a number of flexibility options (see below). Companies newly joining the engineering employers' association, the ASM (*Arbeitgeberverband der Schweizer Maschinenindustrie*), and working more than forty hours a week have a five-year period in which to bring their weekly hours into line with the provisions of the agreement. In times of exceptional economic difficulty firms may depart from agreed provisions with the agreement of employee representatives or, in the absence of a formal structure, following an employee ballot. A forty-two-hour week is common in services, including the financial sector. In the hotel and catering sector the standard week is forty-two hours, which may be increased to forty-five in small establishments. There is some slight movement towards cuts in hours but not on the scale seen elsewhere in Western Europe. For example, the chocolate industry has moved from a forty-one to a forty-hour week from 1 January 1994.

Under the provisions of some collective agreements, employee representatives are granted co-determination rights on the introduction of certain forms of flexible working or other departures from normal working hours.

Breaks   The Labour Code prescribes a minimum unpaid break of fifteen minutes, to be inserted into a working day of five and a half hours or more, thirty minutes for a working day of at least seven hours, and sixty minutes where the working day exceeds nine hours. If the employee cannot leave the immediate work area the break must be paid. However, paid breaks as a matter of course are rare in Switzerland. The customary lunch break is forty-five minutes.

Working time flexibility   Flexitime is very common in both offices and factories, and in all is estimated to embrace some 20 per cent of the work force. The practice is most common in larger workplaces, where it tends to be offered not only to administrative employees but also to production workers.

   Subject to statutory and/or agreed provisions on start and finish times, and the maximum working day or week, there is no legal restriction on the structuring of working hours with flexitime or the introduction of annual hours systems. For example, the agreement on flexible hours in the engineering industry specifies a maximum working week of forty-five hours and a minimum week of thirty hours. (That is, overtime is payable after forty-five hours, and the employee has no obligation to work out any hours below thirty.) The longest permissible reference period is one year, and no more than forty hours may be counted as a time debit or credit. More typically, monthly-based flexitime systems provide for a maximum plus or minus of fifteen hours.

Overtime, night and shift work

There are two understandings of overtime. Hours in excess of the statutory working week are termed *Überzeit*. This is subject to a statutory minimum overtime supplement of 25 per cent of usual rates, and employees may not work more than 260 hours of excess hours a year.

   'Overtime' (*Überstunden*) is work beyond agreed working hours. According to the Code of Obligations, employees may normally be required to work overtime when requested to do so. In most instances, overtime is also paid at 125 per cent of normal rates. Collective agreements frequently allow the parties to agree for overtime to be compensated by time off in lieu.

   Both night work and shift work are subject to official authorisation from the cantonal authorities under the provisions of the Labour Code. Night work, defined as work between 20.00 and 05.00 in summer and between 20.00 and 06.00 in winter, is allowed on a temporary basis, subject to a demonstration of 'urgent need'. For longer-term or regular night work the employer must prove that it is technically or economically indispensable.

   The permission of the cantonal authorities is required for the introduction of two- or three-shift systems, and is subject to limits on individual working hours of nine hours in any twenty-four-hour period. Shift work is allowed on both technical and economic grounds. Workers on shifts must be able to change their shift pattern every six weeks.

Sunday and holiday work

Sunday work is regulated via a blanket ban, but with scope for extensive exemptions. Public holidays are treated as Sundays for statutory purposes. As with night and shift work, Sunday work is permissible on both technical and economic grounds.

Time off

Annual leave

There is a statutory minimum of four weeks' holiday per year for adult employees, and five weeks' for employees aged under 20. Leave must normally be taken in the year in which it is due, and at least two weeks must be taken together. Pay cannot be taken in lieu of this minimum period of leave. Moreover, employees who work during their holidays and who harm the legitimate interests of the employer may forfeit the right to holiday pay (see below).

In practice, holiday entitlement is governed by collective agreement, or by individual contract – often subject to a company's own policies, as set out in its handbook. In both cases, additional leave is usually granted by age and status.

The collective agreement in the engineering industry grants, as from 1 January 1995, a minimum of twenty-two days for employees aged 20–9, rising to twenty-four days at age 40, and thirty days for employees aged 60 or over. Apprentices are granted seven weeks in their first year, falling to five weeks in the third and fourth year of apprenticeship.

Senior employees typically get longer holidays, for their age group, than other grades, and may reach the maximum holiday entitlement usually found in Switzerland of thirty days a few years earlier. Additional holiday may also be granted to employees with arduous or uncongenial working environments.

Holiday entitlement may be cut for lengthy absences for sickness and because of pregnancy.

Public holidays

According to the Labour Code, each canton may grant a maximum of eight public holidays, which for labour law purposes are regarded as a Sunday. Public holidays differ from canton to canton, and there may even be local variations within cantons. The main religious holidays of Good Friday, Easter Monday, Ascension Day, Whit Monday, Christmas Day and Boxing Day, together with New Year's Day, are celebrated throughout Switzerland. In addition, individual employees may take a religious holiday even if it is not granted in the canton in which they work, provided they inform the employer, who may require them to make up the time lost.

Collective agreements may either specify particular public holidays or set a minimum number which employers must allow. In the engineering industry, for example, this is nine days, with extra days allowed by companies, depending on location. In some agreements a maximum number of public holidays is prescribed, in accordance with public law.

In Zurich, for example, in addition to the religious holidays noted above, employees may be granted 2 January (*Berchtoldstag*), 1 May, 1 August (*Bundesfeier*) and *Sechseläuten*, a festival held on the third Monday in April. Collective agreements may leave the choice of days up to local managements and employee representatives, within a given total.

Sickness absence and sick pay

There is a statutory right to continued payment of wages for absence due to illness or other cause where the employee is not to blame (article 324a, Code of Obligations). It requires the employer to pay the employee for at least three weeks during the first year of employment, subject to a qualifying period of three months' service: a longer period may be provided for by individual or collective agreement. After the first year, the law says that pay should continue in cases of illness 'for an appropriate period' which may be set by individual or collective agreement. What is deemed 'appropriate' is set by various scales, relating sick pay to service, which have been proposed by the courts in different cantons and regions. There are three scales: Basle, Berne and Zurich. The Basle scale, for example, provides for periods of sick pay as in Table 4.

Table 4   *Basle sick pay scale*

Length of service (years)	Duration of sick pay
In first year	3 weeks
1–3	2 months
3–10	3 months
10–15	4 months
15–20	5 months
20+	6 months

There is no system of statutory sickness benefit once entitlement to sick pay has expired. Access to sickness benefit is via private insurance, which can be organised in various ways. A number of options are available, some of which deal only with the period after the expiry of sick pay, whilst others deal with the entire period of sickness. Collective agreements may offer companies a number of possibilities through which they can meet their minimum statutory requirements and contribute to a benefit scheme. Where no other provision exists, individual employees take out a personal insurance policy so as to receive a daily sum if they fall ill. Employers may organise a collective scheme with varying contribution regimes – sometimes contributory for the employee, with an employer element, and in other cases wholly financed by the employer. Where a group scheme is available, premiums are generally lower. Such schemes may be mandatory under collective agreements. Under the engineering agreement, for example, employers must insure their employees so as to provide 80 per cent of normal pay for 720 days, financed by a contribution equal to 2 per cent of pay. This is topped up to full pay for a minimum period in accordance with a sick-pay scale similar to the Basle scale.

Insurance against industrial accidents is mandatory for the employer. Benefits paid out include full pay.

Maternity, paternity and parental leave

Absence due to pregnancy or birth is treated in the same way as sickness absence. Once pregnancy is established, a pregnant employee may be absent from work without a doctor's certificate provided she informs her employer. Following the birth, mothers may take leave for a period of eight weeks, which may be reduced to six weeks should the woman wish it and provided a doctor confirms that she is fit for work. Payment is as for sickness, and the period of paid leave will be reduced by any preceding periods of sick leave during the same year. Nursing mothers are also entitled to time off for feeding.

Maternity leave may be provided for by collective agreement. In the engineering industry, mothers with at least ten months' service are entitled to fourteen weeks' leave on full pay, to begin no earlier than four weeks before the expected date of confinement.

Other time off

Additional time off for personal or family needs is typically provided for in collective agreements and/or at company level. Typical provisions would include: two days for marriage, a day for the birth or marriage of a child, up to three days for the death of a spouse, a child, a parent or other close relative, three days for the care of a member of the family.

Employee representatives may be entitled to time off either to carry out their duties or for training and education. The collective agreement in the engineering industry, for example, grants four days' paid training leave a year to employee representatives. Employees who are elected members of trade union bodies are also given paid time off to attend meetings, up to a maximum of three days a year.

Military service

The Swiss army is based on the notion of an armed citizenry and can make extensive demands on employees' time. Military service is compulsory for all men from the age of 20. The initial requirement is for a period of basic training, lasting seventeen weeks. After that, there are eight three-week periods of training which have to be completed by the age of 32. Further training continues until the age of 42 for most individuals, but officers may be called on until the age of 50. There are plans to cut the overall period of training from 1995, with an effective end of military obligations at age 32.

The pay and employment status of those called up for military service are protected under legislation most recently amended in 1988. Employers are required to free employees called upon by the military and pay them at least 80 per cent of their previous earnings whilst on leave. Dismissal during or for a period after military service is also forbidden, and any such dismissal will be null and void. Collective agreements may also grant additional days off with pay for weapons inspection, recruitment or the return of military equipment. Continued payment of wage or salary is also typically governed by collective agreement, company regulations or the individual contract. Some employers may find it irksome to release a senior manager who is also an officer, and, given equally qualified candidates, this may affect recruitment. Conversely, in some sectors – by tradition in banking – there has been a predisposition to build a managerial cadre around officers.

Pay and benefits

There is no statutory minimum wage or system of pay indexation. Minimum pay rates specified in some collective agreements may be binding on companies who are not members of signatory organisations through the procedure of 'extension' (*Allgemeinverbindlicherklärung*), under which the authorities can declare a collective agreement to be 'generally binding'. Such arrangements apply in a few sectors, notably small firms in engineering and in the hotel and catering trade.

Swiss pay and labour costs are among the highest in the world, offset by high productivity levels and the attractions and efficiency of the country as a business location. Non-material factors are also considered important, and Switzerland has a high index of job satisfaction.

Law on pay

Unless otherwise agreed, the Code of Obligations requires pay to be monthly. Payment must be in cash, paid during working hours, unless otherwise agreed. An itemised statement must be provided. However, employees may not be obliged to accept the employer's products as compensation.

Employees on piecework must be given sufficient work to ensure a monthly salary either comparable with that of employees on time rates or in line with their previous piecework earnings.

Employees with a contractual entitlement to a portion of the employer's profit or turnover must be granted access to the company's profit and loss account or other documentation, where necessary to establish profit or turnover levels. Employees working on a commission basis are covered by special provisions which entitle them to a written statement from the employer at each date when payments fall due.

Pay setting

Pay may be set individually or within the framework of a collective agreement. There are no precise figures of coverage by collective agreement in Switzerland, but the percentage of the work force embraced is estimated at 40–60 per cent. However, the forms of pay determination by collective agreement are very diverse, and the mechanisms vary greatly from industry to industry both as regards the category of employee covered and the form in which pay levels are specified, if they are at all. For example, whereas the collective agreement for the chocolate industry sets out minimum pay rates for different employee grades, and the agreement in the banking industry specifies broad pay bands with minima and maxima for four 'functional groups', the agreement in the engineering industry specifies no pay rates at all, stating only that 'Pay shall be determined individually between employer and employee.' (A detailed account of collective bargaining can be found in another volume in this series, on employee relations and collective bargaining.)

The culture of pay is felt to involve a high degree of confidentiality in a context where, at workplace level, pay may be individually determined both for white-collar and, in some companies, for blue-collar employees.

Employers' associations, such as the engineering employers' federation, the ASM, provide member companies with information on pay levels by function, and there are remuneration networks of personnel managers. Where collective agreements specify minimum levels, companies typically pay in excess. One prime concern emphasised by practitioners is the desire to create an element of remuneration which is at the employer's discretion and which can be used to implement merit pay or structure other forms of incentive.

Make-up of the pay package

Seniority can be an important element in determining basic pay, and where collective agreements set out applicable rates they frequently include a set of minimum service-related increments. In the chocolate industry, for example, this extends as far as twenty-five years of service. However, in this instance the absolute levels of service supplements are not large: for example, a worker with ten years' service will receive a monthly supplement of SFr 130 (£61) on a typical skilled worker's monthly pay of SFr 4,500 (£2,122).

A thirteenth month's pay is universal, and is usually simply arrived at by dividing the annual salary into thirteen components. As such it is a fixed part of remuneration and may not be revoked. In some instances, the thirteenth month may be paid as an extra month's basic pay (contractual pay), including seniority and 'household' allowances, but excluding other supplements (such as shift allowances, child allowances and performance-related bonuses).

Child allowances (also termed family or educational allowances) are payable by the employer under cantonal law and usually range from SFr 100 (£47) to SFr 150 (£71) a month. Collective agreements may specify a minimum amount; in the engineering industry it is SFr 150 per month. In some firms and industries a 'household' allowance is payable to employees with responsibilities for dependants. A typical sum might be SFr 30 (£14) a month.

In addition to setting minimum pay levels, collective agreements may also prescribe mechanisms or guidelines for appraisal and the use of any scope for flexibility. For example, the banking agreement sets out minima and maxima for its grades, outlines the percentage of the work force which should be included in each grade and how much of the overall scope for pay differentials should be utilised for each group.

Pay increases and merit pay

Most collective agreements require annual negotiations, usually expressly tied to offsetting consumer price inflation. Additional reviews at company level are carried out along very diverse principles, and may incorporate any collectively agreed increases. There is extensive scope for managerial discretion, and the criteria on which increases are awarded may not always be transparent, although seniority plays a major role in increases to basic pay. Explicitly performance-related pay is growing, as is the tendency to award non-consolidated bonuses: however, tight labour markets in the past have held back both these instruments, as well as frequently upsetting established seniority-based pay.

Overtime, night work and shift pay

Overtime is remunerated in line with the provisions outlined earlier under the same heading – that is, at 25 per cent in addition to normal rates. In many cases there is provision for time off as compensation by agreement. Managers, who are not subject to the Labour Code, may be granted other forms of overtime compensation which are not directly related to the actual time worked in addition to normal hours.

Sunday, holiday and weekend working

Regulations on weekend working are set out above. By law, work on Sunday must be compensated for by at least a 50 per cent supplement to normal rates. Some collective agreements may increase this, in some instances to 75 per cent of normal rates.

Financial participation

Swiss corporations may issue shares or, in the case of non-quoted private limited companies, quasi-equity forms of capital participation to their employees. Under a 1992 amendment of the Corporations Act (*Aktiengesetz*), corporations (*Aktiengesellschaften*) can normally hold up to 10 per cent of their own stock, and in some cases 20 per cent, which may be used for distribution to employees. The precise taxation regime varies between cantons, which levy both income tax on the difference between any preferential price and market value and wealth tax on shareholdings. There is a discount rate on the taxable amount which varies according to the length of time shares are blocked (see below) or, in share option schemes, on the holding period. Social security contributions are payable by employer and employee on the difference between the preferential price and the actual price when the employee has access to the shares.

A typical scheme might be open to all employees, including part-timers meeting a minimum threshold and those on fixed-term contracts. Schemes may offer employees a standard number of shares at a preferential price each year, with an additional number based on length of service: the quantity typically rises steeply with seniority. Senior employees may also enjoy enhanced rights under the plan. Shares are frozen for five years before disposal is possible, although employees have access to dividends.

Share option plans are common, but by no means universal, for top and senior management. Top managers of foreign-owned companies will typically be covered by global stock option plans, offering shares in the parent company.

Main employee benefits

The most important non-pay benefits provided by employers are supplementary pensions (see below) and membership of group insurance schemes to maintain income during sickness, as well as the customary life and dependants' assurance.

Managerial pay

Swiss managers are amongst the highest paid in the world, both in cash and in real terms, and regularly head the lists of international managerial salary comparisons. The past two decades have seen a spread of cash bonuses as a means of rewarding performance, although long-term financial participation through share ownership is less prevalent. The Monks Partnership survey *Incentives and Benefits in Europe 1993–4* found that over 95 per cent of top and senior managers received cash bonuses, with the emphasis on job-related measures of performance rather than a direct relationship to profit or cash flow. Around 40 per cent of executives surveyed received a bonus worth 20 per cent or more of base salary. In contrast, the survey found that only 58 per cent of top managers were involved in a share option scheme, fairly low in international terms.

There are regional pay differences, but they are not particularly large. The Zurich area, with its concentration of manufacturing industry and banking, and Basle, with its highly internationalised chemical undertakings, are high-cost and higher-paying regions.

The most usual benefits include life and dependants' assurance and long-term health insurance. Ordinary employee benefits, such as sick pay and holidays, may also be made available on a more generous scale. For example, the period of sick pay entitlement for non-managerial employees may be doubled for senior staff.

Car provision is low by European standards at all levels of management, but trails off markedly below top management. According to the Monks Partnership survey of company cars in Europe, around 74 per cent of top managers were given a car, but only 30–40 per cent of function heads.

Equal opportunities

Legislation in the pipeline during 1994 set out to assure equal treatment in the areas of recruitment, work allocation, pay, training and dismissal. The law also requires employers to ensure that no employee is the victim of sexual harassment, and gives employees the right to proceed as if discriminated against should the employer fail to take measures to stop acts of harassment. The main area of innovation is seen as enabling cases to be brought, since the underlying principle of equal treatment is already enshrined in Swiss law. In particular, the new law would allow class actions to be taken up by organisations set up to promote sex equality, establish conciliation mechanisms at cantonal level, and place the burden of proof on employers to demonstrate that they had not behaved in a discriminatory way. Women who wished to proceed against their employer would be protected from dismissal during the proceedings and for six months afterwards.

Retirement

Retirement age is 65 for men and 62 for women, but legislation was proposed in June 1994 which would raise the retirement age for women in stages from 2001 to 64 by 2005. Legislation was also passed on vesting and transferability of benefits under occupational schemes in December 1993 to enhance the position of employees leaving schemes early, and to allow scheme members to withdraw some of their benefits to buy a home.

Retirement income is made up of three components (the so-called 'three pillars').

- The first pillar consists of the pension provided under the statutory social security system. This provides benefits in the event of retirement, disability or death.

The basic pension is calculated on the basis of revalued career earnings, subject to an upper limit, with a full pension payable after forty-four contribution years.

• The second pillar is funded occupational schemes, which have been mandatory for employers since 1985. Occupational schemes are required to meet statutory minimum limits, but may offer benefits in excess of the minimum. Reckonable earnings begin at the social security maximum reckonable income (in 1994, SFr 22,560 (£10,642)) and extend up to SFr 67,680 (£31,925). The accepted principle is that the compulsory elements of the state and occupational schemes should provide a retirement income of some 60 per cent of final earnings.

• The third pillar is individual provision, encouraged by a favourable tax regime.

Individual termination of contract

New provisions on individual dismissals came into force on 1 January 1989, in general improving the protection of the individual employee from 'abusive' – in UK terms, 'unfair' – dismissal. Collective agreements at industry level may make provision in a number of areas related to dismissal which will have the force of law. There are no specific procedures for individual economic dismissal which differentiates it from dismissal on grounds of conduct or factors related to the individual employee. However, legislation on collective dismissal was introduced in December 1993 as part of preparations for entry to the European Economic Area (see below). However, a referendum failed to secure approval of entry, although the legislation harmonising Swiss and EU provisions in some areas was put on the statute book.

Termination by mutual agreement

Termination by mutual agreement is possible at any time, and there is no prescribed form which such a procedure should take.

Termination of a fixed-term contract

Under article 334 of the Code of Obligations, a fixed-term contract ends, without notice of dismissal, at the due date, unless the parties agree otherwise. The parties are free to conclude other arrangements if they wish: these might include a probationary period, a right to issue notice before the final date specified in the contract, or a dual approach under which a contract may be fixed and irrevocable for an initial period, then subject to ordinary dismissal (see below). If a fixed-term contract continues to be honoured by both parties after the agreed date of termination it will be deemed to be open-ended. After ten years either party to a long-term fixed-term agreement may terminate it, subject to six months' notice.

Dismissal

The 1989 amendments of dismissal law concretised the protection of employer and employee by listing the circumstances under which notice to terminate the contract would be 'abusive' (*missbräuchlich*). (See below, 'Abusive dismissal'.) Apart from these grounds, which are illustrative rather than exhaustive under the law, together with certain specially protected instances, dismissal with notice is permitted on grounds of the employee's conduct or personal character, and on economic grounds, with no special procedure in the latter case in the event of individual termination. However, there are circumstances in which notice to terminate will be null and void, as indicated below.

Dismissal on grounds of the character of the individual is permissible, except for those factors outlined under 'Abusive dismissal' below. Termination on reaching pensionable age is permitted, or at any other age prescribed as a limit for certain tasks. Termination on grounds of sickness is allowed, subject to the limits set out in the Code of Obligations. The Code states that any notice issued during a period of sickness lasting less than thirty days in the first year of service, ninety days from the second year to the fifth, and 180 days after the sixth year will be null and void. Similarly any termination during pregnancy or for sixteen weeks after confinement is null and void. Notice issued before sickness is suspended for the periods set out above.

Dismissal on grounds of employee conduct is permissible, where the conduct disturbs 'co-operation at the workplace' or entails a breach of duties under the employment contract. If sufficiently serious, misconduct may warrant summary dismissal. Any notice given to an employee on military service, or in service with the Red Cross or civil defence, will be null and void for four weeks beforehand and subsequently.

Employment can be ended on economic grounds in individual instances without special procedures; however, the law allows shorter periods of notice for the employee, should the employer indicate that economic dismissals are possible (see also below).

Summary dismissal

Termination without notice is allowed to both parties for 'an important reason', and must be justified in writing if the other party so requests. The law states that any such reason must be such as to render it unreasonable to expect the party giving notice to continue the employment relationship. Following case law, this could include:

- Repeated refusal to work, despite clear instruction and warnings that employment will be terminated without notice, and in some instances a single refusal

to work when requested (including a refusal of overtime), where urgent work is involved.
- Accepting bribes.
- Repeated drunkenness or incapacity through drugs.
- Repeated lateness or unexplained absence.
- Criminal offences may warrant summary dismissal if they directly prejudice employment (such as embezzlement of customers, violence at the workplace).

Collective agreements may cite particular circumstances which would warrant summary dismissal (such as breaching confidentiality in the banking sector).

The law recognises constructive dismissal by granting the possibility of compensation should the employer be guilty of conduct which breaches the contract of employment.

Although there is no statutory requirement for warnings to be given, the courts would expect the employer to have pointed out the incompatibility of the employee's behaviour with continuing employment and, where appropriate, to have given some scope for rectification.

If the employer dismisses an employee without notice and without an important reason, the employee is entitled to a sum equal to what they would have earned had the contractual notice been worked out or had the contract continued to its agreed end. In such cases the employee must deduct any sums earned elsewhere and any expenses saved during this period. In addition, a court may require the employer to pay compensation up to a maximum of six months' pay.

An employee who terminates the contract without notice and without good reason may be liable to pay the employer a quarter of one month's wages, notwithstanding any claims for other losses.

Periods of notice and form of dismissal

Minimum periods of notice are set out in the Code of Obligations. According to article 335 there is a minimum notice period of seven days during a probationary period. This increases to one month in the first year of service, to two months in the second and up to the ninth year, and to three months thereafter. Unless otherwise agreed, the law requires that periods of notice should be equal for employer and employee. In the event of an agreement which contradicts this, the longer period of notice should apply. However, if the employer has indicated that notice of dismissal may be given on economic grounds, a shorter period of notice may be agreed for employees.

Notice may be given verbally or in writing, subject to individual or collective agreement, with the latter usually requiring written notice. The grounds for dismissal must be given in writing, should the other party request it. Notice must be given to finish at the end of a calendar month.

Periods of notice different from the statutory provisions may be set by collective agreement or individual contract, but in any event a different period must be agreed in writing. Under the Code of Obligations, however, a notice period of less than one month may be provided for only by collective agreement, and only during the first year of service.

Severance payments

Severance payments (*Abgangsentschädigung*) are due to long-service employees by law. Improvements may be made by collective or individual agreement. Under the law, an employee with twenty or more years of service who is at least fifty years old is entitled to severance compensation of at least two months' pay. If no individual or collectively agreed sum is specified, severance compensation may be set by the courts but may not exceed eight months' pay. Compensation may be reduced or cancelled in the event of summary dismissal.

Abusive (unfair) dismissal and appeals

Dismissal will be deemed 'abusive' if it is based on any of the following grounds, as set out in the Code of Obligations and subject to interpretation by the courts. In the instances below it is the employee who is referred to, but the same legal position applies to any notice of termination given by the employee. The factors are:

- Grounds related to a characteristic of the employee which is related to their individual person, unless this characteristic is closely related to the employment relation or is seriously prejudicial to co-operation in the workplace. In general, this excludes dismissal on grounds of sex, race, family status, age, political or religious opinions, sexuality or criminal penalties which have no bearing on employment.
- Because the employee is exercising a constitutional right, unless it entails breaching an obligation under the employment contract or is prejudicial to co-operation in the workplace.
- To frustrate the employee's rights under the employment relationship.
- Because the employee is claiming an entitlement under the employment relationship in good faith.
- Because the employee is carrying out military or other compulsory civic duties.

Moreover, any dismissal on grounds of trade union membership or activity, or of participation in employee representation at the workplace, is also deemed to be abusive. Collective agreements may also establish special procedures in the event of the dismissal of an employee representative, allowing for consultation on the issue with established workplace representatives.

The employee must formally contest the dismissal in writing before the expiry of notice. If no agreement on a continuation of employment is reached, the dismissed person can claim compensation, the claim to be submitted within

180 days of the end of the employment relationship. There is no right to continued employment pending proceedings.

The administration of the system of justice is a matter for cantonal law, although on labour matters the federal government has laid down mandatory procedural rules to ensure speedy and inexpensive treatment in labour tribunals in cases where the sum at issue does not exceed SFr 20,000 (£9,434). Above that sum, the usual civil courts are responsible, with the option of appeal to the federal courts.

Compensation in the event of abusive dismissal is set by the courts in the light of all the relevant circumstances. However, it may not exceed six months' pay. There is no right to reinstatement.

Collective dismissal

Legislation regulating collective dismissal was passed in December 1993, amending articles 335 and 336 of the Code of Obligations. Under the new provisions collective dismissal is defined as economic dismissals over a period of thirty days affecting:

- At least ten employees in establishments usually employing more than twenty and fewer than 100 employees.
- At least 10 per cent of the work force in establishments usually employing at least 100 and fewer than 300 employees.
- At least thirty employees in establishments with at least 300 employees.

The law requires the employer to consult employee representatives or, if none has been elected, individual employees. (Legislation on employee representation was passed on the same date as the law on collective dismissal: details of representation and negotiating arrangements are set out in the volume in this series on employee relations and collective bargaining.) The work force must be given the opportunity to put forward proposals as to how the dismissals could be avoided, their number reduced, and the consequences mitigated for those affected.

The employer must also give either employee representatives or the work force directly all pertinent information, and specifically in writing:

- The reasons for the dismissals.
- The number of employees affected.
- The usual number of employees in the work force.
- The period over which dismissals will take place.

A copy must be forwarded to the cantonal labour authorities. In addition, the employer must inform the cantonal authorities about the consequences of employee consultation: in turn, the authorities are required to look for solutions to any problems created by the dismissals. Employment for those affected ends thirty days after the authorities have been notified, unless a collective agreement or individual employment contract provides for a longer notice period.

Collective agreements may set out consultation procedures in the event of economic dismissal. For example, the agreement for the engineering industry requires all parties to avoid or mitigate any hardship arising out of economic dismissal or major restructuring. In addition to observing statutory regulations, there is a duty to consider measures to provide alternative employment, offer retraining and out-placement, lengthen or shorten periods of notice, offer early retirement, make payments from company provident funds to ease hardship, lift restrictive covenants, accommodate employee needs on such issues as company loans and company-provided housing. Relevant information must be provided to employee representatives comprehensively and as early as possible, and where appropriate the trade union and employers' association should also be notified. Where there are a large number of proposed dismissals, employee representatives have a right to ask for negotiations on measures for those affected.

Employers are required to notify the authorities of any economic dismissals, with the number of employees affected broken down by sex and nationality, for the purpose of compiling labour market statistics.

Transfer of undertakings

Transfer of undertakings is regulated by an amendment to the Code of Obligations, introduced in December 1993, initially as part of preparations for entry to the European Economic Area. The amendment (article 333) provides for employment to continue on transfer, with all rights and obligations, provided the employee does not reject the transfer of the employment relationship. The transferee must respect the terms of any applicable collective agreement for a period of one year, unless the agreement expires or is formally terminated. Both the transferor and the transferee are jointly liable for any obligations arising out of the employment relationship prior to the transfer.

The employer is required to inform either employee representatives or, in their absence, the employees directly of the reasons for the transfer, and its legal, economic and social consequences for the work force. Consultation must take place before any measures related to the transfer are initiated.

Appendix

Social insurance contributions and tax rates

Typical social insurance and related contributions for the employer are approximately 13–14 per cent. Occupational pension contributions, in addition to this, will vary according to age, but may run at 20–5 per cent of salary for employees in their 40s. Employees also pay 13–14 per cent, plus up to 1 per cent for voluntary sickness benefit insurance, and a contribution to pensions of 6–12 per cent of salary, depending on age. In addition, employees must make provision for private health insurance, which in some cases may be arranged through an employer-organised scheme to which the employer may also contribute.

Income tax is levied at federal, cantonal and in some cases at commune level. Different items of expenditure can be set against gross income in each case to arrive at slightly different levels of taxable income. Tax rates, and tax practice for some benefits, will vary from canton to canton. In addition, church tax and other community taxes may be levied. Direct taxation rates are comparatively low, with combined average canton and federal tax of about 25 per cent on high incomes (above SFr 150,000 per annum (£70,755)).

Organisations

Federal Ministry of Industry and Labour
(*Bundesamt für Industrie, Gewerbe und Arbeit*, BIGA)
Gurtengasse 3, 3003 Berne
Tel. + 41 31 322 2948;
fax + 41 31 322 7831

Federal Social Insurance Department
(*Bundesamt für Sozialversicherung*)
Effingerstraße 31, 3003 Berne
Tel. + 41 31 61 91 11

Central Confederation of Swiss Employers
(*Zentralverband schweizerischer Arbeitgeber-Organisationen*)
Florastraße 44, 8034 Zurich
Tel. + 41 1 383 0758

Confederation of Swiss Trade Unions
(*Schweizer Gewerkschaftsbund*)
Monbijoustraße 61, 3007 Berne
Tel. + 41 31 45 56 66

Main sources and legislation

Gerhard Koller and René Kuhn (eds.) *Arbeitsrecht in der Schweiz*, Weka Verlag, Zurich, 1994.

Federal Chancellery, *Arbeitsvertragsrecht* (extracts on collective and individual contracts of employment from the Code of Obligations), Berne, 1992.

Federal Chancellery, *Arbeitsgesetz* (Labour Code), Berne, 1993.

Ronald Pedergnana, 'Überblick über die neuen Kündigungsbestimmungen im Arbeitsvertragsrecht', *Recht*, 2, 1989.

Collective agreements for the engineering industry, banking industry, chocolate industry, metalworking trades, hotels and catering.

14

United Kingdom

Basic rights and labour jurisdiction

General legal framework

The United Kingdom has no written constitution and hence no entrenched constitutional rights in the field of employment or any other area. Individual and collective rights are derived from statute law, over which Parliament is sovereign
subject to the contraints imposed by the law of the European Union, and in the
employment field through the common law of contract. In many areas of
employment regulation there is a complex relationship between statute law and
the law of contract. There is no formal hierarchy of sources of law, although
Parliament through statutes may override the common law. International provisions, such as the European Convention on Human Rights and the Council of
Europe's European Social Charter cannot be directly enforced in the UK.
However, some European Union Directives and clauses in the Treaty on
European Union have been held to be directly applicable.

The legal regulation of employment is primarily through Acts of Parliament.
Although the UK lacks legal regulation of pay, working hours for most employees, and most aspects of collective representation, there is extensive statute law
in the fields of unfair dismissal, redundancy, and sex and race discrimination.
The lack of regulation of substantive terms of employment and of support for
collective bargaining contrasts with the high degree of legislative activity on
industrial action and the conduct and internal arrangements of trade unions during the 1980s. (These issues are taken up in detail in another volume in this
series, *Employee Relations and Collective Bargaining*.)

The bulk of statute law directly covers Great Britain (England, Wales and
Scotland), with parallel arrangements in most areas for Northern Ireland where
there are additional provisions for non-discrimination on religious grounds.

In contrast to mainland Europe, collective agreements are not directly enforceable in law, and as such provide an instrument for the regulation of employment
but do not constitute a source of law. However, if incorporated into the individual
contract of employment, either expressly or in some cases implicitly, they do
become enforceable in the courts through the normal law of contract.

Labour jurisdiction

The UK system of labour jurisdiction provides both a specialised system of labour courts (the industrial tribunals, for hearing cases brought primarily under particular statutes) as well as access to the ordinary civil courts for employment matters which are directly concerned with breaches of the law of contract.

The system of industrial tribunals, initially established in 1964/65 and much expanded since then in terms of their powers, provides a first-instance forum for deciding employment cases. The tribunals are intended to offer a speedy, cheap and informal method for resolving claims: for example, legal representation is not required, and initially it was hoped would not be needed by the parties. However, these principles have been eroded as the law has grown more complex, leading the parties to engage legal representation in many cases. Moreover, because industrial tribunals are judicial bodies, with the possibility of appeal to higher courts, their proceedings have tended to acquire the formality of other courts in areas such as admissibility of evidence.

The system of industrial tribunals is administered by the Central Office of the Industrial Tribunals (see Appendix). There are regional offices; a separate system functions in Scotland. In most cases, tribunals consist of a chairman (who must be a barrister or solicitor of at least seven years' standing) and lay members (usually two) who are appointed by the Secretary of State for Employment. One of the lay members will usually have experience as an employer and the other as an employee representative.

Industrial tribunals are authorised to hear cases brought under specific legislation, primarily the Employment Protection (Consolidation) Act 1978, the Equal Pay Act 1970, the Sex Discrimination Act 1975, the Race Relations Act 1976, the Wages Act 1986, and the Trade Union and Labour Relations (Consolidation) Act 1992. The bulk of cases concern unfair dismissal and redundancy.

Until 1993, an action for breach of the contract of employment had to be brought before the normal civil courts, usually the county courts or the High Court, if the sum at issue was very large. Contractual claims could not be made before a tribunal. This situtation changed as a result of the Trade Union and Employment Rights Act 1993 which allowed some claims for breach of contract to be made via a tribunal, provided the claim arises from, or is outstanding on, the termination of employment. This includes damages for breach of contract, or for a sum due under the contract. The upper limit for claims for breach of contract before a tribunal is £25,000. However, breaches involving non-monetary terms would still need to be heard before the county courts.

Claims must be lodged within a time limit, which varies from issue to issue. In some cases, limits may be extended either if bringing the claim within the required time limit was not practicable or if a tribunal decided that it would not be 'just and equitable' to refuse the case.

The main time limits are:

- Unfair dismissals – three months.
- Sex and race discrimination – three months (six months if the official monitoring body brings a complaint against discriminatory advertisement.

- Redundancy – six months.

Industrial tribunal decisions may, on application, be reviewed by the tribunal itself on procedural grounds, if fresh evidence comes to light, or in the general interests of justice. Formal appeal on a point of law is initially made on most matters to the Employment Appeals Tribunal (EAT): appeals must be lodged within forty-two days of an industrial tribunal decision. The EAT consists of a High Court judge and two lay members (who may be increased to four) with experience as employer and employee representatives. Further appeal, again only on a point of law, may be made to the Court of Appeal, or the Court of Session in Scotland. The final stage of appeal, with leave, is to the House of Lords. In certain circumstances where a point of European Union law is involved, a case may be referred directly from any court or tribunal to the European Court of Justice.

Codes of practice

Codes of practice issued by official or semi-official bodies have played an influential role in shaping employment policy and practice since the early 1970s. Codes are normally issued by bodies such as the Advisory, Conciliation and Arbitration Service (ACAS – see below), the Commission on Racial Equality, and the Equal Opportunities Commission under enabling legislation. Although not legally binding, codes are important because in the event of a complaint by an employee or a collective dispute, industrial tribunals may look at whether the employer or union has taken any relevant code of practice into account in their actions and codes may be admitted as evidence in the proceedings. The main codes of practice are listed below.

- ACAS has issued three codes of practice: 1) *Disciplinary Practice and Procedures in Employment* 2) *Disclosure of Information to Trade Unions for Collective Bargaining Purposes* 3) *Time Off for Trade Union Duties and Activities.*
- The Department of Employment has issued codes of practice on picketing and on the conduct of trade union ballots related to industrial action.
- The Commission for Racial Equality has issued the *Code of Practice for the Elimination of Racial Discrimination and the Promotion of Equality of Opportunity in Employment* (see below, 'Race discrimination').
- The Equal Opportunities Commission has issued a code of practice on the elimination of sex and marriage discrimination and the promotion of equality of opportunity.
- For Northern Ireland, there is a code of practice on fair employment and the prevention of discrimination on religious and political grounds, available from the Fair Employment Commission.

- The Health and Safety Commission has issued codes of practice on safety representatives and time off for training safety representatives.

The Institute of Personnel and Development (IPD) has issued a number of codes of practice for guidance which do not have the status of the codes produced by statutory bodies, but which are nonetheless recognised and endorsed by many organisations active in particular areas of personnel management. There are eighteen codes covering all the main areas of personnel management and they are available as a booklet from the IPD (see Appendix).

The Advisory, Conciliation and Arbitration Service

The Advisory, Conciliation and Arbitration Service (ACAS), established in 1975, offers conciliation services on issues that may come before an industrial tribunal. ACAS conciliation officers play a major role in the resolution of individual disputes and the clarification of issues prior to a tribunal hearing. Settlements achieved as a result of ACAS conciliation are legally binding and exclude further resort to law.

Contracts of employment

Aside from statute law, the individual contract of employment is the primary focus of employment law in the UK. In contrast to many other EU member states, collective agreements are not legally enforceable as such and only acquire a binding character by being 'incorporated' into the individual contract. The contract of employment is governed by the same common law principles that regulate the conclusion and validity of other forms of civil contracts.

In order to establish a contract of employment, the prospective employer must have made an offer, the employee given acceptance, and both parties indicated their intention to be legally bound by what they have agreed. Moreover, the parties must have the legal capacity to contract – a capacity, in general, only restricted in the case of minors (in the UK, those under 18).

Types of employee

Establishing that an individual has become an employee, as opposed to being self-employed, is crucial in determining whether they are eligible to qualify for a number of basic employment rights, such as the right to bring a claim of unfair dismissal, redundancy payments, statutory sickness and maternity pay, and health and safety protection. There is no simple and unambiguous test to establish that the relationship is one of employment (rather than a contract for services etc.) but factors identified by the courts include:

- The degree of control exercised by the putative employer.
- The intention of the parties when concluding the contract.
- The form in which financial consideration is made (for example, a regular sum vs occasional amounts).
- The 'mutuality of obligation' between the parties (for example, whether the 'employee' is bound to attend for work when requested by the employer).
- Whether the putative employee provides their own equipment and supplies other workers.

Company directors   These fall under a broader category of individuals termed 'office-holders' – that is, people occupying a role, the rights and duties of which exist by virtue of the office, independently defined and regulated, rather than exhausted by the individual contract of employment. The categories are not mutually exclusive and office-holders may be deemed to be employees, provided they meet the criteria outlined in case law. The difference may be relevant in defining the tasks of the office-holder (which may be regulated by articles of association etc.) and in regulating removal from office. This may, for example, entail both an administrative decision of the company (vote of shareholders) and the issuing of notice or other form of termination (see below 'Termination of contract').

Labour-only subcontracting   Labour-only subcontracting is widespread in the construction industry.

Employment agency workers   In contrast to many EU member states, employment agency workers ('temps') in the UK are not, in general, regarded as employed by the agency that supplies them to client companies, although many larger agencies offer training and treat temps as if they were indeed employed by them. Some larger agencies have concluded collective agreements with unions, setting minimum terms and conditions for temporary workers. (Agency employment is dealt with in another volume in this series, *Recruitment, Training and Development*.) Nor are temps deemed to be employees of the client. Rather, their contracts are regarded as special and 'of their own kind'. As a result, temps are not covered by unfair dismissal legislation, except in rare circumstances where a tribunal has ruled that a temp had effectively become an employee.

Form of contract

A contract of employment may take any form, and there is no obligation to put it in writing. However, as noted below, there is a statutory obligation to provide written particulars of the contract of employment. There are four main types of contractual term:

- Express terms, which have been specified in writing or orally.

- Implied terms, which are held to be a prerequisite for the contract to function satisfactorily and which the parties may be held to have agreed to by virtue of entering into the contract of employment. These include mutual trust and confidence, a duty of fidelity and the exercise of reasonable care and skill on the part of the employee, and duty of reasonable care on the part of the employer. In the event of a dispute, the courts may imply terms that are required to make the contract workable (known as 'business efficacy'), which are custom and practice for contracts of that type, evident from the performance of the contract or likely to have been included when the parties agreed the contract.
- Incorporated terms, which are taken from other sources: they may be incorporated either expressly, as in terms taken from collective agreements or staff handbooks, or implied.
- Statutory terms, either imposed or implied by statute law into employment contracts. In most cases not only is statute law implied but any attempt to contract out of a statutory provision would be void.

Written particulars   Under the Trade Union Reform and Employment Rights (TURER) Act 1993, which implements the EU Directive on proof of an employment relationship (EC91/533/EEC), employers must provide each employee with a written statement of the main terms of their employment not later than eight weeks after the start of employment; for existing employees, a statement complying with the 1993 provisions must be made available if requested by the employee. (Existing employees will already have a statement of written particulars of their employment under the Employment Protection (Consolidation) Act 1978, replaced by the 1993 provision.) The 1993 Act applies to employees working at least eight hours per week and in employment for at least one month. Under the Act, the terms of employment that must be notified, in addition to basic details of the employer, the employee and the date when employment began, are:

- Pay details (rates, frequency) or the method for calculating pay.
- Hours of work, holiday entitlement, and holiday pay entitlement.
- Provisions on sickness and payment of sick pay.
- Pensions and pension schemes.
- Notice periods for employer and employee.
- Job title or a brief description of the employee's tasks.
- Where the employment is not permanent, the expected duration or, if it is for a fixed term, the date on which employment will end.
- Place of work or a statement whether the employee is expected to work in several locations.
- Any applicable collective agreements.

Where the employee is required to work outside the UK for more than one month, the statement must also define the period involved, the currency in which remuneration will be paid, details of any additional pay or benefits, and any terms and conditions relating to the employee's return to the UK. In addition, the written statement should also set out details of disciplinary and grievance arrangements applying to the employee.

Details may be provided in instalments, using other documents where appropriate, provided there is one 'principal statement' setting out basic employment details.

Variation of terms   Terms in an individual contract of employment may be changed in one of several ways. In the most straightforward case, the contract can be varied by mutual agreement, either explicitly or by implication where the employee continues to work under the changed terms. Variation of terms can also be effected by means of a clause in the contract of employment allowing the employer to change terms. For example, a contractual mobility or flexibility clause would allow an employer to move an employee from one workplace to another or change their activity, even if this involves a drop in pay. Where a collective agreement is held to be incorporated into individual employees' contracts, a negotiated change in terms will also vary contracts. However, if no such presumption or express provision exists, then simply negotiating a new collective agreement will not automatically have an effect on individual contracts of employment.

Most controversially, a change can be imposed unilaterally by the employer, either as a *fait accompli* or by terminating the existing contract and substituting a new one. The employee can respond to a unilateral change in contractual terms by:

- Acquiescing in the change by continuing to work, under the new terms.
- Resigning and claiming constructive dismissal on the grounds of a fundamental breach (see below, under 'Constructive dismissal').
- Continuing to work but refusing the new terms.
- Continuing to work under protest and bringing an action for breach of contract in the High Court or a county court – for example, to recover any loss of pay which the unilateral change in the contract has entailed.

In order to establish that any constructive dismissal was not warranted, the employer must establish that his or her actions were reasonable. However, should the employer terminate the contract, and offer a new contract, the employee may bring a claim of unfair dismissal (see below). An industrial tribunal would then need to assess whether the employer acted reasonably: for example, such a termination to vary the contract might be expected where the employer needed to make drastic economies to prevent closure.

Types of contract

Full-time permanent   According to official figures, only some 62 per cent of the UK work force are currently employed on full-time permanent contracts. So-called 'atypical' work is therefore an important and customary part of the British labour market.

Part-time The incidence of part-time working in the UK is amongst the highest in Europe. According to official figures, 28 per cent of the work force worked 30 hours or less in 1994, of which 81 per cent were women. Part-time employment has grown by 30 per cent since the mid 1980s, with female part-time work the only area of net employment growth. Nine-tenths of part-time work is concentrated in the service sector.

Although there is no statutory right to *pro rata* entitlements with full-time employees, a substantial amount of harmonisation exists. The legal position in the UK has been decisively shaped by EU-level law and judgements, complemented by decisions of the British courts interpreting the law in the light of European Court of Justice rulings on the issue of indirect sex discrimination.

For example, under EU equality law the exclusion of part-timers from a supplementary occupational pension scheme is unlawful, unless it can be objectively justified. In 1993 just under half of occupational pension schemes excluded part-timers entirely; where limits were applied, a threshold of sixteen hours was customary. Following rulings by the European Court in September 1994, part-timers who are excluded from a scheme, and whose exclusion cannot be objectively justified, have the right to claim scheme benefits as from April 1976. In contributory schemes, claiming benefits will entail the employee making contributions backdated to 1976.

A number of statutory entitlements are determined by the number of hours worked and length of service, including rights to bring a complaint of unfair dismissal or claim a redundancy payment. In the past, for example, part-timers working eight to sixteen hours a week were required to work for five years before being entitled to exercise these rights, compared with two years for full-timers. In March 1994 the House of Lords ruled that such qualifying thresholds were in breach of EU law in that they were indirectly discriminatory and not objectively justified. The government has said that it will implement the judgement; in the interim, employees may either bring a claim under the equal pay provisions of the Treaty of Rome (article 119) or claim damages from the government.

Job-sharing Despite the high public profile given to the possibilities for job-sharing, especially in public-sector organisations, the number of posts shared remains relatively small. According to 1991 figures, just over half of 1 per cent of people in employment were job-sharing. Of these, nine out of ten were women. Although formal job-sharing has been most developed in the public sector, where equal opportunities considerations have been a major driving force, private-sector organisations have increasingly turned to job-sharing as a means of retaining skilled female staff – especially because senior posts are more easily converted into a job-share position than covered on a part-time basis. Notable private-sector examples include Boots the Chemists, Barclays Bank and Shell UK.

There is no statutory regulation of job-sharing, and arrangements are therefore determined by company policies, as reflected in individual contracts of employment. In most respects, job-sharers are treated as part-time workers as far as terms and conditions are concerned: this may mean that job sharers fall below the various statutory thresholds for rights to claim unfair dismissal or a redundancy payment (see below).

Fixed-term and temporary contracts   There are no statutory provisions governing the form and substance of fixed-term or temporary contracts, except in the field of dismissal, although case law has ruled on issues such as continuity of employment (and the importance of gaps between fixed-term contracts). Fixed-term contracts have become widespread in scientific and medical research. Temporary work, either directly as an employee or via an agency, combined with fixed-term employment accounts for 6 per cent of total employment.

The law on dismissal distinguishes between a fixed-term contract, which terminates either after a specified term or, if agreed, by a period of notice, and a task-related ('temporary') contract, which ends when the task is completed ('discharged by performance') and which therefore will not entail a dismissal. Non-renewal of a fixed-term contract will normally constitute a dismissal. However, in fixed-term contracts of at least one year's duration the employee may forego the right to claim unfair dismissal; statutory redundancy rights may be waived in contracts lasting more than two years.

Collective agreements and individual contracts of employment

Collective agreements are not legally binding or enforceable as between the signatory parties unless expressly declared to be so: that is, in contrast to most mainland European countries, they do not establish a contractual relationship between an employer (or employers' association) and a trade union. The rights of individual employees to the terms of collective agreements are assured through the 'incorporation' of collective agreements into the contract of employment: this renders substantive – though not procedural – terms legally enforceable through the ordinary law of contract. This may be done expressly, via a clause in the individual contract stating that specific terms will be as determined by collective agreement. It may also operate in an implicit way, where there is a clear custom that terms of collective agreements are incorporated into individual contracts, and that this was evident to the parties when the contract was formed. (Collective agreements and collective bargaining are dealt with in detail in another volume in this series, *Employee Relations and Collective Bargaining*.)

Confidentiality

There is an implied duty on all employees not to divulge to third parties an employer's confidential information and trade secrets which they have obtained during, and because of, their employment. The employee's duty may also be expressed in the form of a confidentiality clause, which may specify those matters deemed confidential by the employer, or in the form of a restrictive covenant, restricting the employee's activities after employment. Irrespective of whether disclosure might damage the employer, such disclosure would not however be regarded as a breach of confidentiality if it was justified in the public interest.

Restrictive covenants

Employees owe their employer an implied duty of fidelity during the contract of employment. Competition by the employee with the current employer would therefore represent a breach of contract (automatically if the work was undertaken during normal working hours), and entitle the employer to dismiss the employee, possibly summarily, and in addition seek damages. However, if the employee was working for a competitor in their own time, the employer would need to establish that serious damage was being done to his or her interests by that activity. Whether making preparations to establish a company to compete with the (former) employer also represents a breach of contract is not definitively established in case law. However, it would be likely to be viewed in this way if the employee had used confidential information.

Employment contracts may also contain an express term restricting the employee's activities and/or stating the terms on which other activities may be undertaken. Provided such clauses are not drawn up so widely as to be seen as an unreasonable restraint of trade, and therefore unenforceable, such clauses may assist both parties to interpret the underlying duty of fidelity and, in the event of a dispute, the courts to ascertain more precisely the intention of the parties in the contract.

Where an employee in possession of trade secrets is employed on a very long notice period and has agreed an express clause forbidding employment for a competitor, the employee may be required to go on so-called 'garden leave' should they give notice to resign to join a competitor and seek to shorten their notice period. That is, they can be required to serve their full notice period, on full pay and benefits but not perform the actual work.

Restrictions on employees' activities after employment must meet two basic conditions to be valid and enforceable. First, the restraint must be reasonable in offering adequate protection to the legitimate interests of the employer in the area of trade secrets and trade connections: should the employee breach the restrictive covenant, the burden of proof will be on the employer to demonstrate this, and the courts have traditionally interpreted such clauses very narrowly.

Second, it must be reasonable in terms of the interests of the public. A restrictive covenant that fails to meet these criteria may be held to constitute a restraint of trade, be contrary to public policy, and hence unenforceable.

Types of restrictive covenant include:

- Restraints on working for a competitor, including a business set up by the employee themselves, if this enables the former employer to protect trade secrets and confidential information.
- A non-solicitation clause, preventing the former employee from seeking the custom of clients of the former employer, or from recruiting former colleagues. Non-dealing clauses may also prohibit commercial contacts with clients of the ex-employer, even where the employee does not solicit custom.

Enforcing covenants can prove difficult, and a covenant solely aimed at preventing fair competition from a former employee is unlikely to be upheld if challenged. The courts would not support a restraint defined so as to prevent an ex-employee from exercising their trade at all. In a recent decision, the Court of Appeal also refused to enforce a restrictive covenant that sought to prevent an ex-employee from exercising their trade at all. The scope and duration of the restraint must also be reasonable: any restraint unduly wide in its application, and prolonged, may be void and unenforceable. For example, an employer choosing too wide a geographical area – such as the whole of Europe – could find the entire clause void if their business was essentially confined to a regional or national market. Similarly, the courts might uphold a one- or two-year restriction on competition within a reasonable area, but would require that the geographical area be limited for any longer period.

Restraints must be clear: vague or uncertain formulations could render a restrictive covenant void. Moreover, the courts will not generally rewrite an unreasonable restraint to make it reasonable, although they may seek to construe a covenant in its proper context. Wrongful dismissal of the employee – that is, without due notice – or resignation of the employee where the employer has fundamentally breached the contract will invalidate any restrictive covenant.

In practice, few cases involving breach of a restrictive covenant ever come to court, and some legal opinion holds that few covenants would be enforceable if tested in the courts. Their perceived value for those employers who insist on them is primarily the likelihood of gaining a temporary injunction to prevent the employee beginning a new employment, allowing the ex-employer to secure confidentiality and repair or avert potential damage.

Individual employee rights

There is no single statutory provision setting out the rights of individual employees at the workplace. Individual rights in specified areas (such as time off, maternity rights, and equal opportunities) are set out separately. Many general individual rights that in other European countries come under constitutional provisions have been afforded to some degree in the UK through the application by the courts of implied terms in the contract of employment (duty of care, confidentiality etc.). Developing case law has, for example, allowed an employee to win substantial damages for a mental breakdown caused by stress at work, on the grounds that the employer breached their duty of care to avoid psychiatric damage to employees.

Data protection

The use of personal data on computers is regulated by the Data Protection Act 1984. The protection provided under the Act has two strands: official supervision of data users, and the individual rights of those about whom data is held and processed.

Data users must register with the Data Protection Registrar, indicating the type of data to be held, the purposes for which it is held, sources of data, and persons to whom it may be disclosed. It is a criminal offence to hold data for any purpose other than that stated to the Registrar.

Individuals have the right to be informed about any personal data held on them and to have a copy of the data. Individuals have the power to ensure that the data is accurate, and – if necessary through the courts – to have material either corrected or erased.

The Act sets out a number of basic principles for data protection. These are:

- Information must be obtained and data processed fairly and lawfully.
- Personal data shall be held only for specified and lawful purposes.
- Data should not be used or disclosed in a way incompatible with the stated purpose.
- Personal data held shall be adequate, relevant and not excessive to the stated purpose.
- Personal data should be accurate and up to date.
- Data should not be held for longer than is necessary.
- Individuals have a right to be informed about whether data is held on them, have access to it, and correct or erase data where appropriate.

The Institute of Personnel and Development (IPD) has produced a Code of Practice on Employee Data which elaborates how the statutory principles should be applied in the workplace.

Exemptions from the Act are allowed for payroll purposes, although the scope is very narrow: the IPD recommends that it is administratively easier to register than to attempt to keep within the bounds of the exemption rules.

There is no statutory framework for personal data stored in paper form. However, there are common law obligations under the law of contract, primarily the duty of confidentiality, that could be invoked by an individual to protect or gain access to personal data held by their employer. (The issue of job references and access to medical records is dealt with in another volume of this series, *Recruitment, Training and Development*).

Discipline and grievance procedures

Under the Employment Protection (Consolidation) Act 1978, there is an obligation on employers to provide written details of disciplinary and grievance procedures; these should be included in the written particulars given to employees under the Trade Union and Employment Rights Act 1993. There is also an ACAS code of practice on disciplinary procedures. This sets out recommendations on the stages of disciplinary procedures, conduct of procedures, appeals and penalties. The employer may only suspend an employee without pay if this is an express or implied term in the contract of employment.

Smoking

Employers in the UK have been in the forefront of developing policies on smoking although, in contrast to France, there is no statutory provision. However, from 1 January 1996 employers must make rest-rooms available for pregnant women, with measures to protect non-smokers from tobacco smoke. In addition to pressure from non-smoking employees, employers have also been spurred on by an out-of-court settlement in which an employee received £150,000 in respect of damages caused by passive smoking. However, no cases on passive smoking have yet been won in the courts on the grounds that employers have breached their duty of care. General insurance costs (life, medical and fire) are also cited by employers as reducible by curbing workplace smoking.

Complete bans on smoking are rare, although smokers do not have any rights to smoking facilities in the UK, and an industrial tribunal is generally unlikely to rule that the resignation of an employee who says they cannot comply with a no-smoking policy constitutes constructive dismissal. Most companies with a smoking policy have adopted the approach of designating a smoking area, as well as in some cases restricting periods of access and banning smoking in shared workplaces. Many companies ease the phasing in of a no-smoking policy by offering support for employees who want to give up. Dismissal on grounds of breaching a no-smoking policy is normally regarded as fair, provided the policy is clear, has been communicated to employees and breaches have been dealt with through a fair procedure.

Employment terms and conditions

Working time

Statutory and agreed provisions   At present there is no statutory regulation of hours of work for adult employees. There are, however, legal restrictions on hours of work for some specific forms of employment (such as miners and drivers of goods vehicles) and for children and young people. As a consequence, working hours for the vast bulk of employees are regulated by the individual contract of employment, subject to the provisions of any applicable collective agreement. The written particulars of terms and conditions of employment, which must be provided to employees within a month of starting work, have to include details of hours of work: changes must also be notified to employees within one month.

The parties to the contract of employment are free to agree any working time arrangements they choose, including provisions on flexibility, overtime, stand-by arrangements and shift patterns (see below). Clauses giving the employer the right to vary hours of work ('flexibility clauses') will be enforceable, provided they are unambiguous. (See also 'Overtime, night work and shift pay', below.)

However, hours of work in general will be subject to the provisions of the EU directive on working time from November 1996. Member states also have up to seven years before implementing the maximum working week of forty-eight hours required by the directive. (For the main points of the directive, see pages 8–9.) The directive has caused particular controversy in the UK on several grounds. First, employees in the UK tend to work longer hours than elsewhere in the EU, principally because of higher levels of overtime. Although contractual hours in the UK are not notably longer than in mainland Europe, average hours worked by all employees, at 43.4 in 1991, were the longest in the EU. Moreover, according to European Commission statistics, 39 per cent of men worked forty-five hours or more a week, and 22 per cent of men fifty hours or more.

Second, UK practitioners have not been accustomed to working within a statutory framework, especially where flexibility arrangements requiring a departure from the law may only be implemented by collective agreement – a common practice in mainland Europe.

However, the UK government is unlikely to proceed to transpose the directive into national law until it has resolved its legal challenge against the European Commission for introducing the directive under the health and safety provisions of the Single European Act, which allow for majority voting in the Council of Ministers.

The most common agreed weekly working hours for manual workers in the UK remains thirty-nine hours, with a substantial minority – probably around one-third – working thirty-seven or thirty-eight hours. The major organised trade union campaign to reduce hours was conducted by unions in the engineering industry in 1989/90, and a large number of company-by-company (and sometimes plant-by-plant) reductions from thirty-nine to thirty-seven hours was agreed, in some cases tied to flexibility provisions (see below). The campaign for further movement to a thirty-five-hour week was suspended because of the recession, and the pace of hours cuts has slowed down markedly. Only a small number of firms offers a thirty-five-hour week to blue-collar workers.

There are still differences between hours for white-collar and blue-collar employees, with white-collar staff typically contracted to work thirty-five–thirty-seven hours a week. The thirty-five-hour week for white-collar employees is virtually the norm in the finance and insurance sector, and is common elsewhere. Some companies have moved towards harmonisation of conditions, with thirty-six or thirty-seven hours the norm.

Overtime and working time flexibility   There are no statutory regulations on levels of overtime, or on shiftworking arrangements.

Overtime work is an institutionalised part of working hours for many employees, especially in manufacturing, where around one-third of employees work overtime. Overtime pay is a significant component of many employees' customary earnings (see 'Overtime, night work and shift pay' below). Blue-collar employees who put in overtime worked, on average, some 9.7 hours of overtime a week in 1993 – the highest individual figure in two decades.

Systems of annual hours have grown in recent years, in particular with the aim of removing the premium element of pay for overtime. They are most commonly found in manufacturing, and especially in continuous process operations – and there most commonly for manual shiftworkers. However, there has been an increase in the number of schemes in the public sector and private services. In a number of cases, annual hours were introduced in association with a move to a shorter average working week. In many systems, employers will roster an employee to work for fewer hours than specified in the annual total, allowing for these 'reserve' hours to be called on to meet production peaks. Some companies operate a predetermined seasonal pattern within the overall number of annual hours.

Time banking for employees, emulating German models, followed the introduction of shorter hours, especially in manufacturing. Under this model, where hours are cut, say, from thirty-nine to thirty-seven, employees will continue to work a thirty-nine-hour week, and 'bank' the two hours until they accumulate into more substantial amounts of time off, which may be taken in accordance with company policy. (See also 'Overtime, night work and shift pay' below).

Annual leave and public holidays

There are few statutory provisions on annual leave and holidays, and – at present – no statutory minimum leave entitlement. The EU Working Time Directive, adopted on 23 November 1993, provides for a minimum of three weeks' paid annual holiday, rising to four weeks three years after the directive's implementation. The main provisions of the directive must be implemented by EU member states by November 1996, although there is provision for the introduction of the fourth week of annual holiday to be postponed for a further three years. In view of the possible delays in transposition (see above), entitlement to annual holiday is likely to continue to be primarily determined by the contract of employment, subject to collectively agreed terms.

The most common basic holiday entitlement for manual and non-manual employees is twenty-five days, with a range of twenty-one–twenty-five days, depending on industry. A basic entitlement above twenty-seven days is rare in the private sector. Around half of employers give service-related extra entitlement. On average, the maximum overall entitlement is four days longer than the basic entitlement, with some 20 per cent of employers offering thirty days or more, although this may require up to twenty years' service in some cases. In a few companies, additional holiday entitlement is related to the employee's age, usually combined with a service requirement. One-off extra entitlements, typically five–ten days, are granted by some companies to long-service employees in particular anniversary years. Extended leave is sometimes granted for visits to overseas relatives.

Many employers, particularly in manufacturing, set fixed holiday times and shut down their plants for normal operations, often accounting for a large proportion – and in rare cases all – of employees' basic entitlement.

Holiday pay is regulated by the employment contract. Employees are usually paid at normal rates, although some firms may average earnings over a preceding period where earnings are customarily much higher than basic pay. In contrast to many countries in mainland Europe, employees in the UK are not paid a thirteenth (or even further) month's salary, and only very rarely holiday bonuses or extra pay during leave.

Entitlement to annual holiday typically accrues with service through the calendar year. Company policy regulates when entitlement lapses and how much untaken leave may be carried over into the next year. Cashing in unused holiday is not a common practice; companies that do allow it impose limits – usually a maximum of ten days – on how much can be claimed in this way.

Employees working out notice of dismissal have a statutory entitlement to paid holiday due to them under their contract, provided their notice period is not longer than the statutory minimum notice period by at least one week (see 'Notice periods' below). In practice, employers allow employees to take accrued holiday up until the date at which employment is terminated.

There is no statutory right to time off on public (usually termed 'bank') holidays, and this, together with payment for the time off, is therefore regulated by the individual contract of employment. The courts have ruled that in the absence of an express provision in the contract of employment, employees are normally entitled to take recognised public holidays and be paid for them.

Public holidays in England and Wales are : 1 January, Good Friday, Easter Monday, the first Monday in May (to celebrate May Day; in 1995 this will be replaced by VE Day, 8 May), the last Monday in May (Spring Bank Holiday), the last Monday in August (Summer Bank Holiday), Christmas Day and Boxing Day (26 December). Scotland has 2 January but not Easter Monday, and Northern Ireland has 17 March and 12 July.

Maternity and paternity leave

Legislative changes providing for a minimum level of maternity leave to all pregnant employees and raising the level of statutory maternity pay (SMP) were introduced from October 1994, in line with the EU directive on the protection of pregnant women at work (92/85/EEC) adopted in October 1992.

Under the Trade Union Reform and Employment Rights (TURER) Act 1993, which amended the previous statute, all employees will have an entitlement to fourteen weeks' maternity leave irrespective of their length of service and hours of work, with a guarantee to return to their previous job. Maternity leave cannot begin before the eleventh week prior to the expected week of childbirth but may start as late as childbirth itself. Employees must have two weeks' leave around the time of childbirth, and maternity leave must be extended if the period of statutory entitlement has been exhausted.

Women who have two years' service at the eleventh week before the expected date of birth are entitled to twenty-nine weeks' maternity leave following the birth, as under the pre-1993 change in the law, yielding a total of forty weeks in all for these employees.

Employees eligible for SMP receive 90 per cent of their previous earnings for six weeks, with twelve weeks at a flat rate of £52.50 (1994 figure). Employers can reclaim statutory maternity pay: the rate is 92 per cent, with small companies entitled to reclaim 104 per cent of their SMP. In contrast to maternity leave, entitlement to SMP is service-related. Employees must have twenty-six weeks' continuous service as at the fifteenth week before the expected week of birth *and* have earnings above the statutory earnings limit of £57 per week (1994 figure).

A significant minority of companies improve on statutory provisions on maternity leave and pay (under the old, pre-1994 arrangements). Enhancements include:

- Longer period of leave, although rarely more than one year.
- Enhanced maternity pay – either through reducing the qualifying period below the statutory two-year period or paying higher than SMP, usually subject to an indication that the employee intends to return to work. A typical enhancement might consist of six–twelve weeks at full pay, followed by the basic rate of SMP up to an overall maximum of eighteen weeks.
- Return-to-work payments are paid by several larger companies as an incentive for women to return to their jobs. Typical provisions might be two months' full pay, paid either in instalments for four–six weeks after return.

There is no statutory entitlement to parental or paternity leave. However, a survey carried out by the Confederation of British Industry in 1992 found that 76 per cent of respondents provided paternity leave on either a contractual or discretionary basis compared with only 32 per cent in 1987. The most common arrangement found in 1994 by an IDS Study was three days, with an increasing number of companies moving to five days.

Career breaks became more common in the UK from the late 1980s, and are seen as an effective and low-cost means of retaining women with young children. Formally, they are usually open to men and women, although most applicants are women. Admission is often at the employer's discretion. The length of break varies considerably, with a usual maximum of five years (one break per career) or two years, but with the option of more than one break. Most companies undertake to provide a job at equivalent pay and status, and often require a short period of work or training each year.

Other time off

There is a statutory requirement for employers to grant paid time off for various purposes including:

- Reasonable paid time off for trade union 'duties', where a union is recognised for collective bargaining purposes, and unpaid time off for trade union activities'. (ACAS has a code of practice giving guidance in this area, and generally urging managements and unions to set out arrangements in workplace agreements.)
- Public duties – such as local government, justices of the peace and members of statutory tribunals, and membership of governing bodies of educational establishments. In most cases, employers grant paid time off, and may limit the total number of days a year. In some cases, official bodies grant loss of earnings payments, which are deducted from the employee's pay by the employer.
- Jury service. Employees have a right to time off, but there is no statutory obligation for this to be paid. Jurors can claim travelling and subsistence allowances, and these are usually topped up to full pay by the employer. Employees can claim exemption from jury service under some circumstances.

There is no statutory entitlement to time off for personal and domestic needs. Typical company-level provision includes: three–four days in the event of bereavement, in some cases varying by the type of relative who has died; some employers give three–five days' paid leave a year for family illness, but others might expect this to be deducted from annual leave or be taken without pay; paid time off is normally granted for medical appointments, but employees might be expected to take sick leave if the appointment is longer than one day.

Paid educational leave may be granted by larger firms, but often only if the course is relevant to the employee's work. Sabbatical leave may be granted in larger organisations (in addition to universities), with varying service requirements (usually at least five years and possibly up to twenty). Periods vary from two to six months. The leave is usually paid (but may be required to be 'banked' periods of annual leave), and there are rarely restrictions on the type of activity.

Individual pay and benefits

There is no statutory or agreed national minimum wage, and no institutional mechanism for setting minimum pay levels at sectoral level since the abolition of the Wages Councils in 1993 (with the exception of agriculture). Pay setting is, therefore, a matter for collective bargaining, individual negotiation or unilateral decision by the employer.

The most notable changes in pay setting arrangements over the past decade have been the fall in the number of employees whose pay is set by collective bargaining and the contraction of collective bargaining at industry level. According to the 1990 Workplace Industrial Relations Survey, 54 per cent of the work force in establishments with twenty-five or more employees were covered by collective bargaining compared with 71 per cent in 1984; given the bias towards collective bargaining in larger workplaces, some commentators have suggested that the overall incidence of collective bargaining is now nearer 40 per cent of the work force. Between 1980 and 1990, furthermore, the number of workplaces affiliated to an employers' association halved, leaving only one in eight members. (These issues are explored in greater detail in another volume of this series, *Employee Relations and Collective Bargaining*.)

Where industry bargaining still prevails, most notably in some areas of the construction industry, pay setting has a two-tier structure, with minimum rates set at industry level supplemented by company-level pay, which often far exceeds the minima.

Although integrated ('single status') pay structures, bringing together all non-managerial employees into a single scale, have grown considerably in recent years, many companies with collective bargaining still negotiate separately with blue- and white-collar unions, and have separate pay arrangements for each category. Harmonisation of conditions between blue- and white-collar has also been a major feature of the past decade or so, although separate provisions still typically exist in areas such as working time and pensions.

The law on pay

Employees have a statutory right to an itemised pay statement, giving details of gross pay, any variable and fixed deductions, and net pay due to the employee. The law does not apply to merchant seamen or to employees who usually work outside Great Britain.

Since the Wages Act 1986 new employees can no longer insist on being paid in cash, and employers can introduce cashless pay for such employees without their express consent. Cashless pay is the practice for virtually all white-collar staff and the bulk of blue-collar employees in large firms.

Deductions from pay may be made only with either the employee's written consent or as required by a statutory or contractual provision. Special arrangements apply in the retail sector, where employers may reserve the right to make deductions to cover cash shortages or deficiencies in stock. In such cases, the employer may not deduct more than 10 per cent of any pay due on a single pay day. Deductions must be made within twelve months of the shortfalls coming to the employer's notice. Under certain circumstances, an employer may be entitled to deduct a proportion of the employee's pay where the employee fails to carry out their full contractual duties.

Attachment of earnings Attachment of earnings is regulated by the Attachment of Earnings Act 1971, with some additional provisions following the introduction of the council tax and new child support arrangements introduced in 1992. Attachment must be made under an attachment of earnings order issued by a court. The court may set a level of protected earnings, below which the employee's take-home pay may not fall.

Main payment systems

Although declining, individual piece-work remains an important payment method for manual workers in manufacturing industry. Where piece-work has been removed, companies have frequently opted to install a flat-rate system, with differentiation according to skill levels. Team-based systems have also made headway, reflecting the desire to retain a tie to output but also mirroring disenchantment with individual appraisal-based reward systems.

One of the most outstanding developments of the 1980s was the growth in performance-related pay from managers into white-collar and supervisory grades. There is as yet relatively little individual performance-related pay for manual workers. This development has begun to displace – but by no means replace – salary progression via increments tied to seniority, although this may be complemented via a merit element either in the form of accelerated progression or additional pay at the top of the incremental scale tied to performance.

Job evaluation Formal job evaluation is widespread in larger companies, with some 70 per cent of companies with over 1,000 employees using such systems. According to the 1990 Workplace Industrial Relations Survey, formal systems were used in 26 per cent of all surveyed establishments, with a slight increase in incidence recorded during the 1980s. Points-rated schemes accounted for just under half the systems in use. Much of the impetus to formalisation came from employer wishes to establish a more equitable pay structure, often from the standpoint of justifying (or avoiding) pay differences which might otherwise foster equal pay claims (see below). The need to establish international comparisons has also been cited as a factor behind increases in the use of formal systems, especially proprietary ones.

Where integrated pay structures have been introduced, a growing trend in the past decade or so, job evaluation has also played a major role in developing new grading systems.

Performance-related pay Individual performance-related pay made great strides during the 1980s. In a 1992 study for the IPM/NEDO it was found to be the main method for salary progression for non-manual employees, with some impact – although still restricted – on manual employees. Most performance appraisal systems with a link to pay for manual workers have been introduced since the mid 1980s. From being largely confined to the private sector, individual performance-related pay spread rapidly in areas of the public sector in the early 1990s, spurred on by the need to meet service objectives under the government's 'Citizens' Charter' programme.

However, the early 1990s have seen some questioning of the validity and effectiveness of performance-related pay: there is evidence that it may be counterproductive, especially where schemes have not been backed up by appropriate training for managers and supervisors entrusted with the task of appraisal, or integrated into a proper performance management culture. The desire to foster teamworking has also given a spur to group-based incentive systems. Nonetheless, in some sectors, most notably finance, there has been a steady advance of merit-only awards.

Competency- and skill-based pay Whilst a number of companies have introduced competencies as a foundation for policy on training and development, and in some cases performance appraisal for clerical and professional employees, few have, as yet, linked competency directly to pay. Where competencies have a role in pay they usually complement other performance criteria as part of an overall performance management system. One example is Abbey Life, which in 1994 introduced a new pay and performance management programme in which competencies are one element in progression.

Skill-based pay, which concentrates more narrowly on the acquisition of identifiable qualifications or passage through a discrete training programme, has been introduced by a small number of pioneering companies primarily for technical and manual jobs. Typically, companies have found it easier to introduce skill-based pay for all employees on greenfield sites, whilst targeting particular groups of employees in established plants.

Annual bonuses and supplements There is no statutory requirement to pay annual bonuses, and employees in the UK do not receive the 'thirteenth-month' salary or bonus virtually universal in mainland Europe. However, Christmas bonuses are common and may be worth *c*. 5 per cent of annual pay. A small number of companies make a payment in mid summer. Profit-sharing payments (see below) have also been widespread, especially in the financial services sector, and these may amount to some 10 per cent of annual salary. Both phenomena have been growing in recent years.

Lay-off and short-time payments There are statutory rights to guarantee payments in the event of lay-off (UK: a temporary stoppage of work). The provisions apply overwhelmingly to manual workers, whose contracts may allow for a suspension of normal payment where no work is available, either for technical or economic reasons, or where lay-offs are customary, as in the construction industry. Under the Employment Protection (Consolidation) Act 1978, an employee with four weeks' continuous service is entitled to a payment if the employer does not provide work on a day on which they would normally be employed, provided the stoppage is not caused by an industrial dispute. The maximum payment is currently £14.10 a day, for a maximum of five days in any three-month period.

Industry and company agreements may provide for supplementary lay-off provisions to offer a guarantee week. This is typically not a full week's pay, and is either defined as a set percentage or comprises only basic pay but not premium payments.

Regional pay differences

With the exception of London and the South-East of England, there are no major regional differences in pay. Pay in the South-East is above the national average, both in terms of basic salaries and through specific allowances paid by some, mostly large employers, in addition to basic pay, to reflect the higher cost of living and labour market pressures: allowances grew rapidly during the boom years of the late 1980s, but in many cases have stagnated, become more targeted or withered away as employers raise basic pay levels (often under more devolved pay-setting arrangements). The level of allowance usually varies, depending on geographical distance from the centre of London, with typically an Inner London, Outer London and 'Fringe' payment, which may extend out to the whole of the South-East of England, and even cover cities and towns well outside the region where there have been recruitment and retention difficulties.

Typical Inner London payments in 1994 in the financial services sector were £3,500 a year with *c.* £2,500 a year for Outer London. Fringe allowances run at £700–£800 a year.

Overtime, night work and shift pay

There is no current specific statutory provision on overtime working or overtime rates, which are set by collective or individual agreement. The contract may specify any, or no, supplements for overtime working, and regulate the employee's obligations to work overtime when requested. However, even if not specified in the contract of employment, a refusal to work overtime may give grounds for dismissal if it is held to represent a breach of the implied terms of a contract of employment under which employees are required to serve the employer faithfully and not obstruct their business. Whether this is the case would need to be determined by a tribunal in the light of the particular circumstances.

In rare cases, overall working hours for groups of employees is limited by law (see above). The implementation of the EU directive on working time (see pages 8–9) may have an impact on practice in the UK because of the prevalence of overtime work.

Eligibility for overtime payment covers the vast majority of manual workers, and white-collar staff up to junior manager level. Higher paid employees more typically may be granted time off in lieu when they work beyond contractual hours. Many companies have embarked on strategies to reduce paid overtime. These have embraced recruiting temporary employees to meet peaks in demand, changing shift patterns – including the introduction of annualised hours – and introducing flexible working.

Typical overtime rates are 150 per cent of basic rates for overtime on weekdays, although some firms pay 125 or 133 per cent. In some cases, up to 200 per cent of basic rates are payable depending on the amount of daily overtime worked. Overtime work at weekends is typically remunerated by 150 per cent for Saturday mornings, and 200 per cent for work on Saturday afternoons, Sundays and on public holidays. Up to 300 per cent of basic rates may be paid for work on Christmas Day, Boxing Day and New Year's Day.

Employee financial participation

There is a wide variety of mechanisms for providing employees with participation in the financial results or capital of the employer, a number of which are tax favoured. However, there is no statutory obligation on employers to operate a system of financial participation for employees.

There are three types of employee share scheme that can be granted approval by the tax authorities and that offer tax privileges: approved profit-sharing schemes, savings-related schemes, both of which are open to all employees, and executive share-option schemes. The latter are much more numerous than the first two: in March 1994 there were 5,680 executive share-option schemes, compared with 2,368 all-employee schemes.

All-employee profit-sharing schemes   These were originally introduced in the last year of the 1974/79 Labour Government during a 'pact' with the Liberal Party. In the year 1992/93 some 740,000 employees were assigned shares, with an average value per employee of £420. Under these schemes, a proportion of profits may be used to acquire shares which are then assigned by the employer to individual employees. All employees who work at least twenty-five hours a week and who have five years' service must be eligible to participate, although schemes may be extended to other employees, and the number of shares allocated may vary by length of service or as a proportion of pay, or by any other agreed objective criterion. The shares are held by trustees. Each employee may be allocated up to £3,000 of shares per year or 10 per cent of the employee's annual earnings, whichever is the greater, up to an annual maximum of £8,000.

Shares cannot be sold for the first two years. If they are sold within a further two years, they attract income tax in full at the original value or the current price, whichever is the less. If shares are held for four years, 75 per cent of income tax due is payable, with no income tax liability if the shares are held for five years or more. Capital gains tax is payable, subject to any current exemption limit (in 1994, £5,800 a year). No capital gains is payable if shares are transferred to a Single Company Personal Equity Plan within ninety days.

Savings-related share-option schemes (SAYE option schemes)   These were introduced by the Conservative Government in 1980. They allow employees to buy shares in the employing company by using savings made under a Save As You Earn (SAYE) savings contract. Schemes must be open to all UK employees working at least twenty-five hours a week and with five years' continuous service. Employees are granted share options with a permitted maximum discount of 20 per cent from the market price. The shares are bought using the proceeds from a SAYE contract, under which employees pay a fixed amount of between £10 and £250 a month for five years into a special account with the Department of National Savings. After five years, the employee may withdraw the principal sum together with a savings bonus worth fifteen monthly instalments or leave the principal for a further two years and then collect an additional thirty monthly payments. The right to take up the option is therefore exercised at five or seven years into the SAYE contract.

Any capital gain realised on the sale of the shares is taxable above the current limit of £5,800, and up to £3,000 a year of shares can be transferred free of capital gains tax to a 'corporate PEP'. Employees leaving the company may exercise their options only if they have held them for at least three years.

Executive share-option schemes   These are share-option schemes run on a discretionary basis, typically for senior managers or even one selected executive. Tax relief for approved schemes was introduced under the 1984 Budget. Such schemes are now common and are operated by around 90 per cent of major quoted companies. However, schemes have been controversial, both in terms of their effectiveness as an incentive and because of the sometimes tenuous links between managerial performance and the potentially large individual gains to be made from options. As a response to the first issue, a small number of companies have replaced their schemes with alternative long-term incentives. On the second issue, in July 1993, the two main representative organisations for institutional shareholders in the UK issued a joint statement saying that they would not approve schemes unless there was a performance test on the exercise of options.

Eligible employees must work at least twenty hours a week (or twenty-five in the case of directors). Executives with more than a 10 per cent stake in a non-quoted company are not eligible. In general, the option price must not be 'manifestly' below the market price at the time the option is granted; however, a discount of 15 per cent on the market price may be granted if the company also has an approved all-employee scheme (such as those outlined above). No income tax is levied on the option or share price growth in an approved scheme (that is, unless the option price is below the market price – subject to the proviso above). Income tax relief will be granted provided the market value of shares does not exceed £100,000 or four times the individual's emoluments subject to PAYE. Options must be exercised not less than three years from the date of granting and no more than ten years thereafter.

The executive is liable for capital gains tax when, and only when, the shares are sold. There is a current annual exemption limit of £5,800, after which the tax is levied at the employee's marginal rate of income tax, currently a maximum of 40 per cent. This reduces the value of the incentive when compared with the previous flat rate capital gains tax of 30 per cent, compared with marginal income tax rates of 60 per cent which prevailed up until 1988.

Employee share ownership plans   There is a legal framework for the operation of Employee Share Ownership Plan trusts (ESOP trust), which enable a block of shares to be held for a group of employees in a trust established by the employer. Funds for acquiring shares are obtained either via loans or grants from the employing company or external loans guaranteed by the employer. However, such schemes are rare and mostly used as vehicles to operate other types of share scheme.

Cash profit-sharing   Under cash profit-sharing schemes the employer simply allocates a proportion of their profits to employees as a cash bonus. In an unapproved scheme, in which there is no link with shares, there are no tax concessions. Many companies with approved profit-sharing schemes (see above) also allow employees the alternative of a cash payment. Payments may be either in the form of a lump sum or be *pro rata* to salary. There are usually minimum length of service requirements, although these vary from three months up to three years. Typical payouts averaged £250–350 in 1993, a year in which recession had squeezed profits. Many companies have replaced cash profit-sharing schemes with approved profit-related pay arrangements to take advantage of the favourable tax provisions.

Profit-Related Pay (PRP)   PRP was originally inspired by Harvard Economics Professor Martin Weitzman, who argued that employment levels could be maintained in downturns if employees' pay was variable, with a proportion tied to corporate performance. Under schemes registered with the Inland Revenue under the Income and Corporation Taxes Act 1988, as amended, any elements of pay that are formally related to a specified measure of profit are tax free up to a limit of one-fifth of total pay or £4,000 a year, whichever is the lower. Other sums paid out as PRP will not attract tax relief. National insurance contributions (see Appendix) are payable on the whole amount. Separate schemes may be set up for any individual business unit which can produce separate profit and loss accounts. In general, registered schemes must cover 80 per cent of employees in the accounting unit, and all employees must participate on equal terms. Payments may not be linked to individual performance.

The number of schemes has risen substantially since the legislation was introduced, and especially following the extension of tax relief arrangements in 1991. At the end of March 1994, there were 7,039 registered schemes covering 1,794,100 employees. Some of this increase is attributable to employers adapting pre-existing schemes for profit-sharing to meet the Inland Revenue's criteria; in some cases, too, employers have lowered employees' basic pay, and made up the difference with PRP to render a portion tax-free. The most recent change to the regulations was made in December 1993, when a number of loopholes was closed.

Sick pay

Some 3.5 per cent of working time was lost through sickness absence in 1993, the equivalent of eight days per employee. Employees, subject to qualifying criteria, are entitled to payments from their employer under the system of Statutory Sick Pay (SSP), and in most cases also receive additional payments from the employer in line with company policies. Recent changes in the system of SSP have shifted the cost of payment during sickness from the state to the employer.

Employers are required to pay SSP to employees who qualify under Department of Social Security (DSS) rules. Before April 1994, employers were able to reclaim 80 per cent of this from the state. From 6 April 1994, this right has been removed, except for small employers. The standard rate of SSP is £52.50 per week (from 6 April 1994). SSP is payable only for periods of sickness of four days or more, including weekends, holidays and days off. The first three qualifying days of sickness are unpaid. The maximum entitlement is twenty-eight weeks of SSP in any continuous period, after which an employee may be entitled to invalidity benefit if they are unable to return to work.

In practice, most organisations also pay employees additional benefits under their own occupational sick pay schemes. Companies have full discretion in this area over eligibility, duration of entitlement and level of payments and other benefits. Employers usually pay full pay during sickness, although the duration of payment varies considerably between employers, and is also typically determined by the employee's length of service, again with wide variation in company practice. In some schemes, full pay is provided for an initial period – typically three to six months – and half pay thereafter, usually for a further three to six months.

Employers are free to choose their own notification procedures, and the DSS has standard procedures in connection with payment of Statutory Sick Pay. In general, companies apply the DSS rules that require employees to notify the employer by the end of the first day of absence, followed by the completion of a self-certification form on return to work for any absence of less than seven days. For absence of more than seven days, the employee must obtain a medical certificate. Firms which impose more stringent regulations may exclude employees from company benefits, but not SSP.

Absence control policies   These are implemented by many employers, and there has been an increase in their incidence in recent years. The typical elements of such policies include return to work interviews, points systems for triggering managerial action depending on the length and frequency of absence, and stringent eligibility and notification criteria in company schemes, such as a requirement for employees to visit a company-nominated physician. (For dismissal on grounds of sickness, see below.)

Maternity pay

(See 'Maternity and paternity leave' above.)

Employee benefits

Company cars   Cars have become a customary and widespread benefit for managers in the UK, extending far beyond employees who need cars for their work. According to the Monks Partnership *European Company Car Survey*, virtually 100 per cent of chief executives, some 95 per cent of function heads, and over 90 per cent of senior managers are eligible for cars. However, from a high point in the late 1980s in terms of tax effectiveness and eligibility, tax changes reducing the value of the benefit combined with company policies during the recession have shifted the overall outlook on company cars. Of these, probably the most important has been the trend offering employees a cash alternative, in some cases allowing employees to alternate between cash and a car. Tax changes have also encouraged companies to grant a 'trading down' option, under which employees can switch to a cheaper vehicle to minimise their tax liability.

Eligibility criteria for status cars – rather than strict job needs – vary widely: in most cases, employees are classified as 'managers', and typically the threshold salary level is *c*. £22,000, although company schemes range from £19,000 to £30,000, according to an IDS Management Pay Review survey of company car policies. Changes in tax arrangements in force from April 1994 mean that company cars are now virtually tax neutral. However, the imputation of status and the conferring of trouble-free motoring, through guaranteed repair and maintenance, have meant that the company car continues to be seen as an attractive benefit.

The tax treatment of company cars is based primarily on the list price of the vehicle. The tax change in each year is based on the 'full cost' of the car, which includes running costs, and major fixed costs such as depreciation and financing. This cost is set at 35 per cent of the list price of the car. Any capital contributions made by the employee, often required to account for private use, will be set off against the list price. The full cost may be reduced to allow for business use: the reduction is one-third for 2,500–17,999 business miles a year, and two-thirds for more than 18,000 miles. There is a further reduction of one-third for cars that are more than four years old. National insurance contributions are payable by the employer only.

Just over half the directors and employees who have a company car receive free fuel. The benefit is taxed via a system of fixed scale charges, based on engine size, at the employee's marginal rate. Since the charge does not vary according to private miles travelled, the benefit can be tax inefficient for the employee unless they drive a substantial number of miles – usually above 12,000 a year, depending on the car's fuel consumption. National insurance contributions are payable by the employer on the appropriate scale charge.

Occupational pensions   The main benefit in terms of cost is the occupational pension, provided by the vast majority of large employers and available to around half the UK work force. The cost to the employer varies from 5–10 per cent of income, depending on whether employees contribute or not. Aggregate contribution rates are expected to rise to 15 per cent in the future, their long-term historic norm. (For details, see 'Retirement' below.)

Insurances   Many employers offer employees a number of insurance options, with death-in-service benefits (life assurance) customarily provided in connection with occupational pensions. Under Inland Revenue rules, the maximum death-in-service benefit is four times current annual salary. Schemes may also contain provisions for long-term disability insurance.

Private medical insurance is typically provided to managers, with over 90 per cent of all middle and senior managers now eligible. Although an increasing number of companies have begun to offer this benefit to all employees, the proportion of blue-collar workers covered remains small. The overall number of employees in schemes has grown by four-and-a-half times since the mid-1970s and now totals some 1.9 million. Senior employees typically may also be able to bring their families within schemes. Typical annual premiums per member are £400–500, with increasing concern at accelerating costs. The employee is taxed on the basis of the cost to the employer.

Child care   Child care emerged as a major issue in the 1980s as skill shortages led employers to look at ways of recruiting and retaining people with family responsibilities. However, despite a great deal of discussion (reflecting problems with public child care arrangements), the number of companies providing child care remains small and workplace nurseries account for only some 1 per cent of all pre-school care arrangements.

Since 1990 workplace nursery places provided for employees have been exempt from tax, and employers can also claim tax relief on the day-to-day costs of providing or subsidising child care. (Companies may group together to provide a tax-favoured nursery.) However, employer assistance to buy a nursery place in an independent nursery, for child minding, or the provision of child-care vouchers is a taxable benefit. Most companies charge for workplace nursery places, with weekly rates ranging from £45–130; subsidies are provided either indirectly, through provision of facilities but not running costs, or on the basis of employee income.

Parental leave to care for a sick child is often allowed on a discretionary basis but is rarely granted specifically or on a paid basis. Where it happens a maximum of five days a year is usually allowed.

Others   Other principal benefits include:

- Relocation expenses – with tax relief up to £8,000 for employees.
- Interest-free or low-cost loans to employees – typically for buying a season ticket: there is no tax liability if the loan does not exceed £5,000. Subsidised mortgages are taxable, with the benefit calculated as the difference between the official rate and the rate paid by the employee. However, employees can claim tax relief on the official rate after adding the value of the benefit to their tax liability. Around 7 per cent of managerial employees are estimated to be covered by such schemes, which are common in the financial services sector.

Managerial pay and benefits

Executive pay has been a fertile source of controversy in the UK, in part because of the proliferation of share option schemes that have enabled the top managers of large companies to earn very substantial additional sums, often seemingly unrelated to their immediate performance; and in part because of the high-profile pay increases awarded to top managers in newly privatised utilities. Basic pay and bonuses also increased markedly in 1994, especially in larger companies, reflecting the recovery of profitability after the UK recession. High pay increases have been a target both of public exhortation by politicians, including the Prime Minister, and of pressure by the institutional investors to tie pay levels and increases more closely to long-term incentives. Some institutional investors have also conducted a campaign, in part successful, to cut the length of notice in top managers' rolling service contracts from three years (very common in large companies) to two years as a means of reducing often spectacularly high severance payments when managers are obliged to leave office prematurely.

Disclosure of information on executive pay has increased in recent years, reflecting greater shareholder interest, the concerns of institutional investors, and statutory requirements. Company reports now should include details of how executive pay is set (presence of a remuneration committee), remuneration of total board earnings, and that of the highest-paid director, with a breakdown between fixed and total remuneration, and a statement of remuneration policy. The Association of British Insurers suggests that reports should also include details of long-term incentive arrangements (cash- or share-based).

The typical top or senior managerial pay package consists of basic salary, a bonus arrangement, and in larger companies a share option plan, together with a range of benefits. In contrast to France and Italy there are no collective arrangements for pay setting for managers, and pay has become increasingly individualised over the past decade.

Share options   Approved share-option plans for senior managers, or even one selected executive, have enjoyed tax relief since 1984 (see 'Executive share-option' schemes above). Such schemes are now common and are operated by around 90 per cent of major quoted companies. No income tax is levied on the option or share price growth in an approved scheme, provided the market value of shares does not exceed £100,000 or four times the individual's emoluments subject to PAYE. Options must be exercised not less than three years from the date of granting and no more than ten years after. The executive is liable for capital gains tax when the shares are sold. There is a current annual exemption limit of £5,800, after which the tax is levied at the employee's marginal rate of income tax, currently a maximum of 40 per cent. This reduces the value of the incentive when compared with the previous flat-rate capital gains tax of 30 per cent, compared in turn with the marginal income tax rates of 60 per cent that prevailed up until 1988.

Concerns about the effectiveness of share options as a motivator have led many companies, spurred on by institutional investors, to subject share options to greater performance review, and in some cases to replace or complement them by other forms of long-term incentive (see below). Reassessment of many share-option schemes has been required in 1994 because schemes set up when relief was first granted in 1984 were typically given a ten-year life. The most common long-term share-based incentive scheme has become the performance share (or executive share incentive scheme), in which shares are released to managers when specific targets are met. Shares may be held in trust.

Management bonus schemes   The vast majority of larger companies operates bonus schemes for top management, a major change from the early 1980s when fewer than one in ten major employers had such schemes. According to a survey carried out by Hay, in April 1993, 74 per cent of industrial and service organisations had schemes for directors. However, the incidence of schemes falls off below director level: 68 per cent of senior managers were covered, but only 20 per cent of other managers.

The proportion of pay at risk varies considerably, with the size of bonus generally proportional to status in the organisation. According to a survey conducted by Monks Partnership, a third of directors were eligible for bonus payments of 20 per cent or more of basic salary for achieving 'acceptable' results. In contrast 55 per cent of senior managers were able to add 15 per cent or less to basic salary. In general, targets for senior management tend to be quantifiable and tied to overall corporate performance: the most common are pre-tax profit, earnings per share, and return on capital. Quantifiable job-related targets or qualitative targets predominate for lower managerial levels.

Long-term incentives have grown considerably since the late 1980s in large companies, following some disenchantment with the effectiveness of share options. The typical period over which performance is measured is three to four years and the most common performance measures are earnings per share or share price. According to a 1994 Monks Partnership survey, a fifth of chief executives in large companies participated in a long-term bonus scheme. A number of companies have moved to introduce 'phantom option' schemes, in which managers receive a cash bonus calculated according to the difference between a fictive option and the share price at future dates, typically with a longer period of review than real share-option schemes: however, managers are not required to buy and sell shares, and the schemes also avoid the Inland Revenue limits.

Main benefits   The principal benefits available to UK executives include:

- Company pensions: most top managers in larger companies are covered by enhanced pension plans that offer more favourable accrual rates than those in normal occupational schemes, allowing them to reach a higher percentage of their final salary within a shorter period, reflecting later recruitment and often a shorter overall career with an employer. (Directors may be subject to special rules for membership of occupational schemes.) Final salary schemes remain the most common option. Since 1989 only pay up to a maximum earnings limit (in 1994, £76,800) may be eligible for tax relief on pensions for people joining schemes after 14 March 1989 (or new members of existing schemes from 31 May 1989). However, employers may offer top-up schemes above this limit for high earners, although these enjoy no tax concessions in most cases. Alternatively, a cash alternative can be provided, allowing the executive to make their own provision through a money purchase or other savings arrangement.
- Cars: provided for 95 per cent of directors or heads of major functions, according to Monks Partnership, with a higher incidence than other European countries for senior managers. For example 96 per cent of senior managers in finance in the UK drive a company car, compared with 74 per cent in Germany and 46 per cent in Switzerland (see also 'Company cars' above).
- Private medical insurance and permanent health insurance.

Flexible or 'cafeteria' benefits have been beckoning for some years, and an increasing number of companies have begun to develop flexible options attached to a core of fixed benefits: employee choice, where granted, usually includes additional holidays, life insurance, private medical and permanent health insurance, and (in the finance sector) subsidised mortgages. Choice over cars, including trading up or trading down, or a cash alternative is common, spurred on by changes in tax arrangements. Cafeteria schemes, where operating, may be open to all employees or restricted to executives.

Equal opportunities

The UK took an early lead in the formulation of legislation on race and sex discrimination, in the former case reflecting the permanence of inward migration in the 1950s and 1960s. The Race Relations Act was introduced in 1965 and amended in 1976. Legislation on sex discrimination was initially introduced in the field of equal pay in 1970 (effective from 1975) and on sex discrimination in 1975: they complement each other very closely, with a number of overlapping provisions. Subsequently, practice and law in the UK have been profoundly affected by EU directives on equal treatment and equal pay, and by judgments of the European Court of Justice (see page 6). For example, following the Marshall case (see page 14), the UK's Sex Discrimination Act 1975 was amended to reflect the European Court's ruling that unequal retirement ages constituted sex discrimination.

The presence of legislation on sex and race discrimination, coupled with the need and desire to recruit members of ethnic minorities and women, has led many larger private and most public organisations to implement non-discrimination and, in some cases, positive action programmes – often evidenced by the statement 'Equal Opportunities Employer' in job advertisements and company literature. Legislation on race and sex discrimination has followed a common format, and case law built up in the area of race discrimination has been used as authoritative in sex discrimination, and vice versa.

Sex discrimination

Discrimination on grounds of sex or marital status is unlawful under the Sex Discrimination Act 1975. The Sex Discrimination Act applies to both men and women.

Discrimination can take three forms (see also 'Race discrimination' below):

- Direct discrimination, where a woman is treated less favourably than a man on grounds of sex (or marital status). Examples include, most notably, sexual harassment and discrimination on grounds of pregnancy. Direct discrimination might also embrace sex stereotypes in formulating policy – for example, selecting women for redundancy on the grounds that 'women are not breadwinners'.
- Indirect discrimination, where requirements are applied to a group of employees which fewer women can meet, which are not justifiable, and which lead to a detriment. Examples include discrimination against part-timers, unless justified by reference to a real need of the organisation; or age limits, which might disproportionately affect women when most likely to be starting familes.
- Victimisation, where an employer discriminates against someone for asserting their rights under the Act.

The 1975 Act established the Equal Opportunities Commission (EOC), which monitors the Act; has issued codes of practice (not binding, but which may be taken into account before a tribunal); may carry out investigations; and assists individuals in bringing complaints, including taking legal action. The EOC may also issue non-discrimination notices, requiring an employer to cease discrimination, with employers required both to comply and to allow for monitoring. The legal route for complaints under the Act is via industrial tribunals, and then on points of law to the Employment Appeals Tribunal, with further appeal possible to the Court of Appeal. Under some circumstances, the EOC will also act on its own to seek a judicial review of government decisions or statutes which it considers discriminatory. In an important case dealing with the rights of part-timers in 1994, the House of Lords upheld the EOC's rights in this area.

The main remedies under the Act are:

- A declaration that the complainant's rights have been violated, possibly specifying action that the employer must undertake to rectify the situation.
- Payment of compensation.

Following the Marshall case (see page 14) the previous limit for tribunal awards was abolished in 1993. Since the abolition large sums have been awarded in some discrimination cases. Employees can now recover all losses attributable to an act of sex discrimination.

Sexual harassment   There is no specific statute dealing with sexual harassment. However, it has been regarded by the courts and industrial tribunals as constituting direct sex discrimination under the 1975 Act. Industrial tribunals have also referred to the European Union Recommendation and Code of Practice on Sexual Harassment, which defines and specifies sexual harassment.

As with direct sex discrimination, a complainant must establish that they have suffered a detriment, with the degree of detriment – and hence level of compensation – a matter for the tribunal. There is no upper limit for compensation, and in 1994 a tribunal awarded a stockbroker £18,000, substantially above the typical award of £3,500.

Equal pay

The Equal Pay Act was passed in 1970 and took effect from 1975. It covers everyone (including men) in an establishment in Great Britain employed on a contract of service or a contract to provide 'any work or labour' (that is, not only employees in the strict sense). Employees in the UK can also rely on the EU Equal Pay Directive, given effect through a 1983 amendment to the Equal Pay Act, and in certain circumstances directly on the equal pay provisions of the Treaty of Rome itself (article 119). As a consequence both domestic and European Court judgments have had a decisive influence on the interpretation of what is a complex statutory framework. 'Pay', for example, has been held by the courts to embrace not simply remuneration in cases brought under article 119 of the Treaty of Rome but also statutory sick pay, pensions and redundancy payments (leading to the important pensions cases ruled on by the European Court; see below). Important cases ruled on by the European Court have also dealt with the matter of objective justification and burden of proof. However, the legal position is complicated by the fact that the wording of EU legislation and UK law in the field is not wholly congruent, although UK law must be interpreted within the meaning of the EU provision, which takes precedence.

Under the Equal Pay Act an 'equality clause' is implied into every contract of employment. This allows a woman to bring a claim if she is treated less favourably than a comparable man in relation to any term or condition in her contract of employment. The woman must be performing one of the following:

- 'Like work', i.e. work of the same or a broadly similar nature to that of the chosen comparator.
- Work 'rated as equivalent' to the chosen comparator's under a job evaluation scheme.
- Work of 'equal value', i.e. the work imposes the same demands on her as on a comparable man when measured on criteria such as effort, skill and decision, and cannot be compared under either of the first two categories.

There is a special, and complicated, procedure for bringing equal value claims.

In looking at terms of employment, a complaint may be brought if there is alleged discriminatory treatment on an individual term, regardless of whether this might in theory be offset by more favourable treatment on other terms.

Employers can defend themselves against a complaint if they can prove that any variation between a man's and a woman's contract is attributable to a 'genuine material difference which is not a matter of sex'. A defence can also be made if the employer can show that the work is rated as unequal under a valid and non-discriminatory job evaluation scheme. A difference that is objectively justified and meets a real need of the employer may be admissible; this could include market forces.

The law is complex, and cases under it can take many years to come to a hearing. The most common remedy will be an award of arrears of remuneration or damages for breach of an equality clause in a contract of employment. In 1993 the EOC requested that the European Commission investigate whether the UK was meeting its obligations in this area under the EU Equal Pay Directive.

Race discrimination

The UK is one of the few European countries with a developed system of law in the area of race discrimination. Discrimination on grounds of race in the fields of employment, education and housing is prohibited under the Race Relations Act 1976. The Commission for Racial Equality (CRE) is charged with monitoring the working of the Act, and may issue codes of practice giving practical guidance. The CRE's 1984 code of practice on employment makes recommendations in the fields of recruitment, training, terms of employment, discrimination and victimisation. The code also recommends that companies adopt positive action programmes. Although not binding, the code may be taken into account by industrial tribunals.

The Act identifies three forms of discrimination:

- Direct discrimination – where an employer treats someone less favourably than other persons on racial grounds; harassment and abuse have been interpreted by the courts to constitute direct discrimination.
- Indirect discrimination – where discrimination results from criteria required of actual or prospective employees that are not essential to the job, and that members of some ethnic groups cannot fulfil; examples include excessive or irrelevant language or qualification requirements.
- Victimisation – where a person receives less favourable treatment because they have sought to assert their statutory rights.

Race discrimination is prohibited in all areas of employment at an establishment in Great Britain, unless the employer can show that membership of a particular racial group is a genuine occupational qualification for the job. Other exceptions include situations in which discrimination is practised in fulfilment of a statutory duty; covers employees working outside Great Britain; or is intended as positive discrimination in favour of an underrepresented racial group (for example, setting up a training programme for ethnic minorities or encouraging job applications from particular ethnic groups). Direct discrimination for reasons of positive action during selection for employment is not permitted. A genuine occupational qualification embraces such areas as the theatre, modelling, working in ethnic restaurants, and directly providing personal services to people of a particular ethnic group.

Action against discrimination can be taken both by the employee and the CRE. The burden of proof rests with the applicant. Cases must be taken to an industrial tribunal, with provision for conciliation by ACAS. Applications must be presented within three months of the alleged act of discrimination. Remedies include:

- A '*declaratory order*' that the employer has violated the employee's rights.
- A *recommendation* to remove or reduce the effects of discrimination. Failure to comply may lead to an order to pay compensation. Tribunals cannot require an employer to appoint an employee or increase pay levels but may instruct the employer to pay compensation and correct their policies.
- *Compensation.* From 1994, there is no upper limit on compensation. Payments

may reflect both quantifiable losses as well as offer redress for injured feelings, with extra amounts ('aggravated' damages) in serious cases. Complainants must mitigate losses.

Appeals may be made on a point of law to the Employment Appeals Tribunal and, where leave is granted, to the Court of Appeal.

The CRE has powers to enforce application of the law through its rights to investigate cases, and can issue a non-discrimination notice that requires an employer to stop the discrimination, inform the CRE about steps taken, and provide the CRE with information to enable it to monitor compliance for up to five years.

Ethnic monitoring is regarded as an important component of positive action policies, and the CRE's code of practice gives guidelines on how to implement ethnic record-keeping.

Fair Employment in Northern Ireland

Under the Fair Employment (NI) Act 1989, which amended legislation dating from 1976, employers in Northern Ireland may not discriminate between employees on religious grounds. Employers must register and monitor their employment practices, ensure that indirect religious discrimination is not practised, and take affirmative action to redress imbalances in their workforces. All private-sector employers with more than ten employees must register with the Fair Employment Commission (see Appendix). Employers with more than 250 employees must monitor and submit annual returns on job applications.

The Commission may investigate companies, set goals and timetables and issue directions for employers to take affirmative action. Employers guilty of bad practice can be debarred from public contracts and grants. There is also a code of practice on fair employment in Northern Ireland: although not binding, failure to implement it could prejudice an employer's case before a tribunal. Employers are also required by law to consider the code when reviewing recruitment, training and promotion practices. Individual complaints of discrimination may be brought to the Fair Employment Tribunal, which may authorise damages and compensation of up to £30,000.

Disability

Under the Disabled Persons (Employment) Act 1944, employers with twenty or more employees must ensure that 3 per cent of their posts are occupied by people with disabilities who are registered under the Act. All employers with 250 or more employees must set out their policies on the employment of people with disabilities in their annual reports. Failure to comply with the employment quota is punishable by a fine, unless the employer is exempted. In practice, the law is barely enforced. A number of organisations, including the IPD, has produced codes on dealing with employees with disabilities.

Age discrimination

There are no statutory regulations on age in the UK, and job advertisements frequently indicate a preferred age range for an applicant. The IPD has a code of practice on age and employment, focusing in particular on the removal of age barriers in selection; the Department of Employment has also run campaigns to deter employers from age discrimination.

Retirement

Post-retirement income in the UK is provided through two state schemes, occupational pension schemes run by employers, and personal pensions. The thrust of public policy over the past decade has been to lower actual and prospective benefits under the state schemes, and encourage occupational and especially personal pensions. The conduct of many occupational schemes caused concern in the late 1980s and early 1990s, highlighting weaknesses in the mechanisms of self-regulation (following the collapse of the Maxwell group of companies), but also connected with issues such as employer access to fund surpluses, and solvency requirements. A new Pensions Act has been proposed to address these issues.

Retirement age

Retirement age under the state schemes is currently sixty-five for men and sixty for women. The retirement age for women will be raised to sixty-five in stages from 2010. Claiming the basic pension may be deferred for up to five years, with entitlement to a higher pension. There are no provisions for early retirement under the state schemes.

Retirement under occupational pension schemes is normally between sixty and sixty-five but must be equalised for men and women, following judgments of the European Court of Justice (see page 6). Provision for women may be worsened in the process of equalisation. Under Inland Revenues rules early retirement from fifty and late retirement up to seventy-five are permitted under occupational schemes.

The state schemes

The current state provision consists of two elements: the basic flat-rate pension and the state earnings-related pension scheme (SERPS).

In April 1994 the basic pension stood at £57.60 for a single person. The rate is raised each year in line with changes in consumer prices (not earnings).

Entitlement is obtained through a contributions record of at least ninety per cent of an individual's working life. The pension may be paid irrespective of whether the employee has retired and is not related to other sources of income.

SERPS, which has operated since 1978, provides an extra earnings-related pension and is calculated on the basis of earnings since 1978, provided full contributions are paid (see the following paragraph on 'contracting out'). The level of SERPS is determined by reckonable earnings over the individual's career. For those currently in the scheme and due to retire before 1998 the pension is set at 25 per cent of average earnings from employment since 1978, subject to upper and lower limits. Benefits will be reduced from 1998.

Employers with an occupational scheme may 'contract out' of SERPS, with the inducement of lower social insurance contributions, provided the benefits offered by the scheme are as good as SERPS. All contracted-out schemes must meet this minimum level, termed the 'guaranteed minimum pension'.

Occupational schemes

Occupational pensions are estimated to cover around half the UK's workforce. Most older schemes, especially with larger employers, provide a percentage of final salary on retirement, usually accruing at 1/60 per year (and hence yielding for example 35/60 = about 58 per cent of final salary on retirement, where employees are in the scheme for up to 35 years). Some companies operate average earnings schemes where revalued career earnings, rather than final salary, are used as the basis for pension benefits. Newer schemes or those with smaller employers are based in contrast on defined contributions leading to a lump sum on retirement (money purchase schemes), used to buy an annuity to provide post-retirement income.

In the past, occupational pension arrangements differed by employee category but the current tendency is for harmonisation between blue- and white-collar employees. However, senior managers may be in schemes with more favourable accrual rates (1/45 or 1/30 for directors). Membership of an occupational scheme cannot be made compulsory (see 'Personal pensions', below). Under Inland Revenue rules a pension paid under an occupational scheme may not exceed two-thirds of final salary (that is, salary earned in the twelve months before retirement), subject to an upper limit for earnings in 1994 of £76,800 for people joining existing schemes from 1 June 1987 or new schemes set up after 13 March 1989. Pension entitlement may be exchanged in part for a lump sum, which may not be more than one and a half times final salary. The maximum death-in-service benefit is four times total salary.

Contributions to approved schemes are tax deductible. Top up schemes for amounts above the limits are fully taxable. In schemes where both employer and employee contribute, around 80 per cent of schemes in all, the current employer contribution averages 6 per cent of earnings, with a broadly matching contribution from the employee. In schemes that are non-contributory for the employee, the average employer contribution is 10 per cent. The long-term average total contribution is some 15 per cent; this may be returned to once the current period of 'contribution holidays', rooted in fund surpluses accumulated during periods of high return, is over.

In contrast to the dominant, statutory, pay-as-you-go schemes (which account for a substantial portion of post-retirement income in mainland Europe) UK occupational schemes are overwhelmingly funded, with a variety of funding mechanisms. In most cases no more than 5 per cent of a fund's assets may be shares of the employing organisation. The UK has the largest accumulation of pension fund assets outside the USA, accounting for some 60 per cent of GDP (compared with 3 per cent of GDP for France and 6 per cent for Germany).

Pension schemes in the private sector are predominantly organised as trusts which must meet minimum statutory conditions for vesting, transferability of benefits, and disclosure of information to members. Proposals under a new Pensions Bill, to be introduced in 1994/95, will tighten standards in a number of areas. The main innovations will provide for: increased supervision by members through rights to nominate up to one-third of trustees; improved information; minimum solvency requirements; and tighter procedures for firms wishing to use pension fund surpluses. A new regulatory body, the Occupational Pensions Regulator, will be given powers to investigate the operation of funds and impose sanctions in the event of abuse. The representative body for occupational pension schemes is NAPF (National Association of Pension Funds). Official supervision is via the Occupational Pensions Board (OPB), to be replaced by a new regulatory body under proposed legislation.

Benefits must be 100 per cent vested after two years, and deferred pensions must be increased in line with consumer prices, up to a maximum of 5 per cent a year.

There is no current obligation to increase pensions in payment in line with prices, except for the element that corresponds to the guaranteed minimum pension. However, this is expected to change under the new Pensions Act. Practice has normally been to uprate pensions in line with consumer price inflation during periods of low inflation, but for pensions to lag during periods of high inflation, with subsequent catching up.

Personal pensions

Personal pension arrangements were encouraged by the government through a number of incentives during the 1980s, leading to widely publicised concerns that the financial services industry used aggressive or misleading sales techniques to induce individuals to leave occupational schemes for poorer individual pensions. Some 5.3 million people had personal pensions in 1992. Since 1988 an employer cannot require an employee to be a member of an occupational scheme.

Contributions are tax free up to a set percentage of income, which varies with the age of the employee, provided the scheme is with an authorised pension provider. The maximum amount that can be invested in a plan is 17.5 per cent of net relevant earnings for employees aged thirty-five or under, rising to 40 per cent for employees aged 61 or over. Personal pensions are money purchase arrangements, creating a fund with which to buy an annuity.

Group personal pensions (GPP), in which the employer facilitates or endorses a particular scheme for their employees, have grown since the late 1980s, especially in smaller firms, and are now estimated to cover neaarly half a million employees.

Individual termination of contract

Termination of contract is subject to the provisions of the law of contract, with protection for employees against unfair dismissal, and a provision for statutory minimum notice periods. The only statutory provision for severance compensation is in the field of redundancy – that is, termination on economic grounds – where employees with 104 weeks' service are entitled to minimum payments.

Termination by mutual agreement

Contracts of employment may be terminated by mutual agreement, without notice and with all obligations under the contract coming to an end. Where termination is by mutual agreement, ex-employees have no rights under employment protection legislation. In the event of a dispute over the nature of the termination, such as alleged pressure on the employee to agree to a termination, industrial tribunals tend to lean towards accepting that the situation is one of dismissal.

Where employees participate in a voluntary redundancy scheme, employment will generally be regarded as having been via dismissal (on economic grounds), notwithstanding the consent of the employee. Under such circumstances, employees are entitled to any agreed and statutory redundancy payment. However, this principle has not always been accepted in the context of early retirement schemes.

Resignation

The employee may terminate the contract, with or without notice, by resignation: the situation in which an employee resigns because the employer has breached the contract of employment is dealt with below under 'Constructive dismissal'. There is no required form for a resignation, aside from any provision in the contract of employment, and simple failure to report for work could be interpreted as such.

Notice periods will be as specified in the individual contract of employment, subject to the minimum requirements of the Employment Protection (Consolidation) Act. Under Section 49 (2), an employee who has been continuously employed for one month or more must give at least one week's notice of termination. If no notice period is specified in the contract of employment, the courts may imply a longer notice period, which may depend on the nature of the employment.

Resignation without notice – unless in response to a fundamental breach of the contract by the employer – will breach the contract of employment. It is very rare for employers to sue ex-employees in such a situation, and the courts are not permitted to compel an employee to fulfil the terms of a contract of employment. In theory, the employer could sue for damages: however, quantifying damages in the event of a single resignation is highly problematic, as would be recovering any compensation. In practice, employees with long notice periods may often negotiate a shorter period before termination. The alternative for the employer is to agree a restrictive covenant with the employee.

Constructive dismissal   Termination without notice by the employee can be construed as dismissal – and thus become subject to dismissals protection legislation – if it is prompted by a fundamental breach of the contract of employment by the employer. This concept of 'constructive dismissal' has common law origins, but is now defined and regulated by statute under the Employment Protection (Consolidation) Act 1978. Three basic requirements must be met:

- The employer's conduct must amount to a fundamental breach of contract, either in the present or where the employer indicates that they do not intend to be bound by an essential term of the contract in the future. Examples of such a fundamental breach include: not paying employees, paying them late, or imposing serious and unilateral cuts in pay and/or benefits; seriously departing from the agreed job description; failing in their implied duty of care, for example, by not taking reasonable steps to protect employees who are victims of harassment, or by unreasonable conduct which undermines trust and confidence between employee and employer.
- The employee must terminate the contract swiftly, otherwise they may be held to have 'affirmed' the contract by continuing in employment. However, the employee may continue in employment but make it clear that they are working under protest: however, undue delay could still be seen as affirming the contract.
- The resignation must be caused by the employer's conduct, and not be for an ulterior reason.

If an employee can successfully establish that their termination can be construed as constructive dismissal, they are entitled to the same remedies as for an express dismissal (see below).

Expiry of a fixed-term contract

A fixed-term contract will automatically terminate when the period for which it was agreed expires. However, the expiry of a fixed-term contract may be regarded as a *dismissal*, and in consequence allow the employee to bring a claim of unfair dismissal (see below). Fixed-term contracts may also contain provision for termination with notice on either side.

Supervening events and frustration

Contracts of employment may be terminated automatically by 'supervening events', such as the appointment of a receiver, the compulsory winding-up of a company, death of the employee and in individual cases of the employer, and permanent closure of the workplace. In some cases such terminations may be deemed to be dismissal, allowing the claiming of redundancy payments. A contract of employment is terminated by frustration when, through neither party's fault, an event occurs which makes it impossible for the contract to be lawfully fulfilled. The most common instances are the prolonged or sudden serious illness of the employee (see 'Termination on health grounds' below), or imprisonment.

Termination by the employer

When terminating employment, an employer must:

- Abide by any agreed or statutory period of notice (see below).
- If requested by the employee, provide a written statement of reasons for the dismissal within fourteen days, provided the employee has two years' continuous service.

Under the Employment Protection (Consolidation) Act 1978, employees have a right not to be unfairly dismissed: that is, the dismissal must be for a good reason and follow a fair procedure. (See 'Unfair dismissal' below.) This section details grounds for dismissal that would be regarded potentially fair under the Act, with examples drawn from case law. Whether the employer acted reasonably in the circumstances, and hence whether the termination could be deemed unfair, will depend on the specific facts of the case.

Employee capability and qualifications Dismissal on grounds of capability or poor performance may take place where employees are slow, inflexible and unadaptable; if they fail to meet performance standards set by management; or if their personal conduct or approach is not conducive to good work relationships. Absolute physical incapacity to do the required tasks would also warrant dismissal. Employees should be warned, in writing, both of their shortcomings and the possible consequences, and given sufficient opportunity to improve. Fair procedures, as set in the relevant ACAS code of practice, should be applied.

Employee misconduct   Employee misconduct may warrant a fair dismissal provided the employer can cite reasonable grounds and has carried out a reasonable investigation. The conduct must be serious or, in the event of minor offences, repeated. Substantial prejudice to the employment relationship must be involved, and dismissal must represent a reasonable penalty. Examples include: persistent absenteeism and lateness, following a warning; abusive language, especially where employee relations are disturbed (racist abuse may also constitute a separate offence under the Race Relations Act); breaching the basic duty of loyalty and confidentiality by disclosing information or setting up in competition; refusal to accept reasonable instructions, including in some circumstances refusal to work overtime; breach of disciplinary rules on drink and drugs, especially where health and safety may be compromised or illegality is involved; personal appearance, if the employee's dress or appearance departs too far from a reasonable assessment of the image of the business, breaches accepted rules on uniforms, or could be regarded as offensive or prejudicial to safety and hygiene; theft and dishonesty; violence and fighting. (See also 'Summary dismissal' below.)

Termination on health grounds   Dismissal on grounds of ill-health is potentially fair either in the event of long-term sickness or because of persistent short-term absences. In the case of long-term sickness, the employer must consult with the employee, conduct a medical investigation, and explore the possibility of alternative employment. In the case of short-term absences, the employer should ascertain reasons for the absence, enable the employee to put their case, and ensure that employees are clearly warned that failure to improve attendance will culminate in dismissal.

For a dismissal to be fair, a number of factors should normally be considered, including: the nature, length and effect of the illness, including the prospects and pace of recovery; the length of service of the employee; and whether a temporary replacement is possible.

Dismissal on the grounds that an employee was HIV+ is likely to be considered unfair, unless there are immediate grounds for fearing that the nature of the employee's work could cause infection to others. Illness caused by an AIDS-related condition would be subject to the procedures for a termination on grounds of ill-health, and where the employee had developed full-blown AIDS this could be deemed to offer grounds for a dismissal. The Department of Employment has produced a guide, 'AIDS and the workplace'.

Dismissal on grounds of pregnancy or maternity is automatically unfair (see below).

Termination on economic grounds ('redundancy')

Dismissal on economic grounds – redundancy – is a potentially fair reason for dismissal. Redundancy is defined in the Employment Protection (Consolidation) Act 1978 as a dismissal wholly or mainly attributable to either of the following:

- The fact that the employer has ceased or intends to cease the business for which the employee was employed.
- The fact that the requirement to carry out work of a particular kind has ceased or diminished at the place where an employee was employed; this covers dismissals occasioned by closure, rationalisation and reorganisation.

Consultation There are consultation requirements with recognised trade unions both in the event of individual and collective redundancies. Following the TURER Act 1993 the definition of redundancy for the purposes of consultation is broader than that still used for eligibility for redundancy payments and embraces all dismissals for reasons not related to the individual. Consultation must take place at the 'earliest possible opportunity' after the employer has framed a proposal to make redundancies. In the case of individual redundancies, there is no prescribed consultation period, although the consultation must meet certain criteria in order to offer a reasonable opportunity to consider the proposals, and some tribunals have insisted on a period of at least twenty-eight days. The courts have also advised employers to consult with individual employees, and have inferred this as a contractual duty.

Where the employer proposes to dismiss:

- One hundred or more employees in one establishment within a period of ninety days or less, the consultation must begin at least ninety days before the first dismissals are scheduled to take effect.
- Between ten and ninety-nine employees within a thirty-day period, the consultation must take place at least thirty days before the first dismissals are scheduled to take effect.

The consultation period is entirely separate from any contractual notice period. The employer must disclose in writing the following information:

- The reason for the dismissals.
- The numbers and description of employees to be made redundant.
- The total number of employees in the establishment.
- The selection procedure to be used.
- Employer proposals for how redundancies are to be implemented and the time-scale involved.

Consultation must include discussions on how to avoid dismissals, how the number of dismissals might be reduced and how the consequences for employees can be mitigated. Consultation should be pursued with a view to coming to an agreement with employee representatives. Should an employer fail to consult, and a trade union brings a complaint to an industrial tribunal, employees may be granted a *protective award*: that is, the employer must pay employees any pay due during the 'protected period' which is set by the tribunal, but which is up to ninety days where ninety days' minimum notice should have been given, up to thirty days where thirty days' minimum notice should have been given, and up to twenty-eight days in any other case. In certain circumstances the employer must notify the Department of Employment.

Selection for redundancy   A dismissal on grounds of redundancy will be held to be unfair if the selection is on trade union grounds (including refusal to join a trade union) or for any other discriminatory reason. Any selection procedure must itself not be directly or indirectly discriminatory on grounds of race or sex, or in Northern Ireland on religious grounds. Length of service ('last in first out') is a common central criterion in redundancy schemes, and up until the mid 1980s was the paramount criterion. In contrast to those in a number of other European countries, UK employers may use performance criteria when selecting for redundancy, as well as conduct-based factors such as absenteeism and lateness, and health record. These have figured increasingly over the past decade; the main requirement is that the criteria be objective and full consultation procedures be observed. There is no positive requirement to retain those most in need of social protection and unlikely to find new employment.

Statutory redundancy compensation   An employee dismissed for reasons of redundancy is entitled to a statutory redundancy payment, payable by the employer, provided they have been continuously employed for two years. However, this right will be forfeited if the employer has offered suitable alternative employment, and the employee has refused.

The basic award is for one week's pay per year of service, up to a maximum of twenty years. There is an upper limit to a week's pay of £205. Employees aged over 41 can claim one and a half week's pay for any service accrued from that age; employees under 22 can claim half a week's pay for any service between 18 and 21. The maximum statutory redundancy payment is £6,150. Payments made in connection with the termination of employment are tax free up to a maximum of £30,000.

Agreed or voluntary schemes may improve on the statutory minima both in terms of the basic cash award, as well as the addition of other benefits as part of a redundancy scheme. These may include outplacement, which is tax free to the employee.

Notice periods

Employees are entitled either to the notice period specified in their contract of employment or the statutory minimum notice period, as set out in Section 49 (1) of the Employment Protection (Consolidation) Act 1978, whichever is the longer. Any employee with at least one month's employment is entitled to one week's notice for each completed year of service, as follows:

Length of service		Notice entitlement
From one month to two years		One week
Two years		Two weeks
Three years		Three weeks
Twelve or more	up to	Twelve weeks

An employee may agree to waive their statutory entitlement on a particular occasion, or accept payment in lieu of notice. This may be insisted on by the employer, where they have reason to believe that the employee may seek to obtain confidential material or create managerial or organisational difficulties at the workplace. (See also 'garden leave' on page 389.)

In practice, most managers and specialists are on three months' notice, with around a fifth of managers on six months' or more. There were some moves to reduce long notice periods for managers during the recession, and also in the light of some disquiet about three-year rolling contracts for very senior managers. During 1993/94 a number of companies cut directors' notice periods from three to two years.

Pay in lieu of notice, if provided for in the contract of employment, will normally be taxable unless it can be established that the payment constitutes compensation for the loss of employment or for the breach of contract and may, therefore, be exempt under Inland Revenue rules on termination payments.

Employees working out notice for redundancy have a right to reasonable time off to find a another job.

Summary dismissal

An employer may dismiss an employee without notice – that is, by summary dismissal – if the employee is in fundamental breach of the contract of employment, such as by committing an act of gross misconduct. As there are no statutory guidelines, and individual cases only give the broadest guidlelines and do not set precedents, employers should spell out in their own rulebooks what sort of behaviour would be deemed to be serious misconduct. In the absence of such express rules, tribunals would normally regard theft, dishonesty, violence, vandalism and serious breaches of health and safety regulations as instances of gross misconduct, but this may depend on the degree or other circumstances specific to the case in hand.

Severance compensation

There is no statutory provision for severance compensation, aside from where a redundancy payment is due (see above) or in the event of an unfair dismissal. However, payment in lieu of notice, or in the case of executives for any unexpired portion of a fixed-term, but rollling, contract, provides an effective means of paying severance compensation, and in some cases is recognised by the tax authorities as a termination payment and will not be taxable.

Wrongful dismissal

Any dismissal which breaches the contract of employment may give rise to action for 'wrongful dismissal' in common law. The most common types of wrongful dismissal are where no notice or inadequate notice has been given (see above), where a fixed-term contract has been ended before the due date of expiry or where a contractual dismissals procedure has not been complied with. As wrongful dismissals involve the law of contract, claims must be made in the county courts, or High Court where the amount of damages at issue exceeds £50,000 or if the law involved is complex. The remedy for a wrongful dismissal, if the claim is upheld, is damages to compensate the employee for losses during the period between the termination of employment and when the contractual notice would have expired. Where no notice is stated in the contract, the courts may imply a reasonable period of notice, subject to the statutory minima set out above. Employees must seek to mitigate their losses, and this may be deducted from damages.

Wrongful dismissal, which is solely confined to the contract of employment, is not to be confused with unfair dismissal (see below) which involves the reasonableness or otherwise of the employer's decision as dealt with in statute law.

Unfair dismissal

Employees who meet certain criteria of eligibility are entitled not to be unfairly dismissed, under the Employment Protection (Consolidation) Act 1978. Complaints of unfair dismissal must be brought before an industrial tribunal, in the first instance, within three months of the effective date of termination.

There are two categories of unfair dismissal: dismissals which are *automatically* unfair because they breach a specific statutory provision; and dismissals which are *potentially* fair, but where the employer has acted unreasonably. In contrast to practice in many other West European countries, an unfair dismissal is not null and void – that is, it remains a dismissal and the employee affected must seek one of the legal remedies available. Moreover, there is no enforceable right to reinstatement, and as a result employers can in theory succeed in dismissing an employee unfairly, provided they are prepared to accept the penalty of compensation payments (see below).

Eligibility   In order to bring a claim of unfair dismisssal, an employee must normally have been continuously employed for a period of two years, be employed in the UK, and be below the normal retirement age in the undertaking, or at most 65 years old. In some cases where the dismissal would be automatically unfair, no qualifying period of employment is needed; this includes dismissals on grounds related to union membership, over the assertion of a statutory right, on health and safety grounds, or for a maternity-related reason.

Special provisions apply in the case of a dismissal connected with industrial action: these issues are dealt with in another volume in this series, *Employee Relations and Collective Bargaining*.

Automatically unfair dismissals A dismissal will be regarded by an industrial tribunal as automatically unfair on the following grounds:

- If it is for a trade union reason: that is, if the reason or principal reason is because the employee dismissed was, or proposed to become, a member of a trade union, had participated in permitted trade union activities, or had refused or proposed to refuse to join a trade union. Selection for redundancy for a trade union reason is also automatically unfair.
- On health and safety grounds: that is, if the reason was because the employee was a safety representative or member of a safety committee, or if the employee refused to work on reasonable safety grounds or to take reasonable steps to protect himself or other persons from danger. Selection for redundancy on health and safety grounds is also automatically unfair.
- For asserting a statutory right, such as protection from unfair dismissal or rights to time off for trade union activities.
- If the dismissal is related to pregnancy or maternity leave, or if the employee is selected for redundancy in contravention of a customary arrangement or agreed procedure.
- If it is in connection with the transfer of an undertaking.

Reasonableness of dismissal If the employee has been dismissed for a potentially fair reason, as set out above, in the event of a claim for unfair dismissal the industrial tribunal must examine whether the dismissal was reasonable or unreasonable. The burden of proof lies neither with the employer nor employee: rather, the tribunal itself must apply the standards required in law by looking at the facts of the case, including the size and adminstrative resources of the undertaking; whether the reason cited by the employer was sufficient to merit the dismissal; and whether the dismissal can be regarded as fair on grounds of equity.

In addition to the reasons for the actual dismissal, tribunals must also take into account whether the procedure used was fair: for example, the tribunal may look at whether the guidelines set out in the relevant ACAS code of practice have been adhered to. Failure to follow agreed procedures, to allow for appeal to higher levels of management, to provide adequate written warnings in the event of poor performance, and where employees have no opportunity to question evidence or scope to provide counter-evidence may all render a dismissal unfair.

Compensation and remedies

There are three basic remedies for a dismissal which a tribunal finds to be unfair. Although there is scope for *reinstatement* – where the employee is reinstated in their previous job with no financial loss – and *re-engagement*, in practice these are never used and cannot be enforced. There is no notion of a null and void dismissal, and an employer cannot be compelled to employ a dismissed employee, no matter how unfair the dismissal. In practice, therefore, the main remedy is *compensation*.

Compensation is broken down into two parts: a basic award and a compensatory award. The basic award is intended to compensate the employee for the loss of job security; the calculation is based on basic weekly pay (subject to an upper limit of £205), length of service and age. A maximum of twenty years' service may be counted. The amount of award is: one and a half week's pay for each year of employment in which the employee was not below the age of 41; one week's pay, excluding the above, where the employee was not below the age of 22; half a week's pay for other periods of employment.

The compensatory award is intended to compensate the employee for any financial losses as a result of the dismissal. Subject to the upper limits set out below, the award is calculated by the tribunal in the light of losses sustained, subject to a judgment of what is just and equitable taking into account all the factors. Losses sustained may include: immediate loss of wages, future loss of earnings and loss of benefits (car, benefits-in-kind, pension rights). The award may be reduced if the employee may have contributed to the grounds for their dismissal (for example, through misconduct), and dismissed employees are also required to mitigate their losses.

Awards are subject to upper limits. The 1994 upper limit on basic awards is £6,150 and on compensatory awards £11,000, although this may be exceeded where arrears of pay or benefits must be paid to the employee. The maximim award in the event of dismissal on grounds of trade union membership or activities, or for health and safety reasons, is also £11,000, but may be increased to £26,800 if the employer fails to comply with a reinstatement or re-engagement order.

Transfer of undertakings

The protection of employee rights in the event of a transfer of an undertaking is provided for in the Transfer of Undertakings (Protection of Employment) Regulations 1981, as amended. The 1981 Regulations were intended to transpose into UK law the 1977 EU Acquired Rights Directive 77/187, with amendments reflecting European Court subsequent rulings. Under these provisions, the rights and liabilities of an employer will pass to any new employer to whom the undertaking is transferred within the meaning of the law. The law applies to all commercial undertakings, and since 1993 also to non-commercial undertakings (such as public-sector services transferred to private contractors – see below).

Individuals who are employed at the time of the transfer automatically become employees of the new owner on their existing terms and conditions: any applicable collective agreement will also be transferred to the new employer, although in practice the enforceable terms of UK collective agreements will generally already be incorporated into individual contracts of employment. Dismissals associated with the transfer are deemed to be automatically unfair, unless effected for economic, technical or organisational reasons entailing changes in the workforce. The question of the precise timing of transfers, and whether employees could be dismissed *en bloc* shortly before the moment of transfer, so as to not to be technically employed when the transfer took place, has proved controversial. Because of deficiencies in the wording of the Regulations, when considering an appeal in 1989 in the case of *Litster v. Forth Dry Dock & Engineering Co Ltd*, the House of Lords departed from the customary literal and textual interpretation of the Regulations, which required employees to be employed at the very moment of transfer, and adopted a 'purposive' interpretation of the law, in the light of a European Court decision which had rejected this as being incompatible with the original directive: that is, the Lords sought to imply the wishes of the legislator, as evidenced by the underlying directive, rather than confine itself to a consideration solely of the wording of the UK Regulations. As well as clarifying the operation of the directive in the UK, by regarding such a dismissal prior to the moment of transfer as unfair if the employee would have been in employment had they not been dismissed in connection with the transfer, the House of Lords' decision also reflected the impact of broadly framed European legislation, designed to state objectives, in contrast to the textual tradition of the interpretation of statutes in the UK.

UK law requires employers whose employees are affected by the transfer, irrespective of whether they are selling or buying the undertaking, to inform and consult representatives of recognised trade unions: information to be provided must include the time of the proposed transfer and the reasons for it; the legal, economic and social implications of the transfer for all affected employees, and any measures proposed in respect of these employees. If the employer fails to consult, trade unions may complain to an industrial tribunal within three months of the date of the transfer. In June 1994 the European Court ruled that UK law was in breach of European directives on transfers of undertakings and collective redundancies because it provides for consultation and information of employees only in undertakings where there is a recognised trade union; in consequence, employees in organisations where the employer does not recognise a trade union will not have a right to be consulted or informed by their representatives. The decision raises the possibility that the government may have to act to provide for some form of statutory system of employee representation or trade union recognition. (These issues are explored in more detail in another volume in this series, *Employee Relations and Collective Bargaining*.)

Appendix

Non-wage labour costs and income tax

Social insurance contributions   The UK social security system is financed both out of general taxation and via social insurance contributions (national insurance contributions, NICs). NICs are payable by employers and employees once gross income has exceeded the weekly lower earnings limit of £57 (1994/95). Once above this limit NICs are payable on the whole of income for the employer, and on the whole of income up to the weekly upper earnings limit for the emloyee of £430 (1994/95). The rates are graduated and also vary according to whether the employee is a member of the supplementary state earnings-related pension scheme (SERPS).

For the employee who is a member of SERPS the rate is 2 per cent for the first £57 and 10 per cent on the balance up to the upper earnings limit. Employees outside SERPS pay 2 per cent of the first £57 and then 8.2 per cent up to the weekly upper earnings limit.

For the employer there are more stages of gradation beginning at 3.6 per cent of gross pay, with the top rate of 10.2 per cent payable on all earnings above £200 per week for employees in SERPS. There is also a lower rate for the employer where the employee has contracted out of SERPS.

The largest single non-statutory, non-wage labour cost is the occupational pension, which currently costs employers on average 6 per cent of pay in a contributory scheme and 10 per cent in a non-contributory scheme.

Income tax   There are three rates of income tax. A 'starter rate' of 20 per cent for the first £3,000 of taxable income; a 'standard rate' of 25 per cent on £3,001–23,700 of taxable income; and a top rate of 40 per cent of earnings over £23,700. In 1994/95 the personal allowance for a single person was £3,445.

Organisations

Department of Employment
Caxton House
Tothill Street
London SW1H 9NF
Tel: + 44 (0)171-273 3000

Advisory, Conciliation and Arbitration
Service (ACAS)
27 Wilton Street
London SW1X 7AZ
Tel: + 44 (0)171-210 3000

Confederation of British Industry (CBI)
Centre Point
103 New Oxford Street
London WC1A 1DU
Tel: + 44 (0)171-379 7400
Fax: + 44 (0)171-240 1578

Equal Opportunities Commission (EOC)
Overseas House
Quay Street
Manchester M3 3HN
Tel: + 44 (0)161-833 9244

Commission for Racial Equality (CRE)
Elliot House
10–12 Allington Street
London SW1E 5EH
Tel: + 44 (0)171-828 7022
Fax: + 44 (0)171-630 7605

Fair Employment Commission for
Northern Ireland
Andras House
60 Great Victoria Street
Belfast BT2 7BB
Northern Ireland
Tel: + 44 (0)1232 240020
Fax: + 44 (0)1232 331544

Data Protection Registrar
Springfield House
Water Lane
Wilmslow
Cheshire SK9 5AX
Tel: + 44 (0)1625-553 5711

Central Office of the Industrial Tribunals
Southgate Street
Bury St. Edmunds
IP33 2AQ
Tel: + 44 (0)1284 762300

The Institute of Personnel and
Development (IPD)
IPD House
Camp Road
Wimbledon
London SW19 4UX
Tel: + 44 (0)181-946 9100
Fax: + 44 (0)181-947 2570

Trades Union Congress (TUC)
23–28 Great Russell Street
London WC1B 3LS
Tel: + 44 (0)171-636 4030

Main sources

Michael Cannell and Stephen Wood, *Incentive Pay*, IPM/NEDO (London 1992).
Jim Hillage, *The Role of Job Evaluation*, Institute of Manpower Studies, Report 269 (Brighton 1994).
Incomes Data Services, *Studies*, various issues.
Incomes Data Services, *Report*, various issues.
Incomes Data Services, *Pension Service: Personnel Manual*.
Incomes Data Services, *Employment Law Handbook*, various issues.
Incomes Data Services, *Management Pay Review*, various issues.
Institute of Personnel and Development, *The IPD Codes of Practice*, available from IPD.
Neil Millward *et al.*, *Workplace Industrial Relations in Transition*, Dartmouth Publishing (Aldershot 1992).
Marc Thompson, *Pay and Performance: the Employee Experience*, Institute of Manpower Studies, Report 258 (Brighton 1993).